THE FINANCES AND PUBLIC WORKS OF INDIA 1869–1881

THE FINANCES AND PUBLIC WORKS OF INDIA 1869–1881

SIR JOHN STRACHEY
SIR RICHARD STRACHEY

Gian Publishing House
29/6 SHAKTI NAGAR • DELHI-110007 • INDIA

GIAN PUBLISHING HOUSE
PUBLISHERS OF BOOKS ON HUMAN CIVILIZATION
29/6 SHAKTI NAGAR, DELHI-110007

First Reprint in India, 1986

Printed at Goyal Offset Printers, Delhi-110035
and published by Smt. Gayatri Garg
for Gian Publishing House, Delhi-110007

CONTENTS

THE

FINANCES AND PUBLIC WORKS OF INDIA.

CHAPTER I.

INTRODUCTORY.

GREAT CHANGES IN INDIA IN RECENT YEARS—DEMAND FOR ADMINISTRATIVE AND MATERIAL IMPROVEMENTS—EXPANSION OF REVENUES AND EXPENDITURE—GROWTH OF IMPORT AND EXPORT TRADE—OUTLAY ON RAILWAYS AND IRRIGATION WORKS—GENERAL PROGRESS OF THE COUNTRY IN WEALTH AND GOOD GOVERNMENT.

THE changes which India has undergone during the last thirty or forty years have been so great, that it is often very difficult to deduce useful inferences from the comparison of its present and past condition. This is especially true in regard to matters of finance.

Comparisons between the revenue, the expenditure, the debt, or the trade of India now and India as she was, though highly interesting in some points of view, have little financial significance, so numerous and profound have been the changes in the condition of the country, its available resources, and its requirements for necessary administrative and material progress.

The territorial extension of the Empire during the last forty years has been enormous. Five great provinces have been added to it, with an area almost equal to that of France and the German Empire put together, and with a population of more than forty millions. This fact is alone sufficient to show how easily we may be misled by general comparisons; but other changes still more important have occurred, and they have been hardly less remarkable in the older provinces than in the new.

Forty years ago there was in India, comparatively speaking, little of what we now think the first necessities of a civilised administration. When I went from Calcutta to my first station in the North-Western Provinces, I was carried about a thousand miles in a box—for a palanquin is nothing better—on men's shoulders, and it took some three weeks to toil through a journey which is now accomplished in two days; there were no other means of travelling through the richest and most civilised parts of India. Speaking generally, roads and bridges had only begun to appear; railways were not thought of; the value of irrigation as a means of affording protection to the people from destruction by famine had hardly been recognised; there were few barracks in which English soldiers could live with tolerable health and comfort; there were few jails in which a sentence of imprisonment did not carry with it a serious probability that it would prove a sentence of death.

But the country at that time was entering on a phase of rapid change. The energies of the Government and its officers, which had at first been unable to do more than secure the bare existence of British power in India, by degrees rendered that power paramount. Then they were applied to its consolidation, and to the evolution of an organised system of administration out of the chaos bequeathed to us by the old rulers of the country. The firm establishment of order was followed by improvements in all directions. A vigorous impulse was given to material progress, and among the most active causes of the great changes which were beginning must be ranked the introduction of new and rapid means of communication. These not only directly developed the resources of the country, increased the wealth of the people, and profoundly altered the conditions of life, but they stimulated the vitality of every branch of the administration; they brought the various provinces of the Empire closer together, and England closer to India; English influence became stronger and stronger, and all classes set before themselves new and higher standards, as they were more frequently and immediately brought into contact with European habits and civilisation.

Even before the mutinies of 1857 this process of change had made great progress. After that revolution, which for a time nearly swept away our Government through a large part of India, the change went on with enormously accelerated speed. Thousands of Englishmen, not only soldiers, but Englishmen of almost every class, poured into India. Ten thousand things were demanded which India had not got, but which it was felt must be provided. The country must be covered with railways and telegraphs, and roads and bridges. Irrigation canals must be made to preserve the people from starvation. Barracks must be built for a great European army, and every sort of sanitary arrangement which could benefit the troops must be carried out, for we did not choose to let our soldiers go on dying like sheep in the old fashion. In fact, the whole paraphernalia of a great civilised administration, according to the modern notions of what that means, had to be provided.

This was true not only in regard to matters of imperial concern. Demands for improvement, similar to those which fell upon the central Government, cropped up in every city and in every district of the country.

Compare, for instance, what Calcutta was twenty years ago, and what it is now. This city, the capital of British India, supplies an excellent type of what has been everywhere going on. The filth of the city used to rot away in the midst of the population in horrible pestilential ditches, or was thrown into the Hooghly, there to float backwards and forwards with every change of tide. To nine-tenths of the inhabitants clean water was unknown. They drank either the filthy water of the river, polluted with every conceivable abomination, or the still filthier contents of the shallow tanks. The river, which was the main source of supply to thousands of people, was not only the receptacle for ordinary filth; it was the great graveyard of the city. I forget how many thousand corpses were thrown into it every year. I forget how many hundred corpses were thrown into it from the Government hospitals and jails, for these practices were by no means confined to the poor and ignorant; they were followed or allowed, as a matter of course, by the officers of the Government and of the municipality. I remember the sights which were to be seen in Calcutta in those days, in the hospitals, and jails, and markets, and slaughterhouses, and public streets. The place was declared, in official reports by the Sanitary Commission in 1864, in language which was not, and could not be, stronger than the truth required, to be hardly fit for civilised men to live in. There are now few cities in Europe with which the better quarters of Calcutta need fear comparison, and there is hardly a city in the world which has made more extraordinary progress.

I do not mean to say that Indian cities generally were so bad as Calcutta. This was far from being the case, but Calcutta affords, not the less, a good illustration of what has been and still is going on in India. Illustrations of the same sort might easily be multiplied. Fifteen years ago, for instance, in the great city of Rangoon, containing more than 100,000 people, with half a million tons of shipping, there was not a single public lamp, no supply of wholesome water, not a single drain except the surface drains at the sides of the streets, and no means of removing the night-soil and filth out of the town. About the same time, the Royal Commission for inquiring into the sanitary state of the army in India declared that thousands of the lives of our soldiers had been and were still being sacrificed in consequence of bad and insufficient barrack accommodation, and neglect of every sanitary precaution. So again, the Government was told, and in many parts of India it was certainly true, that, in consequence of the insufficiency of jail accommodation, the prisoners were dying at a rate frightful to think of, and that the necessary proceedings of the courts of justice involved consequences repugnant to humanity.

Thus arose demands for the requirements of civilised life and of modern administration, which had to be provided, and to a great extent for the first time, within the space of a few years. This was true not only of material appliances, of roads, and railways, and canals, and barracks, and city improvements, and so forth ; for the demand for improved administration became so strong, that it is not too much to say that the whole of the public services have been reorganised. Thus, for example, the police, which was in a shameful condition throughout India, has been placed on a completely new footing. The changes in the judicial service, and in the laws which it administers, have been as great; Lord Lawrence, when he was Viceroy, declared that the inadequacy of the pay given to the native judges, and to the chief ministerial officers of the courts, was a public scandal; many of these officers receiving salaries less than the wages earned in most parts of India by the better class of bricklayers and carpenters. No honest or satisfactory administration of justice was, under such conditions, possible.

The demands for every sort of public improvement, moral and material, which thus sprung up, could not be resisted. Whatever might be the cost, remedies had to be provided in the most complete way, and in the shortest time possible. There were doubtless those who thought and said that as these demands involved the expenditure of millions, compliance with them was impracticable or would be ruinous. Happily the Government of India decided otherwise.

It might perhaps have been better, in regard to some of the reforms which have been carried out, if the work of improvement had been more gradual. But the fault has been on the right side. A greater or more admirable work was never conceived in any country than that which has been undertaken, and in a great degree accomplished, by Englishmen in India during the last twenty-five years, and which is still going on. That mistakes should have been made in dealing with a country as large and as populous as the whole of civilised Europe was inevitable, and no doubt money has sometimes been needlessly or wastefully expended. Nevertheless, the work has been excellently done, and with this further merit, that there has been little talk about it. For all this the credit is not due to the initiative of the Government alone. India has indeed been fortunate in her Viceroys, but still more fortunate in the possession of a most admirable and hardworking body of public servants, to whose intelligence, devotion to their duties, and self-sacrifice, the results actually obtained are greatly due.

The magnitude of the work that has been accomplished is extraordinary. The England of Queen Anne was hardly more different from the England of to-day, than the India of Lord Ellenborough from the India of Lord Ripon. The country has been covered with roads, her almost impassable rivers have been bridged, 9,000 miles of railway and 20,000 miles of telegraph lines have been constructed, 8,000,000 acres of land have been irrigated, and we have spent on these works, in little more than twenty years, some 150,000,000*l*. Our soldiers' barracks are now beyond comparison the finest in the world; quarters which twenty years ago had a reputation little better than that of pest-houses are now among the healthiest in the British Empire, and the rate of mortality among the troops is not one-half what it was. The improvement in the jails and in the health of the prisoners has been hardly less remarkable. The cities and towns are totally different places from what they were.

Simultaneously with the progress of all these and a thousand other material improvements, with the increase of trade, the creation of new industries, and a vast development of wealth, there has gone on an equally remarkable change in every branch of the public administration. The laws have been codified, and improved, and simplified, until they have become the admiration of the world. The courts of justice and the police have been revolutionised, and, however far they may still be from perfection, India has obtained, to a degree unheard of and unthought of before, protection for life and property, and an honest administration of justice. All over India we have been building schools, and hospitals, and dispensaries. The natives of India have been admitted to a far larger share in the government of their own country. Municipal institutions, the first practical step in political education, have been established in all considerable towns in British India, and more than 12,000,000 of people live within their limits. It is needless to continue this catalogue of the changes that have taken place; but it is not the least remarkable part of the story that the accomplishment of all this work, and the expenditure of all this money, which have increased to an extent absolutely incalculable the wealth and comfort of the people of India, have added nothing to the actual burden of their taxation.

It will be plain that in the circumstances which have been described, comparisons between the statistics of Indian revenue and expenditure at the present time with the statistics of thirty or forty years ago have little financial meaning, but they will illustrate forcibly the immense change which has taken place in the condition of the country and the position of its government. Thus, for instance, the gross revenues of India, which were 21,000,000*l.* in 1840, were 40,000,000*l.* in 1860, and 65,000,000*l.* in 1878.[1] The total expenditure, which was 23,000,000*l.* in 1840, was 50,000,000*l.* in 1860, and 63,000,000*l.* in 1878. The public debt was 30,000,000*l.* in

[1] These and the figures immediately following are not strictly comparable, because many changes have been made in the system of accounts, and for other reasons; but for my present purpose, which is one of illustration only, they require no correction.

1840, 90,000,000*l.* in 1860, and is now 160,000,000*l.* The increase in all these cases has been enormous, yet it would be a complete mistake to suppose that growth of the revenue has been due to increased taxation, or that the real burden of the debt has become heavier. The land revenue, for instance, was 12,500,000*l.* in 1840, 18,700,000*l.* in 1860, and it is now about 22,000,000*l.*; but there is no province in India in which, measured by its incidence on the area actually assessed, the land revenue is not, where it has been altered at all, lighter than it was. The gross salt revenue was 4,600,000*l.* in 1860, and it now exceeds 7,000,000*l.*; yet in the greater part of India the rate of duty was higher in 1860 than it is now. In 1860, the customs revenue was 3,200,000*l.*, and there was hardly a single article of the import or export trade of India which was not heavily taxed; the customs now yield a million less, and it will be shown further on how great have been the remissions and reductions of duty, and how great the relief to the people and to trade. The income tax in 1861-62 yielded a revenue of nearly 2,000,000*l.*, and it was levied on every description of income and property without exception. The present license taxes and the new land cesses put together yield about half the revenue yielded by the income tax of twenty years ago; they affect a far smaller number of people, and they are levied at less than one-third the rate. This is not the place to pursue these comparisons, but it is a fact not open to question, that although the revenues have enormously increased, the burden of taxation is now lighter than it was twenty-five years ago.

Other statistics illustrate in a remarkable way the changes that have occurred in India.

In 1840. the total value of all the imports into

British India was about 8,000,000*l.*; in 1880 it exceeded 50,000,000*l.* In 1840, the total value of the exports was about 11,000,000*l.*; in 1880, it was nearly 70,000,000*l.* The trade of India is as great now as that of England was some forty years ago. In 1854, the first year for which any figures are forthcoming, the number of letters passing through the Post Office was 19,000,000, while in 1879 it was 132,000,000. It might be stated how many millions of people and how many millions of tons of goods are now carried on the railways, and how many telegraphic messages are despatched; but as twenty years ago railways and telegraphs in India had only begun to exist, there would be no comparison to make. In the last thirty years more than 150,000,000*l.* has been spent on railways, irrigation works, and other permanently useful objects, from which a gross yearly income of more than 15,000,000*l.* is now earned, and, as will be shown in the sequel, not only without causing any present appreciable burden on the finances, but concurrently with a large virtual reduction of the charge for debt.

The intention of the present volume is not to describe in detail the progress of British India during the last thirty or forty years, but to supply information as to the actual condition of the finances; and the growth of the revenues and expenditure during the last twelve years will be fully discussed further on. The foregoing figures are therefore given as illustrations merely of the fact that India is a totally different country now from what it was.

And this implies no disparagement of the work of our predecessors. On the contrary, great as, with the aids of modern science and capital, our own progress has been, it is hardly doubtful that each successive period since our countrymen first established themselves as the dominant power in Southern Asia, would, when viewed in relation to the circumstances of the time, yield in one direction or another results as great as those here recorded. How great they have been, and how vastly beneficial to the people we have taken under our rule, may best be seen by a comparison of the neighbouring Asiatic countries with British India, which has not only been rescued from the incessant sequence of foreign conquest, plunder, and anarchy which marked its past history, but has in little more than a century acquired a position of peace, good government, and wealth, which will compare favourably with many of the older States of Europe.

There have always been, and perhaps always will be, people who, according to the unfortunate English fashion of decrying the great achievements of their countrymen, endeavour honestly and persistently to show that, in consequence of the wickedness or stupidity of our Government, India is in a state bordering on bankruptcy; that its people are becoming poorer and poorer, more and more miserable, more and more exposed to ruin and death by famine; that crushing taxation goes on constantly increasing; that an enormous and ruinous tribute is exacted from India to be spent in England, and I know not what else. I have neither the time nor the inclination to reply to statements of this sort. 'I know,' said the wisest of English statesmen, 'the obstinacy of unbelief in those perverted minds which have no delight but in contemplating the supposed distress, and predicting the immediate ruin of their country. These birds of evil presage at all times have grated our ears with their melancholy song; and, by some strange fatality or other, it has generally happened that they have poured forth their loudest and deepest lamentations at the periods of our most abundant prosperity.'[1]

It is not pretended that, unlike any other country, the social, material, and political conditions of India now leave no room for improvement. Defects of many sorts can readily be pointed out. But it is through the very progress made that these become known. In the arts of administration, as in all other applications of knowledge, our views widen with each successive step we take; and the emphatic recognition that much yet remains to be done for the people of India, neither dims the lustre of what has been accomplished nor should cool the ardour of those who there continue the strife with human misfortune, weakness, or ignorance.

That India has gone on, with a speed hardly surpassed in any country, steadily increasing in knowledge, in wealth, and in all the elements of progress, that every branch of the public administration has constantly improved in honesty and efficiency, and that of all the things for which England deserves honour in the world, her government of India is the greatest and best—these are to me facts not requiring to be argued about. It is, broadly speaking, these facts which explain the enormous increase which has taken place in the revenue and expenditure and trade of India, and which have brought about such extraordinary changes in the condition of the people.

[1] Burke's *Third Letter on a Regicide Peace.*

CHAPTER II.

PROGRESS AND PRESENT CONDITION OF THE REVENUES AND EXPENDITURE.

Preliminary Explanations.

PUBLIC INCOME OF INDIA LARGELY DERIVED FROM SOURCES OTHER THAN TAXATION—LAND REVENUE AND FORESTS—TRIBUTES—OPIUM—ADMINISTRATIVE SERVICES—PUBLIC WORKS—OTHER RECEIPTS—TAXATION PROPER — EXCISE — CUSTOMS — SALT — STAMPS — DIRECT TAXES — PROVINCIAL RATES—INCIDENCE OF TAXATION ON PEOPLE—LOCAL TAXATION—CHANGES IN FORMS OF ACCOUNT—DIFFICULTIES IN WAY OF COMPARISONS BETWEEN PAST AND PRESENT.

THE gross annual revenues of British India at the present time exceed 68,000,000*l.*, but the larger part of this great income is derived from sources independent of taxation. This fact cannot be too clearly stated or steadily remembered, for, if it be forgotten, no accurate conception of the Indian finances, or of the incidence of the public burdens, is possible. We hear a great deal that is undeniably true regarding the poverty of the people of India and their inability to bear heavy taxation; and to persons accustomed to judge by an English standard it seems a terrible thing that this poor country should be forced to raise every year a revenue exceeded only by that of two or three of the greatest and richest of European nations. The truth is, however, that the public burdens in India are light to a degree absolutely without precedent, because the State has reserved to itself resources which in other countries belong to individuals, and possesses sources of revenue which render it in a great measure independent of taxation.

The most important of these resources is the land revenue, a rent-charge in favour of the public, a portion of the rent of land reserved by the State from time immemorial for its own purposes.

The State in India has always possessed, both in theory and in practice, the greater share of the property in land, and has been entitled to receive from the occupier such portion of the surplus profit after defraying the expenses of cultivation as it has appeared possible or expedient to take. The land revenue of India is this portion of this surplus. It has been the policy of the British Government to encourage the growth of private property in land, and even to create such property when no private rights of ownership could be found, and it has been an essential part of that policy to limit, either for a term of years or in perpetuity, the share of the rent or profit which the State is to receive. The remainder is private property. The rights of the State and of the private proprietor are identical in their nature, both being founded on long established custom. The object of our so-called settlements of the land revenue is to define the portions of the rent which the State and private proprietors shall respectively receive, and to give security to the latter that improvements made by them on their estates shall not lead to an increased demand on the part of the Government. A settlement of the land revenue has nothing to do, except indirectly, with questions of taxation, although the determination of the share of the rent which the private proprietor is to retain has of course the greatest possible effect in determining the value of his property, and affects immensely his capacity of meeting taxation.

These facts have been clearly explained by Mr. Fawcett.[1] The Government in India, he says, exercises over a great portion of the soil 'the same rights of property as those which an English landlord exercises over his own estate. The Government in India takes the place of individual landlords, and the cultivators of the soil rent their land from the Government instead of from private landowners. . . . As far as the cultivators of the soil are concerned, it can be a matter of no consequence whatever to them whether they pay a land tax to the Government, or whether they pay rent to private landowners. Hence a land tax is no harder upon the cultivator, nor does this impost cause any loss to the rest of the community. It therefore follows that a land tax, as long as it does not exceed a rack-rent, cannot increase the price of products raised from the land, for those who grow the products would not sell them cheaper if they paid rent to a private landlord instead of paying the same amount to the Government in the form of a land tax. A land tax consequently differs from all other taxes, for it possesses the excellent quality of providing a large revenue for the State without diminishing the wealth of any class of the community. Those, therefore, are completely in error who quote the aggregate amount of taxation which is raised in India in order to prove how heavily the people of that country are taxed. At least 20,000,000*l*. per annum is obtained in India by the land tax; but it would be as unreasonable to consider this amount as a burden laid upon the people as it would be to consider that the whole rent which is paid

[1] *Manual of Political Economy*, 5th edit. p. 568.

to English landlords in this country is an impost levied upon the cultivators of the soil.'

If, indeed, as Mr. Fawcett goes on to show, the land tax should exceed a rack-rent in amount, the effect would be to increase the price of agricultural produce, and there would be a tendency to throw land out of cultivation. It has never been pretended that any such results have followed from the very moderate assessments of the land revenue which now prevail in India. Their moderation, even in those provinces where settlements have been made for a term of years and not in perpetuity, is shown by the enormous increase that has taken place in the area under cultivation, and by the great and rapid increase of the selling price of land.[1] Under the native governments the right of the State to the whole of the surplus profits of the land, leaving to the occupier no more than was sufficient for his subsistence and for the expenses of cultivation, was and still is frequently exercised. The British Government never takes more than a fixed share, varying in different parts of India from four to eight per cent. of the gross value of the produce, and for many years past the tendency has been to diminish the share of the State, and to leave a larger share to the private co-proprietor. Although the gross land revenue has increased from 12,500,000*l.* in 1840 to 22,000,000*l.* in 1880, there is no province of India in which its incidence is not lighter now than it was forty years ago. This increase, says Mr. Cunningham, 'is owing partly to the addition of 36,000,000 of people, or twenty-five per cent., and 242,000 square miles of territory, with a land revenue of more than 6,000,000*l.*, partly to an increase of fifty to a hundred per cent. in the area of cultivation, partly

[1] *Report of the Indian Famine Commission*, 1880, part ii. p. 125.

to the increase in the price of agricultural produce, and in no instance to the enlargement of the share claimed by Government in the profits of the soil. In Madras, for instance, the area assessed has increased from 9,750,000 acres in 1850 to 20,000,000 in 1875-76, and though the land revenue is 1,000,000*l.* sterling higher, its incidence per acre is reduced by 4½*d.* on dry land, and 5*s.* on irrigated land. Similarly, in Bombay, the assessed area has increased from 12,500,000 acres in 1856 to 20,300,000 in 1875-76, and an increase of three-quarters of a million in the land revenue has resulted, notwithstanding an average reduction of 4½*d.* per acre in the assessment.[1] In the same manner in the North-Western Provinces, where the land revenue is calculated on the supposed value of the rental, there is no doubt that the share of the rent claimed by the Government has much decreased. Originally the theory was that the Government took eighty-five or ninety per cent. of the net rental, leaving the landowner only fifteen or ten per cent. for his own enjoyment. Under the settlements made by the British from 1833 to 1843, the Government proportion was reduced to two-thirds of the existing rental, the proprietors being further left in enjoyment of any increment which might occur during the thirty years of the settlement. When the period of the settlement expired, this

[1] The following figures are given by Mr. Cunningham in explanation of these results.

MADRAS.

	Assessed Area. Acres	Land Revenue. £	Average rate per Acre. Dry Land. R. A. P.	Average rate per Acre. Irrigated Land. R. A. P.
1852–53	9,780,000	2,502,000	1 3 11	7 0 11
1875–76	20,021,000	3,426,000	1 0 11	4 8 11

BOMBAY.

	Assessed Area. Acres	Land Revenue. £	Average rate per Acre R. A. P.
1856–57	12,550,000	1,647,000	1 5 4
1875–76	20,340,000	2,330,000	1 2 4

proportion was again reduced, and was fixed at fifty per cent.; but notwithstanding this reduction in the share claimed by the Government, the result of the general prosperity of the province and the increased out-turn of the crops has been to raise the land revenue from 3,680,000*l.* to over 4,000,000*l.* In the Punjab it is notorious that the land revenue is infinitely lighter than that in any previous period, and the fact is corroborated by the enormous increase in the price of land since it passed under our rule from the cruel rack-renting of the Sikh Government. In Bengal the land revenue has necessarily remained unchanged, notwithstanding the increase of the landlord's share of the rental from a few hundred thousand pounds to more than 10,000,000*l.* sterling.'[1]

The truth is that there has been a tendency of late to take too little rather than too much as land revenue, and to forget that, at any rate in a country like India, this is the best of all possible sources of public income, and better than taxation in any shape. A lamentable mistake of this sort (I refer of course to the permanent settlement) has led in Bengal not only to the sacrifice by the State of several millions of revenue a year, but to the still worse result of impoverishing the agricultural population of the most productive province in the Empire.

The gross amount brought to credit under the head of Land revenue in 1879-80 (including that due to irrigation) was 22,463,548*l.*, of which, however, 283,326*l.* was Capitation tax levied in British Burma, leaving 22,180,222*l.* Land revenue proper.

Besides this sum, the Indian Government derives a gross income of nearly 26,500,000*l.* from other sources

[1] *British India and its Rulers*, 1881, pp. 141-142.

altogether distinct from taxation. The following this shows these receipts for 1879-80 :—

Tributes and contributions from native states		702,45
Forests (sale of timber and other products, &c.)		676,234
Opium		10,319,162
Services :—	£	
Minor departments . .	99,282	
Mint	230,569	
Post office . . .	1,004,372	
Telegraph	505,552	
Law and justice (fines and receipts from convict labour, &c.) .	658,902	
Police	227,657	
Marine	258,187	
Education	139,414	
Medical	56,329	
Stationery and printing . .	56,019	
		3,236,283
Public works (railways, canals, and other works)		8,540,439
Receipts in aid of superannuation, retired and compassionate allowances . . .		525,141
Miscellaneous		337,370
Army (excluding £50,499 due to the Afghan war)		1,029,483
Gain by exchange		320,580
Interest on investments of the Paper Currency Department, loans to native states, municipalities, &c.		748,050
Total . . .		£26,435,193

Further details will be given subsequently of some of the more important of these sources of income; in this place it is only necessary to point out the fact that out of the whole gross revenue of 68,484,666*l.* received by the Government of India in 1879–80, more than 48,500,000*l.* was derived from sources other than taxation, and that less than 20,000,000*l.* was raised by taxation properly so-called. This latter sum was distributed as follows :—

Excise	2,838,021
Capitation tax in British Burma . . .	283,326
Assessed taxes	785,318
Provincial rates	2,882,125
Customs	2,280,793
Salt	7,266,413
Stamps (judicial and commercial) . . .	3,193,739
Registration	269,239
Total . . .	£19,798,974

The taxes levied under the heads of Assessed Taxes, Provincial Rates, Customs, and Salt will be fully discussed hereafter; and it will be shown how, with the exception of assessed taxes and provincial rates, the policy of the Government has been of late years to reduce, and not to increase, the rate of their incidence. With regard to the other items in the list of taxes properly so called, the Excise duties, yielding more than 2,800,000*l.*, are mainly paid by the lower classes to whom the consumption of drugs and spirits is for the most part confined. Stamps produce more than 3,000,000*l.*, two-thirds of which falls on litigation and one-third on commercial documents. The incidence of the Excise duties is $3\frac{1}{4}$*d.* per head; that of the Stamp duties is about $3\frac{3}{4}$*d.* per head. The incidence of the Customs duties is about $3\frac{1}{3}$*d.*, and of the Salt duty $6\frac{3}{4}$*d.* per head. The total incidence of taxation on the 185,000,000 persons constituting the population of British India, is 2*s.* per head. Adding the land revenue, the total burdens are about 4*s.* per head. Distributing the several items of taxation among the different classes of the population, according to their probable incidence, the following results have been arrived at. The land-owning classes pay about 5*s.* 6*d.* per head, or excluding the Land revenue, 1*s.* 6*d.* The agricultural labourer may pay in the shape of taxes on liquor and salt 1*s.* 6*d.*

a head, or for each family a fortnight's wages in the year. The artisan may pay 2*s*., or the earnings of five working days. Traders pay 3*s*. 3*d*.[1]

'The landowner,' writes Mr. H. S. Cunningham, 'pays for land revenue a sum ranging between 3 per cent. and 7 per cent. on the gross produce of his lands, and a further fraction by way of provincial rates. If he goes to law, he may contribute something to stamps; if he drinks, to excise; and, if he prefers English to native cloth, to customs; but when he has paid his land revenue, his only imperative tax is 7*d*. for salt. He is probably the most lightly taxed subject in the world, except the owner of personal property in India—money in the funds, &c.—who, though a millionaire, may under like conditions of abstinence from the luxuries of drink, litigation, and English cloth, contribute nothing but 7*d*. to the expenses of the State; such a man is obviously absurdly under-taxed. The artisan's position is the same; the trader when he has paid 7*d*. on salt, and, if his gains are over 50*l*. per annum, his license tax, may go free of further taxation; the only imperative tax on the agricultural labourer is the annual 7*d*. which he pays for salt. He is no doubt a very poor man, but his poverty can scarcely be said to be grievously enhanced by the exactions of the State.'[2]

There is another point of importance to be noticed. In all civilised countries heavy taxes are raised for local purposes, in addition to those collected for the purposes of the central government, and the two accounts are ordinarily quite distinct from each other. In India this is not the case: the receipts from all provincial and local taxation, excepting that raised in

[1] *Report of the Famine Commissioners*, part ii. pp. 91, 92.
[2] *British India and its Rulers*, 1881, p. 149.

municipalities for the service of the towns,[1] are incorporated in the imperial accounts, which show therefore nearly the whole of the burdens imposed for all purposes on the country.

Although, for the reasons before explained, attempts to compare the revenues and expenditure of British India at the present time with those of many years ago are likely to mislead, yet the same difficulties will not attend the examination of the variations which have occurred during the last twelve years, the period to which the present review is intended specially to refer.

There have been in this period no important territorial changes, and during it the existing system of financial administration has been more or less in force. The policy of constructing productive public works with borrowed money first took a practical shape in 1868–69, the year immediately preceding the selected period, and in 1870 it was decided that the construction of railways should be undertaken directly by the State. The year 1869–70 also was that immediately preceding the great fresh departure in Indian finance, which was taken by the introduction of the measures of decentralisation, which will be described further on. The gradual development of these measures has produced financial and administrative results of extreme importance, and the time of their introduction forms a convenient landmark. An examination into the state of the finances between 1869–70 and the present time will enable the reader to form an accurate conception of the changes for good or evil that have occurred in the interval.

Attempts have often been made to compare the

[1] There were, in 1878–79, 868 municipalities in British India, with an income of 1,305,442*l.*, of which 1,022,402*l.* was derived from taxation.

financial condition of India at various periods, and the results have been very variously stated. The fact is that, for many years past, there has been going on a constant process of improvement in the published abstracts of the accounts, and a constantly increasing amount of information and of detail has been given. Heads of accounts which used to be lumped together have been separated, while others have been consolidated, and instead of merely the net result of the differences between revenue and expenditure being shown, the actual revenue and expenditure have been entered on the two sides of the account.

For example, in Mr. Wilson's Budget statement in 1860, there were only six revenue heads. The first was 'land revenue, sayer, and abkaree,' and it included land, forest, and excise revenue, all lumped together; then came, separately, 'customs,' 'salt,' and 'opium;' then 'miscellaneous,' a large item of more than 4,000,000*l.*; and lastly 'receipts from railway companies,' which at that time were only 330,000*l.* On the expenditure side the charges on account of collecting the revenue from land, forest, excise, customs, salt, opium, post-office and stamps, and on account of political pensions, allowances, assignments, and charitable grants, were all included under one head; the remaining heads were 'interest on debt in India,' 'military charges,' 'marine,' 'civil charges' (which included all political, judicial, and police establishments, and all public works, except military and marine), 'miscellaneous,' and 'guaranteed interest on railway capital.' The charges incurred in England were not classified at all.

From that time the published abstracts of the accounts have been, from year to year, amplified and improved. The changes have been considerable, involving the entry of large gross amounts on each side of the account, which were previously shown net on one side only. For instance, until recently, the excess of the guaranteed interest on railway capital over the net earnings of the railways, was shown in one entry on the expenditure side, instead of the net earnings being entered on the revenue side, and the full guaranteed interest on the expenditure side. This obvious improvement has caused an addition to each side of the account of some 5,000,000*l.* So, again, the provincial revenue and expenditure is now entered in the gross, under the appropriate heads, instead of net on one side only of the account. This has added about 1,000,000*l.* to both sides. Finally, local revenue and expenditure, which, although as much public transactions as any other, used to be excluded altogether from the financial statements, have now been included, adding more than 2,500,000*l.* to each side of the account. Thus, under these three heads alone, the totals of the accounts of revenue and expenditure have been increased by about 8,500,000*l.*, without any addition whatever to the revenue or expenditure

Changes of this kind of course affect in no way the actual financial position of the country, or alter the surplus or deficit of the year. Even now, the form of the published abstracts is not perfect, but it gives immensely more information than it was possible to obtain from the abstracts as formerly framed. But it cannot be reasonably contended that the difficulties which changes of this kind throw in the way of persons who wish to make comparisons, whatever they be, ought to have deterred the Government, or should in future deter it, from rendering the published accounts as perfect and comprehensive in form as possible, or that, because our published statements were incomplete ten or twenty years ago, they ought to have remained incomplete for ever.

It should be added that the Government, having in view the great importance of trustworthy comparisons of the revenues and expenditure from year to year, has recently caused the accounts of the series of years from 1869–70 to the present time to be revised and brought into a properly comparable form, and a summary of them has recently been made public as a Parliamentary paper. The results thus obtained constitute the basis of the discussions contained in this volume, and it is believed that the figures, which have been obtained at the expense of great labour and attention in the office of the Comptroller-General (of Indian accounts) at Calcutta, may be fully relied upon. Abstracts of these accounts will be found, with other illustrative statements, in the Appendix.

It is further necessary to explain that in proceeding to discuss the progress of the revenues and expenditure it has been thought best, when treating of the main heads of revenue, to deal with the net income after setting off all necessary charges of collection and the like; and in like manner, when treating of the main heads of expenditure, to deal with the net charge after setting off all contingent receipts. The net charges under those heads of the administration which commonly cost more than they yield are classed as net expenditure, though it may be an essential condition of the service rendered that it shall be paid for, as in the case of the Mint, the Post Office, or the Telegraph.

It is also to be remembered that the two following Chapters, III. and IV., treat only of the ordinary revenues and recurring expenditure, on the due balance of which the equilibrium of the finances primarily depends; and that in them such extraordinary and disturbing causes of outlay as famine relief or war have been excluded from consideration, though their serious importance and influence on the general financial position will receive full attention afterwards.

CHAPTER III.

PROGRESS AND PRESENT CONDITION OF THE REVENUES AND EXPENDITURE.

The Revenues from 1869 *to* 1881.

LAND REVENUE—TRIBUTES FROM NATIVE STATES—FORESTS—OPIUM—MISCELLANEOUS RECEIPTS—TOTAL RECEIPTS OTHER THAN TAXATION—EXCISE—SALT—STAMPS—CUSTOMS—CAPITATION TAX IN BURMA—LICENCE TAX—PROVINCIAL RATES OR CESSES—TOTAL RECEIPTS FROM TAXATION—TOTAL REVENUES.

IN this Chapter I proceed to show the progress of each of the great branches of revenue during the last twelve years, and their present condition.

For reasons before explained the revenues will be arranged in two groups, those which are not, and those which are, derived from taxation properly so called.

The *Land revenue* (*a*) recorded in 1869–70 was, after deducting the capitation tax, 20,811,905*l.*, but this included an accidental credit of 408,764*l.*, the accumulated sale price of waste lands. The normal land revenue at that time did not exceed 20,400,000*l.* The amount of land revenue collected between 1876–77 and 1879–80 was so greatly disturbed by remissions or postponements of the demand made in consequence of famine that no comparisons can usefully be made between the figures for particular years. The amount realised in 1879–80 was 22,125,807*l.*, of which 338,657*l.* was on account of arrears in Madras due to past famine. The regular estimate for 1880–81 gives 21,414,000*l.*, including 65,200*l.* famine arrears, but the collections for the year have been retarded owing to the census operations, and the receipts are thereby diminished by about 445,000*l.* The normal land revenue, exclusive of the capitation tax, is now at least 21,750,000*l.* a year, or 1,350,000*l.* more than it was twelve years ago I have already explained the causes to which this great increase is due, and have shown that not only has there been no enhancement of the assessments, but that the demand of the State, in relation to the value and extent of the culturable area, has diminished, and continues to diminish.

The *Tributes and contributions from native states* (*b*) do not vary much from year to year. In the last twelve years they have never been lower than 675,120*l.*, or higher than 768,544*l.* The contributions are chiefly for the maintenance of local troops. The Government of India preserves peace throughout the native states under its protection, which have an area of more than 575,000 square miles, and a population of about 50,000,000. The sums paid by these states to the Government of India are insignificant compared to the benefits which they receive.

The net *Forest revenue* (*c*), which is almost entirely derived from the sale of timber and other forest produce, the property of the Government, was 158,854*l.* in 1869–70, and 223,000*l.* in 1880–81, and it has only once exceeded 237,000*l.*, namely, in 1875–76, when it reached 274,551*l.* The stationary condition of the net forest revenue has been rather a matter for satisfaction than otherwise. The forest administration, which is of comparatively recent creation, looks to the future interests of the community more than to present profit, and is more occupied in the preservation and improvement of the State forests than in realising an immediate large revenue. The gross revenue is now, however, close on 700,000*l.*

The net *Opium revenue* (*d*) has grown from 6,132,387*l.* in 1869–70 to 8,466,000*l.* in 1880–81, an increase of 2,333,613*l.* The annual average for the first period of four years from 1869–70 to 1872–73 was 6,672,756*l.*; from 1873–74 to 1876–77 it was 6,267,746*l.*; and from 1877–78 to 1880–81 it was 7,734,044*l.* The greater part of the increase has taken place in the last three years. Evidence will be adduced further on to show that this increase in the opium revenue has been neither temporary nor accidental, and that it is likely to continue.

There are many other branches of the administration which, though they yield a revenue, cost more than they yield, and they will therefore be discussed under the head of expenditure. It may here, however, be mentioned that the Mint, although not administered with that object, frequently yields a small surplus. Recently the Telegraph has also begun to do so, and the Post Office may perhaps do so before long, while the Productive Public works are rapidly approaching the time when they also will not only cover the entire amount expended on them—that is, their working expenses and the interest on the capital invested in their construction—but when they will yield a surplus revenue to the State.

There are certain small items of revenue and expenditure which do not belong to any of the main heads of account, and are therefore recorded as *Miscellaneous* (*e*). The average net revenue yielded by them for the last four years has been 21,532*l.*

The total net receipts from sources other than taxation, namely; Land revenue, Tributes, Forest, Opium, and Miscellaneous, were in 1869–70 28,009,878*l.*, and in 1880–81 they were 30,885,000*l.* Their average amount from 1869–70 to 1872–73 was 28,127,152*l.*; from 1873–74 to 1876–77 it was 28,113,932*l.*; and from 1878–79 to 1880–81 it was 30,020,036*l.*

The receipts derived from taxation proper will next be considered.

The net *Excise revenue* (*f*) has grown from 1,991,039*l.* in 1869–70 to 2,967,000*l.* in 1880–81, an increase of nearly 1,000,000*l.* The average receipts from 1869–70 to 1872–73 were 2,122,783*l.*; from 1873–74 to 1876–77 they were 2,317,999*l.*; and from 1877–78 to 1880–81 they were 2,640,766*l.* This increase of 50 per cent. in the last twelve years is not to be attributed to the increase of intemperance, but to improvement in the condition of the people, and, still more, to better administration. For obvious reasons it has everywhere been the policy of the Government to increase the rates of excise duty on spirits and drugs, as far as possible, consistently with avoiding the risk of illicit traffic.

The *Capitation tax* (*g*) in British Burma, which in the accounts is incorrectly credited under the head *Land Revenue*, gradually increases with the population, and has risen from 201,395*l.* in 1869–70 to 266,000*l.* in 1880–81. This tax is indefensible in principle, and being a direct tax is vexatious in the method of levy. It falls at the rate of 5 rupees on every married, and 2 rupees 8 annas on every unmarried man. Reference will again be made to this tax in connection with the salt duties.

Under the head *Assessed taxes* (*h*) the net revenue from income tax was 1,026,400*l.* in 1869–70, and the licence tax yielded 497,000*l.* in 1880–81; a decrease of 529,400*l.* The net amount levied under this head in 1870–71 was 1,988,023*l.* In 1861–62 it was 1,850,897*l.* In the first period of four years, from 1869–70 to 1872–73, the average annual receipts were 1,098,341*l.*; and in the last period, from 1877–78 to 1880–81, they were 531,965*l.* In the second period, from 1873–74 to 1876–77, neither income tax nor licence tax were levied, excepting some trifling arrears.

The largest net amount yielded in any year by the licence tax was 837,312*l.* in 1878–79.

The net receipts under the head of *Provincial rates* (*i*) were 1,235,496*l.* in 1869–70, and 2,731,000*l.* in 1880–81; an increase of 1,495,504*l.* In the four years from 1869–70 to 1872–73, their average annual amount was 1,484,330*l.*; in the next four years, from 1873–74 to 1876–77, it was 1,788,422*l.*; in the last four years, from 1877–78 to 1880–81, it was 2,576,856*l.* About 500,000*l.* of this increase was caused by the new rates imposed, for famine purposes, in 1877 and 1878. The remaining increase, amounting in the twelve years to nearly 1,000,000*l.*, has partly arisen from the natural growth of the older local revenues, but it has been chiefly due to increased local taxation, between 1869 and 1871. In Bengal, in 1871, rates yielding 340,000*l.* were imposed for the construction and maintenance of district roads and communications. In the Punjab, in 1871, rates yielding 137,000*l.* were imposed for local roads, education, hospitals, wells, and other useful purposes. In the same year the old rates, which had long been levied for similar objects in the North-Western Provinces, were placed on a legal basis, and slightly increased in amount, and rates yielding 35,000*l.* were imposed in Oudh. The local taxation in Madras and

Bombay was also increased to the extent of about 500,000*l.* by acts of the local legislatures passed in 1869 and 1871. In some of these cases the new rates took the place of various so-called voluntary and irregular cesses, which were not brought to account at all, and the change rather gave relief than otherwise.

With the single exception of the rates levied for the protection of the country against famine, yielding 510,000*l.* a year, the whole increase of taxation under this head has been for local purposes, of the kind just stated, not on account of the central government.

It must also be explained that under this head of Provincial rates are included receipts from rates on land, to the amount of about 500,000*l.* applied to payments for village services, such as in the greater part of India are not brought to account at all, although they are assessed and collected with the land revenue; they are therefore not in the nature of taxation. Excluding this sum, the total amount of taxation, properly so called, levied under the designation of Provincial rates, is about 2,200,000*l.*, of which about 1,700,000*l.* is wholly appropriated to provincial and local purposes.

The licence tax and the additional rates imposed on the land made up together, as will be explained elsewhere, the so-called famine taxation of 1877 and 1878, and they then yielded together 1,109,200*l.* The whole of the famine taxation yielded in 1880–81 about the same amount as that yielded by the income tax in 1869–70; and about one-half the sum yielded by that tax in 1861–62, and in 1870–71. In 1870–71 the income tax was levied at the rate of $3\frac{1}{8}$ per cent. or $7\frac{1}{2}d.$ in the pound. The present average rate of the licence tax is about $1\frac{1}{2}$ per cent. or $3\frac{3}{5}d.$ in the pound, and it affects immensely fewer people than the income tax.

The net amount derived from *Customs* (*j*) exclusive of the import duties on salt, which are under a separate head of account, shows little change. It was 2,167,797*l.* in 1869–70, and 2,269,000*l.* in 1880–81. The average for the first period of four years from 1869–70, was 2,316,284*l.*; for the second four years it was 2,371,656*l.*; and for the last four years it was 2,176,287*l.* In no year has the net revenue been so low as 2,000,000*l.*, or so high as 2,500,000*l.* Although the variations in the amount of the customs revenue have been so small, the changes made during the last twelve years have been numerous and important. Further details will be given hereafter on this subject, but it may here be noticed that all the changes have been for the relief of the taxpayer.

Before 1867, the law regulating the customs tariff imposed a general rate of duty on every article imported into or exported from British India. Such articles as were free, or were subject to special duties, were enumerated. The general rate from 1859–60 to 1863–64, was on imports 10 per cent. and on exports 3 per cent. The special duties were for a time on some large and important classes of goods as high as 20 per cent. In April 1864 the general import rate was lowered to 7½ per cent. The Act passed at the commencement of 1867–68 changed the plan on which all former tariff Acts had been drawn, and specified all the dutiable articles, leaving everything else free. The rate on imports, however, remained generally at 7½ per cent., and on six classes of articles the export duty continued to be 3 per cent., on two it was 4 per cent., while indigo and grain were subject to fixed duties.

In 1870 shawls, in 1873 wheat, and in 1874 lac dye, were freed from export duty. In 1875 the general rate of the import duties was reduced from $7\frac{1}{2}$ per cent. to 5 per cent.; and cotton manufactures, oils, seeds, spices, and all grains except rice, were exempted from export duty. In 1878 twenty-nine out of the sixty-two major heads of the list of articles on the import tariff, including some of the coarser kinds of cotton goods, were altogether exempted from duty, and in the same year the inland customs duties on sugar, which had yielded an annual revenue of 150,000*l.*, were abolished. In 1879 the whole of the coarser grey cotton goods were exempted from import duty with a sacrifice of 300,000*l.*, and the export duties on indigo and lac were removed, leaving nothing except rice subject to export duty. Notwithstanding these reductions, amounting altogether to nearly a million,[1] the revenue was, in consequence of the great increase of trade and prosperity, larger in 1880–81 than it was twelve years before.

The net *Salt revenue* (*k*) has increased from 5,462,501*l.* in 1869–70, to 6,573,000*l.* in 1881, or more than 1,000,000*l.* In the four years, from 1869–70 to 1872–73, the annual average net receipts from salt were 5,562,064*l.*; from 1873–74 to 1876–77 they were 5,717,465*l.*; and from 1877–78 to 1880–81 they were 6,461,454*l.* Although the increase has been more rapid during the last four years, it has gone on steadily through the whole period, since 1869–70; and, as will be shown further on, this has been accompanied by a reduc-

[1]
1875-76.	Import and export duties removed, and general rate of imports reduced .	. £308,000
1878-79.	Import duties and inland sugar duties removed	. 232,000
1879-80.	Import and export duties removed	. 351,000
	Total .	. £891,000

besides remissions of duty previous to 1875 on shawls, wheat, and lac dye exported, and on various articles imported.

tion of duty, and of the price of salt in the greater part of India.

The net revenue from *Stamps and Registration* (*l*) has increased from 2,280,670*l*. in 1869–70 to 3,243,000*l*. in 1880–81, an increase of nearly 1,000,000*l*. The growth of these branches of revenue has been steady. They yielded an average sum of 2,400,733*l*. from 1869–70 to 1872–73; 2,695,655*l*. from 1873–74 to 1876–77; and 3,098,359*l*. from 1877–78 to 1880–81. The stamps are both judicial and commercial. Before 1879–80 registration was included in the accounts under the head *Law and Justice*, but for the past two years a separate head has been specially made for this branch of the administration, the net revenue from which is expected to increase. In 1880–81 it amounted to 112,000*l*.

The total net sum received from all kinds of taxation properly so called was 14,365,298*l*. in 1869–70, and 18,546,000*l*. in 1880–81; an increase of 4,180,702*l*. From 1869–70 to 1872–73, the average annual receipts were 15,189,588*l*.; from 1873–74 to 1876–77 they were 15,137,106*l*.; from 1877–78 to 1880–81 they were 17,740,792*l*. Thus the whole increase has taken place in the last period of five years.

With the exception of the famine taxation, however, no fresh taxes have been imposed in India during the last ten years, and although the old taxes have become greatly more productive, this has been the result of increased prosperity and improved administration, and not of any enhancement of their rates. The truth is that although there has been some redistribution of the public burdens, with the object of making their incidence more equitable, the total weight of taxation has not been increased, but reduced during the last twenty years. The remissions of Customs duties alone, in the last five years, have nearly equalled in amount the whole sum now yielded by the licence tax and the famine rates put together.

Taking together all sources of revenue, the net receipts have risen from 42,375,176*l.* in 1869–70 to 49,431,000*l.* in 1880–81. This increase of 7,055,824*l.* has been spread in the most satisfactory way over all the great branches of the revenue. There is every sign that this will continue, but whatever may happen hereafter, we may, at least for the present, dismiss as erroneous all statements regarding the absence of elasticity in the revenues of India. If they have not shown themselves to be elastic it is difficult to conceive what elasticity means.

Abstract of Net Revenues from 1869 to 1881.

Head of account	Averages of four years			First and last years	
	1869–73	1873–77	1877–81	1869–70	1880–81
	£	£	£	£	£
(*a*) Land revenue, excluding capitation tax	20,617,402	20,649,879	21,352,047	20,811,905	21,414,000
(*b*) Tributes and contributions from native states	742,512	728,660	708,058	765,126	751,000
(*c*) Forests	140,905	203,614	204,355	158,854	223,000
(*d*) Opium	6,672,756	6,267,746	7,734,044	6,132,387	8,466,000
(*e*) Miscellaneous	*46,423*	264,033	21,532	141,606	31,000
Total revenue other than taxes	28,127,152	28,113,932	30,020,036	28,009,878	30,885,000
(*f*) Excise on spirits and drugs	2,122,783	2,317,999	2,640,766	1,991,039	2,967,000
(*g*) Capitation tax	205,053	227,085	255,105	201,395	266,000
(*h*) Assessed taxes	1,098,341	18,824	531,965	1,026,400	497,000
(*i*) Provincial rates	1,484,330	1,788,422	2,576,856	1,235,496	2,731,000
(*j*) Customs	2,316,284	2,371,656	2,176,287	2,167,797	2,269,000
(*k*) Salt	5,562,064	5,717,465	6,461,454	5,462,501	6,573,000
(*l*) Stamps and registration	2,400,733	2,695,655	3,098,359	2,280,670	3,243,000
Total taxes	15,189,588	15,137,106	17,740,792	14,365,298	18,546,000
Total net revenues	43,316,740	43,251,038	47,760,828	42,375,176	49,431,000

N.B. Figures in Italics signify expenditure in excess of revenue.

CHAPTER IV.

PROGRESS AND PRESENT CONDITION OF THE REVENUE AND EXPENDITURE.

The Expenditure from 1869 *to* 1881.

CHARGES UNDER LAND REVENUE INCLUDE COST OF INTERNAL ADMINISTRATION—ADMINISTRATION AND MINOR DEPARTMENTS—TOTAL CHARGES FOR EFFECTIVE CIVIL SERVICES—NON-EFFECTIVE CIVIL CHARGES—INTEREST ON DEBT—PUBLIC WORKS CHARGES—GUARANTEED RAILWAYS—PRODUCTIVE PUBLIC WORKS—ORDINARY PUBLIC WORKS—LOSS BY EXCHANGE—ARMY—INCREASE OF MILITARY CHARGES AND NECESSITY FOR REDUCTIONS—PROVINCIAL SURPLUS AND DEFICIT—EXPLANATION OF THESE ENTRIES—GENERAL CONCLUSIONS AS TO GROWTH OF EXPENDITURE.

THE progress of the net expenditure during the same twelve years will next be considered.

The head *Land Revenue* (1) has been exhibited in the statements given in the Appendix, both on the revenue and expenditure side of the account, instead of appearing net on the revenue side only, because the expenditure recorded under the head Land Revenue does not truly or exclusively represent the cost of collecting that revenue, but is incurred, to a large extent, for the internal general administration.[1] There

[1] For the year 1879–80 the total expenditure recorded under the head 'land revenue' is 2,937,185*l*. Of this 22,209*l*. was commission on collections of capitation tax, which should properly be deducted from the former and charged to the latter head. Of the remainder, 623,559*l*. represents charges for revenue survey, settlement, commission on land revenue collections, management of government estates, process-serving, and *malikana* to proprietors; these might properly be set off against land revenue. There are also charges amounting to 796,310*l*., described as 'allowances to district and village officers,' of which about 536,000*l*. would in most provinces be excluded from the land revenue account, the balance belonging to the general

are numerous departments of the public service which are administered by the Collectors of the land revenue, the connection of which with that revenue is only indirect. The greater part of the direct charges connected with the actual collection of the land revenue does not appear in the accounts at all. They form a part of the village expenses, and in most provinces, though assessed with the land revenue, are paid directly by the landholders to the village servants. A portion of the salaries of the district officers is now shown under the head 'Law and Justice,' on the ground that they have also magisterial duties to perform, the division of the charges between 'Land Revenue' and 'Law and Justice' being, however, quite arbitrary. In most provinces a moiety is charged under each head, but in Madras four-fifths is charged to Land revenue, and one-fifth to Law and Justice. These arrangements are complicated and misleading, and it would be an improvement if the expenditure on account of the salaries of the district officers and their establishments, now recorded under Land Revenue, and Law and Justice, were shown under the general head Administration.

The expenditure charged under 'Land revenue' has varied little during the last twelve years. It was 2,790,375*l.* in 1869–70, and 2,956,000*l.* in 1880–81. This slight increase of 155,625*l.* has been due, for the most part, to the creation of new districts in British Burma, the North-Western Provinces, and Oudh, and to various administrative improvements. The recent regulations for the admission of natives of India to the higher ranks of the civil administration, on a lower

administration. The remainder, or 1,520,685*l.*, is the cost of the district officers (collectors, assistant commissioners, &c.) and their establishments, and other general charges relating to the administration of the districts.

scale of emolument than that applied to officers who enter the service by competition in England (among whom no distinction of salaries is made, be they English or Indian), will tend to future economy, and as the heavy charges connected with settlement operations are likely soon to cease, no considerable future increase of expenditure under the head of Land revenue is probable.

Under the head *Administration* (2), the cost of the whole civil administration, down to the grade of Commissioners of division, is shown. It includes all the charges, both in England and India, on account of the Secretary of State, the Viceroy, Governors, Lieutenant-governors, Councils, &c. There has been little variation in the amount during the twelve years; it was 1,434,728*l.* in 1869–70, and 1,543,000*l.* in 1880–81. It is satisfactory to see that under this head the increase has been so small.

For the *Minor Departments* (3), such as the trigonometrical and topographical surveys, model farms, cinchona plantations, census, &c., it is unnecessary to give details. The whole net charges incurred are small, and are less now than they were in 1872–73, in which year they stood highest, at 377,217*l.*

The *Mint* (4) charges are in many years more than covered by the receipts, which consist of seigniorage and gain on the coinage and miscellaneous items. The highest net expenditure in the twelve years was 32,859*l.*, and the highest net revenue was 311,776*l.* The principal cause of variation is the quantity of money coined. The smaller the amount coined the more is the net cost to the government. In the twelve years ending March 31, 1881, nearly 70,000,000*l.* was coined in the Indian mints, almost entirely in silver. The net receipt realised during that period was nearly 650,000*l.*

Taking the *Post office* (5), and *Telegraph* (6), together, there has been a net reduction of expenditure of 119,649*l.*, the former showing an increase and the latter a decrease. The net cost of the Post office was 33,409*l.* in 1869–70, and 153,000*l.* in 1880–81, an increase of 119,591*l.* Its administration has been excellent. The development of the business performed by the post office, and of the efficiency of the service, is out of all proportion to the increase of charge. It has hitherto not been the policy of the government to treat the post office as a source of revenue, but to use the constantly growing receipts in increasing the usefulness and efficiency of the department. In no country in the world are lower charges made than by the Indian post office for the many and great public services which it performs. Under the head of Telegraph the net charge was 296,267*l.* in 1869–70, while in 1880–81, after providing a large sum for capital outlay, there was a net revenue of 35,000*l.*, an improvement amounting to 331,267*l.*

It was mentioned that the charges under *Law and Justice* (7) include a portion of the pay of district officers. The creation of new districts has thus led to an increase in these charges; but the general judicial administration has been much improved and the courts have been made more efficient, and much of the increase under this head has been due to the increased cost of maintaining prisoners in jails, owing to the prevalence in many parts of the country of famine and war prices. The net expenditure under this head was 2,145,233*l.* in 1869–70, and 2,595,000*l.* in 1880–81, an increase of 449,767*l.*

The net charge for *Police* (8) has varied very little during the twelve years. In 1869–70 it was 2,223,837*l.*, and in 1880–81 it was 2,282,000*l.*

The charge under *Marine* (9) was 989,793*l.* in 1869–70 and 325,000*l.* in 1880–81, but in the former year there were exceptional and nominal charges under this head, amounting to 320,000*l.*, on account of certain Bengal marine funds which were written off. The net expenditure in subsequent years has varied a good deal; the highest amount was 466,934*l.* in 1876–77, and the lowest was 272,653*l.* in 1879–80.

Under *Education* (10), the expenditure was 756,445*l.* in 1869–70 and 839,000*l.* in 1880–81; an increase of 82,555*l.* It is to be regretted that the increase has not been larger. Too much money is spent by the Government in giving to the richer classes a superior education for which they ought to pay themselves, while too little is spent on elementary instruction for the masses of the poor. It is true that in this respect matters are better than they were. Excepting in the North-Western Provinces, where an excellent system of village schools had already been established by Mr. Thomason and other enlightened men, there were, twenty-five years ago, in British India only about 2,000 schools maintained or aided by the Government, with about 90,000 scholars. Including the North-Western Provinces, there were about 8,000 schools, and 190,000 scholars. In 1879, the number of schools was 63,600, and the number of scholars was 1,800,000. But much remains to be done.

The net expenditure under the head of *Ecclesiastical* (11) has remained practically unaltered. Under *Medical* (12) the expenditure was 445,360*l.* in 1869–70, and 628,000*l.* in 1880–81, an increase of 182,640*l.* This signifies a greater number of hospitals and dispensaries, and is matter for congratulation. The *Political expenditure* (13) has slightly increased. The expenditure for *Stationery and printing* (14) is large, but it is difficult to overstate the advantage to the administration and to the despatch of public business resulting from the free use of printing. A considerable reduction under this head was made in 1871–72 and 1875–76, but it was not maintained. The expenditure under the four heads ecclesiastical, medical, political, and stationery and printing, was 1,383,640*l.* in 1869–70, and 1,736,000*l.* in 1880–81, an increase of 352,360*l.*

Taking altogether the fourteen heads under which the effective civil services are distributed, and which have been detailed above, the average net annual expenditure was 11,771,842*l.* from 1869–70 to 1872–73; 12,403,268*l.* from 1873–74 to 1876–77; and 12,457,158*l.* from 1877–78 to 1880–81. The expenditure was 12,188,152*l.* in 1869–70, and 12,723,000*l.* in 1880–81, an increase of 534,848*l.*—a moderate sum when we consider the immensely improved efficiency of the administration, and the fact that much of the increase has been due to a rise in prices.

The net charges for *Furlough allowances* (15) have increased since 1869–70; in that year they were 157,918*l.*, and in 1880–81 they were 224,000*l.* But this is only nominal, and is due to a change of system in the accounts. During the last eight years they have been stationary and have shown no tendency to increase.

The charge for *Superannuation allowances* (16) has gone on steadily growing during the last twelve years. The charges shown in the Appendix under this head are larger than those in the published returns in consequence of the omission in the former of a portion of the receipts, which are only book entries, and which prevent a proper comparison of the actual charges. The charge thus corrected was 993,581*l.* in 1869–70, and 1,864,000*l.* in 1880–81. This increase has been mainly due to the growth of the civil establishments during the past half-century, and it is, to some extent, a sign of greater efficiency in the public service, and of the determination to get rid of worn-out and incompetent officers. The large reductions lately made in the public works establishments have been a serious cause of increase under this head.

Taking the furlough and superannuation allowances together, the charges were 1,151,499*l.* in 1869–70, and 2,088,000*l.* in 1880–81; an increase of 936,501*l.* The average annual amount was 1,278,130*l.* from 1869–70 to 1872–73; 1,660,286*l.* from 1873–74 to 1876–77; and 1,975,490*l.* from 1877–78 to 1880–81. Thus there was an increase of 382,156*l.* in the second four years, and a further increase of 315,204*l.* in the last four years.

The payments under the head *Allowances and Assignments under treaties* (17) fell from 1,863,615*l.* in 1869–70 to 1,646,093*l.* in 1877–78, chiefly by the gradual lapse of political pensions, which form a large portion of this charge. In the last three years the amount has again increased owing to the payments made to some of the states of Rajputana on their transferring their right to collect salt duties to the British Government. The expenditure for 1880–81 is 1,908,000*l.*, of which about 700,000*l.* is for political pensions, 350,000*l.* for compensations of various descriptions, and the remainder represents alienations of the land revenue, chiefly in Madras and Bombay, which in other parts of India would be dealt with as deductions and not appear in the public accounts at all. These charges have no tendency to increase.

The apparent net charge for *Interest on debt* (18) has risen from 5,245,187*l.* to 5,655,000*l.*, or 409,813*l.*

In fact, however, there has been not only no real increase, but, as will be presently shown, a large reduction of burden on the taxpayer, because we must set off against the charge for interest on the money borrowed for productive public works, the net income received from them.

The growth of the income from railways and canals has not been the sole cause which has led to the virtual diminution of the interest charge notwithstanding the increase of the debt. Owing to the steady improvement in the credit of the Government of India, a large amount of interest has been saved by the repeated conversion of debt bearing higher interest into debt bearing lower interest. In India, in 1869, there was 30,500,000*l.* of the debt bearing interest at 5½ and 5 per cent.; in 1880 there was in place of it, 23,500,000*l.* debt at 4½ per cent. and 7,000,000*l.* at 4 per cent. A similar improvement has taken place in the Home debt. In 1869-70, 22,200,000*l.* of this debt bore interest at 5 per cent. Practically no part of the sterling debt now bears interest above 4 per cent., and the success last year of the 3½ per cent. loan shows that further reductions may be anticipated. The capital of the debt in England has increased by about 40,000,000*l.*, but the interest has increased by little more than 100,000*l.* The general result is that the average rate of gross interest charge on the whole Indian debt has fallen from 4·6 per cent. in 1869–70 to 3·8 in 1880–81, or about ¾ per cent.

Although, however, the burden of interest has diminished, the policy of constructing productive public works with borrowed money has necessarily led to a constant growth of the capital of the debt. At the commencement of 1869–70 the total debt in India and in England was 97,379,000*l.*; at the end of 1880–81 it was 157,149,000*l.*, an increase of 59,770,000*l.* During these twelve years 38,415,000*l.* has been spent on productive public works, besides 10,208,000*l.* provided in part payment for the East India Railway on its purchase in 1880, and 7,456,000*l.* advanced as loans to Native states, corporate bodies, and individuals, on interest; this accounts for nearly the whole increase.

The total net expenditure on *Public works* (19) of all kinds met from revenue, including payments of guaranteed interest, but excluding the public works portion of the interest on debt, and the credits received on account of increased land revenue due to irrigation, was in 1869–70 6,635,796*l.*, and in 1880–81 it was 3,852,000*l.* Combining the charge for interest on debt and for public works, it will be seen that the total net outlay under these two heads has been reduced from 11,880,983*l.* in 1869–70 to 9,507,000*l.* in 1880–81, that is, by 2,373,983*l.*, a result essentially due to the growth of the public works income.

The accounts are now prepared so as to distinguish the part of the interest chargeable on the borrowed capital spent on public works from the other interest. Making this division, the net interest on ordinary debt was 5,151,579*l.* in 1869–70, and in 1880–81 it was reduced to 3,300,000*l.*, a decrease of 1,851,579*l.* The public works portion of the interest increased in the same time from 93,608*l.* to 2,355,000*l.*, or by 2,261,392*l.*, the net increase being, as before stated, 409,813*l.*

Including the charges on account of the guaranteed railways and the public works portion of the interest on debt, and taking credit for the increased land revenue due to irrigation, the net public works expenditure on all accounts was 6,601,000*l.* in 1869–70, and 5,506,000*l.* in 1880–81, showing a decrease of 1,095,000*l.*

The net charge for guaranteed railway interest, including the East Indian railway (after allowing for the set-off obtained from the net traffic receipts), which in 1869–70 was 1,498,000*l.*, was converted in 1880–81 into a net receipt of 337,000*l.*, showing an improvement of 1,835,000*l.*

The public works classed as productive, or those yielding revenue, taking account of all interest charges and all net income, led to a net revenue of 299,000*l.* in 1869–70 and to a net charge of 532,000*l.* in 1880–81. In this period the net income had increased from 443,000*l.* to 1,529,000*l.*, the interest charge at the same time having grown from 144,000*l.* to 2,061,000*l.*

The public works expenditure under all heads not classed as productive, including roads and buildings of all descriptions, was 5,311,000*l.* in 1869–70 and 5,312,000*l.* in 1880–81, exclusive of the large outlay in the last year on the frontier railways, which has been treated as a contingency of the Afghan war. This class of outlay was summarily reduced by Lord Mayo in 1870-71 by more than 1,000,000*l.*, as he was satisfied that it had become more than the country could afford, but it was again increased, until in 1873–74 it stood at 5,382,000*l.* From 1876–77 to 1879–80 it remained at about 4,500,000*l.*, in 1880–81 rising again to 5,312,000*l.* The reduced expenditure between 1876 and 1879 was in some measure due to restrictions imposed in consequence of the pressure, first of famine relief, and afterwards of the Afghan war, and the increase in the last year has followed on the removal of those restrictions, and will be met, to a great extent at least, from the accumulated balances of the Provincial governments.

The whole subject of the expenditure on public works, and its effect on the public debt and the charges for interest, will be more fully gone into subsequently, but the foregoing summary will show that so far from there having been any increase of the public burdens on this account, there has been a relief now amounting annually to nearly 2,800,000*l.* sterling.

The next head of expenditure requiring notice is *Loss by Exchange* (20). It arises partly upon the transactions with the guaranteed Railway companies, but chiefly upon the sale of the Rupee bills of the Secretary of State. The difficult problems suggested by this most serious burden, over which the Government of India is unable to exercise any control, are treated of in another chapter. Here it will only be remarked that among all the causes of financial anxiety in India there has been, for some years past, no cause which can for a moment be compared with this in importance. In consequence of the great fall in the gold price of silver, the loss incurred by the Government of India on its remittances to England has assumed most formidable proportions. In 1869–70, the loss by exchange was 102,786*l.*; in 1880–81, it was 2,553,000*l.*; an increase of 2,450,214*l.* In the four years from 1869–70 to 1872–73 the average annual charge was 270,152*l.*; from 1873–74 to 1876–77 it was 951,170*l.*; from 1877–78 to 1880–81, it was 2,364,050*l.*

The cost of the *Army* (21), apart of course from war, has increased during the twelve years by 218,866*l.* It was 15,247,134*l.* in 1869–70, and 15,466,000*l.* in 1880–81. It was intermediately reduced by more than a million; and was at its lowest point, 14,218,378*l.*, in

1873–74. From 1869–70 to 1872–73 the average annual charge was 14,922,773*l.*; from 1873–74 to 1876–77 it was 14,433,550*l.*; from 1877–78 to 1880–81 it was 15,636,006*l.* This increase has for the most part been caused, directly or indirectly, by changes of system which have been introduced at various times, and has fallen chiefly on the non-effective charges, the growth of which has more than swallowed up the important economies carried out in the effective charges. The additional payments in the shape of pensions and their capitalised values, which have been unavoidable consequences of the abolition of the old Indian army, have increased the yearly non-effective charge by 750,000*l.*, and the increase in payments on account of the European troops who have served in India amounts to about half that sum. This increase of military expenditure, which from its nature has been beyond the power of the Government of India to control, is the most unsatisfactory part of the financial history of the last few years. No subject was more anxiously considered by Lord Lytton. He was convinced that the military charges were excessive, while at the same time the army in India was, in some respects, far from being as efficient an instrument as could be desired. I am not competent to criticise the details of military organisation and administration, but there can be no doubt that many of the highest military authorities concur with this opinion of Lord Lytton. In 1879 he appointed a special commission to inquire into these subjects. It had for its president Sir Ashley Eden, one of the most eminent of Indian administrators, and it included among its members some of the most distinguished of Indian soldiers, among whom may be named Sir Frederick Roberts and Sir Peter Lumsden. There were some subjects, in a great measure political in their nature, on which there was a difference of opinion in the commission, but on almost all the important military questions its conclusions were unanimous. It declared its belief that, if its recommendations were adopted, the strength and efficiency of the army in peace and war, and the popularity of the service, would be greatly increased, and that without the sacrifice of anything that had any value, the military expenditure in India might be reduced by 1,250,000*l.* a year.

I know how the powers of obstruction and prejudice and *laissez faire*, both in India and in England, are apt to stop attempts at army reform, and to frustrate efforts to diminish the immense military charges now imposed on the country. I am not sanguine that we shall soon see them very largely decrease, but that they ought to be decreased there can be no doubt whatever. It is not only in India that attention to the subject of Indian military expenditure is required. The Government of India has never concealed its opinion that in apportioning the charges which have to be shared between the two countries, and when the interests of both English and Indian taxpayers have been at stake, India has sometimes received a scant measure of justice. This feeling has been increased by the knowledge, learned by the experience of the past, that this is a matter in which India is helpless. It is a fact, the gravity of which can hardly be exaggerated, that the Indian revenues are liable to have great charges thrown upon them without the Government of India having any power of effectual remonstrance. The extension to India of the numerous measures taken in England to improve the position of the officers and soldiers of the army was no doubt right and unavoidable, but the fact that heavy additional expenditure has thus been incurred by India gives her a claim to expect that no efforts shall be spared to diminish charges which are unnecessary, or of which she bears too large a share.

The heading *Provincial and Local Surplus or Deficit* (22), requires a few words of explanation. Under the system of Provincial finance initiated under the Government of Lord Mayo, of which a full description will be given in the sequel, contracts are made in respect of certain branches of revenue and expenditure between the Imperial and Local Governments, the Local Government being entitled to receive credit in their account with the Imperial treasury for any saving they may effect, and, per contra, being bound to make good any excess charge they may incur, the balance at their credit remaining at their disposal from year to year, and not lapsing to the Imperial treasury as in the case of ordinary grants from the revenue. The Provincial surplus thus in fact represents an addition to be made to the Provincial balance by the Imperial Government, and the Provincial deficit a payment to be made from the Provincial balance to the Imperial Government. In this way, while the Imperial and Provincial revenues and expenditure are brought into one combined account, the true separate surplus or deficit for the year is shown, both on the Imperial and Provincial accounts. In the four years 1869–70 to 1872–73 there was an average net surplus on the Provincial accounts of 338,967*l.*, in the next four years from 1873–74 to 1876–77 there was an average annual net deficit of 279,714*l.*, and in the last four years from 1877–78 to 1880–81 there was an average annual net surplus of 446,074*l.* The final result of the twelve years was an accumulated net surplus due to the Provincial Governments of 2,021,309*l.* It is from this accumulation that the Local Governments are enabled to meet the increased expenditure before noticed, for ordinary public works, many of which, though not productive in the restricted and conventional sense of that term, will nevertheless yield direct returns and develop the resources of the country.

I have now referred to all the permanent heads of expenditure. For reasons which will be more fully stated hereafter the charges on account of Famine relief and War are not here included, and the general result is that, apart from these, the net expenditure which was 42,418,230*l.* in 1869–70 was 44,335,000*l.* in 1880–81, an increase of 1,916,770*l.* For more full details reference may be made to the statements in the Appendix.

That this result, always excepting the increase in the last five years of the normal military expenditure, and the increase in the last six years of the loss by exchange, is, when analysed, highly satisfactory, it is impossible to deny. It shows, in the first place, that in the total cost of those branches of the Civil Administration over which the Government of India has had complete control there has been no increase whatever; there has been, on the contrary, an actual diminution of charge. This has, to a great degree, been due to the measures of decentralisation, by which while the powers and responsibilities of the Provincial Governments have been largely increased, their inducements to strict economy have at the same time been equally stimulated. Next it is seen that the apparent increase of expenditure includes 410,000*l.* of interest, but that in reality the burden under this head has been reduced by about 3,500,000*l.* The whole of the remaining increase has been caused under the head Loss by Exchange by the fall in the gold price of silver, a matter absolutely beyond the control of the Government.

ABSTRACT OF THE NET EXPENDITURE FROM 1869 TO 1881.

Head of account	Average of four years			First and last years	
	1869–73	1873–77	1877–81	1869–70	1880–81
	£	£	£	£	£
1. Land revenue, exclusive of capitation tax	2,772,482	2,877,573	2,935,138	2,790,375	2,956,000
2. Administration	1,439,065	1,552,158	1,503,268	1,434,728	1,543,000
3. Minor departments	279,430	342,413	292,701	190,575	323,000
4. Mint	*793*	*36,607*	*123,785*	*56,150*	6,000
5. Post office	39,249	153,110	132,361	33,409	153,000
6. Telegraph	251,979	155,712	33,071	296,267	*35,000*
7. Law and justice	2,247,062	2,485,274	2,639,769	2,145,233	2,595,000
8. Police	2,168,964	2,227,548	2,247,209	2,223,837	2,282,000
9. Marine	538,358	366,166	301,703	989,793	325,000
10. Education	717,166	835,029	838,231	756,445	839,000
11. Ecclesiastical	157,438	163,978	157,063	161,126	159,000
12. Medical	504,101	604,083	627,727	445,360	628,000
13. Political	371,223	426,781	467,359	415,367	521,000
14. Stationery and printing	286,118	250,051	405,343	361,787	428,000
Total effective civil services	11,771,842	12,403,268	12,457,158	12,188,152	12,723,000
15. Furlough allowances	165,519	235,089	227,004	157,918	224,000
16. Superannuations	1,112,611	1,425,197	1,748,486	993,581	1,864,000
Total non-effective civil services	1,278,130	1,660,286	1,975,490	1,151,499	2,088,000
17. Allowances and assignments under treaties	1,773,747	1,745,334	1,798,803	1,863,615	1,908,000
18. Interest	5,419,945	5,106,542	5,700,467	5,245,187	5,655,000
19. Public works, including guaranteed interest	6,221,088	5,870,744	3,852,876	6,635,796	3,852,000
Total interest and public works	11,641,033	10,977,286	9,553,343	11,880,983	9,507,000
20. Exchange	270,152	951,170	2,364,050	102,786	2,553,000
21. Army	14,922,773	14,433,550	15,636,006	15,247,134	15,466,000
22. Provincial and local surplus or deficit	338,967	*279,714*	446,074	*15,939*	90,000
Total net expenditure	41,996,644	41,891,180	44,230,924	42,418,230	44,335,000

N.B. Figures in Italics signify receipts in excess of expenditure.

CHAPTER V.

PROGRESS AND PRESENT CONDITION OF THE REVENUE AND EXPENDITURE.

General Results.

REASONS FOR EXCLUDING CHARGES FOR FAMINE AND WAR FROM REVIEW OF REVENUES AND EXPENDITURE—GENERAL RESULTS OF PAST TWELVE YEARS—AMOUNT OF SURPLUS EXCLUDING FAMINE AND WAR—CORRECTIONS TO BE APPLIED TO INSURE PROPER COMPARISONS—EFFECT OF FAMINE AND WAR EXPENDITURE ON THE BALANCE OF ORDINARY REVENUE AND CHARGES—STATEMENT OF ULTIMATE DEFICIT—MEASURES TAKEN TO MEET FUTURE FAMINE OUTLAY—HOW FAR SUCCESSFUL—INFLUENCE ON FINANCIAL POSITION OF EXPENDITURE OF BORROWED MONEY ON PUBLIC WORKS—PRESENT NORMAL SURPLUS SUFFICIENT TO ADMIT OF FURTHER FISCAL REFORM.

THE charges arising from famine and war, which have been excluded from the review of the ordinary expenditure contained in the preceding chapter, although uncertain and adventitious, are as real as any others, and adequate provision has equally to be made for them. Heavy expenditure for war is, however, so exceptional in its occurrence that it is neither necessary nor would it be practicable to make special provision, in anticipation, for meeting it from the ordinary yearly revenues. But no such plea can be urged in regard to famine. Drought and scarcity or famine are calamities which, under present circumstances at least, must be expected to recur periodically and at comparatively short intervals, and the cost of relieving them must obviously, under a sound system of finance, be provided from the annual revenues. The only way, however, of making such provision is by securing a sufficient surplus of revenue assets over the ordinary recurring liabilities of expenditure; and it is as true of charges for famine relief as it is of those for war, that unless they are separately shown the normal condition of the finances cannot be understood, nor can any comparison be made between the financial position in different years, or groups of years, unless these great disturbing elements are eliminated. Thus, for example, the expenditure on Famine relief in the last three years has been 464,691*l.*, while in the previous two years it was 7,512,306*l.* It would give a totally incorrect idea of the comparative condition of the finances in the two periods, if we were to treat the famine expenditure as an ordinary incident of the first period, and were to ignore the fact that in the second period, although little such expenditure was actually incurred, it was necessary to store up, so to speak, during this time of prosperity resources to meet the inevitable requirements of the future.

While, therefore, due consideration will be given in the sequel to the actual charges for famine and war in the last twelve years, and the effect produced by these charges on the finances, it has been deemed preferable, in the first instance, to show the progress of the revenues and expenditure apart from these causes of disturbance. The net figures have also been taken because they give a more accurate idea of the real condition of the finances than figures representing the gross receipts and charges.

The total net revenues derived not only from the taxes, but from Land, Tributes, Forests, Opium, and Miscellaneous sources amounted in 1869–70 to 42,375,176*l.*, and in 1880–81 to 49,431,000*l.*, showing an increase of 7,055,824*l.* In the four years from 1869–70 to 1872–73 the average annual net revenues were 43,316,740*l.*, in the next four years, from 1873–74 to 1876–77, they were 43,251,038*l.*, and in the last four years, from 1877–78 to 1880–81, they were 47,760,828*l.* Thus this great increase has taken place in the last four years. Before 1878–79, the net revenues never reached 44,250,000*l.*

Making a similar comparison on the other side of the account, the total net expenditure, exclusive of the charges on account of famine and war, and omitting certain exceptional credits of the assets of the military funds was 42,418,230*l.* in 1869–70, and in 1880–81 it was 44,335,000*l.*, an increase of 1,916,770*l.* In the four years from 1869–70 to 1872–73 the average annual net expenditure was 41,996,644*l.*; in the second four years, from 1873–74 to 1876–77, it was 41,891,180*l.*; in the last four years, from 1877–78 to 1880–81, it was 44,230,924*l.* Thus, as with the net revenue, the greater part of the increase of net expenditure has occurred in the last four years. It reached its maximum in 1878–79, when it amounted to 45,820,198*l.*

Apart, therefore, from famine and war, a comparison between 1869–70 and 1880–81 shows that while the net revenue increased by 7,055,824*l.*, the net expenditure increased by 1,916,770*l.*; thus the financial position was, putting aside the charges for famine and war, better in 1880–81 by 5,139,054*l.* than it was twelve years before.

Setting off the net expenditure against the net revenue, exclusive always of war and famine, the general results for the twelve years would be to show an aggregate surplus of 24,839,433*l.*, distributed over the three periods of four years as follows:—

	£
In the first period, an average of . . .	1,320,096
„ second period „ . . .	1,359,858
„ third period „ . . .	3,529,904

There are, however, certain corrections to the foregoing comparisons which a severe criticism of the financial position might appear to demand, and which it may be well to notice.

One such correction, and it is the most important, has indeed been already applied by excluding from credit sums amounting in the aggregate to 3,599,212*l.*, which were transferred to revenue under the head 'Receipts in aid of superannuation, retired, and compassionate allowances,' from the book balances of the military funds when the liabilities of those funds were taken over by the Government. This departure from the published figures was before mentioned. It is unnecessary to discuss the question whether the procedure adopted in regard to these funds was, as a mere matter of account, accurate. It was not approved by the Government of India, but was ordered by the Secretary of State. Instead of the whole assets being credited to revenue as soon as they became the property of the State, they were credited piecemeal year by year in sums varying from 250,000*l.* to nearly 600,000*l.*, and thus the annual revenue was, for a number of years, artificially increased. These nominal credits which added nothing to the revenue have therefore in the present review been excluded. The whole of these assets have now been brought to credit, and no further disturbances on this account will occur. It may be mentioned that a sum of 3,051,918*l.*, the balance of the Civil Service Annuity fund, taken over by the Government in 1874–75 under very similar circumstances, was not credited as ordinary revenue, and has not, therefore, disturbed the comparison of the accounts.

There are two other items of expenditure which are treated in the accounts in a manner to which, on examining and comparing the annual financial results, objection might be taken. These are the Loss by Exchange and the expenditure on Bengal Opium.

The sums recorded annually as Loss by Exchange show the loss on the actual remittances to England to meet the home charges. But the remittances during the twelve years fell actually short of the whole current requirements of the Home treasury by 28,578,135*l.*, and this amount was provided by borrowing in London. In the finance and revenue accounts, the loss by exchange on this sum, amounting to 1,773,427*l.* is not charged; but clearly this advantage was not wholly real. It is true that apart from the direct diminution of expenditure thus caused under the head Loss by Exchange, the current finances have indirectly benefited from the short remittances and the borrowings, which may have led to some improvement in the rates of exchange, but no estimate of the amount of this advantage could be made. But on the other hand, the home charges have been increased by the interest on the money borrowed to replace the short remittances; and to make the comparison between the several years really fair, there should be added to the recorded net loss by exchange, the sum by which it would have been increased if the whole current requirements of the Home treasury had been met by remittances from India year by year, while the interest paid on the money borrowed to make good the deficiency should be deducted from the amount recorded under the head of Interest.

The expenditure charged in each year under the head of Opium does not represent the actual cost of opium sold during the year. The conditions of the opium revenue will be explained more fully hereafter, but it may here be stated that the recorded expenditure of each year represents the cost of the crop produced and manufactured in that year; while the quantity of opium sold in the year has no direct relation to the crop of that year, but is fixed with reference to the average crop of a number of years, and to the necessity of keeping a reserve stock to meet short crops. For the purposes of a comparison of the general financial position in different years, it is not right that the finances of any particular year should benefit by the accidental small outlay on a short crop, or suffer by the large expenditure on a bumper crop. During the twelve years we have paid 1,105,299*l.* more than the actual cost of the opium sold, and this sum is invested in the reserve stock of Bengal opium actually existing at the end of the year 1880–81. To make the comparison correct, therefore, the expenditure under the head of Opium should be adjusted so as to counteract this excess charge.

The effect of excluding from credit the amounts saved by short remittances to England, and of excluding from expenditure the amount invested in the reserve stock of opium, would on the whole be to lessen the accumulated surplus by 668,128*l.* Such an amount, however, is of little importance in relation to the total surplus, which amounts to nearly 25,000,000*l.*, and it may be disregarded for practical purposes.

Introducing now the exceptional expenditure due

to famine and war, it will be found that in the twelve years in question 14,788,819*l.* was spent on famine relief, and that the net charge on account of the Afghan war was 18,072,353*l.*, or in all 32,861,172*l.* These charges therefore convert the calculated surplus of 24,839,433*l.* on the ordinary account into an actual deficit of 8,021,739*l.*

Against this deficit, however, may be set the surplus amounting to 2,021,309*l.*, which has in the same period accrued to the local governments, so that the ultimate deficiency on the Imperial and Provincial accounts together is only 6,000,430*l.* This has been the result not only after meeting the very large direct expenditure before stated (32,861,172*l.*) for famine and war, but after losing about 2,000,000*l.* in land revenue in the Madras presidency, and after being subjected to the vast loss by exchange, which has amounted in the last six years to 12,000,000*l.* Thus the annual revenues have been nearly sufficient to cover all these great and exceptional charges, and if there had been neither famine nor war the accumulated surplus of the twelve years would have not been far from 30,000,000*l.*

A careful examination made in 1877 into the condition of the finances, based on the accounts of the preceding seven years, satisfied the Government that, applying the strictest tests, the income and expenditure of the State might, with one reservation, be then considered, for practical purposes, to be in a condition of equilibrium. This reservation was a serious one. It was that there was no sufficient surplus of income over expenditure to meet the obligation caused by the periodical occurrence of famine. The Government thought it necessary, therefore, to improve the financial position by 1,500,000*l.* a year on account of famine liabilities alone; and, in addition to this, to provide a margin on the annual estimates of about 500,000*l.* to meet unforeseen contingencies. The measures consequently taken will be described further on. There can now be no question not only that the improvement aimed at in 1877–78 has been secured, but that India now possesses an annual surplus greatly exceeding the normal surplus of 2,000,000*l.* then declared to be necessary. Apart from the expenditure on the Afghan war, there was a surplus on the ordinary account of 2,710,465*l.* in 1878–79; of 4,917,525*l.* in 1879–80; and of 5,075,893*l.* in 1880–81.

In fact, the annual revenues have not only been sufficient to meet the whole cost of famine relief, which properly falls among the ordinary charges, but also to cover a very large part of the cost of the war. As, however, most of the famine expenditure was actually incurred before the commencement of the last period of four years, and as the greater part of the improvement of the revenues has taken place within this same period, it is more correct to say that the greater part of the money spent on the war has been provided from the revenues, and that a portion of the famine charges was met by borrowing.

The average annual charge on account of famine, if distributed over the twelve years, would be 1,232,400*l.*, or rather less than the sum of 1,500,000*l.*, which the Government of India estimated to be the average burden for which provision must be made. It may reasonably be hoped that even if future seasons should be as adverse as they have been in the past, yet the constant improvement in the means of irrigation and of transport will greatly facilitate the relief of distress and may reduce its cost. We may also fairly hope that war expenditure on anything like the scale of that which we have lately had to meet is not likely to recur for some years at least.

I know of one argument only which may be held to support the opinion that these conclusions convey too favourable an impression of the state of the Indian finances, but whatever weight may be attached to it affects the past and not the present or the future. The policy under which it has been determined to borrow money for the construction of productive public works will be fully discussed further on. It is sufficient in this place to notice that the rule has ultimately been adopted of constructing by this means no works but those in regard to which there is a reasonable certainty of their earning, within a moderate period of time, an equivalent to the interest on the capital invested in them.

Although, speaking generally, the policy followed has been, as will be shown, in the highest degree successful, some of the works constructed with borrowed money do not fulfil the conditions now prescribed for productive public works. In several cases, some years ago, it was determined to undertake great works required for political or military reasons, the cost of which could not be met from ordinary revenues. It might be held, therefore, that the exclusion from the ordinary expenditure of the cost of these works, from which a net return is not now obtained equal to the interest on the capital invested in them, has benefited the account in a manner which is misleading. But these works already yield a considerable and an increasing revenue, and their construction can hardly be treated as an ordinary incident of the administration. If they had not been undertaken with borrowed funds, they would have been constructed very slowly, if at all.

There would be no advantage in now discussing the hypothetical question of the amount of advantage which has accrued to the current revenues in consequence of the exclusion of the cost of these works from the ordinary account. If an extreme view be taken, and we say that no part of this partially profitable expenditure ought to have been so excluded, the financial results of the period under review would no doubt appear less satisfactory than those shown by the figures given above. Thus, to give one illustration, there was in the year 1876–77, apart from expenditure on famine relief, and after making the other corrections which have been described, a small deficit of 37,347*l.* But in that year 1,457,881*l.* was spent on works not strictly answering to the present technical definition of productive, and if this sum had been included in the ordinary account there would have been a deficit of 1,495,228*l.*

It is needless, however, further to discuss this matter, which is wholly of a speculative nature, nor would it be possible to estimate the correction which might be made on this account. The important fact is that such causes of disturbance have now almost entirely ceased, nor is there any probability of their recurrence.

I have thought it right thus to state the case, in order to guard against the suspicion of exaggeration. But it will probably be conceded that the safest course is to take the figures exactly as we find them, without any reservations whatever, the result, as before stated, being this, that while the net annual expenditure has increased, during the last twelve years, by 1,916,770*l.*, the net annual revenue has increased, during the same period, by 7,055,824*l.*, and therefore that the financial position was better by 5,139,054*l.* in 1880–81 than it was in 1869–70.

Although the whole improvement has taken place during the last part of this period, for which the Government of Lord Lytton was responsible, I am far from wishing it to be inferred that I attribute this immense improvement in the financial condition of India to better administration in the last few years, for its main cause has undoubtedly been the rapid increase in the wealth and general prosperity of the country, which, with favourable seasons and other beneficial influences, has rapidly recovered from the effects of the preceding period of drought and depression.

Excluding the charges for War and Famine, the surpluses for the last two years, as shown on the accounts, have been for 1879–80 5,021,515*l.*, and for 1880–81 (regular estimate) 5,123,174*l.* The figures of the Budget estimate for 1881–82, if treated on the same principles as those followed in the accounts of those years, would give a surplus of 2,355,000*l.* But to compare this last amount with the corresponding figures of former years it is necessary to add 1,500,000*l.*, the sum by which the opium revenue has been intentionally under-estimated (see paragraph 77 of Financial Statement for 1881–82), and the surplus shown on the accounts when thus increased would therefore stand at 3,855,000*l.* As certain restrictions were placed on the Provincial expenditure in the years 1879–80 and 1880–81, the normal surplus in those years would be somewhat less than the sums shown on the accounts, and the general result therefore is that the figures for the three years are fairly concordant, and that the present normal surplus, in excess of obligatory expenditure, excluding War and Famine, stands at somewhat above 4,000,000*l.*

In 1877–78 it was decided, as already noticed, and as will be more fully explained hereafter, that to cover liabilities for famine, provision ought to be made for virtually reducing the public debt by 1,500,000*l.* a year, and that a further margin of 500,000*l.* should also be provided to meet unforeseen contingencies; 2,000,000*l.* a year has thus to be reserved for these purposes from the surplus of 4,000,000*l.* There remains, therefore, at the present time, after providing for famine and all other liabilities, excepting always any further possible charge under Loss by Exchange, an available surplus of at least 2,000,000*l.* It may be hoped that this will be increased by the reduction of the military charges, and if a remedy be applied to the exchange difficulty, the surplus may be expected to become still larger.

It is evident therefore that the Government of India enters upon the future with ample resources, though it is fully recognised that there are possible causes of financial disturbance. No remedy may be applied to the difficulty regarding exchange, and the loss instead of diminishing may increase. Also, although no branch of the revenue now is more steady and seems less precarious than that derived from opium, there may be room for some anxiety about its future. But the financial position of India is now so satisfactory and so promising that it has become possible, for the first time in the late history of British India, to contemplate without anxiety all probable contingencies of the future; and I trust that this prosperity will enable the

Government of India to give relief to the people from those taxes which press to some extent on the springs of industry and on the poor, and to complete the great fiscal reforms which have been commenced.

If I am asked why, four years ago, I advised the Government of India to impose fresh burdens upon the country to enable it to meet its obligations on account of famine, and whether, as a fact, sufficient provision for that object would not have been made without any new taxation, I reply that the subsequent progress of the revenue has undoubtedly rendered the proceeds of that taxation financially superfluous. But the condition of the finances, four years ago, when the taxes in question were imposed, was very different from what it now is, and it was then impossible to predict that the revenue would improve with such extraordinary rapidity. Moreover, I consider that even if this improvement could have been foreseen, much of the new taxation would have been necessary and right, because a more equitable distribution of the public burdens was then, as now, urgently required. That taxation, with some small exception perhaps, ought not only to be maintained but extended, because it falls on the comparatively rich and not on the poor. When the time comes, and in my opinion it has come already, for reducing taxation in India, it is not with the taxes imposed in 1877 and 1878 that we should begin, but with taxes like those on salt and on clothing, which add to the cost of the necessaries of life, or which fall on the materials of industry. These are matters to which I shall return hereafter.

Abstract of the Net Revenue and Expenditure from 1869 to 1881.

Head of Account	Averages of four years			Total 12 years
	1869–73	1873–77	1877–81	
	£	£	£	£
Net revenue (Chapter III.)	43,316,740	43,251,038	47,760,828	537,314,423
Net expenditure (Chapter IV.)	41,996,644	41,891,180	44,230,924	512,474,990
Surplus excluding war and famine expenditure and military fund credits	1,320,096	1,359,858	3,529,904	24,839,433
Famine relief expenditure	22,493	2,216,820	1,457,892	14,788,819
Surplus or deficit including famine expenditure	1,297,603	*856,962*	2,072,012	10,050,614
Net expenditure on Afghan War, including frontier railways	—	—	4,518,088	18,072,353
Surplus or deficit, including war and famine expenditure	—	—	*2,446,076*	*8,021,739*
Military funds credited	325,274	356,386	218,143	3,599,212
Actual surplus or deficit as shown in the published accounts	1,622,877	*500,576*	*2,227,933*	*4,422,527*

N.B. Figures in Italics signify deficits.

CHAPTER VI.

THE HOME CHARGES.

THE HOME TREASURY HOW REPLENISHED—THE DISBURSEMENTS CLASSIFIED—INTEREST ON DEBT—CHARGES FOR CIVIL ADMINISTRATION—ARMY—NON-EFFECTIVE—EFFECTIVE—STORES—GUARANTEED RAILWAYS—GENERAL RESULTS—INCREASE HOW ACCOUNTED FOR—LARGELY DUE TO RAILWAY TRANSACTIONS—SECRETARY OF STATE'S BILLS—THEIR AMOUNT—MEANS OF REDUCING THE HOME CHARGES—REDUCTION OF DEBT—TRANSFORMATION OF STERLING INTO RUPEE LIABILITIES—SUMMARY OF CONCLUSIONS.

ALTHOUGH the review that has been given of the past and present expenditure of India includes the whole of the Home charges, the special interest attaching to this part of the public outlay will justify a more detailed examination into its character and amount. Besides a natural and reasonable jealousy in regard to the application of the revenues of India outside the country, a strong additional argument for the reduction of such outlay to a minimum has of late years been supplied, by the heavy charges brought on the revenues through the Loss by Exchange on the remittances made from India to supply the Home treasury. To this loss reference has already been made, and it will call for further separate discussion.

Besides the remittances obtained by the sale of the Secretary of State's Bills on India, the ordinary receipts of the Home treasury include repayments of advances made in India on account of the British Government; miscellaneous receipts of comparatively small importance; large deposits of the capital funds of the guaranteed railway companies; and lastly money borrowed in England.

Excluding from consideration transactions which arise from the discharge of debt accompanied by simultaneous re-borrowing, and from the similar disbursements and receipts consequent on the discharge and renewal of railway debentures, the total amount of the home disbursements has since 1868–69 never fallen below 15,500,000*l.*, and has often exceeded 17,000,000*l.*

For the purpose of the present discussion, it is necessary to consider not only the final charges against the revenues of the several years, technically spoken of as 'expenditure,' but also all other payments for which provision has to be made by the Secretary of State. In this view the disbursements may conveniently be grouped as follows: 1. Interest on Debt; 2. Charges for the Civil Administration; 3. Army; 4. Stores; 5. Guaranteed Railways and Madras Irrigation Company.

The charge under 'Interest on Debt' has risen from about 2,209,000*l.* in 1869–70 to 2,685,000*l.* in 1880–81, a result which apart from its causes is very satisfactory, considering that the sterling debt, on which interest is payable in London, excluding that due to the purchase of the East Indian Railway, has meanwhile increased by not less than 26,500,000*l.* The whole question of debt will be discussed hereafter; in this place the only points that arise are the direct consequences involved in the shape of interest charge.

The charges under 'Civil Administration,' which represent the payments for all services in all the civil departments, have increased during the same period, excluding certain exceptional payments for Public Works, from about 2,800,000*l.* to 3,300,000*l.* The cost of the 'India Office' has remained steadily at about 220,000*l.* The charge for 'Furlough Allowances' of all civil departments is now about 300,000*l.*; before 1873–74 it did not exceed 180,000*l.*, but the increase is apparent rather than real, being chiefly due to the inclusion of the allowances of military officers in civil employ, which had previously been shown under 'Army.' The charge for 'Superannuation and Pensions' of all sorts paid in England has grown from 1,000,000*l.* to 1,400,000*l.*; it is under this head that nearly the whole increase under 'Civil Administration' has occurred, and it has been due to the gradual increase of the European establishments in India. The outlay for miscellaneous services connected with 'Indian Departments' has fallen from 500,000*l.* to 360,000*l.* The charges under 'Public Works,' include some large payments for the purchase of the Calcutta and South-Eastern Railway, and the Orissa Irrigation Works, but apart from these, and without the cost of stores, which is separately shown, the outlay under this head only amounts to about 40,000*l.*, chiefly for Cooper's Hill college (which, however, shows a set-off of about 17,000*l.* income), and the special staff for the provision and inspection of stores for the State Railways.

Certain charges have been shown in the statements in the Appendix under the head 'Civil Administration' which in the published accounts appear as 'Remittances.' They are payments made in England, either in consideration of sums paid into the public treasuries in India, or for services the accounts of which are kept and settled by transfer payments in India. The chief heads are 'Postage' due by India to England, 100,000*l.*; 'Family Remittances,' allowed under a long-established custom to officers and men in the army, varying from about 400,000*l.* to 700,000*l.*; and 'Miscellaneous' amounting to about 200,000*l.*, of which more than half is usually the price of stores ultimately paid for in India from local funds. The aggregate of the 'Remittance' heads is about 1,000,000*l.*, and has not varied much.

The next main head, 'Army,' shows an increase from 2,627,000*l.* in 1869–70 to 3,416,000*l.* in 1880–81, excluding stores; or, including stores, the amounts would be 3,505,000*l.* and 4,200,000*l.*

Separating the army charges into 'Effective' and 'Non-effective,' it is found that there has been since 1869–70 a small reduction under the former head, with an increase of rather more than a million under the latter. This increase is, to the extent of 600,000*l.*, due to payments in the shape of pensions, or their capitalised value, to the officers of the old Indian army to induce the supernumerary field officers to retire; the remaining 400,000*l.* arises from the charges for retired pay and pensions of the British troops that have served in India.

Under 'Effective' the 'Furlough Allowances' have stood at about 200,000*l.* since 1873–74, when the allowances to officers in civil employ were transferred to the Civil head, and they do not exhibit any tendency to grow. The charges under 'Pay,' being the contribution for the British troops, were at a minimum in 1875–76, standing at 474,000*l.*, since which they have risen to about 750,000*l.* The payments for some years past, however, have been made without any fixed principle of apportionment between India and England, and little more can be said on the subject than that it is not probable that the settlement when made will lead to a reduction of this element of charge. The charges under 'Transport' have remained without much variation between 300,000*l.* and 350,000*l.* The large increase under 'Stores' (military) between 1874 and 1878, averaging about 250,000*l.* yearly in excess of the preceding four years, was due to the cost of the new arms and ordnance supplied to India during those years, and this head of charge has again fallen to its former rate. The Afghan war has not led to any material addition under these heads, the charges falling almost entirely on the Indian accounts.

The fourth head, 'Stores,' has been dealt with in the aggregate, in order to show clearly the magnitude and nature of the transactions it embraces. The charge is of necessity liable to vary greatly, and has increased from about 1,500,000*l.* as it stood in 1869–70 to 2,600,000*l.* in those years in which the supply of railway materials has been on a large scale. Excluding this last class of stores, there has been a decided tendency to diminish the outlay under this head, a result to a considerable extent due to the constant efforts of the Government to prevent demands being made on England for stores which can be procured in India. The details of the outlay under the chief departmental heads will be seen in the Appendix, on which a few comments may be useful. The reduction under 'Army Commissariat' is largely due to the consumption of beer brewed in India in place of imported English beer. Under 'Marine' the charges are chiefly for coals and for vessels of various descriptions required for service in Indian waters. Under 'Stationery' are included printing materials. The growth of the charge under this head is considerable, and is probably unavoidable. Under 'Stamps,' the increased use of stamps for fiscal purposes accounts for the growth of the outlay, and there are obvious advantages of economy and security in conducting their manufacture in England. Under 'Miscellaneous' is included the cost of postage stamps, envelopes, and cards, all of which have to be procured in England. Under 'Public Works' the largest outlay was in 1880–81, when it rose to 1,266,000*l.*, chiefly for railway materials; in the three previous years the charge had slightly exceeded one million, and the average for fourteen years has been about 700,000*l.*

The last main head of the Home charges, that of 'Guaranteed Railways,' is a most important one. The first entry under it is 'Interest.' The charge under this head has risen steadily from 4,138,000*l.* in 1869–70 to 4,787,000*l.*[1] in 1879–80, the capital under guarantee having increased in the same time from 86,500,000*l.* to 98,000,000*l.* The next item of railway charge is the supply of funds to the companies for their English expenditure, whether for capital or revenue account. This outlay is met from the corresponding deposits of capital. In the earlier years of railway construction these deposits, which included the whole paid-up capital of the companies, largely exceeded the sums required for expenditure in England, and the surplus was available for supplying the Home treasury; funds were advanced for the railway expenditure in India by the Government there, and a corresponding amount was treated as a remittance from the funds in England. During the years between 1868 and 1874 there remained a floating surplus balance of railway capital in the hands of the Government amounting to rather more than 3,000,000*l.*; since that time the drawings

[1] These charges include, in both cases, a sum of 50,000*l.* yearly, guaranteed interest, paid to the Madras Irrigation Company.

have exceeded the deposits, and the average yearly balance is now not more than 750,000*l.* Previous to 1865 the balances of capital, after meeting the demands of the companies, sufficed to meet the charge for guaranteed interest, which had not then exceeded about 2,500,000*l.* yearly. The subsequent rapid growth of the interest and the gradual falling off in the balances led to a great change, and since 1869–70 there has been a large permanent excess of the aggregate disbursements on account of the capital and revenue expenditure in England, and of the guaranteed interest, over the receipts on account of guaranteed railways. Since 1874–75 the withdrawals from the Home treasury for the capital and revenue accounts, irrespective of interest, have always been in excess of the deposits, so that the old position is now entirely inverted, and the Secretary of State, instead of being relieved of a considerable part of his liabilities by help of the railway transactions, is now charged by reason of them with a considerable sum, varying from 500,000*l.* to 1,500,000*l.* yearly, in addition to the largely increased payments for guaranteed interest, which now amount to 4,750,000*l.* The combined charge for interest and capital and revenue purposes, in excess of all receipts from the companies, has in this way grown from about 2,250,000*l.* in 1869–70 to about 5,500,000*l.* at the present time; and thus the burden caused by the guaranteed railways is now about one-half of the whole charge for administrative purposes, or one-third of the entire home disbursements.

The general result of this discussion is to show that the total outlay classed as administrative (excluding certain exceptional payments for public works) has risen from 9,000,000*l.* in 1869–70 to 10,450,000*l.* in

1880–81. The increase of 1,450,000*l.* is accounted for as follows:—

			£
Interest on debt .	. more	. .	500,000
Civil—superannuations .	,,	. .	500,000
Army—non-effective .	,,	. .	800,000
Stores . . .	. less	. .	*350,000*
	Total	. .	£1,450,000

Excluding the cost of railway stores, the total administrative charge remained, with very small variation, a little above 9,000,000*l.* (9,150,000*l.*) from 1869–70 to 1875–76. From the last-named year to 1880–81 the charge has varied between 10,000,000*l.* and 10,500,000*l.* (average 10,300,000*l.*).

These figures indicate a careful management of the details of the administrative expenditure, and leave no possible doubt that the chief cause of the large increase of the home charges in recent years has been the guaranteed railway liabilities. The combined railway requirements, which in 1868–69 left a surplus of railway capital in the Home treasury amounting to 194,000*l.*, led in the next year to a net charge of 2,241,000*l.*, and this has gradually increased till in 1881–82 the charge had become 5,603,000*l.*

Altogether, therefore, comparing the first and last years of the series, the demands to be met by the Home treasury are greater in the last year by 5,000,000*l.*; of this one-fourth is due to actual increase of administrative expenditure, and three-fourths to liabilities caused by the guaranteed railways, which, however, do not involve ultimate increased charge on the revenues of India, but only increased disbursements in England.

The sources from which the Home treasury has been supplied have next to be examined. The years 1867,

1868, and 1869 were rendered abnormal by large repayments of advances on account of the Abyssinian war. These repayments led to a reduction of the amount of the Secretary of State's Bills, which had, since 1861, averaged about 6,000,000*l*. yearly. After 1869–70, when the Bills were about 7,000,000*l*., they were gradually increased in amount, till 1872–73, when they were about 14,000,000*l*. The financial pressure caused by the heavy famine expenditure in 1873–74 and subsequent years, and by the great loss by exchange, led to a considerable contraction of the Bills after that year, and, as a consequence, to the necessity for supplementing the Secretary of State's funds by borrowing in London. In 1878–79 the sale of Bills was again pressed to the full extent thought practicable; they then yielded about 15,500,000*l*, and they have since been kept at about the same amount.

From these causes hardly a single year has passed since 1869–70 without considerable additions to the sterling debt, the aggregate increase to the end of 1880–81 (excluding that caused by the purchase of the East India Railway) being rather less than 26,000,000*l*. net, of which about half was incurred before 1875–76. The miscellaneous receipts hardly amount on the average to 500,000*l*. a year, and, as already shown, the railway capital has altogether ceased to be a source of supply.

It is apparent from these facts that the normal yearly charge to be met by the Home treasury cannot at the present time be reckoned at a smaller sum than 17,500,000*l*. or 18,000,000*l*., without making any allowance for extraordinary demands, or providing for the discharge of debt. Further, since the miscellaneous receipts, including railway capital, cannot now be reckoned to produce more than one-half or three-quarters of a million, it is obvious that unless the full amount to meet the home disbursements be obtained by the sale of Bills on India the necessary result will be an addition to the home debt to make good the deficiency, with a still further increase to the permanent home charges.

It will likewise be readily perceived that there are only two directions in which any really important reduction of the amount of these home charges can be sought—first, through diminishing the charge for interest on debt, and second, through obtaining relief in some way from the obligations arising from the guaranteed railways.

As to the interest charges, such relief as has hitherto been obtained has rather been by the reduction of the rate of interest on the capital of the debt, than by any actual discharge of the debt itself. In the present condition of the currency of India, which virtually precludes bullion remittances from that country, and of the exchange with England, which is essentially dependent on the varying value of silver in the London market, it would manifestly be extremely difficult, if not impossible, to make any sensible impression on the home debt, by remitting surplus revenue from India for its discharge. The addition of even 2,000,000*l.* or 3,000,000*l.* yearly to the sum to be remitted through the sale of the Secretary of State's Bills would at present be an operation of very questionable expediency. Any pressure on the exchanges would be viewed with great alarm by the commercial community, and in present circumstances could hardly be justified. Nor is it probable that the operation could be carried out on a scale to give results commensurate with the risk and discontent that would attend it. It is plain that with interest at 4 per cent. the remittance of 2,500,000*l.* yearly would only serve to extinguish 100,000*l.* of the home charges; operations such as this would aggravate the evil they were designed to mitigate, and instead of giving relief would add to the practical difficulties of the situation.

If, then, the home debt is to be reduced, it must be accomplished otherwise. The recent announcement that it is the intention of the Secretary of State to apply the sum received from England as a contribution to the cost of the Afghan war, to the extinction of sterling debt, is no doubt a right step; but the two millions first given as a loan have already been disposed of, and the rest of the grant will be spread over so many years, that the practical effect produced will be insignificant.

The extent to which the Secretary of State's Bills could be increased in amount without bad results depends mainly on the condition of the trade of India, and the subject cannot be conveniently discussed in this place. But it may be affirmed, without risk of contradiction, that so long as the currency of India remains as it now is, in relation to the currency of England and continental nations, no reduction of the sterling debt can be hoped for through remittances by the Secretary of State's Bills, in the face of the risk of still further forcing down the Exchanges, and of the certain additional burden which would be thrown on the revenues of India by such transactions.

Nor indeed is it likely that in any future improved condition of the Exchanges it would be expedient to adopt this means of providing for the extinction of the sterling debt. There seems no room for doubt that in the event of the Exchanges assuming a character of tolerable stability, the best, if not the only practicable, method of dealing with the matter would be to raise the money required to discharge sterling debt by the sale in Europe of Rupee securities; to operate in short by transforming the sterling into Rupee debt, and then to carry out in India and not in England all possible measures for the reduction of the debt. The Rupee paper enfaced for the issue in London of interest Bills payable in India now amounts to nearly 20,000,000*l.*, having increased since 1874 from 14,000,000*l.* It is probable that by extending the issue of debentures or stock with attached coupons, an amount of Rupee securities could without difficulty be placed on the European market sufficient to replace the whole of the sterling debt likely to be redeemable for many years to come. Such coupons would form a convenient means of remittance in place of that portion of the Secretary of State's Bills which would be set free by the discharge of the sterling debt, and by the consequent cessation of the payment of interest upon it.

It would, however, be difficult to carry out operations such as these with success, unless some fundamental change takes place in the relations of the currencies of India and England, and in some way or other a common standard of value be established between the two countries, which shall insure fair stability in the exchanges. It would be out of place here to dwell more on this aspect of the subject. But it is desirable to direct attention to the great importance to India of enabling her to establish a free and unrestricted market in Europe for her securities, so that she may be in a position to obtain in the future the aid of European capitalists without incurring the objectionable liability of having to discharge her debts in a currency other than her own. There is no reason why India should not acquire this position, and when she does so there will be an end, once for all, to the ever-recurring difficulties which now attend the financial operations of the Secretary of State in London.

That relief must in some shape be obtained from the constantly growing burden placed on the Home treasury by the Guaranteed Railways is a truth so obvious, and of such urgency, that it is surprising how little attention has been paid to it. The obligations which the Secretary of State has incurred towards the companies must no doubt be faithfully discharged in every particular, but so far as this condition will admit, every possible step should be taken, not only to prevent the further accretion of sterling liabilities, but to transform those that exist into Rupee charges to be paid in India.

It must of course be recognised that there are likely to be difficulties in accomplishing either of these results, and in any case it must be a work of time before the Secretary of State, consistently with the terms of the contracts with the companies, can acquire the powers without which no remedy could be effectually applied. It may probably happen in dealing with the Railways, as with the sterling debt, that the transformation of the existing sterling payments in London into Rupee payments in India, will not be possible without some addition to the immediate charge. But the difficulty to be overcome does not to any important degree consist in the actual amount of the burden on the revenues of India. It lies essentially in the form of the charge, and in the extreme inconvenience of its incessant and insidious growth. In the nature of the case the railway capital must continue to expand, and, so long as a guarantee of interest continues, the charge for interest must expand also. The actual growth of capital has not hitherto been such as would justify a complaint that it has been excessive, and its further growth at a somewhat similar rate cannot be avoided. It is essential, therefore, that protection should be afforded to the Home treasury against the increase of disbursements which, however necessary in some form, may certainly be otherwise met, and this protection will be well worth whatever additional charge may be necessary in transferring the payment from England to India.

In what has gone before, all questions as to the policy which has given rise to the various elements of the home charges have been intentionally set aside as appertaining to a set of ideas different from those before us. It has been simply assumed that certain charges have to be met, and their nature and incidence have been examined and explained. There are, however, a few points to which attention may properly be drawn.

First may be noticed the comparatively moderate and stationary charge for the India Office establishments; it amounts to about 1¼ per cent. on the net home disbursements, while the total charge for administration in the combined home and Indian accounts is about 2½ per cent. on the total expenditure. Next may be observed the growth of the charges under civil superannuations and pensions; this indicates the financial consequences of the expansion of the European administrative staff in India, a subject which on other grounds has of late years most properly received increased attention, and which manifestly demands cautious procedure in the future. Another marked feature is the heavy cost of the changes of military system; these have involved a large increase in the non-effective charges of the army, through the necessity for getting rid of the superfluous officers of the old local army, and the great expense which has followed the introduction of the short service system of the British army. However important may have been the increase of efficiency consequent on this change, the necessity is none the less but the more urgent for adopting every reasonable measure for reducing the cost of the army, and for removing all elements of charge which are not directly conducive to efficiency, but are relics of a condition of things belonging to the past.

The transactions under the head of 'Stores' show that apart from the requirements of the railways, the outlay has a tendency rather to diminish than to increase. There is every reason to believe that the cost of agency, including all contingent charges, but little exceeds 2 per cent., and is considerably less than would be incurred if the purchases were arranged through private trade in India. The quality of the supplies is decidedly better than could at present be ensured under any other system, and notwithstanding occasional shortcomings, many serious causes of failure and loss are avoided, the risk of which would indeed in some cases render reliance on ordinary trade impossible.

At the same time it is indisputable that every possible encouragement should be given to extending the local supply of stores for Government purposes, whether produced in India or obtained from England, in substitution for the present system of supply through the India office. With this object it may even be expedient for the present to pay a somewhat higher price for articles locally supplied. The correct rules would seem to be, that purchases should always be made locally when suitable articles, at reasonable prices, can be obtained in the local market; and that no payments should be made till after delivery and approval of the supply. Stores which must be manufactured under inspection in England should be procured through the India Office. These principles have been accepted by the Government, though their practical application is still incomplete.

The Guaranteed Railway charges show the results of a policy which, while its benefits to India have been extremely great, has placed a burden on the home financial administration of India that could hardly have been anticipated; the true character of which has too long been overlooked, and which now demands earnest and immediate attention. There is no reason to think that insurmountable difficulties would arise in dealing with this matter, but its gravity increases year by year, and the importance of removing or alleviating this constantly growing burden cannot be exaggerated.

It may also be noticed that the growth of the Home debt has fortunately not been accompanied by corresponding growth of the interest charge. Reductions in the rate of interest have secured this result; it has been the more acceptable as it was obtained during the period in which India lay under the load of an enormous expenditure for famine relief, and in which a disturbance of the gold value of her currency increased in a few years the annual expenditure by sums varying from 2,000,000*l.* to nearly 3,000,000*l.* sterling, without securing any increased advantage to the State. Though the actual results of the large addition to the debt, which has taken place since 1869–70, are less serious than might have been anticipated, the fact must be steadily borne in mind that there are many great difficulties in the way of redeeming debt incurred in England; the lessons of the past should be read as inculcating the importance of avoiding all borrowing in sterling, unless as an inevitable necessity, and of meeting the home requirements of every year as they arise by the sale of Bills on India, or (when borrowing is unavoidable) of Rupee securities, the payment of interest on which would be made in India.

Lastly, the important fact must be remembered, that although the Loss by exchange appears in the public accounts as a Rupee payment in India, it is in reality a contingency of the Home expenditure, and might not improperly be regarded as an addition to those charges. The average amount of this item for the last two years has been about 2,750,000*l.*, and if distributed proportionally it would lead to the following additions to the main heads of the Home expenditure:—

	£
To interest on debt . . .	400,000
„ administration . . .	1,250,000
„ guaranteed railways . . .	900,000
„ productive public works . .	200,000

This subject will be more fully considered in a subsequent chapter.

Abstract of the Home Receipts and Disbursements from 1869 to 1881.

Head of account	Averages of four years			First and last years	
	1869–73	1873–77	1877–81	1869–70	1880–81
	£	£	£	£	£
Net receipts:—					
Revenue	204,000	278,000	347,000	194,000	533,000
Advances repaid	630,000	203,000	877,000	1,568,000	2,503,000
Bills	10,061,000	12,303,000	14,187,000	6,980,000	15,388,000
Debt	1,842,000	2,955,000	1,601,000	3,538,000	503,000
Total receipts	12,737,000	15,739,000	17,012,000	12,280,000	18,927,000
Net disbursements:—					
Interest	2,366,000	2,276,000	2,620,000	2,209,000	2,685,000
Civil	2,794,000	3,100,000	3,261,000	2,754,000	3,320,000
Army	2,662,000	2,575,000	3,291,000	2,627,000	3,416,000
Stores (Civil and Military)	1,308,000	1,461,000	1,208,000	1,414,000	1,035,000
Total	9,130,000	9,412,000	10,380,000	9,004,000	10,456,000
Guaranteed railways	3,207,000	5,530,000	5,377,000	2,241,000	5,603,000
Productive public works and State railway stores	407,000	868,000	966,000	1,169,000	1,266,000
Total disbursements	12,744,000	15,810,000	16,673,000	12,414,000	17,325,000

CHAPTER VII.

PRODUCTIVE PUBLIC WORKS.

EXPENDITURE ON PUBLIC WORKS BEFORE 1867-68—BORROWING AUTHORISED IN 1864 TO CARRY ON IRRIGATION WORKS—EXTRAORDINARY PUBLIC WORKS—EXTENSION OF SYSTEM IN 1870 TO RAILWAYS—PRINCIPLES ADOPTED AND PRECAUTIONS TAKEN—FORECASTS OF EXPENDITURE—CHANGES OF SYSTEM SUBSEQUENTLY INTRODUCED—PRODUCTIVE PUBLIC WORKS—POLICY CONSIDERED BY COMMITTEE OF THE HOUSE OF COMMONS AND CONCLUSIONS ADOPTED—COMPARISON OF ACTUAL RESULTS WITH FORECASTS—GREAT IMPROVEMENT IN FINANCIAL POSITION DUE TO SUCCESS OF WORKS—PRACTICAL UTILITY AND VALUE OF WORKS—GUARANTEED AND STATE RAILWAYS—IRRIGATION WORKS—THEIR PRESENT POSITION AND PROSPECTS—GENERAL CONCLUSIONS—COMPLETE SUCCESS OF THE POLICY.

THE policy pursued by the Government of India during the last twenty-five years in respect of Public Works has had so important an effect on the expenditure and revenues, as well as on the material prosperity of India, while the further progress of the country will depend so greatly on the policy that may be followed in the future, that some time and space may well be given to tracing its history, and discussing the lessons which that history should teach us.

Before 1850 the expenditure on public works other than military and civil buildings had been very small, and the average yearly charge for the whole of India hardly exceeded 250,000*l.* The decision to undertake the construction of railways under a system of guarantee, which dates from about that time, indicated that a more liberal policy had then begun to find favour, and the commencement of the Ganges Canal, and other irrigation works in Madras and the Punjab, and of some important lines of road, gave further evidence of this fact. In 1854 the growing importance of this branch of the administration led to the constitution of a special Public Works department under the Government of India, and the outlay shown under the head of Public Works in that year rose to nearly 2,000,000*l.*, exclusive of the capital spent on the railways under guarantee.

The occurrences of 1857, while they for a time tended to suspend all progress, gave such manifest proof of the enormous utility of improved communications, that the systematic extension of roads in connection with the main lines of railway which were gradually coming into operation, was among the measures most earnestly taken up when the financial pressure caused by the Mutiny had subsided. For some years, however, the urgent necessity of providing barracks for the increased force of British troops took precedence of other demands, and eventually led to an outlay on so large a scale as to force on the Government the question of how the requisite funds could be provided for the numerous works of improvement, the pressing need of which was indisputable.

In 1860–61 the Public Works expenditure had risen to 4,800,000*l.*, and in 1865–66 to more than 5,000,000*l.*, and it had become apparent that the ordinary revenues could not furnish funds for carrying out works of permanent improvement on the scale that was felt to be desirable. The large outlay which was unavoidable in the years immediately following the Mutiny, for providing temporary quarters for the European troops, was still further increased when the building of the permanent barracks began; an operation which is reckoned to have cost altogether between ten and twelve millions, of which one-half was estimated to have been spent before 1869. Under the pressure thus caused it was at one time contemplated to provide for the new barracks by borrowing, and though this idea was in form given up, the heavy deficits which marked the three years preceding 1869 made the actual result little different from what it would have been if special loans for this purpose had been obtained.

The severe famine of 1837–38 in Northern India, and the terrible destruction caused by it in many districts, afforded signal proof of the value of irrigation canals in protecting the tracts through which they passed, and the importance of works of this class was strongly brought out as a means both of affording protection to the country from the frightful results of widespread famine, and of adding permanently to the resources of the people and the State. Similar experience obtained in Madras in the scarcity of 1853 enforced these lessons, and they were again repeated in the North-Western Provinces in the severe drought of 1859–60. After a discussion which extended over several years, the Secretary of State in 1864 at length accepted the conclusion that the Government should carry out all the irrigation works it could practically manage, and that when the surplus revenues and available cash balances proved insufficient to supply the requisite funds, loans should be raised for the purpose. But before this decision was acted on, another extreme drought had fallen on the province of Orissa in Bengal, to be followed in the next year by a similar calamity in Northern India extending over a vast area, and once more affording practical proof of the efficacy of irrigation canals in giving complete protection against the effects of drought to the country which they water.

Thus originated the policy of carrying out irrigation works, by direct State agency, with borrowed funds. The necessity for extending irrigation wherever it was practicable, as a protection against famine in districts liable to drought, which had been enforced by the sad and recurring experience of thirty years, was at last definitively accepted, and it was recognised, almost without a dissentient voice, that the State must itself undertake the construction and management of the works, the agency of companies for such purposes being manifestly unsuitable in the actual condition and circumstances of the Indian agricultural population.

These conclusions first took a practical shape during the Government of Lord Lawrence, and in 1867–68 the supply of funds by borrowing for what were originally called 'Extraordinary public works' commenced. The Government accepted as the basis of their action proposals put into a definite form by one of the authors of this work, then Colonel R. Strachey and Secretary in the Public Works department, and they were to the following effect. It was reckoned that the sum which the revenues could supply for these purposes would probably not exceed 500,000*l.* yearly, while it was estimated that the sum which could be beneficially spent during the next ten years on the extension of irrigation was not less than 30,000,000*l.*, so that it would be necessary to borrow largely in order to carry out the scheme satisfactorily. It was proposed that the accounts of the expenditure on works so constructed should be kept separate from those of works supplied with funds from the ordinary revenues. Though the aim was to protect the country from famine, no project was to be taken up which did not promise to be fairly remunerative in a reasonable time; and it was calculated, from the data supplied by similar works, that the earnings would gradually overtake the expenses, and that before long the whole interest on the borrowed capital would be covered, any charge meanwhile being met from the general revenues. The essential considerations which were held to justify this policy were, that the works would really be worth the sum spent on them, that the financial risk was small, and one which the Government was bound to run for the sake of giving to the country the best possible protection against drought and famine, while the present charge until the works became remunerative was not likely to be in excess of what the revenues could bear without inconvenience, and would soon cease.

The total expenditure on irrigation works from borrowed money during the first five years amounted to about 3,300,000*l.*, excluding a sum of about 1,000,000*l.* paid to the Orissa Company on the transfer of their undertakings to the Government, a measure which the financial position of the company rendered unavoidable. For the next few years the grants were increased, and were somewhat in excess of 1,000,000*l.* yearly, but they have again been reduced; the whole outlay from borrowed funds to the end of 1880–81 was about 12,500,000*l.*, including the purchase of the Orissa works, so that the actual charge incurred during the first ten years has been much less than that originally contemplated.

In 1869 it was proposed by Lord Lawrence to extend the system thus introduced for irrigation works to the further development of railways. His conclusions to this effect were recorded in a minute, dated January

9, 1869, which it is now no breach of official reserve to say was drafted by Colonel Strachey and accepted by Lord Lawrence without reservation. The plan sketched out in this paper was substantially adopted by the Secretary of State, and by Lord Mayo who succeeded Lord Lawrence as Governor-General, and in 1870 the first steps were taken to give it effect. The principal motive in this case was the desire to extend as widely as possible the great commercial benefits which railways were seen to confer on the country, their extreme importance in meeting the pressure of famine not having been yet clearly recognised. It was considered expedient, in the interests of economy, that new lines should, as a rule, be undertaken directly by the State, instead of by an extension of the old system of guarantee, the financial and other inconveniences of which had been strongly felt; while without a guarantee capitalists would not come forward for the purpose. The outlay on railways has much exceeded that on irrigation works. In 1874–75 the yearly expenditure had risen to about 3,000,000*l.*, at which rate it remained until the reduction of the sum borrowed for Public Works was enforced under the orders issued by the Secretary of State in 1879. The total outlay on State railways up to the end of 1880–81 has been about 26,689,000*l.*, including a sum of 675,000*l.* paid to the Calcutta and South-Eastern Railway Company, which surrendered its line under the provisions of its contract, as it did not pay its working expenses.

When the Government of India entered on this policy, with the determination to provide such a system of irrigation and railways as the safety and progress of the country appeared imperatively to demand, it distinctly recognised the fact that for a time at least some not inconsiderable burden would be placed on the revenues. It was held that in making financial provision for these great works of material improvement consideration must be given to general rather than to particular results, and that so long as the aggregate net charge on their account, after taking credit for the income they earned, did not exceed a sum which the revenues could meet without inconvenience, it would not be an undue sacrifice on the part of the people of India to make, for some years, a contribution sufficient to secure the important objects in view, in the confident expectation that before long the growing income of the works would reduce the burden, if not extinguish it. The guaranteed railways were regarded as forming a portion of the general scheme of works, and the charges that had arisen, or were likely to arise on their account, were held to be undistinguishable in their financial character from those that might arise from the new works to be undertaken. It was known that for several previous years a net charge, varying from 1,500,000*l.* to 1,750,000*l.* had been met from the general revenues on account of the interest on guaranteed railway capital, and it was argued that a charge of some such amount could, without objection, be further continued for a limited period.

It was, however, obvious that satisfactory results could not be secured in carrying out the policy, unless the general financial position was at the same time placed on a thoroughly sound basis, and a substantial surplus of ordinary income over expenditure maintained. With this view the expenditure on ordinary public works was largely reduced, and chiefly that on military works and buildings of all sorts, which in 1868–69 had absorbed 2,380,000*l.* out of a total grant (excluding outlay from local funds) of 5,440,000*l.* Security was at the same time taken against the expansion of other branches of outlay by the adoption of the provincial financial system, the general scope of which has already been noticed, and which will be more fully discussed in a subsequent chapter.

Further, to guard as far as possible against the risk of involving the finances in inconvenient or dangerous charges for interest on the money to be borrowed, the Government caused a forecast to be prepared, for some years in advance, of the irrigation and railway expenditure which it proposed to authorise. The estimate thus framed in 1873 embraced the proposed outlay to 1878. For irrigation works an expenditure of 8,500,000*l.* was anticipated, and this, it was reckoned, would lead to the charge for interest in excess of net income gradually increasing from 38,760*l.* in the first year to 214,560*l.* in the last. For railways an annual outlay of 3,000,000*l.* was contemplated, to result in 2,125 miles of new lines to be opened by 1878, with an excess of interest charge over net income at the end of the period amounting to 378,000*l.* It was estimated, however, that during the same interval the annual net charge for guaranteed interest would be reduced from 2,200,000*l.* as it stood in 1872–73 to 1,400,000*l.* in 1877–78, so that the general result would probably be a reduction of total charge of about 200,000*l.*

The experience of the next two years led to a revision of this forecast, and in consequence of the actual result being more favourable than the anticipation, it was thought possible to increase the yearly expenditure of borrowed money to 4,000,000*l.*, to be applied,

2,700,000*l.* to railways, and 1,300,000*l.* to canals. The estimate thus modified in 1875, and extended to 1880, indicated a result not materially differing from the former, and still showing a reduction of total charge at the end of the period embraced of about 200,000*l.* yearly.

Such were the original plans for the extension of railways and irrigation works. But in carrying them out considerable modifications were by degrees introduced. The term 'extraordinary,' which was applied both to the works and to the expenditure supplied from borrowed money, signified in the conventional language of Indian accounts that these charges were to be excluded from the 'ordinary' expenditure, which is that met from the revenues of the year. Hence it was thought proper to treat as 'extraordinary' all expenditure on railways and canals which could not be met from the revenues, whatever might be the conditions or circumstances under which they were undertaken. The question of the probable early, or even ultimately remunerative character of the works was in some important cases altogether set aside, the justification for the outlay having been found in considerations of a political or administrative nature. The forced purchase of the Calcutta and South-Eastern Railway, which was an admitted financial failure, and the somewhat similar transfer to the Government of the Orissa Irrigation Works, as well as the prosecution of the railways through Sindh and from Lahore to the North-west frontier, and the Madras Harbour, are instances in which very large sums were expended, and treated as extraordinary outlay, almost irrespective of any hopes of early financial success. Such burdens have necessarily weighed heavily on the general results, adding as they have done almost one-fourth or one-fifth to the total outlay.

In 1876 the great fall in the value of silver in relation to gold, and the consequent large increase to the cost of the remittances to England, together with the heavy burdens which had been created by the famine in Bengal, led the Government somewhat to reduce the expenditure on 'Productive Public Works' (as they were then for the first time called), and it was resolved to restrict the outlay of this description to the amount which it was thought could be borrowed in India without unduly pressing on the market, and this was then estimated at 2,000,000*l.* or 2,500,000*l.* per annum.

From this time also increased restrictions were imposed on the application of borrowed money to new works, in order to guard more completely against the risk of entering on undertakings which would not be remunerative, and which might therefore lead to a permanent charge for interest on the borrowed capital being thrown on the general revenues. In 1878 and 1879 the whole question of supplying funds by borrowing for public works was considered by a committee of the House of Commons, and the policy of the Government, since the issue of their report, has been to comply with the recommendations it contained. The committee adopted the conclusion that the principle on which the Government of India had initiated its policy, namely of limiting and regulating the expenditure of borrowed money by reference to the dead weight of interest uncovered by the net income of the works as a whole, could not be accepted; and they proposed instead to place an absolute limit on the yearly outlay, with increased stringency as to the character of the works to be sanctioned. They further advised that all debt incurred for public works should be separated from the general debt; that all capital expenditure on productive works supplied from the revenues should be dealt with in the accounts as though it had been borrowed; and that a sum equal to that which was thus provided should be transferred from the 'Ordinary' debt to the 'Productive Public Works' debt, and interest charged against the works accordingly.

Mainly as the result of these recommendations there have been introduced into the public accounts, entries which show under the heads of 'Productive Public Works Revenue,' and 'Productive Public Works Expenditure,' the whole income and charge arising from these undertakings. It is, however, only in the last year of our series, 1880–81, that these principles have been fully carried out, and the results for previous years are consequently not properly comparable with them. Nor do the accounts admit of an immediate or exact comparison with the forecasts of 1873 and 1875, which were based on estimates differently treated from the figures shown in the published accounts.

Notwithstanding these differences the figures[1] are very instructive; they give complete evidence of the caution with which the forecasts were prepared, as well as of the soundness of the principles of the policy, so far as the practical financial results afford a test, and it is impossible to see what better test could be found.

For the Irrigation Works the accounts of past years are incomplete, and the true income of the Madras and Bombay works is shown for the first time in 1879–80; the whole interest on borrowed funds, wherever spent, is included throughout; but the interest on capital supplied from revenue is first shown in 1880–81.

[1] See the table at page 97.

Actual net charges on account of Guaranteed and State Railways and Irrigation Works classed as Productive Works compared with the forecasts.

Year	Actual net charges, including interest on capital				Estimated charges, 1873–75			
	Guaranteed Railways	State Railways	Irrigation Works	Total	Guaranteed Railways	State Railways	Irrigation Works	Total
	£	£	£	£	£	£	£	£
1872–73	2,215,000	109,000	*55,000*	2,269,000	2,210,000	130,000	40,000	2,380,000
1873–74	1,529,000	174,000	*61,000*	1,642,000	1,840,000	220,000	70,000	2,130,000
1874–75	1,244,000	239,000	4,000	1,487,000	1,630,000	360,000	110,000	2,100,000
1875–76	992,000	313,000	31,000	1,336,000	1,570,000	460,000	150,000	2,180,000
1876–77	278,000	441,000	113,000	832,000	1,490,000	470,000	180,000	2,140,000
1877–78	*675,000*	536,000	69,000	*70,000*	1,380,000	500,000	210,000	2,090,000
1878–79	740,000	686,000	82,000	1,508,000	1,310,000	530,000	210,000	2,050,000
1879–80	*110,000*	724,000	*337,000*	277,000	1,220,000	570,000	240,000	2,030,000
1880–81	*337,000*	608,000	*76,000*	195,000				

N.B. Figures in Italics imply receipts in excess of charges.

H

From this table it will be seen that (excluding 1880–81, which is not comparable with the earlier years) the total yearly charge was reduced from 2,269,000*l.* to 277,000*l.*; or excluding the Madras and Bombay net income, shown for the first time in 1879–80, and amounting to 300,000*l.*, the total charge in that year would be 580,000*l.*, still showing a reduction of more than 1,500,000*l.* Taking the aggregate of the eight years, whereas the forecast contemplated an excess charge of 17,100,000*l.*, the actual charge was only 9,281,000*l.*, or 7¾ millions less. These results have followed an expenditure since 1872 of 6,600,000*l.* on Guaranteed Railways, of 22,800,000*l.* borrowed money on State Railways, and of 7,400,000*l.* borrowed money on Irrigation Works; while in both of the last classes of works there are many, on which large sums have been laid out, which are still incomplete or not fully brought into operation, and which are therefore earning up to the present time little or no income.

The true practical results of the whole policy will, however, be better seen by reviewing together the whole of the charges arising from the ordinary debt, from the guaranteed railway interest, and from the public works outlay of all descriptions which have to be met from the revenues; thus there can be no risk of losing sight of any part of the burdens which the policy may have caused, and its influence on the general financial position will be rendered more apparent. In the Appendix will be found in detail the figures from 1868–69, when the policy was initiated, to the present time, and these will be better understood with the help of the following remarks.[1]

The entry 'Net interest on debt' indicates the whole

[1] An abstract will be found at the end of this chapter.

amount paid as interest on the public debt proper, excluding service funds and deposits; and after deducting the receipts under interest.

The net interest is divided so as to separate the interest on the borrowed Productive public works capital, which in the last year includes interest on the capital supplied from revenue, from the interest due to the ordinary debt.

Under 'Guaranteed railways' has been still included (to facilitate comparisons) the East Indian Railway, though its financial position was much changed after its purchase in 1880. The entries under interest show the true gross guaranteed railway interest paid; those under net income give the net traffic receipts after deducting the share of surplus profits paid to the companies and all other contingent charges. The published accounts have commonly included, with the guaranteed railway interest, the interest on the Madras Irrigation capital (which is placed under 'Irrigation works' in the present statement) and the payments of the surplus profits; the net traffic receipts being shown in the gross. But this gives an inaccurate view of the facts, for the true liability of the State is only in respect of the guaranteed interest, and the true set-off is the net traffic receipts after deducting any share of surplus payable to the companies.

The entries under 'State railways' are properly comparable throughout, though the rate of interest charged on the borrowed capital, which is 4 per cent. in the earlier years, and has been taken from the return of net revenue and expenditure presented to the House of Commons, June 2, 1881, differs from that shown in the Indian separate accounts, which is 4½ per cent.

In the two last years large sums have been spent

from 'revenue' on railways, treated as due to the Afghan war; the cost of these is not included in the present figures, and, as it is not added to the Productive works capital, interest has not been charged on it in the accounts.

Under 'Irrigation,' until 1879–80, the true income on the Madras and Bombay works, which is mainly received as land revenue, is not shown. For the other provinces the figures are approximately correct, and they include the portion of irrigation income received with the land revenue so far as it has been ascertained; they will therefore not agree with the published accounts which, until 1879–80, do not include this element of income under the head of 'public works.' The aggregate of the public works charges of all descriptions is, however, left unchanged, and will be found to agree with the sums entered in the Parliamentary return just mentioned.

The guaranteed interest on the Madras Irrigation Company's capital is included with interest, under 'Irrigation works,' at the rate of 50,000*l.* yearly, and the losses on the working of the company's canals have been added to the working charges of the State canals.

In the last year only has interest been charged on the capital supplied from revenue, spent in past years on the irrigation works classed as 'productive;' and, as the published accounts do not show the years in which this expenditure took place, this defect cannot be properly corrected. The net income of 1879–80 may therefore, by reason of this, be regarded as exaggerated (in comparison with the figures of previous years) to the extent of about 200,000*l.*; as, however, in the earlier years the income is understated by the omission of the Madras and Bombay net revenues, which would exceed the understated charges for interest on the capital obtained from revenue, the correction if made would no doubt make the result still more favourable than that shown in the statement.

The 'Ordinary public works' expenditure is for all purposes other than the productive works, and it is charged against the revenues of the year. Since 1868–69 the outlay on military buildings and works of all sorts has been rather more than 1,000,000*l.* yearly, and about the same amount has been provided for local works from local funds, leaving from two to three millions as the sum supplied from the general revenues for all civil buildings, roads, and miscellaneous objects. The increase in 1880–81 is in part due to the railway expenditure from revenue before noticed, and in part to an expansion of the provincial and local outlay on public works.

The general results may be stated as follows:—

1. The capital outlay on all classes of productive works has been increased in the thirteen years since 1868–69 from 80,409,000*l.* to 142,223,000*l.*

2. The net yearly charge on all accounts for the same works, including all interest on capital, has fallen during the same period from 1,791,000*l.* to 195,000*l.*

3. The net interest on the ordinary public debt, excluding that due to public works, has fallen from 4,785,000*l.* to 2,898,000*l.*

4. The total charge for the productive works and debt together has fallen from 6,576,000*l.* to 3,093,000*l.*

5. The outlay on ordinary public works after 1868–69 was reduced from 6,471,000*l.* to a yearly amount varying between 4½ and a little more than 5 millions.

6. Comparing 1870–71, the year in which the pro-

vincial system was established, with 1880–81, the aggregate charge for debt and public works of all sorts fell from 10,643,000*l.* to 8,405,000*l.* Comparing 1868–69 with the last year of the series, the reduction in the aggregate yearly charge has been from 13,047,000*l.* to 8,405,000*l.*, or no less than 4,642,000*l.*

7. To sum up: The outlay of 62,000,000*l.* on Irrigation works and railways has been accompanied by an ultimate yearly reduction of charge of 3,000,000*l.* sterling. India has now obtained works to the value of 142,000,000*l.*, which produce a gross income of 15,500,000*l.* and (excluding interest charges on capital) a net income of 7,000,000*l.*; and consequently yield a return of $4\frac{2}{3}$ per cent. on the capital outlay, which pays all interest except a present net residual yearly charge on the State of 195,000*l.*, or less than 3 shillings per 100*l.* per annum on the capital invested. These results have been secured in a period during which India has experienced a succession of famines, unparalleled in history, leading to an extraordinary expenditure of about 14,800,000*l.*; during the same time the fall in the value of silver has led to an exceptional outlay, in excess of the average of former years, amounting to not less than 10,000,000*l.*; and lastly the war in Afghanistan, after deducting the grants made by England, has cost 18,000,000*l.* net, which has been met from the revenues.

It is difficult to understand how facts such as these should have been so completely misconceived or overlooked, and that the utterly mistaken idea should have been so widely disseminated and accepted, that the public works policy of the last ten years has been leading India to financial difficulty, if not ruin. It is only by the most complete neglect of proper inquiry into the facts that such ideas could have been formed; the opinion that the expenditure from borrowed funds has in the period under review been dangerously large cannot be sustained for a single instant by the financial results, which prove conclusively that following this expenditure, and as its immediate consequence, there has been a positive improvement of the resources of the State amounting to 3,000,000*l.* yearly. During this period there has been virtually no increase of taxation, and notwithstanding the very heavy extraordinary demands of late years, the effective debt of the country, so far from having been increased, has been largely reduced. Further elucidations of this point will be supplied in the sequel.

But it is not on the purely financial aspect of the policy under consideration that its full justification rests. We must turn also to the actual results of the works, and inquire what has been their effect on the country, and how their construction and management have been carried out as regards economy and efficiency.

Commencing with the railways, it will be found that, on a capital outlay of 124,417,000*l.*, the gross receipts in 1880–81 amounted to 14,240,000*l.*, and the net receipts to 6,096,000*l.*, or close upon 5 per cent. on the capital, results which compare favourably with those of any other country. In the United Kingdom the average return for 1879 was 4·15 per cent., and it has never been above 4·74 per cent.; in England and Wales out of a total capital outlay of 442,000,000*l.* only 122,000,000*l.* earned more than 5 per cent., and only 41,000,000*l.* earned more than 6 per cent.

The guaranteed railways in India in 1880–81 earned 5,495,000*l.* net on a capital of 97,728,000*l.*, being at the rate of 5½ per cent. The State lines on a capital of 26,689,000*l.* will earn about 2½ per cent. in 1880–81. But only one of these lines had been open more than six years, whereas the older guaranteed lines have been at work twenty-five years, and at a corresponding period of their existence they hardly gave such good results as the State lines now give. Comparing the older lines with the new it must also be remembered that the latter pass through relatively poor districts, and that as the former receive valuable additions to their traffic from the newer State lines, the whole advantage obtained from the latter cannot be properly estimated without making some allowance for the traffic they contribute to the older lines.

On the whole it may confidently be affirmed that there is no country in which the railways, taken as a whole, have been constructed with more economy, or, having regard to the conditions to be dealt with, offer better present financial results, or more encouraging prospects for the future. The gross receipts have increased from 5,750,000*l.* in 1868–69 to 14,240,000*l.* in 1880–81, and the net receipts have grown from 2,500,000*l.* to more than 6,000,000*l.*, or nearly in the same proportion; which, bearing in mind the immature condition of many of the lines last constructed or still under construction, is eminently satisfactory.

It is fair to reckon the cost of transport by rail at about one-fourth of the cost by carts, so that on this standard India now benefits, by reason of its railways, to an amount which may be taken at thrice the gross receipts, or 40,000,000*l.* yearly.

The soundness of this view is confirmed by the great expansion of the foreign trade since the railways have come into operation. The first lines were opened in 1854. In the five years before that time the average yearly imports of merchandise were valued at 11,000,000*l.*; for the last five years the average has been upwards of 39,000,000*l.*, and in the year just closed the value has risen to 52,000,000*l.* For the first-named period the exports of merchandise averaged 19,000,000*l.* yearly, for the last five years the value has been 62,000,000*l.*, and for the year just ended they have risen to 70,000,000*l.* Thus in the last twenty-six years, or since the railways have come into use, the aggregate foreign trade has grown in value from thirty millions to more than 130 millions sterling. The weight of goods carried has increased between 1868 and 1880 from about 3,000,000 tons to more than 10,000,000, and the number of passengers from 16,000,000 to more than 47,000,000.

Bearing in mind that this remarkable expansion of trade and traffic has been contemporaneous with years of altogether exceptional pressure on the population, caused by the extreme droughts and consequent high price of food over very large areas, it is impossible to avoid the conclusion that a great advance has been made in the producing and purchasing power of the people, or to doubt that this advance has been in a very important degree due to the improved and cheap means of transport given by the railways, and to the increased production and security provided by the extension of irrigation works. The position of railways in relation to the protection of the country against the effects of famine will be more fully dealt with in the sequel; their value in the recent great calamities of season, in bringing food supplies to districts where the people without their aid must have had their sufferings vastly aggravated, has been incalculable; in many cases, indeed, without the railways, millions of the population must have been left in a position almost beyond the possibility of relief.

On the larger irrigation works which are classed as 'productive,' about 18,000,000*l.* have been spent, 12,500,000*l.* from borrowed funds and 5,250,000*l.* from revenue. There are also other works of the same character, not classed as 'productive,' for which borrowed money has not been granted, the capital outlay on which has been about 2,500,000*l.* In all, the capital invested in irrigation works for which accounts of revenue are prepared is something less than 20,250,000*l.*; the estimated net income from them for 1880–81 is 1,100,000*l.*; or about 5½ per cent. on the outlay, divided in the proportions of 900,000*l.* from the productive works class, and 200,000*l.* from the others.

The accounts for 1879–80 give the following results for the irrigation works classed as productive in the chief provinces.

Province	Capital	Net revenue	Interest at 4½ per cent.	Surplus	Excess charge
	£	£	£	£	£
Bengal . .	4,980,000	18,000	220,000	—	202,000
North-west Provinces	5,346,000	269,000	237,000	32,000	—
Punjab . .	3,544,000	170,000	155,000	15,000	—
Madras. .	1,720,000	427,000	77,000	350,000	—
Bombay .	1,333,000	10,000	59,000	—	49,000
Total .	16,933,000	894,000	748,000	146,000	—

The bad results in Bengal arise from the Orissa and Sone works which, as before mentioned, were purchased by the Government from the company that began them. The relatively large returns in Madras are due to the high average rates paid on the irrigation of rice, which is the staple crop, and to the small capital outlay. The Bombay works are not giving a satisfactory return.

In the North-Western Provinces, for which the accounts are available in a more complete shape than elsewhere, we find that in 1872–73 the capital outlay on all works in operation (including some which are not technically classed as productive) was close upon 3,000,000*l.*; the net profits amounted to $5\frac{1}{2}$ per cent. on that capital, and the irrigated area was 941,000 acres. In 1878–79 the capital outlay on all works in operation had risen to 4,500,000*l.*, with an increase of profits to $8\frac{1}{2}$ per cent., and an extension of the irrigation to 1,737,000 acres. Besides this, about 1,500,000*l.* of capital had been spent on the Lower Ganges Canal, which had not come into operation, but even including this outlay the net income would still amount to 6 per cent. on the entire sum.

In the year 1877–78 a sum of 2,260,000*l.* had been spent on irrigation works in the Punjab, the irrigated area being 1,324,000 acres. The value of the food crops raised on the two principal canals in that year was estimated at 2,000,000*l.*, and of other crops about 1,000,000*l.*, in all 3,000,000*l.*, and of this it is considered that at least one-half was saved by irrigation. Thus, in a single year, these two canals added to the wealth of the Punjab a sum not less than two-thirds of their entire original cost. The net canal revenue shown in the accounts for this year was, however, only 119,000*l.*, being about $5\frac{1}{2}$ per cent. on the capital outlay on works in operation, a result which obviously supplies a wholly inadequate test of their real value to the country. In the North-West Provinces, in 1877–78, the whole capital outlay being about 4,500,000*l.*, the value of the crops raised was 6,000,000*l.*, and it is reckoned that one-half would have been lost without the canal irrigation. The net revenue received was 315,600*l.*, a result, again, which in no way indicates the true value of the works, for here, too, the value of the produce saved by them was 3,000,000*l.* sterling, and equalled about three-fourths of the first cost of the works. Similar results might be gathered from almost every province.

Though the results of irrigation are not so favourable in Bengal as in the North-West Provinces and Punjab, there is even there abundant evidence of its value. Up to the end of 1878 the outlay on the Sone canals had been 1,908,000*l.*, of which probably 20 per cent. is due to the elaborate provisions made for navigation. In the drought of 1873–74 these canals were very incomplete, and water was rudely poured over the fields through cuts in the banks. The result was that 159,500 acres of rice were saved, worth not less than 600,000*l.* Were a similar season of drought to occur again, 1,000,000 acres might be watered, the value of which would approach 4,000,000*l.* sterling, or about double the cost of the works. It may still be long, under the existing system of management, which avowedly looks to the proceeds of the public works land cess as supplying a contribution from the landholders in aid of the necessary charges for this and other similar works in Bengal, before a direct return is obtained equal to the interest on the 3,110,000*l.* spent, or remaining to be spent, to complete the canals of Orissa; but should another severe drought occur after they are completed, their value would be incalculable. In 1865–66, when there were no canals, about 1,500,000*l.* was spent on famine relief in this province; yet about 1,000,000 persons perished from starvation, and the province was enriched by no single public work to set against the outlay incurred.

From the hilly character of the Deccan districts of Bombay, their broken surface, and the absence of constantly flowing rivers, the construction of large irrigation works has been more difficult and more costly there than in other parts of India; but some of the works by which the waters of the minor streams are utilised, though on a small scale, are extremely productive, and the value of watered crops is, in ordinary years, not less than four times that of others.

In Sindh we find a large province in which, it being almost rainless, agriculture and population would be alike impossible without irrigation, but with this protection it has 1,800,000 acres of cultivated land, has reached a fair condition of prosperity, and gives evidence of far greater capacities in the future.

The two great deltaic systems of irrigation in Madras originated by our Government, the Godaveri and the Kistna, yield returns of 15 and 11 per cent. respectively on the capital spent on them. During 1876–77, a year when every unirrigated district was importing the food of a large portion of its population, the value of the rice produced in the deltas of the Godaveri and Kistna is calculated, at the prices then prevailing, to have been not less than 5,000,000*l.* sterling; the quantity exported by sea from Coconada, the port of the Godaveri delta, was valued at 870,000*l.*, while an equal quantity is believed to have been exported by land. The Caveri works are still more profitable, but the revenue they produce cannot properly be compared with their recorded cost, as they are very largely the result of the labour of years antecedent to British rule, the value of which cannot be estimated.

It is needless to dwell further on the value of the larger class of irrigation works in time of drought. The advantages obtained by irrigation are, however, far from being limited to such seasons. Even where the rain is most abundant, it is reckoned that a command of irrigation will increase the produce of rice by 40 per cent. The ordinary rental of land in Northern India is doubled by irrigation, while, on an average of eleven districts in Madras, the increase is fourfold, and in Tinnevelly it is said to be tenfold. In Mysore the selling price of irrigated land, under favourable conditions, is quoted at 35*l.* per acre, while land which is unirrigated would only fetch 2*l.* or 2*l.* 10*s.*

In almost every part of India artificial irrigation is practised with great advantage to most crops, and to many of the most valuable this aid is essential. It is estimated that out of a total area usually under cultivation, amounting to 200,000,000 acres, about 30,000,000 are irrigated; 8,000,000 from the better class of irrigation works, 12,000,000 from wells, and the residue from other less trustworthy sources of supply. Whether as a means of increasing the necessary food supply of the people, or of stimulating the production of the agricultural staples of commerce, the extension of irrigation must be pronounced to be almost the greatest blessing that can be bestowed on the country, and the construction of the great works which have been carried out in conformity with the policy now under discussion, must unquestionably be classed among the most truly beneficent acts of the British government in India.

A retrospect of this chapter of our administration shows that, notwithstanding many unforeseen obstacles, the results obtained have greatly surpassed in their success the moderate anticipations of those who initiated the policy of carrying out works of permanent utility with borrowed money. The modifications which have by degrees been introduced into the original scheme, mainly as consequences of the very fluctuating opinion which regulates the action of Indian administration, and of the unfortunately small amount of real knowledge of the essential facts to be dealt with, which is possessed by persons influential in forming and directing that opinion, have constantly tended to throw heavier burdens on the profit and loss account of the projected system of works than was at first contemplated; but the thoroughly sound character of the scheme has been most significantly proved by the ultimate financial results obtained, notwithstanding the continually increasing severity of the tests applied to it. All that was first asked was that this policy should not lead to any increase of the public burdens. It has already reduced these burdens by a yearly amount of 3,000,000*l.* sterling.

That an outlay between 40,000,000*l.* and 50,000,000*l.* could be incurred without some blunders or failures was not to have been anticipated. But there is no reason for regarding the failures which have occurred as more conspicuous than those which necessarily attend all human action, or than those which have arisen in the efforts to supply India with education, good laws, efficient courts of justice, and the like. On the contrary there is the best ground for thinking, on the evidence which has been adduced of the practical results, that no portion of the public expenditure has more completely and certainly repaid the people by whom it has been provided than that which has been devoted to works of the productive class; while it has been directly most beneficial to the people, it has greatly added to the resources of the State, and has led to an important improvement in the general financial position of India.

Nor can the thorough success of this policy be challenged because an analysis of the elements of income and charge shows how large a portion of the effective income is due to the older irrigation works, which naturally took advantage of the more easily accessible sources of water supply, and to the older railways, which occupied the main lines of traffic; or because that analysis indicates that the largest returns are mainly derived from a comparatively small number of conspicuously profitable undertakings. Nor will the principal conclusions be shaken if allowances are made for cases like that of the Caveri irrigation works, in which perhaps 100,000*l.* of the income now obtained is not due to any action taken by our Government. A policy of this description must be judged by its results as a whole. In its nature its success depends on balancing the unusually good against the bad. The object in view was not merely to supply the more wealthy parts of the country with conveniences for which they could readily pay, but to give to the poorer tracts what to them were essentials of well-being, or even of existence, and which were quite beyond their means if they were left unassisted. Such an end could only be secured by treating the undertaking as a whole, and dealing with India as a whole. Thus, without putting undue pressure on any part of the community, the more prosperous have silently, but efficiently, aided the poorer, and the prospects of the future have been everywhere improved.

ABSTRACT OF FINANCIAL RESULTS OF PRODUCTIVE PUBLIC WORKS FROM 1868 TO 1881.

Head of Account	Averages of four years			First and last years	
	1869–73	1873–77	1877–81	1868–69	1880–81
	£	£	£	£	£
Net interest on ordinary debt	4,687,000	4,031,000	3,709,000	4,785,000	2,898,000
Guaranteed railways:—Capital	—	—	—	79,168,000	97,728,000
Gross interest	4,405,000	4,640,000	4,693,000	3,878,000	4,599,000
Net income less surplus and charges	2,554,000	3,629,000	4,789,000	1,966,000	4,936,000
Net charge	1,851,000	1,011,000	—	1,912,000	—
Net receipt	—	—	96,000	—	337,000
State railways:—Capital	—	—	—	553,000	26,689,000
Net income	—	56,000	324,000	*17,000*	602,000
Interest	61,000	348,000	962,000	10,000	1,210,000
Net charge	61,000	292,000	638,000	27,000	608,000
Irrigation works:—Capital	—	—	—	688,000	17,806,000
Net income	360,000	331,000	670,000	217,000	927,000
Interest	180,000	353,000	605,000	69,000	851,000
Net receipt	180,000	*22,000*	65,000	148,000	76,000
Total productive public works:—Capital	—	—	—	80,409,000	142,223,000
Net income	2,914,000	4,016,000	5,783,000	2,166,000	6,465,000
Interest	4,646,000	5,341,000	6,260,000	3,957,000	6,660,000
Net charge	1,732,000	1,325,000	477,000	1,791,000	195,000
Total interest on debt and productive public works charges	6,419,000	5,356,000	4,186,000	6,576,000	3,093,000
Ordinary public works	4,545,000	5,061,000	4,595,000	6,471,000	5,312,000
Grand total	10,964,000	10,417,000	8,781,000	13,047,000	8,405,000

N.B. Figures in Italics signify receipts less than charges.

Note to Chapter VII.

In the Accounts of the last two years the manner of treating the guaranteed railway receipts has been changed, so that the figures are not properly comparable with those of the earlier years. The net traffic receipts now appear without modification, in the conventional currency of 10 rupees to 1*l.*, instead of being converted into sterling at the contract rates of exchange. The new procedure is no doubt more correct. Its effect is to make the railway receipts appear larger, as they now include the amount which was before shown as 'Gain by exchange,' and treated as a deduction from the 'Loss by exchange;' this last head being now to the same extent increased. To bring the years before 1879–80 into harmony with the two last years, an addition of rather more than 200,000*l.* should be made to the net traffic receipts for each year from 1869 to 1872, of about 300,000*l.* for the next three years, and of 400,000*l.* for the next three. It has been thought better to deal with the figures as they appear in the published accounts, making this explanation, rather than to alter them in what might appear a somewhat arbitrary manner. Complications of the accounts are unavoidable in dealing with the adjustment of the rupee and sterling currencies, and the guaranteed railway transactions.

The figures in this chapter will not be found to agree with those given in Mr. J. Danvers' reports on Indian railways, those reports stating the traffic receipts and expenditure at the contract rates of exchange, and not in rupee currency, and being also for the calendar and not for the financial year.

Further, it should be noticed that in the table on the preceding page, and in this chapter generally, the amounts of interest on debt are those shown in the published accounts, without the corrections explained at pages 118 to 120.

CHAPTER VIII.

THE PUBLIC DEBT OF INDIA.

THE TRUE CRITERION OF THE POLICY OF BORROWING FOR PUBLIC WORKS—INVESTMENTS ON REPRODUCTIVE WORKS SHOULD BE DISTINGUISHED FROM ORDINARY DEBT—REVIEW OF INCREASE OF DEBT AND ITS PRESENT AMOUNT AND CONSTITUENTS—ORDINARY DEBT AND CHARGE FOR INTEREST GREATLY REDUCED—INTEREST ON PUBLIC WORKS INVESTMENTS HOW FAR COVERED BY NET INCOME—GENERAL POSITION OF DEBT AND PUBLIC WORKS CAPITAL—RETURNS FROM THESE INVESTMENTS—DISCHARGE OF DEBT HOW FAR DESIRABLE—STERLING DEBT—ITS LARGE INCREASE—IMPORTANCE OF PREVENTING ITS GROWTH—DIFFICULTIES IN WAY OF ITS REDUCTION—RUPEE DEBT—EXPEDIENCY OF ESTABLISHING A SINKING FUND FOR DISCHARGE OF DEBT INCURRED FOR PUBLIC WORKS—MARKET PRICE OF SECURITIES INDICATES COMPLETE MAINTENANCE OF CREDIT—GUARANTEED RAILWAY CAPITAL—THE OBLIGATIONS IT CREATES—IMPORTANCE OF EXERCISING POWERS OF PURCHASE—RESULTS OF PURCHASE OF EAST INDIAN RAILWAY.

It has already been remarked that the true criterion of the financial success of the policy of borrowing money for the prosecution of public works, and the true test of how far provision has been made for future expenditure on famine relief by present reduction of debt, will be found in the actual burden caused from time to time by the public works and debt taken together. It is, of course, true that many other causes besides the two just referred to operate in determining the amount of debt incurred or discharged, and of the interest charge arising from the debt; but if it be found that the charge on account of debt is not increased, and, *a fortiori*, if it is directly reduced, it may be unhesitatingly affirmed that the measures of the

Government have been successful, in proportion to the value to the country of the works provided for its material improvement and protection against famine.

Though the evidence already adduced in proof of the success of these measures, and of the wisdom which dictated their adoption, might be considered sufficient, yet it is desirable that every possible light should be thrown on so important a subject, and the more so because it has been freely asserted that the increase of late years in the public debt of India has become a great danger, and that, whatever be the importance of the objects aimed at by those who advised borrowing to extend public works, this course ought altogether to be abandoned.

It is a manifest misuse of language to speak of outlay on works of permanent utility, which, as a whole, already meet all the expenses arising from them, and yield a surplus after paying the ordinary rate of interest on the capital laid out on them, as though such investments, if provided for by borrowing, were undistinguishable, or rather ought not to be distinguished, from debt for which no return can either be obtained or hoped for. The debt which has been incurred for the productive public works of India, viewed as a whole, is debt which involves neither the obligation of reimbursement nor a charge for interest, but which brings a direct profit to the debtor; and it would be as little rational to describe the capital outlay on the railways of Great Britain as a grievous burden on this country, as to speak of the similar investments in India as a danger or an evil.

It is no doubt a fair question for discussion whether the Government, in adopting the system of constructing these works directly through its own agency, did what was best in the actual circumstances, and this will be more fully considered subsequently. But the point more immediately in view is to ascertain the actual results of the course that has been pursued.

Statements will be found in the Appendix which show the position of the debt of India since 1868–69. The total amount of the permanent debt appearing in the accounts has increased from 97,379,000*l.* at the end of that year to 157,149,000*l.* at the end of 1880–81, or in all by about 60,000,000*l.* The above amounts include the debt incurred for productive public works, which has increased from 1,241,000*l.* to 39,656,000*l.*, or by 38,415,000*l.*; and the sum raised in part payment for the East Indian Railway and for subsequent capital outlay, amounting to 10,208,000*l.* Allowance must also be made, as a set-off against the addition to the debt, on account of the loans and advances to municipalities, public trusts, Native States, and others which, in the first-named year, were little more than 680,000*l.*, but in the last exceeded 8,000,000*l.* These loans and advances are covered by corresponding payments of interest, and, as no ultimate liability or charge on the revenues can arise from them, they create no permanent burden. In the last year of the series a sum of 5,306,000*l.* was transferred from the ordinary debt to the productive public works debt (under the rules that have been before explained), to cover the capital outlay from revenue on the productive public works which have been aided by borrowed money. Consequently the whole debt in the last year, stated in round numbers, may be thus divided — ordinary debt, 93,839,000*l.*; productive public works, 44,962,000*l.*; East Indian Railway, 10,208,000*l.*; loans and advances, 8,140,000*l.*; total, 157,149,000*l.*

To make a proper comparison between the first and

last years of the series, it becomes necessary, however, to point out that in 1874 a sum of 4,579,416*l.* was added to the debt to complete the sum required for the discharge of the East India Company's stock in that year, the capital amount of which was not entered in the account as debt. The residue of the sum, about 7,500,000*l.*, was obtained by the investment of the guarantee fund formed in 1834, which was dealt with altogether outside of the public accounts. Consequently, for a proper comparison, the sum of 4,579,416*l.* should be looked on as having formed part of the public debt in 1868–69, instead of having been incurred only in 1874. Further, the sum of 5,306,000*l.* transferred from the ordinary to the productive public works debt in 1880–81, was, in fact, spent in a long series of years, commencing before 1868–69. It is not now possible to say how much of this amount is due to the earlier period, and for purposes of the present comparison it will be best to omit the transfer entirely, thereby assuming that no reduction of the ordinary debt has taken place from this cause since 1868–69, which is a view unduly unfavourable to the period after that year.

Making these allowances, it will appear that the ordinary debt in 1868–69 stood at 100,033,000*l.*, and in 1880–81 at 99,145,000*l.*, or was reduced by nearly 1,000,000*l.*, and this reduction will be an effective one if the interest on the rest of the debt is adequately covered by corresponding receipts. To ascertain how this is we must turn to the interest charges.

In dealing with the interest charges, that item of interest which is paid on service and other funds and deposits must be excluded from consideration, as it represents payments of a totally different character from that of interest on the debt proper; the former being more or less optional in their nature, and in no way representing liabilities caused by borrowing to meet the financial exigencies of the State.

The gross interest on debt proper (with which is included in the accounts, till 1874, the payment of 630,000*l.* yearly to the proprietors of India stock) was a little in excess of 5,000,000*l.* in 1868–69, and rose to 6,096,000*l.* in 1880–81, the average rate (excluding the payment on India stock, the capital of which is not included with debt) having, at the same time, fallen from 4·6 per cent. to 3·8 per cent.

The net interest rose from 4,814,000*l.* to 5,251,000*l.*, or only by 437,000*l.*; the net rate paid (excluding the loans and advances on which interest is charged by Government to its debtors) being 4·3 per cent. in the first year, and 3·2 per cent. in the last.

For purposes of comparison a correction of the interest charge, similar to that above made in the account of the capital debt, will be needed. Of the 630,000*l.* entered in the earlier years for the payment to proprietors of India stock, 450,000*l.* may be properly regarded as the sum which was covered by the accumulated guaranteed fund, and 180,000*l.* as the true interest charge corresponding to the capital sum of 4,579,416*l.* added to the debt in 1874, as before explained. In like manner the interest on the capital amount of 5,306,000*l.*, transferred to productive public works in 1880–81, amounting to 238,000*l.*, should follow the capital debt, and be deducted from the interest charge on the ordinary debt in 1868–69. Making these corrections the net interest charge in 1868–69 on ordinary debt will be 4,097,000*l.*, and in 1880–81, 2,896,000*l.*, showing a reduction of 1,201,000*l.* yearly.

The interest charge on productive works (excluding the guaranteed interest) will in like manner be 267,000*l.* in 1868–69, and (excluding also 344,000*l.* on account of the East Indian Railway) 2,011,000*l.* in 1880–81, showing an increase of 1,744,000*l.* It remains to be seen how far the receipts cover this charge.

The net income of productive public works, excluding the guaranteed railways and canals, rose from 199,000*l.* in the first year to 1,534,000*l.* in the last, an improvement of 1,335,000*l.*, leaving, therefore, a net increase of charge of 409,000*l.* in 1880–81 for interest not covered, and reducing the improvement under ordinary debt, from 1,201,000*l.* to 792,000*l.*

As, however, the policy contemplated the inclusion of the guaranteed railways and canals in the general category of productive works, the charge or income, as the case may be, due to them must also be considered. The net charge for the guaranteed works in 1868–69 was 1,961,000*l.* while there is in 1880–81 a net receipt of 626,000*l.*, making (after deducting 344,000*l.* for interest on account of the East Indian Railway which appears as a charge under interest on debt) an improvement of 2,243,000*l.*; this, combined with the net improvement of 792,000*l.* before arrived at, produces a total reduction of 3,035,000*l.* of net yearly charge for interest and productive works together.

On the whole, therefore, it is not only true that the capital of the ordinary debt may be regarded as having been reduced in 1880–81 by 1,000,000*l.* below what it was in 1868–69, and the interest on it by about 1,200,000*l.* yearly; but besides this, after paying the whole interest on the money actually borrowed for productive works, and on 5,250,000*l.* spent from revenue, and meeting the whole charge arising from the guaranteed railways, the net income of the works is such that there now remains only the small deficiency of 195,000*l.* as compared to a deficiency of 1,791,000*l.* in 1868–69, and of 2,269,000*l.* in 1872–73.

That the full significance of these results may be felt, it must be repeated that during the eight years 1873–74 to 1880–81 there has been spent, as before said, from the revenues, on famine relief the sum of 14,700,000*l.*, and in the three years 1878–79 to 1880–81 on the Afghan war 18,350,000*l.* So that it has been possible in this period of thirteen years to meet the entire charge arising from the most disastrous series of famines on record, and to provide an increase of the capital laid out on productive works and other useful objects of no less than 68,000,000*l.*, with an absolute reduction of debt instead of any increase, after having paid upwards of 18,000,000*l.* of war charges.

Looking to the actual position in 1880–81 we find it to be as follows:—

Total amount of ordinary debt . . .	£93,839,000
Net interest thereon	2,898,000
Total guaranteed railway capital, including the East Indian Railway	£97,728,000
Gross receipts therefrom	12,065,000
Net receipts	5,495,000
Net Government receipts, after payment of all interest	337,000
Total State railway capital	26,689,000
Gross receipts therefrom	2,175,000
Net " "	602,000
Net charge after payment of interest on capital .	608,000
Total irrigation capital (excluding Madras Company)	17,806,000
Gross receipts therefrom	1,357,000
Net " "	927,000
Net income after payment of interest on capital .	76,000
Total capital	£142,223,000
Gross receipts	15,597,000
Net "	7,024,000
Net State charge after paying all interest .	195,000

Viewing the aggregate public debt and guaranteed railway capital as investments for the benefit of India, we shall find that the whole amount stood in 1868–69 at 176,547,000*l*., and at 244,669,000*l*. in 1880–81, with a corresponding charge on the revenues of India in the former year of 6,576,000*l*., being at the rate of 3·8 per cent., and of 3,106,000*l*. in the last, being at the rate of 1·3 per cent.; thus, with an increase of 40 per cent. in the amount of the investment, the charge on the public has been reduced to one-third of its original rate.

The sums paid yearly as interest on debt and as the interest and surplus profits of the guaranteed railways, which constitute the return upon the investments of the capitalists who have furnished the amount above mentioned, have increased from 8,984,000*l*. to rather more than 11,000,000*l*. in the year 1877–78 and those following it. Setting aside the 3,000,000*l*. which is, so to speak, the burden placed on India for its unprofitable debt, there remains a sum of 8,000,000*l*. which, therefore, represents the yearly profits on the capital invested in the great public works; profits, moreover, obtained without causing any burden on India, India, on the contrary, obtaining the vast advantages of the works with no payment excepting that which is voluntarily made for the conveniences supplied in return.

Such results show conclusively how little foundation there is for the allegation, on the one side, that the recent public works policy of the Government of India has been leading to consequences of an alarming nature, from the burden they are throwing on the country; and on the other, that this policy has proved a bar to the profitable investment of capital in India.

In closing this part of the discussion, it may be well to indicate more precisely what has been the amount of the burden which has actually been placed on the revenues during this series of years, and which it was from the outset foreseen would be a necessary consequence of the measures adopted. It may easily be calculated that the accumulated net charge due to the productive public works, guaranteed railways, State railways, and irrigation works from 1868–69 to the end of 1880–81, with compound interest yearly at 4 per cent., would amount to rather more than 22,000,000*l.* If the whole of this sum had been borrowed, and no charge whatever had been thrown on the revenues by the payment of interest, the present result would be that the net yearly interest charge for productive works would be increased from 195,000*l.* to 1,037,000*l.* Hence, in such an event, the aggregate net charge for productive works, together with all interest, including that on the ordinary debt, would have been increased from 3,091,000*l.*, as it now is, to 3,933,000*l.* Comparing this with the total charge in 1868–69, viz. 6,576,000*l.*, we should still find an improvement of more than 2,500,000*l.* yearly, so that from this point of view also the result remains thoroughly satisfactory.

Further, it becomes obvious that so far from Lord Lytton's Government having failed to make provision for the future possibilities of heavy charges for famine by the present reduction of debt and of net interest, to secure which the measures of so-called famine insurance were designed, as will be subsequently explained, such has been the elasticity of the revenues that the ordinary debt is less now than it was in 1877–78 by 6,000,000*l.*, and the net charge for interest less by 1,000,000*l.*, while the net charge for productive public works of all sorts, including all interest on capital, has virtually disappeared. That this has been accomplished in the midst of a time of extreme financial pressure, consequent on the war in Afghanistan, and immediately following the recent years of most severe droughts, has doubtless been mainly due to the rapid increase of the wealth of India during this period; but the success is complete, and those by whose action and whose counsels the way has been opened for it may confidently abide by the verdict which facts have thus already pronounced.

The foregoing statements supply a firm ground on which to rest the consideration of the policy which India may best adopt in future in relation to its public debt. It is not necessary here to reproduce the well-known truisms which are so often repeated as to the importance of paying off debt from surplus income. The practical question which needs attention is how best to secure a reasonable diminution without interfering with the progress of the country, and without placing undue burdens upon the revenues for providing works of permanent utility by which posterity will benefit even more than the present generation of taxpayers.

Attention has elsewhere been directed to the increase of the home charges which has attended the growth of the Sterling debt and of the guaranteed railway liabilities, and an opinion has been expressed that everything possible should be done to reduce this branch of the expenditure. The sterling debt has increased from 31,698,000*l.* in 1868–69 to 71,335,000*l.* in 1880–81, that is, by 39,637,000*l.* If from this be deducted the 4,579,000*l.* required to complete the discharge of the sum due to the proprietors of India stock, and the 9,576,000*l.* raised in connection with the East India Railway purchase, there will remain nearly 25,500,000*l.*

as the addition to the sterling debt caused by the financial exigencies of the period, and it is difficult to avoid the conclusion that this is the one serious blot on the administration of Indian finance in this period.

That the additions to the home debt thus made were regarded as unavoidable in the actual circumstances is not questioned, and indeed such were the difficulties of the time, in consequence of the great fall in exchange, that it is possible that no other course could have been followed. But unless a recovery in the exchange takes place, the relief obtained by borrowing in London may in the end be very dearly purchased. Excluding the last two years of the series, there has been little advantage gained by borrowing in sterling, other than that secured by avoiding the loss by exchange on an equivalent rupee remittance, and sooner or later this must be made good again, if not on the discharge of the debt then on the payment of the interest on it, unless some fortunate turn of events shall once more raise the value of the rupee to something like its old rate.

Considering the very obvious importance of reducing the home disbursements of the Indian Government to a minimum, and the equally obvious difficulties in the way of making remittances by the sale of the bills of the Secretary of State on India, in sufficient amount to pay off any important part of the sterling debt, it is not easy to see what objection could be taken, on grounds of general policy, to any measures that could be devised for transforming the sterling into rupee debt, and thus obtaining indirectly those means of discharging the debt which cannot be obtained directly. Though it may be true that English constitutional practice requires the sanction of Parliament to the raising of loans in England by the Secretary of State for India, there would be no apparent cause for jealousy of a power to transform sterling into rupee debt, or to sell rupee securities, subject to the condition that the proceeds should be applied to discharge sterling debt or other similar sterling liabilities.

In dealing with the rupee debt there are no such technical difficulties to be overcome, and the main question with reference to it is to consider what are the conditions under which it is possible or expedient to continue borrowing for the prosecution of public works, and at the same time to discharge debt. It can hardly be said that the debt of India at present causes any very heavy burden on the country, or that there is any particular urgency in its reduction. The net charge for interest is hardly in excess of 3,000,000*l.*, out of a total net expenditure of 46,000,000*l.*

The part of the debt due to public works may be taken at 55,000,000*l.*, or, excluding the East Indian Railway portion, 45,000,000*l.* It would not appear unreasonable to provide for the gradual discharge of this by the action of some form of sinking fund, which should distribute the burden over a series of years. One per cent. on the capital, with interest at 4 per cent., would pay it off in about forty years, and some such rate appears likely to be suitable. For reasons which will be stated subsequently it would probably be preferable to place the responsibility for the gradual discharge of the capital debt incurred for public works, on the Provincial Governments under which they are constructed and kept in operation. Such a sinking fund would at present involve an actual discharge of debt to the extent of about 450,000*l.* yearly, and the changes which occur from time to time by the lapse of old securities would commonly give the opportunity of applying the accumulating contributions in a convenient manner. The powers which are possessed by the currency department to invest the currency reserve in Government securities to the extent of six crores of rupees would give facilities for such operations.

As the discharge of debt can only take place when there has been a surplus of revenue over expenditure, the continuance of any policy of reducing debt necessarily implies a succession of years of surplus, and involves the recurrence of a consideration of the relative expediency of reducing taxation, or applying a realised surplus to the discharge of debt; but it would manifestly be out of place here to enlarge on such a subject, which can only be usefully dealt with as the occasion actually arises.

An examination of the market price of the securities of the Government of India during the period under review gives no useful indications of the extent to which the increase of the total amount of the debt may have affected the selling price. The fluctuations appear to have been mainly dependent on the varying rates of interest in the money market, and the rates of exchange between India and England, and the latest results are altogether opposed to any idea that the markets have been overweighted with such securities either in this country or in India. How little the credit of the Indian Government has been affected by the clamours of the past year or two is sufficiently demonstrated by the fact that the issue price of the loan issued in Calcutta in the spring of last year, immediately after the announcement of the serious error that had been made in the war estimates, was actually higher than the market price immediately before; and the success of the Secretary of State's $3\frac{1}{2}$ per cent. loan, which immediately rose to a premium, points to the same conclusion.

Before leaving this part of the subject reference may perhaps usefully be made to the position of the Indian Government in relation to the guaranteed railway capital. The obligation to pay interest on this at the stipulated rate, commonly 5 per cent., with a set-off of the net traffic receipts, operates of course in a way which, when there is any deficiency in the net receipts, is identical with a liability to pay interest on ordinary debt. This charge at present is from 500,000*l.* to 700,000*l.* yearly, of which more than half is due to the Madras Railway. The Great Indian Peninsula Railway causes a charge of less than 100,000*l.* in one half-year, in the other half-year giving a surplus, and may so remain for some years. The Oudh and Rohilkhund and the South Indian lines will probably continue to bring a charge, from 50,000*l.* to 100,000*l.* each, for several years. The Punjab and Sindh line has improved considerably, but is still likely to cause a burden of about 100,000*l.* The East Indian and the Eastern Bengal lines are permanently yielding a surplus income. The Bombay and Baroda line will certainly reach this condition almost immediately.

The conditions of the contracts with these companies are complicated, and it is not necessary to explain them in detail. But in all cases they are such as to make it to the interest of the Government to exercise the power of purchase, which is among the conditions, at the earliest date possible. It happened, very unfortunately for the interests of India, that owing to a misconception on this point the Secretary of State some years ago gave up his first power of purchase in the case of the Great Indian Peninsula, Bombay and

Baroda, and Madras railways, and cannot exercise it for twenty-five years to come. The money value of the loss caused by this error can hardly be estimated at less than several millions sterling, but it is now beyond remedy, and all that can be done is to take care that no such blunder is again permitted. On the whole it seems probable that, at least for the next ten years, the aggregate burden caused by the less productive of these railways will not be reduced much below 500,000*l.* yearly; but the set-off that is even now obtained from the more profitable lines covers the deficiency, and yields a direct surplus, and the ultimate advantage to the State, though in a somewhat distant future, and paid for by considerable present sacrifices, will certainly be very large.

The power of purchase has been already exercised with the most satisfactory results, in the case of the East Indian Railway, and a brief explanation of the manner in which this was done, and of its present and probable future financial effect, will afford the best indication of the way in which other similar operations may be expected to work.

The Secretary of State, under the contract with the East Indian Railway Company, was able to purchase their undertaking by creating an annuity for seventy-four years in their favour, equal in capitalised value to the amount of their share capital, taken at the average price during the three years preceding the purchase. This price was by agreement settled at 125*l.* for 100*l.* stock, and the rate of interest for calculating the annuity at 4*l.* 6*s.* per cent. The capital having been 26,200,000*l.* an annuity of 1,473,750*l.* was created, which is at the rate of 4½ per cent. on 32,750,000*l.* At the same time the Government took over the debentures of the company, aggregating in amount 4,450,000*l*. The purchase having been thus disposed of a working lease of the railway was given to the company, on the following basis. A nominal sum of 6,550,000*l*., which is one-fifth of the purchase-money on which the annuity was reckoned, was to be left with the Secretary of State during the currency of the lease, a corresponding deduction being made from the amount of the annuity. On this sum interest was guaranteed at the rate of 4 per cent. on the security of the revenue of the railway. The net receipts of the line after paying all working expenses, and a contribution to a Provident fund, were then to be dealt with as follows. From the receipts were to be deducted the following sums: (1) the amount paid by the Secretary of State on account of the annuity, (2) the guaranteed interest to the working company, (3) interest on the debentures taken over from the old company, and (4) interest on all moneys advanced by the Secretary of State for the purposes of the working company. The Secretary of State was to supply all needful capital required for extensions of the undertaking, being paid interest thereon as just stated. The residue was then to be divided, in the proportions of one-fifth to the working company and four-fifths to the Government. All sterling payments of interest and annuities, &c., made by the Secretary of State were also to be converted into rupee currency at the current rate, instead of at the old fixed conventional rate of 1*s*. 10*d*. per rupee.

The general result of the change thus made will appear by comparing the actual amounts received by the Government and the company respectively for the year 1880, under the new arrangement, with what they would have been under the old one.

Under the new arrangement, the net traffic receipts for the year, after the payment to the Provident fund, being 2,84,66,849 rupees,[1] they were distributed as follows:

Annuity and Interest	Rs.1,90,71,220
Surplus to Company	Rs. 17,72,690
Residue to Government	Rs. 76,22,939

Under the old contract the result would have been:

Guaranteed Interest, 1,498,000*l.* at 1*s.* 10*d.* .	Rs.1,63,41,818
Surplus to Company	Rs. 59,94,107
Loss by Exchange on Guaranteed Interest .	Rs. 11,23,102
Residue to Government, net	Rs. 50,07,766

Therefore the Government direct advantage is 26,15,173 rupees, or about 260,000*l.* in the year. But as this profit will be made after paying the instalments of the purchase-money included in the annuity, the average amount of which for the 74 years is about 440,000*l.* yearly, the whole advantage may be taken at 700,000*l.* yearly. The present yearly Government income from the railway being about 760,000*l.*, about 53,000*l.* has to be deducted from that sum as the interest on Government capital advanced for the undertaking, so that the present yearly clear income may also be taken at 700,000*l.* This will go on increasing as the receipts of the railway improve, and at the end of the term of seventy-four years, with the lapse of the annuity, the Government, having completed the purchase of the railway, will come into the receipt of a clear yearly income which cannot be less than 2,500,000*l.* sterling, and probably will be much more.

[1] The Indian system of reckoning money is by crores, lakhs, and thousands of rupees, so that this sum would be read as:—Two crores, eighty-four lakhs, sixty-six thousand eight hundred and forty-nine rupees.

CHAPTER IX.

DECENTRALISATION OF FINANCIAL ADMINISTRATION.

GREAT EXTENT OF INDIA—DIFFERENCES AMONG ITS PROVINCES—FORMATION OF SEPARATE ADMINISTRATIVE GOVERNMENTS—BUT WITHOUT FINANCIAL POWER—NECESSITY FOR SUCH POWERS RECOGNISED—DIFFICULTIES CAUSED BY ITS ABSENCE—MEASURES FOR ITS INTRODUCTION SUGGESTED—CARRIED OUT BY LORD MAYO IN 1871—HIS MEASURES DESCRIBED—FIRST APPLIED TO EXPENDITURE—THEIR EFFECT—THEIR DEFICIENCIES—EXTENDED IN 1877 BY INCLUDING REVENUE—THE SCOPE OF THESE EXTENSIONS—FURTHER EXTENSIONS CONTEMPLATED—GENERAL RESULTS OF POLICY OF DECENTRALISATION—SHOULD BE APPLIED TO MANAGEMENT OF PRODUCTIVE PUBLIC WORKS—SIR A. EDEN'S OPINION ON RESULTS OF POLICY IN BENGAL—PROPOSALS MADE BY MR. BRIGHT.

ALLUSION has more than once been made to the measures which have been taken for increasing the financial authority and responsibility of the Local Governments. Their extreme importance has not been understood or appreciated by the public, which sees little of their practical working, but they have in fact revolutionised not only the financial relations which formerly existed between the Supreme and Provincial Governments, but the whole system of Indian administration. Of these measures a more particular account will now be given.

India, it ought always to be remembered, is no homogeneous country, but a continent containing many nations, the differences between which are as great as those which exist between the nations of Europe. It is further from Lahore to Calcutta than from London to Naples, and wide as is the difference between England and Italy in physical conditions and in the character of their inhabitants, the differences between the Punjab and Bengal are hardly less. We should think it absurd to suppose the same plans of administration to be necessarily applicable in all their details to all the countries of Europe, and it is not less absurd to suppose it of India. And it may here be observed that this consideration may often afford the explanation of divergencies between high Indian authorities on matters not only of opinion but of fact. We frequently hear complaints of the impossibility of learning anything certain about India; we are told that statements made yesterday, by men who ought to know, differ entirely from statements made by men of equal knowledge to-day. These uncomplimentary comments of English critics often have their origin in forgetfulness of the vast extent and the varying conditions of the provinces comprised under the common name of India.

The necessity for dividing the country into separate governments, and entrusting the chief local authorities with large executive responsibility, arose very early. But so long as the British power was in the transition state mentioned in the first chapter of this work, the much smaller amount of the revenues, and simpler character of the administration, rendered the management of the finances a matter of comparatively small difficulty. It was not until after the Mutiny in 1857 that anything deserving the name of a regular financial administration was established in British India. The enormously costly measures adopted for the restoration of authority and order, followed by the hardly less imperious demands for funds to meet the rapidly growing wants of the country, then made it apparent that a system of strict financial control over all parts of the empire, and all branches of the executive government, had become essential. This control was naturally centered in the Supreme Government of India, and almost of necessity it was, at the outset, exercised in the form of a very severe repression of expenditure.

At that time[1] the Local Governments, which practically carried on the whole administration of the country, were left with almost no powers of financial control over the affairs of their respective provinces, and no financial responsibility. Everything was rigorously centralised in the Supreme Government, which took upon itself the entire distribution of the funds needed for the public service throughout India. It controlled the smallest details of every branch of the expenditure; its authority was required for the employment of every person paid with public money, however small his salary; and its sanction was necessary for the grant of funds even for purely local works of improvement, for every local road, and every building, however insignificant.

The evils of this system became more and more manifest as time went on. There grew up gradually, among the most competent advisers of the Government, a strong conviction that radical changes were necessary. By no one was this opinion more forcibly urged than by Lieut.-General Dickens, then Secretary to the Government of India, in the department of public works, who in a memorandum written in

[1] The following account of the measures of financial decentralisation adopted by Lord Mayo is, for the most part, extracted from Sir John Strachey's Financial Statement for 1877-78, which was founded on papers written by General Strachey.

September 1860, when serious discussions on the subject had already begun, proposed to confide to Local Governments a large share in the management of the finances. He protested against a system under which the exercise by the Supreme Government of constant and minute control in matters of petty detail was 'regarded with feelings of aversion by the local governors, whose powers it curtails, and with whose acts it interferes. The consequence is, as might be expected, that the Local Governments render at best to the Supreme Government a cold and languid support in financial vigilance and reform; they too often exhibit a passive resistance, and even countenance evasions of regulations intended to be conducive to economy. The Supreme Government is always suspicious and dissatisfied; the Local Government, always sulky and discontented.'

In the financial statements for 1861–62 and 1862–63 Mr. Laing dwelt strongly on the evils of the existing system; and in the latter of those years he spoke as follows:—

'If this great empire is ever to have the roads, the schools, the local police, and other instruments of civilisation which a flourishing country ought to possess, it is simply impossible that the Imperial Government can find either the money or the management. The mere repair of the roads, where anything like a sufficiency of good roads has been made, is matter altogether beyond the reach of any central bureau. It is of the first importance to break through the habit of keeping everything in dependence on Calcutta, and to teach people not to look to the Government for things which they can do far better for themselves. . . .

'It is most desirable to break through the system of barren uniformity and pedantic centralisation, which has tended in times past to reduce all India to dependence on the bureaus of

Calcutta, and to give to Local Governments the power and the responsibility of managing their own local affairs. The great branches of the expenditure, such as the army and national debt, are imperial; and while this is the case, the great branches of revenue must remain imperial also. But there is a wide field, both of revenue and expenditure, which is properly local, which in England is met by local rates, and which, in fact, must be met locally, or not at all.'

Mr. Laing made no actual change in this respect, but the necessity for some measure of reform became daily more apparent. The business of supervising in a central office all the details of the receipts and expenditure of the empire had become so enormous, that its proper performance was impossible. 'I do not think,' wrote Sir Henry Maine, 'that anybody can have observed the recent workings of our system of financial control without coming to the conclusion that, if it be not on the point of an inevitable collapse, it is, at all events, in great danger of going to pieces, unless the strain be lightened somewhere.'

For many years the ordinary financial condition of India had been one of chronic deficit; and one of the main causes of this state of affairs was the impossibility of resisting the constantly increasing demands of the Local Governments for the means of providing every kind of improvement in the administration of their respective provinces. Their demands were practically unlimited, because there was almost no limit to their legitimate wants, and the Local Governments had no means of knowing the measure by which their annual demands upon the Government of India ought to be regulated. They had a purse to draw upon of unlimited, because unknown, depth; they saw, on every side, the necessity for improvements; their constant and justifiable desire was to obtain for their own provinces and people as large a share as they could persuade the Government of India to give them out of the general revenues of the empire; they found by experience that the less economy they practised, and the more importunate their demands, the more likely they were to persuade the Government of India of the urgency of their requirements. In representing and pressing those requirements, they felt that they did what was right, and they left to the Government of India, which had taken the task upon itself, the responsibility of refusing to provide the necessary means.

The Government of India had totally failed to check the constant demands for increased expenditure; there was plainly only one remedy—to prevent the demands being made—and this could only be done by imposing on the Local Governments a real and effectual responsibility for maintaining equilibrium in their local finances. There could be no standard of economy until apparent requirements were made absolutely dependent upon known available means. It was at that time impossible for either the Supreme or Local Governments to say what portion of the provincial revenues was properly applicable to local wants; for the revenues of the whole of India went into a common fund, and to determine how much of this fund ought fairly to be given to one province, or for one object, and how much to others, was impracticable. 'The distribution of the public income,' General Strachey wrote, 'degenerates into something like a scramble, in which the most violent has the advantage, with very little attention to reason; as local economy leads to no local advantage, the stimulus to avoid waste is reduced to a minimum; so, as no local growth of the income leads to an increase of the local means of improvement, the interest in developing the public revenues is also brought down to the lowest level.'

The unsatisfactory condition of the financial relations between the Supreme and the Local Governments led to other evils. Constant differences of opinion about petty details of expenditure, and constant interference of the Government of India in matters of trivial importance, brought with them, as a necessary consequence, frequent conflicts with the Local Governments, regarding questions of provincial administration, of which they were the best judges, and of which the Government of India could know little. The relations between the Supreme and Local Governments were thoroughly inharmonious, and every attempt to make financial control more stringent increased an antagonism the mischief of which was felt throughout the public service.

It was not until 1867, when Mr. Massey had charge of the financial department that the subject began to assume a clear shape. Definite proposals were then for the first time made for the adoption of specific practical measures which should accomplish the object in view. Their author was General Strachey; the principles laid down in papers written by him in 1867 are those which have since received so wide an application, and the practical course he suggested has been followed in the proceedings taken up to the present time for conferring on Local Governments a larger measure of financial responsibility and power. Although Mr. Massey was unable to carry those proposals into effect, he gave them his firm and constant support, and this contributed greatly to their ultimate adoption.

To Lord Mayo belongs the honour of having

actually applied the only effectual remedy for these serious evils. He resolved to carry out, so far as circumstances allowed, the reforms which General Strachey had proposed; to give to the Local Governments the economical standard which they required; to make over to them a certain income within which they must regulate their local expenditure; and to leave to them, subject to certain general rules and conditions, the responsibility of managing their own local affairs.

From the commencement of the official year 1871–72 the financial control of the following services was transferred to the Local Governments: gaols, police, education, registration, medical services, printing, roads, and civil buildings.

The objects in view were stated by Lord Mayo himself in the Legislative Council on March 18, 1871, as follows:—

'Under these eight heads it is proposed to intrust the administration, under a few general conditions, to the Provincial Governments, and a fixed contribution will be made from imperial revenue every year. . . . It is impossible to prophesy or say at present what can be done in the far future; but I should be misleading the Local Governments if I were not to say that it is our opinion that these sums are now fixed at an amount which cannot be exceeded for at least a number of years. I think it desirable that this should be perfectly understood, because one of our objects is the attainment of as great an amount of financial certainty as is possible. . . . But, in addition to the increased power of administration which it is proposed to give to the Local Governments, an administrative change will take place, which I think they will be able to exercise with advantage. They will have a large sum to devote to local objects; the power of allotment will be left absolutely to them; and they will be able to vary their grants for roads, civil buildings, education, and other heads, from year to year, as they may think most desirable; in some provinces it may be desirable in one year to spend a larger sum on roads; in others it may be desirable to fill up some shortcomings with regard to education or other objects. The Local Governments will thus be able to exercise that power of allotment with much greater satisfaction to themselves and to the public than they did under the old system, when they were obliged to consult the Supreme Government, not only as to the allotments that were made in the beginning of the year, but also with regard to any appropriations that were thought desirable within the year, provided that those appropriations exceeded a certain amount.

'. . . I have heard it stated that, by the proposals which we make, there may arise a separation of interests between the Supreme and Local Governments; I fail to perceive any strength whatever in this assertion; I believe that, so far from there being a separation of interests, the increased feeling of responsibility and the feeling of confidence which is reposed in them will unite and bind together the Supreme and Local Governments to a greater extent than before. . . . I believe that we shall see, in place of greater uncertainty, greater certainty; we shall see works and objects carried on with more vigour, enthusiasm, and with less hesitation, when these works and these objects are effected under the immediate responsibility of those who are most interested in them.'

The gross sum made over yearly to the Provincial Governments for these services, and some few others transferred between 1871–72 and 1877–78, amounted to about 5,600,000*l*.

The original distribution of the provincial grants was strictly based on the then actual expenditure under the heads transferred. That there were great differences in the incidence of the public burdens in different provinces was well known, but it would manifestly have been quite impracticable to have attempted any re-adjustment at that time, and all idea of dividing the available revenues among the several governments, on theoretical conceptions of supposed equity, was deliberately rejected. Nor is it indeed apparent how any more satisfactory principle could have been adopted than to start from the status quo of each province, leaving the removal of inequalities to be effected by degrees and by a readjustment of local burdens.

When Lord Lytton became Viceroy, and Sir John Strachey took charge of the financial department of the Government, six years' experience of the new system had been gained, and there was not, nor had there ever been, a dissentient voice, either in the Supreme Government or in any of the Local Governments, in regard to its success. The only fault ever found with it was that, although an excellent beginning, it did not go far enough. Every object with which the change of system was made had been gained; the old friction between the Supreme and Local Governments had been diminished; the authority of the Supreme Government, and its power of general control, instead of being weakened, had become stronger and more real since the attempt to interfere in all sorts of petty details had been abandoned; and the Local Governments had been able to carry out many measures of improvement which would otherwise have been impracticable.

The most important object of all, so far as the imperial finances were concerned—that of economy and the prevention of increased expenditure—had been completely gained. The charges made over to the Provincial Governments had been selected because they were specially liable to increase. Between 1863–64 and 1868–69 the cost of the services in question rose from 5,112,000*l.* to 6,030,000*l.*, or at an average of nearly 200,000*l.* a year. In 1870–71, in consequence of the determined efforts of Lord Mayo's Government the charges which had been growing at so alarming a rate were reduced to 5,197,000*l.*, but until the new system was introduced, there was little reason for hoping that the process of constant increase would not immediately recommence. Five years after the change of system had been made, the expenditure on the whole of the assigned services remained almost unaltered. The total charges only exceeded by 200,000*l.* the sum to which, by extraordinary efforts, they had been reduced in 1863–64, and they were less in 1875–76 by 700,000*l.* than they were in 1868–69. When the figures were examined in detail they were still more satisfactory, for they showed that there had been a reduction of expenditure under nearly all heads excepting 'Education' and 'Medical,' or, in other words, that the people had got more schools, hospitals, and dispensaries, although less money had been spent on gaols and police.

When Lord Mayo's measures were taken in 1870, there was much ignorant talk about their leading to an increase of local taxation, and it has been loudly asserted that in consequence of those measures new burdens had been imposed on the country, which were none the less serious for being called local. There is no foundation for such statements. The Local Governments obtained no powers of taxation which they did not possess before, and excepting in the North-Western Provinces, Punjab, and Oudh, where new rates for local purposes were imposed to a very moderate extent, the measures of 1870 led to no fresh taxation. It is true that a considerable increase to local taxation was made about the same time in Bengal, Madras, and Bombay, but this was an accidental coincidence, and had no connection whatever with the introduction of the new system of administration and finance.

The chief defect of these measures, excellent so far as they went, was that they dealt almost exclusively with expenditure, and hardly at all with income. If it was certain that provincial responsibility would lead to economy in expenditure, it was equally certain that it would lead to improvement in those sources of revenue which depend for their productiveness on good administration.

For example, the two great heads of income, excise and stamps, yielded in 1876–77 5,360,000*l.* The whole of this went into the Imperial treasury; the increase or decrease in the receipts mainly depends, in the long-run, on good or bad management; and bad management of such resources means not only the wasteful throwing away of revenue without any relief to the country, but very possibly the needless imposition of other and more objectionable taxation. In the financial statement for 1877–78, Sir John Strachey referred to this subject in the following terms:—

'How is this better management to be obtained?—The answer seems to me simple: it can be obtained in one way only; not by any action which gentlemen of the financial department, or any other department of the Supreme Government, can take while sitting hundreds or thousands of miles away in their offices in Calcutta or Simla; not by examining figures and writing circulars; but by giving to the Local Governments, which have in their hands the actual working of these great branches of the revenue, a direct and, so to speak, a personal interest in efficient management. It may be very wrong, but it is true, and will continue to be true while human nature remains what it is, that the local authorities take little interest in looking after the financial affairs of that abstraction the Supreme Government, compared with the interest which they take in matters which immediately affect the people whom they have to govern. When Local Governments feel that good administration of the excise and stamps and other branches of revenue will give to them, and not only to the Government of India, increased income and increased means of carrying out the improvements which they have at heart, then, and not till then, we shall get the good administration which we desire; and with it, I am satisfied, we shall obtain a stronger and more real power of control on the part of the Central Government than we can now exercise.'

Lord Lytton had always, from the time of his assumption of office, desired to carry out to its full legitimate extent the policy which had worked so successfully, and consequently in 1877 he effected a further important application of the original scheme, which on grounds of expediency Lord Mayo had not attempted in 1871. The services which were the subject of the settlement of 1871 were gaols, registration, police, education, medical services, printing, miscellaneous public improvements, and civil buildings, with the connected receipts. In 1877 the system was extended to all the remaining services, excepting the few administered directly by the Central Government, or in the management of which the Local Governments could manifestly exercise no influence. At the same time, the revenues from stamps, excise, law and justice, and some other items, were surrendered, under certain conditions, to the Local Governments. To these was added the licence tax as soon as it was imposed. Moreover, the management of some of the railways and all of the canals within their jurisdiction was made over to the Local Governments. The object of all that was done was, as far as possible, to renounce on the part of the Government of India all responsibility for the detailed management of these revenues and services, and to intrust this responsibility to the Local Governments.

These new arrangements still left the Local Governments without any separate interest in the land, the forest, and some other items of revenue. As regards the Governments of Assam and Burmah, this defect was cured in the settlements made with them in 1879. By these settlements, all the revenues and all the services which could possibly be made provincial were so treated; and for the balance, instead of a fixed sum, a fixed proportion of the land, forest, and other revenues was assigned to the provincial treasury.

It will give a better idea of the practical scope of these measures, and of their administrative importance, to mention that the revenues assigned under them to the Provincial Governments amounted in 1880–81 to close upon 10,000,000*l.* sterling, to which were added supplementary grants from the revenues reserved as Imperial of about 4,250,000*l.*; thus the sum of about 14,500,000*l.* was placed at the disposal of the Local Governments, for provincial purposes, besides the more strictly localised income designated as Local amounting to nearly 3,000,000*l.*, or altogether more than 17,000,000*l.*, out of the 69,000,000*l.* which constitutes the whole gross public revenue.

The latest settlements have worked most satisfactorily; still they are not perfect. On the one hand, the Central Government has not always reserved a sufficient share in the increase of such revenues as those from excise, stamps, and registration. On the other hand, the interests of the Local Governments in the land revenue, and in the other revenues now shared between them and the Central Government, are not substantial enough. It is also felt that it would be desirable, without insisting on any unmeaning identity, to make the arrangements with the several provinces more uniform. The existing settlements having been made separately at various times, the terms of one settlement sometimes differ needlessly from those of another. The Government of Madras, moreover, has, since the original settlement of 1871, declined to enter into any extended arrangements, and none of the recent measures apply to that Presidency. No reason for this was apparent to the Government of India, except that chronic and invincible dislike of change by which the Madras Government has been so often distinguished.

Sir John Strachey had hoped, before leaving India, to complete the policy described in this chapter by a revision of the settlements with all the Local Governments upon a uniform and comprehensive basis. What he contemplated was as follows. The revenues and charges arising from tributes, salt, and opium, allowances and assignments, the administration of the post office and telegraphs, the political department, the East Indian Railway, the guaranteed railway companies, and all items recorded only in the accounts of the Central Government, would have remained wholly imperial. The revenues from forests, excise, and assessed taxes, stamps, and registration, and the import duties on liquors, would have been shared equally between the Local and Central Governments. Each Local Government would have received a fixed proportion of the net land revenue to make good the difference between its assigned revenues and expenditure; and the rest of the revenue and expenditure, with a few exceptions, would have been provincial. The assignment of a share of the land revenue formed a part of General Strachey's original scheme, but was deliberately avoided at first in order to remove as far as possible all objections to the practical adoption of the measure, and to introduce it in a form that should not excite opposition, or risk failure, from its too large dimensions.

To complete this scheme the Local Governments ought to have some interest in the salt revenue also; there are, however, difficulties in arranging this Except in Burmah the salt revenue brought to account in each province is not the duty levied upon the consumption of salt within the province; it would be difficult to ascertain the true local consumption, and objectionable to allow to a Local Government a share in the duty levied on salt consumed beyond its jurisdiction.

The foregoing is an outline of the measures for completing the policy of financial decentralisation which Sir John Strachey proposed, and the needful details of which have been worked out by Mr. Chapman in the department of Finance with much care and labour. The plan awaits the consideration of the Government of India.[1] Under it, instead of the general allotment now made, amounting to about 4,250,000*l.*, specific proportions of the separate items of revenue would be assigned for provincial purposes, amounting in all to about 7,000,000*l.*, with a corresponding addition to the charges that would become provincial, so that the provincial income and expenditure would be raised from 14,500,000*l.* to 17,000,000*l.*

The facts and figures given in this chapter and elsewhere show how completely successful this policy of decentralisation has been. Viewing it in its financial aspect, we find that in the last twelve years there has been, on the whole, no increase in the charges

[1] While these pages were passing through the press, the decision of the Government to carry out arrangements based on these plans has been announced.

under the chief provincial heads, the only exceptions being a moderate growth of the expenditure upon education, medical services, the internal civil administration, and gaols. The provincial revenues are flourishing, and show every indication of successful management. The aggregate surplus of provincial revenue over expenditure during the twelve years has amounted to more than 2,000,000*l.*, so that the provincial treasuries were able without difficulty between 1879 and 1881 to contribute 670,000*l.* towards the necessities of the central treasury arising from the war. The total amount standing to credit as the provincial and local balances was at the end of 1880–81 rather more than 3,000,000*l.*, and in 1881–82 is estimated at 2,500,000*l.*, after providing for an increased expenditure, compared to the previous year, of nearly 1,000,000*l.*

The administrative results are equally satisfactory. Controversies between the Central and the Local Governments are now almost unknown; the transaction of public business has been greatly facilitated; and the Local Governments are generally well content, not only with their financial position, but with the wide measure of administrative independence which they have obtained. And this last is the greatest result of all. Interference with the petty details of expenditure necessarily involved interference in all the details of administration. The Local Governments are incomparably stronger than they were, and the efficiency of all the most important branches of the public service has been increased. As was said at the beginning of this chapter, the whole system of Indian administration has been profoundly affected by this change. The Viceroyalty of Lord Mayo will be honourably remembered for its introduction; to that of Lord Lytton belongs the honour of its accomplishment. The reform is now not far from complete, all that remains being to make final improvements of detail, and to give the policy an extension in a direction which Lord Lytton's Government had desired, but was unable to accomplish. The nature of this extension will be briefly stated.

The arrangements which have been described relate almost exclusively to the receipt and expenditure of the ordinary revenues. They should be supplemented by others, more completely handing over to the Local Governments the responsibility for applying borrowed funds to works of public improvement. It would have been the aim of Lord Lytton's Government to appropriate suitable sums, proportional to the ascertained wants of the several provinces, in a manner that would have secured to the Local Governments reasonable continuity in their operations, and would have freed them in respect to this part of their duties from the necessity of constant references and appeals to the Central Government, in a way similar to that which has been accomplished in dealing with the ordinary funds derived from the revenues. The measures of Provincial decentralisation will not be complete until the Local Governments have been invested with full responsibility for the financial administration of all branches of the public service, the executive management of which is placed in their hands; and with this responsibility should be joined that of originating all measures needed for the good government of their respective charges. Were this done, the Government of India would be freed, as it should be, from all details of local business, and would assume its proper position of a controlling authority only.

One direction in which the efforts of Lord Lytton's Government thus to extend the powers of the Local Governments were frustrated calls for special notice. It is plainly an object of considerable importance to obtain the co-operation of local capitalists in the prosecution of useful works. In the North-Western Provinces, Sir W. Muir, when Lieutenant-Governor, undertook a branch railway on this principle. A large part of the requisite capital was supplied by persons locally interested in its success, the residue being made up from the Provincial funds. A moderate guarantee of interest, to be met from Provincial revenues, was promised on the capital locally subscribed, as well as the right to participate in half the profits in excess of the guaranteed interest. A local committee of native gentlemen was formed from among the subscribers of the capital, which was consulted as to the tariff and business arrangements of the line.

The success of this undertaking, which almost from the outset gave a return a little in excess of the guaranteed rate of interest, and caused no burden on the Provincial revenues, made it clear that the plan might be usefully adopted in other cases, and the Local Governments, generally, were invited to adopt the system, under certain rules which were framed to secure financial regularity, and prevent the undue extension of the Provincial liabilities. Two or three works of local interest were immediately brought forward for prosecution in this manner; considerable sums were subscribed locally for them; and the subsequent great success of one of them, the Patna and Gya Railway, shows that the plan was one of much promise. But before it had received such a development as would certainly have rendered most valuable assistance in the extension of works of local improvement, and would have initiated a system of true local co-operation for such purposes, the Secretary of State issued orders which had the effect of arresting all further progress in this direction. He required that all money raised locally, under engagements by the Local Governments to pay interest from the Provincial revenues, should be treated as though it had been borrowed by the Imperial Government, and that the amount thus provided should be deducted from the limited sum to which he had restricted the loans for the prosecution of Public Works. It followed that the Local Governments could not increase the means at their disposal by thus receiving local aid. All inducement to seek it was removed, and a plan of the greatest promise fell—still-born. The centralising power of the Government of India, and of the Secretary of State acting through that Government, which it had been desired to relax in a new direction, was strictly maintained, and the means of developing a healthy and useful spirit of local co-operation and self-support, which it had been proposed to give to the Local Governments, were withheld.

The reduction of the total amount to be spent on productive works, and the refusal to authorise this useful extension of the powers of the Local Governments, were subsequently followed by still further restrictions, both on the classes of works that might be undertaken with borrowed money, and on the application to them even of funds obtained from the revenues of the year. It is hardly necessary to point out how little such a restrictive policy finds any justification, either in the present state of the finances, or in the actual results of the different course that was till lately followed in this matter; how manifestly it stands in the way of the reasonable development of Provincial administrative and financial responsibility, on which the future progress of India essentially depends; nor how seriously it must interfere with the early provision of those means of protection against future calamity, which a true perception of the demands of good government and ordinary humanity alike require.

The following extract from a Resolution of the Government of Bengal, reviewing the position of that province at the commencement of the present financial year, affords the best possible corroboration of the views expressed in this chapter. The able Lieutenant-Governor of Bengal, Sir Ashley Eden, whose independence of judgment and freedom from all disposition to exaggeration are beyond question, and whose cordial co-operation with the Government of India in all matters affecting the financial administration calls for special acknowledgment, uses these words:—

'That the system of decentralisation has been thoroughly successful in Bengal is sufficiently clear from the foregoing sketch. The revenues have rapidly increased, independently of any new taxation; useless expenditure has been curtailed; and funds have been made available for improvement under all branches of the Administration. All grades of the service have shown the deepest interest in increasing the resources of Government, under the belief that the surplus revenue would be available for the good of the province. The three heads of improvable revenue made over to the management of the Provincial Government, with an income of 165¼ lakhs in 1876–77, will stand with an income of not less than 217¼ lakhs in 1881–82. In the meanwhile, the Lieutenant-Governor has been able to carry out numerous works of improvement on his own responsibility, many of which, under the previous system, would have been indefinitely postponed. Besides making a special contribution of 20 lakhs to the Imperial treasury in time of need, he has been able during these five years to increase the staff of executive and judicial officers; to provide increased facilities for the administration of justice; to increase the grant for education; to make grants in aid of district communications and of works of drainage, sanitation, and municipal improvement; to build schools, colleges, and hospitals; to replace the huts in which the public business was transacted, or prisoners were confined, by substantial masonry court-houses and gaols; to spend 20 lakhs on railways which will bring in a large return, 5½ lakhs on tramways, ¾ of a lakh on a steamer service to improve communications with Assam, and 2 lakhs on a road to develop the trade with Thibet; to spend 11 lakhs on the first portion of a work which will develop the trade of Orissa and protect it from famine; and to spend 38¼ lakhs on improving navigation and providing a supply of pure water for the people. While 77½ lakhs have thus been expended on great measures of material improvement, and the expenditure on Ordinary Public Works has been increased from Rs. 25,12,000 in 1877–88 to Rs. 63,53,000, exclusive of expenditure on preliminary works of railway construction, in 1881–82, and while no legitimate outlay has been spared to strengthen every department of the Administration, the five years' period, which opened with a credit balance of Rs. 2,88,000 only, will close with a credit balance of at least Rs. 14,46,000. When it is recollected that under the system which prevailed before 1871 every new charge required the sanction of the Imperial Government, that the decision on the demands of each province took no cognisance of the extent to which it had contributed to the general Exchequer, that nothing was to be gained by economy, because money left unspent by any one Government was practically lost to it and only went to increase the amount to be scrambled for by all, some idea may be gained of the advantages which Bengal has reaped from the control of its own finances. There is no department of the service which has not felt the benefit of the financial independence conferred on the Government immediately responsible for its administration.'

It may not be out of place here to point out how the measures of which this chapter gives an account, differ from certain proposals made by Mr. Bright some years ago. He told us in eloquent terms that it was folly to suppose that so vast a country as India, with all its different nations and languages, could ever be bound up into a single State. 'What you want,' he said, 'is to decentralise your Government. What would be thought if the whole of Europe were under one Governor who knew only the language of the Feejee Islands?' The basis of truth in these observations is obvious and undisputed. But the projects by which Mr. Bright would have abolished the Governor-General in Council, and established half-a-dozen separate Governments in India having little or no connection with each other, and each of them directly subordinate to the Government at home, would if carried out have hardly failed to destroy our Indian Empire. Although it is true that we ought to decentralise our administration, the last thing we ought to desire is to diminish the authority of the Central and Supreme Government. The one thing most essential to India is a strong Central Government. We shall certainly never get such a government except in India itself, and it is difficult enough to get it even there. Experience has fully established that the only way to secure this object, and to maintain a true imperial control, is for the Central Government to refuse to meddle with details which the local authorities alone can understand, and with which they alone can intelligently deal.

CHAPTER X.

FINANCIAL MEASURES FOR MEETING FAMINE LIABILITIES.

FAMINE LIABILITIES MUST BE MET FROM REVENUES—THEIR HEAVY AMOUNT—LORD SALISBURY'S OPINION OF NECESSITY FOR LOCALISING THEM—DANGER OF MEETING THEM BY BORROWING—PROVINCIAL REVENUES OF BENGAL MADE LIABLE FOR CHARGES ARISING FROM RAILWAYS AND IRRIGATION WORKS—SIMILAR STEPS IN NORTH-WESTERN PROVINCES—LORD NORTHBROOK'S VIEWS—FAMINE EXPENDITURE ESTIMATED AT ONE-AND-A-HALF MILLIONS YEARLY—DECISION TO OBTAIN SPECIAL YEARLY SURPLUS OF THIS AMOUNT—TO BE APPLIED DIRECTLY OR INDIRECTLY IN REDUCTION OF CHARGE FOR DEBT—FRESH TAXATION HOW FAR NEEDED—ACTUAL RECEIPTS FROM NEW TAXES—MISCONCEPTIONS AS TO FAMINE INSURANCE—CREATION OF A FUND NOT PROPOSED—PLAN NECESSARILY INOPERATIVE IN ABSENCE OF REAL SURPLUS—CHANGES OF POLICY MADE BY HOME GOVERNMENT—SUBSTANTIAL REALISATION OF SCHEME OF INSURANCE.

AMONG the measures which have engaged the attention of the Government of India during the last ten or twelve years, none have surpassed in their importance those which had their origin in the distinct recognition of the obligation to provide against the liabilities, financial as well as administrative, arising from the destructive seasons of drought to which almost all parts of India are periodically subject. These liabilities included not only the necessary direct relief of the population which suffers from scarcity or famine, but the obligation to carry out those public works which, as experience has proved, afford the only true safeguard against such calamities. The very heavy expenditure which famine has entailed has been already referred to. How the administration of Lord Lytton dealt with these matters will now be described.

Shortly after Lord Lytton assumed the office of Viceroy, the south of India was visited by a most destructive drought and famine, the measures for the relief of which were necessarily on such a scale of magnitude, and followed so closely on the enormously costly operations thought requisite for meeting the famine in Bengal in 1874, that it became evident to the Government that one of the most obvious and important duties which the State was called upon to discharge, was that of maturing and carrying into execution plans for guarding against the financial consequences of the outlay on relief, which threatened to become ruinous. This question had to be taken up in a time of great difficulty, while the most serious drought of modern times was devastating the provinces of Madras and Bombay.

In a despatch, dated November 25, 1875, reviewing the relief measures adopted in Bengal in 1874, Lord Salisbury had called the attention of the Government of India to the question of the proper incidence of the charges which have to be incurred for the relief of famine. These, he argued, should be localised as far as possible. He said that, however plain may be the primary obligation of the State to do all that is possible towards preserving the lives of the people, it would be most dangerous, either to make the general revenues bear the whole burden of meeting all local difficulties and of relieving all local distress, or to supply the needful funds by borrowing in a shape that establishes a permanent charge for all future time.

The first practical recognition of the principle on which Lord Salisbury thus insisted was given in March 1877 by measures which had for their object the imposition upon the several provinces of responsibility for the charges incurred in providing canals and railways to give protection to the people against famine.

The famine which prevailed in Southern India rendered it impossible at the time to think of imposing fresh burdens on Madras and Bombay; and the first measures of the Government were confined to the Bengal Presidency, including Bengal, the North-Western Provinces and Oudh, the Punjab and the Central Provinces.

It was estimated that in Lower Bengal the capital outlay incurred by the Government on canals and railways, in operation or under construction, would be at least 8,000,000*l.* To enable the Local Government to discharge the interest on the capital expended on these works, and to meet similar obligations in the future, a provincial cess, of which more will be said further on, was imposed upon the land in Bengal.

Similar obligations for the same purpose were at the same time imposed in the North-Western Provinces, but they were much lighter than in Bengal; and to enable the Local Government to meet its new liabilities, all that was thought necessary was the introduction of a very light licence tax upon traders, estimated to yield 50,000*l.* a year.

This was in the beginning of 1877. In December of the same year the Government announced the measures by which it hoped to complete a sufficient insurance of the whole country against the financial consequences of famine; and early in 1878 those measures were carried into effect. The principle which underlies the policy they involved had been publicly recognised by Lord Northbrook after the famine of 1874 in Northern Bengal. He said that famines could no longer be treated as abnormal or exceptional calamities, and that sound financial principles required that the grave obligations which they entailed upon the Government should be explicitly recognised and provided for among the ordinary charges of the State. Within the previous ten years three serious famines had occurred. The drought of 1866 led to famine in Behar and Orissa; the failure of the rainy season in 1868 and 1869 caused severe distress over a great tract of country in Northern India; and in 1874 came the famine in Bengal. As it could not be doubted that India was liable to the periodical and not unfrequent occurrence of such calamities, Lord Northbrook justly concluded that to attempt to meet them merely by borrowing without a simultaneous increase of income would be financially ruinous. 'Whatever means,' he said, 'we may take to obviate or mitigate them, it must, under present circumstances, be looked upon as inevitable that famines will from time to time occur.' He therefore declared that, to enable the State to meet the obligation of preventing and relieving famine, it was necessary to secure, in prosperous times, a substantial surplus of revenue over expenditure, in addition to that necessary margin which a prudent administration always requires for the ordinary service of the State. Due provision would thus be made for meeting occasional expenditure on famine. He said that if this surplus were devoted in years of prosperity to the reduction of debt, or to preventing the increase of debt for the construction of productive public works, there would be no objection to the public expenditure exceeding the public revenue in occasional years of adversity, so that we might then meet the charges on famine from borrowed funds to the full extent to which our surplus had permitted the discharge of debt or prevented its increase. The principles thus enunciated by Lord Northbrook were fully accepted by the Secretary of State, Lord Salisbury, but no steps were taken to put them in practice until they were made the basis of the policy carried into effect by Lord Lytton.

The actual expenditure on famine relief, including remissions of land revenue, in the five years from 1873 to 1878, was nearly 16,500,000*l.* But there was good reason for believing that this had been a period of exceptional disaster, and the Government came to the conclusion, necessarily in a somewhat arbitrary manner, that, taking an average of years, the annual cost of relieving famine, including loss of revenue and actual expenditure, was not likely to exceed 1,500,000*l.* It is satisfactory to find that the probable sufficiency of this assumption has been confirmed by the subsequent elaborate inquiries of the Famine Commission, which has estimated the yearly average charge at 1,250,000*l.* 'Considering,' the Commission says, 'the doubts that must necessarily surround any such estimates, the accordance of the sum thus obtained with the 1,500,000*l.* adopted by the Government of India in 1878, seems to justify the belief that this last-named amount is not likely to be exceeded as the average charge for famine relief over a series of years.'[1]

The Report of the Famine Commission gives so clear and succinct an explanation of the policy adopted, of the principles laid down, and of the objects aimed at by Lord Lytton's Government, that it may usefully be quoted here:—

'The Government,' it says, 'has, with good reason, pro-

[1] *Report of Indian Famine Commission*, part i. paragraph 100.

ceeded very cautiously in its arrangements for localising the expenditure which famines must involve. It was declared that the Local Governments should henceforth be regarded as responsible, to the full extent of what was possible, for providing the means of protecting the people of their own provinces against famine, and of meeting the cost of relief when famine actually occurred. As to the first of these objects, arrangements were made under which a guarantee might be given by each province for the interest on the capital expended on its own railways and canals, and the sources of income necessary for the discharge of this liability being at the same time entrusted to it. As to the second, it was expected that, by economical and judicious control of the expenditure on the numerous branches of the administration which have been transferred to Provincial Governments, a balance would be secured which would be available for purposes of relief, and that such balances standing to the credit of provincial revenues should be exhausted before the imperial treasury could be drawn upon. But it was recognised that there was a limit beyond which the provincial revenues could not supply relief, and that resources must be created from which the central authority could supplement provincial funds on occasions of widespread and severe famine; and it was to this end that arrangements were made to secure a surplus of 1½ millions of income over ordinary expenditure, in addition to the annual surplus of half a million otherwise regarded as proper. It was determined that this surplus should not take the form of a fund specially allocated to meet the cost of famine relief, because such an arrangement would be financially inconvenient and objectionable. The intention was simply that a source of revenue should be provided which would enable the Government to carry out the principle on which it had for some years insisted —that the relief of famine distress must be regarded as a charge constantly liable to recur, which must be met like all other obligatory items of State expenditure. The money obtained, or so much of the 1½ millions as remained after meeting charges for famine during the current year, was to be applied to the discharge of debt, or the prosecution of remunerative public works of a character likely to give protection to the country against the effects of drought. Such works might be expected to produce an income equal to the interest on the capital spent on them, and thus lead to a result financially identical with the discharge of debt, but otherwise more beneficial from the protection given by the works. As the Government was engaged in carrying out productive public works, the expenditure on which involved annual loans to the extent of three or four millions, the plan practically operated in reducing, to the extent of the surplus, the sum to be thus borrowed. We see no reason to doubt that the general arrangements thus made were in the actual circumstances well suited to meet the difficult problem that had to be solved, nor is it easy to see how such heavy and irregularly recurring charges as those that arise from the relief of famine on a great scale of severity and extent, could otherwise be met than by borrowing when the calamity occurs and by discharging the debt in times of prosperity, or securing such an increase of revenue from productive works as shall cover the interest on the debt.'[1]

According to this plan, the Government, when the country is free from famine, would virtually reduce the public debt by 1,500,000*l*. a year, or prevent debt to that amount, and resources would thus be stored up in years of prosperity, by means of which, when famine actually occurs, it would be possible to discharge the heavy obligations which then fall upon the State.

The Government in 1877 came, as elsewhere stated, to the conclusion that the ordinary income and expenditure of the State might at that time be considered to be, for practical purposes, in a state of equilibrium. It was therefore, in the opinion of the Government, necessary to improve the financial position by 1,500,000*l*. a year on account of famine liabilities alone, and in addition to this to provide a margin on the annual estimates of at least 500,000*l*. to meet unforeseen contingencies.

A considerable portion of this total sum of 2,000,000*l*. was supplied, without any addition to the

[1] *Report*, part i. paragraphs 175, 176.

public burdens, either imperial or local, by the transfer of charges to the Provincial Governments under the measures of financial decentralisation of which I have spoken; but fresh taxation was thought necessary to complete the whole amount required.

The new taxes actually imposed will be described elsewhere; it will now be shown what financial success has attended these efforts of the Government towards insuring the country against the liabilities entailed by the periodical occurrence of famine.

The question whether this object has been gained is practically identical with the question, which has a much simpler appearance, and which has already been answered in a previous chapter of this work, whether we have really secured a substantial annual surplus of income over ordinary expenditure of not less than 2,000,000*l.* a year.

This was to be ascertained on a comparison of the revenue with the expenditure, after excluding the expenditure on productive public works, which, to whatever extent was necessary, might be provided for by loan. That portion of the surplus which was especially required to meet famine liabilities, or 1,500,000*l.*, would be subject to reduction by any amount which might be expended on famine relief, or which might be lost in the shape of remission of revenue on account of famine. The remaining 500,000*l.* of the required surplus might be reduced by expenditure of an obviously abnormal and extraordinary character. In other words, it was desired to secure an income sufficient to meet all ordinary charges year by year, besides 1,500,000*l.* for famine, and also all extraordinary charges up to 500,000*l.* More than this was not aimed at. For heavy war expenditure, for instance, no provision was made beforehand, and it would have been absurd to attempt to do so.

The amount of new taxation actually imposed amounted originally to 1,345,000*l*., and is now about 1,000,000*l*. Whether the public accounts have shown deficit, surplus, or equilibrium, it is indisputable that if the new taxes were not applied to stimulate fresh expenditure, they must have prevented debt, or permitted its reduction, to the exact amount which they have yielded, and that, when famine occurs, our resources for meeting it will be increased by an amount exactly equal to the amount obtained from those taxes, with compound interest upon them.

The actual sum which they are estimated to have yielded in the aggregate in the three years since they were imposed is 3,393,891*l*. In the same period the actual or estimated expenditure on famine relief was 417,420*l*. Therefore the taxation thus levied in these years has enabled us to defray the expenditure on famine relief, and to prevent debt to the amount of 2,976,471*l*. with interest on this sum, and therefore to improve the general financial position to the same extent apart from other independent causes of expenditure, and to obtain a corresponding resource available in the future. That this result has been achieved is self-evident; it is independent of the surplus or deficit of the revenue as a whole, and requires no further demonstration.

It has been asserted that the proceeds of these taxes have not been expended on the objects for which they were imposed, but on the prosecution of the Afghan war. Such assertions are based on misconception of the facts. These taxes were imposed to enable the State to meet its future liabilities for the relief of famine. Their proceeds have been devoted to meeting these liabilities as certainly as if they had been actually expended on famine relief, or had been applied to the direct repayment of debt. If these taxes had not existed during the last three years, the revenues would, as was shown, have been less by nearly 3,000,000*l.* than their actual amount; consequently the amount available for meeting the whole public expenditure, including that on the war, which has obviously not been affected in any way by these taxes, has been increased by this sum, and the amount to be borrowed has been reduced by the same sum: in other words, the public debt is now 3,000,000*l.* less than it would have been. It is plain, therefore, that when serious famine next occurs we shall be able, if necessary, to borrow 3,000,000*l.* for its relief, without creating liabilities of a larger amount than that by which the present increase of the general liability has been prevented; any increase of debt due to the war is beyond the present discussion.

There has been much misunderstanding in regard to the so-called Famine insurance fund or surplus, which, in fact, was never designed to be anything more than a mere surplus of annual revenue over expenditure, though the necessity for it arose from a particular cause. It was impossible for the Government, even if it had desired to do so, to have given a different character to this surplus, unless, indeed, the expedient had been adopted of paying the proceeds of the new taxes into a separate fund to be applied only to specified purposes. From the very first, and at all times, every idea of this sort was repudiated by the Government as out of the question, foolish, and impracticable, and no doubt will be equally repudiated in the future.

In further explanation of this point reference may be made to the following extract from the Budget Resolution of 1879–80.

'The propriety of the course followed by the Government last year in refusing to constitute any separate fund in connection with the famine arrangements has thus, it may be added, been justified by the event. Foreseeing the possibility of such a contingency as that which has actually occurred (namely, the anticipated failure of the surplus in consequence of the heavy fall in the exchange and the cost of the Afghan war), Sir John Strachey spoke in the Legislative Council on February 9, 1878, as follows:—

"Any other decision might lead to results probably not contemplated by those who have suggested the establishment of a separate fund; I mean that this might involve the necessity for imposing fresh taxation. Suppose, for instance, that the produce of the new taxes were, by law, strictly set apart from the general revenues and paid into a separate fund only to be applied to specified purposes; if then any sudden change of circumstances arose, calling for seriously increased expenditure, or causing a considerable falling off in the revenue, we should have to choose between the imposition of fresh taxes and the abrogation of the law constituting the fund, for I set aside the idea of meeting the ordinary charges by borrowing as a course financially inadmissible. This dilemma might arise, though the pressure was likely to be only temporary; nor can any one say that such a contingency would be at all improbable, or that it might not occur at any moment. With all my desire to see the pledges maintained that we have given as to the application of a sum not less than 1,500,000*l.*, as an insurance against famine, I think it would be irrational, under many circumstances that I can conceive, to object to the temporary diversion of any necessary part of the revenue from this purpose with the view of obtaining relief which might be no less urgently required than that which experience has taught us to be requisite in meeting famine. Without thinking of a future far removed from us, events might of course happen which would make it impossible even for us who have designed these measures to maintain our present resolution."

In the very nature of the case, a real sinking fund involves the existence of a real surplus, and the above extract clearly shows that this was well understood. Indeed in circumstances such as had been foreseen, and were very soon to arise, the only effect which the specially created resources could have, would be the indirect one which has already been explained. It is obvious that the measures which were proposed could have no effect in averting other causes of expenditure, or in preventing debt being incurred for other objects, and that so long as the surplus was dissipated never mind how, or as debt was increased never mind why, no real sinking fund operations could be carried out.

That the misunderstanding which has been alluded to may have been due to want of precision in the original explanations of the policy of the Government is not denied. When these questions were first brought forward, being, as they were, new and complicated, they were not in their financial aspect very easy to comprehend, and some things were undoubtedly said which not unnaturally gave rise to misinterpretation. Moreover, the difficulty which the public has had in understanding this matter has been increased by the fact that the original policy was afterwards greatly modified by Her Majesty's Government, and some of the statements of the Government of India thus ceased to be applicable. This observation applies especially to the orders of the Secretary of State, given in accordance with the recommendations of a Committee of the House of Commons, by which the Government of India was obliged greatly to reduce its expenditure on those works the construction of which it had looked upon as the best safeguard against famine. If Lord Lytton's beneficent and admirable schemes for the protection of the country have been abandoned or postponed, it has certainly not been his fault. So far as his Government has been concerned, there was at no time any change of policy in regard to the subject of famine insurance, or to the construction of necessary public works, or any failure to carry out any of the intentions with which the new taxation was imposed.

But no apology or explanation is in truth needed for any part of these measures. So far from the famine insurance policy having failed through the faults of its originators, the fact is indisputable that notwithstanding all the difficulties of the actual situation, the net charge for interest on the public debt, after making allowance for the receipts from public works, has actually been reduced during the past three years by a much larger sum than had been aimed at. The net charge for productive public works and interest on debt fell from 4,070,000*l.* in 1877–78 to 3,093,000*l.* in 1880–81; that is, more than 900,000*l.*, which is equivalent to a discharge of debt of about 20,000,000*l.*, so that instead of there having been any failure in the policy, it has obtained an altogether unexpected measure of success, and in the precise manner that had been from the first designed.

CHAPTER XI.

MEASURES FOR GIVING PROTECTION AGAINST FAMINE.

RECURRENCE OF FAMINE STILL UNAVOIDABLE—MEASURES OF ALLEVIATION AND PREVENTION POSSIBLE—NECESSITY FOR APPLYING THEM—LORD NORTHBROOK'S OPINION—EXTENSION OF RAILWAYS AND IRRIGATION REQUIRED—INSUFFICIENCY OF MEASURES ACTUALLY TAKEN—LORD LYTTON'S PROGRAMME—EMIGRATION NOT APPLICABLE—IMPORTANCE OF EARLY EXTENSION OF CHEAP RAILWAYS—VALUE OF IRRIGATION—CO-OPERATION OF LOCAL GOVERNMENTS TO BE SECURED—STEADY SUPPLY OF FUNDS ESSENTIAL—PLANS FRUSTRATED BY ORDERS FOR REDUCTION OF OUTLAY ON PRODUCTIVE WORKS—OTHER RESTRICTIONS IMPOSED—APPLICATION OF HALF OF FAMINE SURPLUS TO UNREMUNERATIVE WORKS PROPOSED—OBJECTIONS STATED TO THIS ARRANGEMENT.

THE periodical recurrence of seasons of drought in India must be regarded as a physical necessity, and, in the present condition of the country, famine in an extreme form must at times be unavoidable. The gradual advance of the economical position of the people can alone bring complete remedies; nor need we doubt that a security may some day be attained equal to that now enjoyed in other countries, which, as their past history shows, long remained liable to periodical famines hardly less disastrous than those which have recently devastated India.

But it is certain that it is already possible to prevent, or very greatly to alleviate, by remedial measures the worst effects of scarcity. When provision had been made against the financial liabilities to which it had become obvious that the State was exposed in the future by the recurrence of famine, it still remained, therefore, to supply such direct means of protection and prevention as were practicable, and Lord Lytton regarded this object as being, if possible, even more important than financial security.

After the famine in Bengal Lord Northbrook had insisted upon the duty which rested on the Government of sparing no efforts to provide railways and canals for this purpose. In the financial statement for 1874–75, reference having been made to the necessity of providing a sufficient surplus of income over ordinary expenditure to meet periodical charges on account of famine, it was said that there remained—

'the further and more important consideration, whether the disastrous effect of periodical failures of rain may not be mitigated, and to a great extent obviated, by the extension of irrigation works, and of railways or other means of communication. This subject has constantly received the attention of the Government of India. Already a vast area of country has been rendered secure from the effect of a failure of rain by the irrigation works which have been originated or renewed by the British Government. Had it not been for the large expenditure upon the construction of the guaranteed railways, it would have been physically impossible to have taken adequate precautions to preserve the lives of the people in Behar. In the forecast of expenditure upon reproductive public works, published in July last (1873), it was announced that 2,700 miles of railway and irrigation works, calculated to secure from liability to drought 50,000 square miles of country, would be constructed during the five years ending with 1877–78 at a cost of 22½ millions sterling. This programme is sufficient to show that, before the occurrence of the drought of last year, the Government of India were fully alive to the necessity of a vigorous prosecution of such works. A general view is now being made of the position of the whole of Her Majesty's dominions in India as regards liability to famine from the want either of the works of irrigation or of means of communication. It will be the duty of the

Government to consider how far it may be desirable to accelerate the construction of reproductive public works, and, if so, how the necessary funds shall be provided.'

But, as has too frequently been the case on other occasions, these promises were not followed up by any sufficient action. After the immediate pressure caused by the occurrences of 1874–75 had passed away, things went on in their old routine. If such a review of the wants of the country as was spoken of was actually made, nothing came of it, and so far from any acceleration of the construction of productive public works having ensued, a disposition to reduce the available funds began to find favour.

The subject, however, was once more taken up by Lord Lytton, with the serious intention of doing all that it was possible for a Government to do towards preventing famine, and furnishing the country with the machinery by which, when it occurred, the largest practicable amount of relief could be most speedily and effectually distributed. The new taxation, and the other measures by which the finances were improved, gave the means of carrying out these objects with a certainty and rapidity which it would otherwise have been impossible to insure.

A nobler, more humane, or wiser programme was never devised by any Government for the benefit of a country than that put forth by the Government of India in 1878 for the protection of India against this most terrible and ruinous and far-reaching of all natural calamities; and until it is brought into far more complete operation than has hitherto been permitted, the most urgent of the duties of the British rulers of India to the vast population they have undertaken to govern will be left unfulfilled. The following extract from Lord Lytton's speech before the Legislative Council[1] is quoted at length, as containing the clearest exposition of the whole subject of providing the country with protection against famine, through the instrumentality of public works, and his words deserve to be remembered among the wisest utterances of Indian Governors.

'The statement made by Sir John Strachey will, I trust, have satisfied the Council that the additional revenue now required by the Government, and the increased burdens which must consequently be borne by the people of India, are the inevitable consequences of famine, and of famine only. I will not abuse your sympathies by harrowing your feelings with any description of the ghastly scenes I have witnessed this year in Southern India; scenes which, horrible as they were, only partially revealed the mass of unseen, unuttered misery that lay behind them. I feel sure you will believe that no such sights were needed to impress me, and I am equally confident that no such descriptions are needed to impress this Council, with a profound sense of the paramount obligation now resting on us all to spare no effort for preventing the recurrence, or mitigating the effects, of such calamities. But of one thing I am convinced—our efforts must fail if they be merely the uneducated offspring of casual impulse and indefinite sentiment. The primary condition of successful effort is the strictly sympathetic subordination of it in all directions, and in all details, to the verified results of experience, and the carefully ascertained conditions of what is practically possible. It is not by the indulgence of that morbid sensibility to the dramatic elements of horror which so unconsciously simulates compassion, it is not even by exclamatory utterances of a generous impatience, or a genuine grief, under the painful contemplation of the sufferings of our fellow-creatures, that we can practically prevent or alleviate such national calamities as those through which Southern India has been passing during the last two years. I am profoundly persuaded that every rupee superfluously spent on famine relief

[1] Some sentences have been omitted which are not of importance to the present argument.

only aggravates the evil effects of famine, and that in all such cases waste of money involves waste of life.

'The measures now before the Council have for their principal object the provision of that increase of the public income which experience has proved to be the first condition of any practical insurance against famine; and, therefore, it is only proper that the Council should know how we intend to employ the resources which its adoption of these measures will place at our disposal for that purpose.

'Our first duty must be, I fear, to recognise and face, with all its consequences, the sad but certain fact that, in the present social condition of India, famines cannot, for many years (I might almost say for many generations) to come, be entirely prevented. The population of this country is still almost wholly dependent upon agriculture. It is a population which, in some parts of India, under those securities for life which are the general consequence of British rule, has a tendency to increase more rapidly than the food it raises from the soil. It is a population whose consumption, in many places, trenches too closely on the crops already provided by its industry; and which, therefore, runs great risk of having no accumulated produce to depend upon, whenever the earth has failed "to bring forth her fruit in due season." A people permanently living under such conditions—a people, that is to say, whose entire labour provides only just food enough for its own annual sustenance—is, it must be confessed, a people removed only a few degrees from a state of barbarism. Until the accumulated fruits of industry exceed the current requirements of the population for its own subsistence, there can be no growth in the wealth of the community; and until the national wealth —that is to say, the exchangeable surplus produce of the country—has been increased up to a certain standard, there can be no adequate security against famine. To the attainment of this object, therefore, all our efforts, in every department of the administration, must be constantly directed. But, at the same time, it must also be always borne in mind that, until this object has been attained, no exertions and no expenditure on the part of the State can practically do more than provide for the restriction and mitigation of periodical scarcity. It is not yet in the power of human science to foresee, still less to control, the uncertainty of the seasons; and this uncertainty, which is so constant and violent in India, must always afflict with exceptional severity any population that is habitually living from hand to mouth. Fortunately, however, the material appliances which already exist, and only need to be prudently developed, in order to provide us with an effectual insurance against the worst consequences of famine, are also those which, if rightly employed, will most rapidly promote that general increase of the national wealth on which alone we can reckon for the permanent prevention of famine.

'Now, of the countless suggestions made from time to time, and more especially during the present year, for rendering less bitterly ironical than it still seems, when read by the sinister light of recent events, that famous inscription on the huge granary built at Patna for "*the perpetual prevention of famine in these provinces*," there are only three which merit serious consideration. These are, *firstly*, EMIGRATION; *secondly*, RAILWAYS; and, *thirdly*, IRRIGATION WORKS.

'We must practically exclude the first expedient from the list of those on which we mainly rely as a means of insuring the population of India against the calamities of periodical famine. The conclusion thus arrived at forcibly confines our immediate efforts to the most rapid development, by the cheapest methods, combined with the most appropriate and efficient application, of the only two remaining instruments for increasing the produce of the soil, facilitating its circulation, and thereby improving the general social condition, and augmenting the collective wealth, of the whole community. Those instruments are railroads and irrigation works.

'Now, the incalculable value to India of her present railways has been unmistakably demonstrated during the past year; and the Government is unquestionably bound to stimulate the extension of this class of works to the greatest extent, and with the greatest rapidity, consistent with the requirements of financial prudence. The capital expenditure on the guaranteed railways, during a period of 28 years, has amounted to not far from 95 millions sterling, with a result to be measured by about 6,000 miles of broad-gauge line. During the last nine years the outlay on State railways has amounted to about 18½ millions, producing 1,050 miles of broad and 1,200 miles of narrow-gauge line, more or less finished. I need not here re-open the once-vexed question of broad *versus* narrow gauge. For all practical purposes that question has long ago been settled. Had we now to consider the construction of long lines of rail solely, or chiefly, for military purposes, I doubt not that many arguments might be forcibly urged in favour of a broad-gauge system. But when the object in view is to stimulate the exchange of commodities, and provide for a goods traffic with special reference to local needs and local means, then, I think, it cannot possibly be doubted that any extension of our railway system must be carried out in strict conformity with that method which experience has proved to be the cheapest, and indeed the only one financially possible in the circumstances of a poor country with a languid commerce. The importance of strategic railroads to such an empire as this is not, in my opinion, open to question. But it is not for the construction of strategic railroads that we are now seeking assistance from the local populations and Governments of India.'

. . . .

'It is an unquestionable fact that the railways, and the railways alone, were the salvation of the situation in North Behar during the famine of 1874; and that they have again been the salvation of the situation in Madras during the present year. The sea, no doubt, would have thrown rice into the town of Madras; but, with the cattle dying of drought, it would have been impossible to move the grain up-country; nor, if every possible mile of navigable canal had been completed throughout the Madras Presidency, would it have greatly helped us to throw grain into those very districts where the famine has been at its worst; for the broken upland country of Bellary and Kurnool, and the Mysore plateau, are physically impracticable for big canals; and had there been no railway within reach of these districts, the people, where they have now died by hundreds, must have assuredly succumbed by thousands.

'I am satisfied that the development of a network of subsidiary lines of railway, giving the means of transport through every district of British India, has become a matter of vital necessity for the attainment of the great object now before us. To accomplish this, in accordance with the financial and administrative policy already explained, we propose to call upon the various Provincial Governments to undertake at once the preparation of such a scheme of local railways, with plans for their gradual and systematic execution, carefully made out by the best-informed local authorities. Our present object is to render available, within the shortest possible time, a maximum length of line specially constructed for a slow goods traffic, rather than to provide those more ample conveniences for passengers and goods which have been commonly deemed necessary for all Indian railways hitherto constructed. We have every reason to believe that, by restricting the works at the outset to the essential requirements of a slow goods traffic, we can, without any sacrifice of durability, or sound constructive principle, reduce the first capital outlay even below the amount which was found sufficient for the execution of the Hathras and Muttra Railway in the North-Western Provinces—a line which furnishes us with a most instructive illustration of what may be done, under a local Government, in the way of thoroughly useful work executed at a small cost. We have also in the United States of North America an encouraging example of the rapidity and financial ease with which cheap railroads may be constructed over vast tracts of sparsely populated territory, and of the incalculable benefits conferred by them on every part of a continent even more spacious in extent and various in climate than our own.

'During my visit to Madras and Mysore I had many opportunities of obtaining information about the distribution of grain into the distressed provinces. I cannot doubt that but for the main trunk lines of railway there must have been an appalling, and quite irremediable, failure in the supply of food to those provinces; and, for all purposes of famine relief, I am equally convinced that the proved utility of these great arterial lines will be immensely increased by the cheap internal railroads we now propose to commence, with the intention of completing them as rapidly as may be compatible with the extent of the financial resources at our disposal for that undertaking.

'The early conclusion of such an undertaking must necessarily depend upon its financial practicability; and for this reason all minor considerations must be subordinated to the most rigid economy in construction, and the most severe limitation of the works to what is indispensable for the efficient exercise of their special function. But if these conditions be duly complied with, I have confidence that, at a comparatively early period, we shall, without any strain upon our financial resources, have extended to all parts and provinces of our Empire the most efficacious protection, not indeed from dearth (for that is impossible), but from those terrible effects of dearth which now generally terminate in famine.

'These, then, are the principles on which we are prepared to apply at once to the extension of our railway system, as a means of insurance against famine, an adequate proportion of the resources at our command for that purpose. We cannot, indeed, solely for the sake of developing local commerce, undertake to build railroads on the commodious and costly scale of our present main lines, which have been constructed with a view to their general utility in many other ways. But with the active co-operation of the Local Governments, and by steadily adhering to, and prudently developing, the great principle of provincial responsibility which is the backbone of our financial policy, we are persuaded that the resources of the State will now be sufficient for the early and continuous construction of a wide network of cheap provincial lines well adapted to the special object for which they are required.

'It remains to explain to the Council the manner in which we propose to apply to the extension of irrigation works precisely the same principles and policy.

'It is certain that throughout the greater part of India the produce of the soil may still be very considerably increased by artificial irrigation. But it is equally certain that in many parts of India, and for many kinds of Indian crops, irrigation could only be employed at a cost which would render it unremunerative. Canal irrigation cannot everywhere be supplied from permanent sources; and, wherever it is not supplied from permanent sources, it frequently proves altogether abortive as a preventive against famine. Again, in the second year of the drought from which we have been suffering throughout Southern India, tank irrigation generally failed. Moreover, even were it physically possible to apply irrigation to all the cheap millet crops now grown upon the uplands of Madras, the expense of their cultivation by that means would render them quite unpurchasable by the classes who at present derive from them their chief means of subsistence. The difficulties and disasters of the recent famine have been greatest in Madras. But Madras is, taken as a whole, the best irrigated part of India. Out of a total area of 22,000,000 acres under cultivation, that Presidency has some 4,000,000 acres artificially irrigated; and its entire irrigation system is supervised by professional officers who, in their own line, are unsurpassed. One part of the irrigation system of Madras is supplied by the permanent rivers; and of these the number is limited. All the rest of it is derived from the local rivers and storage tanks which are scattered in profusion over the whole Presidency. Now, the experience of the present year has proved that the latter source of supply is only one degree less dependent on the normal rainfall than are the dry crops of the unirrigated districts. If, therefore, we are to insure Madras against future famines by largely increasing its present water supply, it is exclusively upon the permanent rivers that we must reckon for our attainment of that object. Assume (and from all the inquiries I have yet been able to make this is the most I feel justified in assuming) that the waters of the permanent rivers might be so employed as to irrigate another half million of acres: what effect would the produce of half a million of acres have had towards preventing the famine in Madras? It would not represent one-third of what the railways alone have carried down from Northern India, and it is about equal to what was landed by sea during only two and a half months out of the twelve through which this famine has lasted. So far, then, as it was possible to render irrigation a protection against famine in a second year of drought, Madras has received, within a narrow margin of some 20 per cent., all the benefit which the nature of the case and circumstances of the country permitted, and yet Madras has this year suffered from a worse famine than has afflicted any province of India during the present century. In view of such facts as these, we cannot safely lay down any fixed rule for universal application. Whether the value of increased produce will, in any particular case, be sufficient to justify the requisite outlay of capital on providing irrigation; whether the necessarily limited amount of capital available for works of improvement is best applied to irrigation works; or, again, whether the physical conditions of the locality will practically admit of irrigation at all—to these and many similar questions no general answer can be given. Each case must be decided in reference to its own merits, and on a careful review of many conflicting considerations.

'But, though I feel that, for all these reasons, we must be constantly on our guard against premature generalisations and impulsive action in such matters, I am none the less most fully persuaded that, next to the facilitation of transport, our greatest safeguard against future famine will be found in a well-considered and widely developed system of irrigation works. The surplus produce of industry is the foundation of national wealth: and irrigation is the most certain means of improving and extending agricultural industry. It enables the cultivator to accumulate produce; and, if combined with navigation, it also enables him to transport produce.

'Every country which produces only just enough for its own consumption is a poor country. So is every country which cannot export its surplus produce, and exchange it for other commodities. Therefore, admitting even that in many parts of India irrigation cannot appreciably augment the local food-supply, it by no means follows that irrigation cannot largely augment the wealth of the whole community; for if this Empire be adequately provided with the means of transport, it is not so much by increasing the actual food-supply of the people as by helping to create other and different produce, not required for the consumption of the people, and possibly not even adapted for such consumption, that extensive irrigation will promote the social and financial prosperity of India. It is only by the gradual and continued improvement of their material condition that the people of this country can permanently escape the calamities they now suffer from the uncertainty of the seasons.

'To look to irrigation works as a panacea for our misfortunes would be to trust to an illusion; to hesitate to recognise them as among the most certain of our means of protection would be to reject the irrefutable evidence of prolonged experience.

'A memorandum has been placed in my hands showing from the latest returns of the actual operation of the irrigation works in the North-Western Provinces that the whole area now irrigated by them is about 1,500,000 acres, which, under pressure, might be extended to 1,600,000 acres, producing respectively 775,000 or 800,000 tons of grain, and providing food for eight months for six million to six and a half million persons. The progress of these works will add half a million of acres; and this addition would yield one quarter of a million tons of food, and feed for eight months two millions of people. Thus these works will secure the food for the period named of between eight and nine millions of persons.

'I conclude, then, that we shall be certainly right in carrying out irrigation works wherever the water-supply is both sufficient and constant, and wherever the material difficulties to be overcome do not involve an outlay that interposes insurmountable financial obstacles; so long of course as due attention be, at the same time, given to the means of communication. But we cannot, and do not, undertake to provide irrigation gratuitously to those for whose special benefit it is required. We cannot afford to apply to new irrigation works the financial policy which has hitherto rendered so costly, and so unremunerative, the works of that kind which are already constructed. Here, again, we can only proceed in strict accordance with the principle of provincial responsibility and self-support. As the only funds at the command of the Government for irrigation works are derived from the country itself, the cost of such works must fall to a great extent upon those who derive from them immediate benefit. I repeat that it is on the co-operation of the whole community we reckon for the means of securing the whole community against the worst consequences of periodical scarcity. But it is to the local Governments that we look for the execution of local works of a preventive character; and it is upon local resources that we must depend for the ultimate supply of the funds necessary to provide and maintain such works. I am aware that there are already some parts of India whose exclusively local interests are practically secured by the bounty of nature, or the industry of man, from the direct effects of famine. In the nature of things the population of those particular localities may, and probably do, derive some immediate advantage from the periods of scarcity which so fearfully afflict their fellow-subjects in other provinces. But it would be an insult to suppose that their fortunate exemption from the perils and sufferings common to the rest of the community can furnish any argument they would stoop to urge in favour of exempting them from their fair participation in the support of any general burden imposed for the protection of the whole community from such sufferings and perils. Whilst, therefore, I do not doubt that the chief cost of protective works ought to be borne by those who most need them, and will chiefly benefit by them, I must maintain that no province of the Empire, and no class of the community, can be legitimately relieved of the national obligation to contribute to the means required for the construction of such works.

'And here I would ask the Council to listen to the testimony of my honourable friend the Lieutenant-Governor of Bengal, who, speaking of the measures he contemplated last spring for dealing with irrigation works in the province he so ably administers, observed that—

'"During the last five years the Government of India has spent nearly 20 crores of rupees in alleviating famines caused by deficient water-supply. When I say that the Government of India has spent this money, you will understand that this expenditure has fallen, not upon the Viceroy and the Council, but upon the people; and that, if the necessity of expending their money had not been forced upon the Government, the taxation of the people would have been diminished to this extent. Now, the only way of averting famines arising from drought is to make the greatest use which science and experience can suggest of the supply of water which fortunately nature has given us in Behar. . . . This, of course, cannot be done without the expenditure of money; and the question is who, in fairness and justice, should find this money.

'"After very careful consideration, I come to the conclusion that, as the whole of the province of Bengal suffered when there were such famines as have occurred of late years in Orissa and Behar, it was fair that a large proportion of the cost should be borne by a tax laid upon the public at large. But it also seemed to me fair, and I believe you will agree with me if you will give the subject your unprejudiced consideration, that a share of the cost should fall on the people who directly benefit by the introduction of water to the neighbourhood of their fields, and are thus assured of a good crop at all seasons, instead of being exposed to the risk every few years of absolute failure. When I proposed this, I was told that the people did not want water; that they would sooner be left alone to bear the risk of famine; and I was even told that the water of the Sone was destructive to fields. Shortly after this discussion took place, the periodical rains were suspended, and then we had practical proof as to whether or not the Sone water was considered injurious or prejudicial. The people clamoured for water, and to meet this demand we were forced to open our unfinished canals, by means of which we have irrigated, during the last few months, 200,000 acres of land, which would otherwise have remained waste for the year, but which are now covered with luxuriant crops. The produce of this land represents food grain of the value of 55 lakhs of rupees, 550,000*l.*, and of this crops to the value of 40 lakhs, 400,000*l.*, certainly would have been entirely lost if it had not been for the supply of canal water; but it also represents the rent of the land, of which the landholder would have been otherwise deprived; and to this must be added the outlay which would fall on him if he had again to give relief to his tenantry in consequence of famine."

'To sum up, then: the Government of India is convinced, upon a careful review of its financial position and prospects, that the heavy obligations imposed upon it by the calamitous circumstances of recent years can only be discharged, without serious risk to its financial stability, by a strict and patient adherence to the principle affirmed in the financial measures we introduced last year, and developed in those which are now before the Council. That principle involves the enlargement, with adequate precautions, of the financial, and consequently also of the administrative, powers and responsibilities of the local Governments. In the next place, we believe that, if this principle be fairly carried into effect, the new imposts, which the Council is now asked to sanction, will, when added to the resources already created, provide the State with sufficient means for the permanent maintenance of a national insurance against famine, without heavily increasing the pecuniary burdens of its subjects. For the attainment of this object the material appliances we intend to promote, by means of additional revenue, are cheap railroads and extended irrigation works. We are conscious of the reproach we should justly incur if, after such a declaration as I have now made, the prosecution of these necessary works was commenced, suspended, or relinquished according to the increased or relaxed pressure of annual circumstance, or the intermittent activity of spasmodic effort. We therefore propose to entrust, in the first instance, to the local Governments the duty of framing a sufficient and carefully considered scheme of local railroad and irrigation works. We are prepared to provide them with the means whereby they may from year to year work systematically forwards and upwards to the completion of such a scheme. The funds raised for this purpose will be locally applied. But provincial Governments will have to meet the cost of provincial famines out of provincial funds to the fullest extent those funds can bear. They will find that thriftless expenditure in one year may involve the risk of diminished allotments in subsequent years; and I cannot doubt that the unavoidable recognition of this fact will make them wisely eager to spend the requisite proportion of their annual income upon well-planned and carefully estimated railway and irrigation works, which will be their best insurance against the losses of famine, and the postponement of all administrative progress which famine generally entails. It will be the special duty of the Public Works Department of the Government to keep those objects constantly in view of the local Governments, and to assist them, no less constantly, in their endeavours to give a rational preference to really useful and remunerative works, over those more captivating, but less compensating, subjects of expenditure which, in all comparatively small communities, so powerfully appeal to provincial pride, professional proclivities, or popular pleasure.

'The specific projects now announced to this Council I have not presumed to put forward as the enunciation of any new policy. On the contrary, I should have spoken with much more hesitation if I imagined myself to be treading upon ground not long since surveyed by experienced authorities; and the strongest recommendation I can claim for the views I have expressed is that they differ in no important particular from those of the eminent statesmen who have preceded me in the office I now hold. But between the present and all previous occasions on which the Government of India has declared its policy and principles in reference to the prevention of famine, there is one essential difference which I am anxious to impress upon your attention. We have been told over and over again by the highest authorities that India is to be insured against famine in this way or in that; but when famines come upon us we find that the promised way is still wanting. The current claims upon the activities and resources of the Government of India are so numerous, so pressing, so important, official forces and imperial funds so necessarily limited, that when once the daily, hourly strain of a great famine has been removed from a wearied administration and impoverished treasury, its fearful warnings are soon forgotten.

'Well, then, I think I am entitled to point out to the Council that we are not now fairly open to this customary criticism. We do not speak without having acted; and we promise nothing which we have not, after long and anxious consideration, provided ourselves with the means of performing. I must have very imperfectly explained myself thus far, if I have failed to make it clearly understood that I am not now speaking of what we ought to do, or would do, to insure this country against the worst effects of future famine, had we only the means of doing it; but of what we can do, and will do, with the means already provided for in the measures now before the Council. I do not mean to say that the construction of such an extensive system of local railroads and irrigation works as we propose to undertake will not be the gradual task of many years. But I do mean to say that, in the manner and on the principles already explained, we are now providing for the prompt commencement, and uninterrupted continuation, of this great and necessary task. We are systematising a policy the principles of which have been repeatedly approved and proclaimed by our predecessors. We are associating with it the interests, the powers and the duties of our local administrations. We are providing them with the means of permanently prosecuting and developing it, not without reference to our financial control, but exempt from the distressing uncertainty which has hitherto been inseparable from the practical execution of this policy, in consequence of the obligation which till now has rested on the Government of India, with the very limited funds at its disposal for the prosecution of public works, to choose, from year to year, between the conflicting claims upon its purse of the various and dissimilar localities of this spacious empire. If you look back over a wider and a longer tract of experience than that which is covered by the history of India, if you embrace in one view our own history with the past history of other countries in other climates, you will find that the principles on which we have lately acted, and on which I trust we shall continue to act, in dealing with seasons of calamitous drought, have been found no less applicable, no less efficient, in other countries similarly affected, than they have proved to be in this country, wherever they have been intelligently understood and loyally carried out. There is, I venture to think, no more striking illustration of this truth than the history of the scarcity that occurred in Central France during the year 1770–71. That great statesman, Turgot, was then Minister. His administrative ability was equalled by his philosophical power of thought; and, fighting with difficulties in many respects almost identical with those which we ourselves have lately had to deal with—difficulties partly material, but greatly aggravated by the prevalence of extremely erroneous economical conceptions—Turgot conceived, developed, and, in the face of great opposition, carried into effect, views no less identical with those which have guided our own action, as to the essential importance of guarding the perfect freedom of inland trade in grain, of improving the internal communications of the country, and of providing relief works of permanent utility upon which to employ the suffering population. Here, to-day, in India, those views are as sound, and as applicable, as they were in the Limousin a century ago. If, then, from the past we look forward into the future, why, let me ask, may we not hope that, under improved conditions of administration, and with increased development of those material appliances which civilisation creates for the provision of national wealth, India will eventually enjoy as complete an immunity from the worst results of scarcity as that which now exists throughout those regions of France where but a century ago such a result might have seemed as difficult of attainment as it now appears to be in many of our own provinces?'

It was the confident hope of Lord Lytton that he would soon see the rapid fulfilment of these plans. Their execution, which the imperative requirements of humanity prescribed, not only involved no financial risk, but was certain to prove financially sound and prudent and profitable. Notwithstanding mistakes, which after all have not been numerous, and which in transactions of such magnitude it was impossible altogether to avoid, the policy by which, for many years past, we have been constructing railways and canals in India was wise and statesmanlike in its conception, and its practical results have, as already shown, been triumphantly successful. The wealth of the country, and the prosperity and happiness of its people, have been increased by it to an extraordinary extent; the consequent gain to the country and to the public finances has been immense, and is not to be measured by figures showing only the direct returns from the works which have been constructed. There are no drawbacks, and no disadvantages which deserve to be weighed for one moment against the benefits which have been derived. It is certain that limits can hardly be assigned to the increase in wealth and prosperity which it is in our power to bestow upon India by the construction of works of material improvement. The exercise of careful judgment and of all possible caution are of course essential; but if these conditions be duly observed, the boldest policy will be financially the safest. Other counsels, however, have temporarily prevailed. Lord Lytton was prevented from fully executing the plans which have been described; he was compelled, by orders from the Secretary of State, largely to reduce the expenditure which, for many years past, the Government of India had incurred on works of necessary improvement, and to leave unexecuted measures by which he had hoped to facilitate their more rapid progress.

Similar partial failure attended other efforts of Lord Lytton's Government to supply protection to the country.

The arrangements described in the last chapter were intended to secure a surplus revenue, to the average amount of 1,500,000*l.* a year, which should be applied either directly to the actual relief of famine, or to the reduction or prevention of debt; and this amount, or any part of it, might be invested in the construction of productive works, likely to produce an income equal to the interest of the capital spent on them.

But it was apparent that, under the strict rules laid down for the application of borrowed funds, no facilities existed for meeting a very important class of cases, in which, although it is obviously necessary to construct certain works for the prevention of famine, it cannot be assumed that they will be so directly remunerative as to yield a net income equal to the interest on the capital expended on them. The question therefore arose how to provide means for the construction of this class of works, called for the sake of distinction protective, when the required expenditure was too large to be met from ordinary income.

The province of Bandelkhand supplies an illustration. It suffers frequently from serious drought, and is peculiarly exposed to failure of the periodical rains and consequent famine. It is cut off from the existing railway system, and its means of communication are very imperfect. Designs for irrigation works and for cheap railways had been completed, which would render the province secure against serious danger, and would make its relief in case of necessity easy. But the country being naturally poor, it could not confidently be said that the direct money return from these works would cover the interest of the capital expended on their construction. It might, perhaps, for a good many years cover only half of it, and leave, say 20,000*l.* or 30,000*l.* a year unprovided for. Under the existing rules these works could not be undertaken, except from the ordinary revenues, and, in the absence of funds from this source, Bandelkhand was left exposed to the dangers of famine.

The first suggestion for dealing with such cases was that these protective works might properly be constructed from the famine insurance surplus, which would be reduced to a corresponding extent. But, although this plan had been proposed by the Secretary of State, the Government of India considered that it was not admissible. 'It is essential,' they wrote to the Secretary of State,[1] 'that the limited amount of that surplus should not be trenched upon to an extent that will frustrate the main object of its creation, namely, the prevention of any permanent increase of the public debt by reason of the public expenditure upon famines. If the assumption be true upon which our recent measures were founded, namely, that 1,500,000*l.* sterling is the amount which it is necessary to secure as a yearly surplus to provide for the cost of counteracting famines,

[1] Despatch from Government of India to Secretary of State, dated September 16, 1878.

it is plain that, if unremunerative works were carried out under conditions which caused a reduction of that surplus beyond a certain limit, additional taxation would be eventually required to make good the loss. This result could only be avoided if the works were found so useful as, when famine occurred, to cause a diminution of the expenditure which must otherwise have been incurred for purposes of relief, sufficient to compensate for the cost of the construction and maintenance of the works at other times.'

The suggestion that the supply of funds from the famine surplus for the construction of protective works may be justified by such an expectation as that just referred to should be received with much hesitation. The true object of these works is to give increased security against the greatest dangers that arise in extreme drought, to supply the means of saving life and of averting suffering and misery, rather than to cause an eventual reduction in the cost of famine relief. Experience indicates no valid ground for hoping for any important diminution of the burden of such relief. On the contrary, the probabilities of the future, within any period to which for practical purposes we can now look forward, assuredly are in the direction of a constantly growing demand for a more bountiful administration, and of increased efficiency rather than for reduced cost. In short, no reduction of any insurance fund against future liabilities could be prudently accepted on grounds such as those just noticed.

Further, one of the most essential conditions to be observed in the construction of great public works is that, when they have been commenced, they should be carried on to completion without interruption, at a certain and steady rate of expenditure; the neglect of this condition has notoriously been already a fruitful cause of wasteful expenditure in India; and consequently if the construction of protective works depended on the possession of a sufficient surplus, there could be no certainty that they would go on uninterruptedly for a single year, for their progress might at any time be disturbed by famine, or war, or other causes.

For such reasons, to which no reply can be given, the Government of India rejected the proposal to provide from the famine special surplus the capital required for protective works demanding a large expenditure, or in other words to provide the money from ordinary revenues, making an equivalent reduction from the surplus of 1,500,000*l.*

Lord Lytton's Government considered that there was only one way in which these works could be made with the speed which the necessity of protecting the country against famine required, and at the same time without financial risk. In any case, they said, in which it would be justifiable in principle, although not expedient in practice, to diminish our annual famine insurance surplus, with the object of defraying the capital expenditure on protective works, it would be unobjectionable to apply a portion of that surplus in payment of interest on the capital required. It was therefore proposed to allow, in case of necessity, money to be borrowed for these works, subject to the condition that the net charge for the interest on their capital cost, and for their maintenance, after setting off the income yielded by them, should not exceed a specific maximum amount, to be provided from the ordinary standard surplus. The amount of the liability thus admitted might be altered, from time to time, as experience was gained; but to be on the safe side, it was proposed, in the first instance, to fix at

250,000*l.* the sum by which the yearly charge for interest and maintenance might exceed the net revenue from the works. It was believed that the annual surplus of 1,500,000*l.*, reserved for famine, might safely be reduced by this amount, not only because the construction of these works would reduce the ultimate liability for the relief of famines when they occur, but because, as the inquiries of the Famine Commission have since more decidedly shown, there is reason to think that, in originally determining the standard amount of that surplus, it was fixed at a sum somewhat higher than was really essential.

This sum of 250,000*l.*, to be annually expended in paying interest on fresh capital for protective works, would have been distributed between the Local Governments according to the urgency of their wants; and as soon as the quota of any province became exhausted, the further capital outlay in that province would have been suspended until the growing income from the provincial works as a whole, or, under certain conditions, from other sources of provincial income, again relieved the provincial revenues and supplied a surplus.

Even if the works should produce no net income at all, and should merely cover their working expenses—a supposition so improbable that it does not really deserve to be considered—a capital sum of about 6,000,000*l.* might, under this plan, be gradually expended, and such a sum would go far towards providing the protective works most urgently required. But, in fact, the growing income would, without the least doubt, rapidly provide the means of extending the capital expenditure, while, as already said, the gain to the country from the improvement of its communications would far outweigh any deficiency in the direct return from the works. The adoption of this plan would create no fresh ultimate obligation beyond what has already been accepted; the interest payment would be nothing more than an indirect contribution of the capital itself, and no greater risk would be incurred than if the capital had been directly supplied from surplus revenue.

These proposals were not sanctioned by the Secretary of State. Not being able to appreciate the force of his reasons for this, and wishing not to misrepresent them, I quote his orders on the subject in extenso:—

'I have given a most careful consideration to this important question, and regret that I am unable to give my consent to the modification proposed. . . . The events of the last few months, and their effect on our financial position, have compelled me to reconsider the question of public works expenditure; and I propose to address your Excellency in another despatch on this subject. In the meantime, however, I deem it necessary to express the opinion that the present condition of the finances does not justify any loan for outlay on protective works, or any expenditure on them beyond what may be met from the receipts from the special taxation recently imposed. The first claim on those receipts being that of the Home Government for the repayment of debt already incurred on account of famine, I am of opinion that not less than one-half, or, say, 750,000*l.*, should be held available for remittance to England in the next ensuing years on that account. The remainder may be appropriated, at your discretion, to the extinction of debt, to the relief of famine, or to the construction of protective works, not necessarily remunerative, but obviously productive in the sense of guarding against a probable future outlay in the relief of the population. I cannot, however, under present circumstances, sanction the raising of capital by loan for the construction of works which do not distinctly fall under the regulations laid down for productive public works.'

It must be understood that the proposals of Lord Lytton's Government were made on the assumption that the regulations referred to in the last words of this quotation would be maintained, and that it was useless to advise their alteration. So long as this assumption remained true, no other satisfactory means of providing the funds required for protective works could be suggested. But a far better solution of the difficulty would have been found in the abandonment of the system under which the assignment of borrowed funds for the construction of irrigation works and railways was made to depend solely on the immediate financial prospects of each individual undertaking. It would be a much more reasonable and beneficial plan, and one attended with no financial risk whatever, as has been shown in Chapter VII. of this work, to revert to the principles originally laid down in the time of Lord Lawrence and Lord Mayo, and to regulate the expenditure of borrowed money on great public works of improvement on the broader considerations, of what are the true requirements of the country, and what the amount which can wisely be contributed from the general revenues in payment of interest on capital laid out for such purposes. Under such a system there would be an end to the misleading and really meaningless distinctions now drawn between productive and protective works, to the arbitrary lines laid down for determining what are and what are not remunerative works, and to the artificial and inconvenient complications in the accounts which are now growing up as a result of these distinctions, and which can only tend to make the facts unintelligible to the public.

It appears from the Budget Statement for 1881–82 recently published, that effect is about to be given to the views expressed by the Secretary of State in the quotation above given, and that a sum of 750,000*l.*, to be taken from the famine surplus, is assigned for expenditure in the coming year on the class of works that have been spoken of as protective; and among these will be some of the works before mentioned as required in Bandelkhand. I have thought it right to notice this in connection with what has been said on the subject of protective works; but it may be added that the object of this book is to state the policy of Lord Lytton's Government, and it forms no part of my plan to discuss the acts of their successors.

CHAPTER XII.

TAXATION IMPOSED IN 1877 AND 1878.

TAXATION FOR FAMINE RELIEF SHOULD BE GENERAL—REIMPOSITION OF INCOME TAX IMPRACTICABLE—CLASSES SPECIALLY LIABLE—TRADERS HITHERTO UNDULY EXEMPT FROM TAXATION—LICENCE TAX PROPOSED—ADDITIONAL RATES ON LAND IN BENGAL—IN NORTHERN INDIA—AMOUNT RAISED FROM LAND—INCIDENCE OF LICENCE TAX—ITS EXTENSION TO OFFICIALS AND PROFESSIONS—DIRECT TAXATION HOW FAR NOW APPLICABLE AND DESIRABLE—FREQUENT CHANGES IN PAST ARRANGEMENTS MOST MISCHIEVOUS—RETENTION OF CESSES IN BENGAL AND LICENCE TAX ON TRADERS NECESSARY FOR PROPER ADJUSTMENT OF BURDENS—TAXATION FIRST NEEDING REDUCTION.

WHEN the Government of India resolved, in 1877, that it was necessary to make a permanent addition to the public revenues, with the object of enabling the State to meet its obligations for the relief of famine, it declared that there was no class in the whole community, and no sort of property or income, which might not properly be made to contribute for a purpose of such general interest as the protection of the country against the consequences of famine. But there were special reasons which at the time rendered it hardly possible to reimpose an income tax, and their sufficiency could not be denied even by those who have always regretted the loss of that tax, and have always believed that it might with great advantage have been maintained as one of the permanent sources of Indian revenue. Lord Lytton could not avoid the conclusion that its reimposition was impracticable, and the Secretary of State had declared that he would not assent to it. There was, therefore, an income tax having been set aside, no way in which any universal liability could be enforced, and there were good reasons for considering that the trading and agricultural classes should be the first to bear the new taxation which was considered necessary.

These reasons were fully explained by Sir John Strachey at the time. It was shown that when scarcity affects one part of India, the dealers in grain and the producers of grain in parts of the country not so affected make large profits; and that while the agricultural and trading classes are, on the one hand, those that require large measures of relief in a region suffering from extreme scarcity, so, on the other hand, these are the classes which are in a position to obtain large profits when their own provinces are flourishing and others are suffering. The less wealthy members of the professional and official classes, on the other hand, who depend on fixed incomes for their support, or on incomes little affected by competition, as well as the labouring class paid by wages, suffer from the pressure of high prices, not only when scarcity prevails in their own provinces, but when it prevails elsewhere. The high prices which, under such circumstances, serve to enrich the producing and trading classes, entail suffering on the small officials, and on those subsisting on wages the amount of which they are powerless to regulate. Also, though it was never suggested that the richer members of the official, or professional, or any other classes, might not equitably be taxed, yet it was con sidered that the class of European officials, from which the professional classes could hardly be distinguished, were for the moment placed under such special disadvantages by the recent sudden and heavy fall in the exchange value of the rupee, that it would be inexpedient then to subject them to any fresh burden. These considerations did not apply to the trading and agricultural classes, to which, for the reasons above stated, a special liability was held to attach, and as regards the former there were other reasons of a more important and more permanent character.

It has always been admitted that the trading classes in India are the least heavily taxed portion of the population. They have ordinarily contributed almost nothing to the expenses of the State, while they derive perhaps the largest share of benefit from our administration, and from the railways and other works of improvement provided at the cost of the country at large. The exemption which these classes have enjoyed has long been felt to be one of the most indefensible and inequitable peculiarities of our Indian system of taxation.

It was not an easy task at once to apply a remedy, and to introduce a system under which a fair share of the public burdens should be placed on the commercial and trading sections of the community; but the Government resolved that the task must be undertaken. It was clear that until it was accomplished the condition of our fiscal administration would always be unsatisfactory. The Government believed that at least the foundations might be laid for a better apportionment of the public burdens, and that, although mistakes might be made at the outset, they would be corrected as experience was gained. They accordingly endeavoured to frame a scheme which, although it might be imperfect, should, as far as possible, be equitable in principle, and which might be capable of future development into a system which would secure many of the objects aimed at by a general income tax.

It was therefore decided to impose a licence tax on all traders whose presumed annual profits exceeded a certain amount. This amount varied in different provinces. The average rate of the tax on annual profits was about 1½, and was in no case to exceed 2 per cent. This Indian licence tax, it should here be explained, has no analogy with the licence duties levied in England. Here persons are required to take out licences to carry on certain occupations or to perform certain acts. The fees paid for the licences are comparatively small in amount, and have no relation whatever to the income of the person paying them. Bankers pay 30*l.*, auctioneers 10*l.*, game dealers 2*l.*, wine merchants 10*l.* 10*s.*, and the like. But the Indian licence tax is a tax assessed on persons engaged in professions, commerce, or trade, with direct reference to their income. The persons who are chargeable are divided for purposes of assessment into classes according to their presumed income. All persons in the same class pay the same tax. Thus the so-called licence tax is in fact a limited income tax assessed on a system of classification according to approximate income.

The propriety of placing fresh taxation on the land might seem, at first sight, more open to question; but the Government was satisfied that no room for doubt existed. In Bengal an additional cess on the land had been already imposed in 1877, under the name of the Public Works Cess, to cover the liabilities caused by the works constructed in that province to protect it from famine. A new rate was placed on the land in all other provinces, excepting Madras and Bombay, which were at the time actually suffering from famine.

In the permanently settled province of Bengal, the land revenue, which was fixed nearly a century ago, has notoriously become a very small and often hardly appreciable burden. There is certainly no important class of persons in any civilised country in the world which enjoys such a virtual immunity from taxation as the Bengal zemindars, and Bengal, although the wealthiest, is the most lightly taxed of all the provinces of the Empire. There was also a special propriety in insisting that when the Government was obliged to impose fresh taxation for such a purpose as the protection of the country against the consequences of famine, Bengal, in which, within the last few years, nearly 7,000,000*l.* had been expended from the general revenues of India on famine relief, should not escape its just share of the common liability. It was inevitable that on this as on every other occasion on which the zemindars of Bengal have been called upon to bear their share of fresh public burdens, it should be loudly asserted that the Government was infringing the conditions of the permanent settlement of the land, and was committing a breach of faith. On these grounds, the zemindars had demanded to be exempted even from the income tax, which was imposed on all kinds of property throughout India, without exception. Lord Lytton was not disposed to listen to such extravagant claims. They have received, during the last ten or twenty years, much more consideration than they deserved. It is sufficient to say here that it has been repeatedly and finally decided that (to quote the words of the Duke of Argyll, when he was Secretary of State) 'the levying of such rates upon the holders of land, irrespective of the amount of their land assessment, involves no breach of faith upon the part of the Government, whether as regards holders of permanent or temporary tenures.'

In Northern India, the imposition of the new rate, at one per cent. on the rental of the land, to meet famine liabilities, was approved by all the Local Governments. It is payable by the landlord and not by the tenant. It cannot, of course, be asserted that this or any other taxation is not disliked by those who have to pay it, but it is so slight a burden that it certainly constitutes no real hardship. The debate of February 9, 1878, in the Legislative Council, and especially the speeches of Mr. Thornton and Mr. Bazett Colvin and Sir Ashley Eden, than whom no men could speak with higher authority, indicates the opinions of the Government on this point.

Mr. Thornton showed that 'the landholders of the Punjab could well afford the proposed insignificant addition to the local rates,' that the agricultural population was 'eminently prosperous and thriving,' and that land had so increased in value that the people were, as a rule, more than six times as well off as they were twenty years ago. 'What,' he said, 'does the Government ask? Why, it asks a body of landowners, whose property has more than sextupled in value, to pay a famine insurance rate for that property amounting on an average to one farthing per acre per annum.'

Mr. Colvin showed that similar facts were true in the North-Western Provinces. He said that 'everywhere there has been an extraordinary rise in the value of land,' that 'the great advance in wealth and prosperity of the agricultural classes is too plainly evident to be called in question,' and that 'whatever the industry and intelligence of the proprietary class may have been, this improvement in their position is, in very great measure, due to the direct action of our Government. It is scarcely too much to say that it has created proprietary rights in the soil. It has secured them by maintaining good order and tranquillity; and it has added indefinitely to their value by furnishing marvellously improved and accelerated means of communication, and by opening markets for the produce of the land, of which the people of two generations back never even dreamed.' Mr. Colvin declared his belief that the landowning class, as a body, are four or five times as rich as they were at the beginning of the century.

The Lieutenant-Governor of Bengal, Sir Ashley Eden, gave similar testimony. He stated his opinion that 'no measures could have been devised more likely to be efficient, equitable, and inoppressive,' and with reference to the position of the landholders of Northern India, who, as Mr. Colvin had shown, had prospered greatly under former settlements, when they paid to the Government two-thirds of their collections, instead of one-half as at present, he made the following remarks:—

'For no very apparent reason, when the new settlement was made the zemindars were only called upon to pay half of their collections, keeping one-half. Admitting, as I do, that it is sound policy in the Government of India to limit its demands on the country to its actual requirements, and to distribute the burden of taxation as evenly as is practicable on all classes of the people, I should be sorry to condemn the principles of the present settlement; but the fact remains that if the present settlement had followed the lines of the old settlement in respect of the shares of the Government and the landholders, the Government would, setting new cesses aside, have received 2,000,000*l.* more than it receives now. And making all allowances for new cesses, including those now imposed, the landowners of the North-Western Provinces are receiving 1,500,000*l.* more than they received before. And now that its imperative requirements have increased, I do not consider that there is anything unjust or unreasonable in Government imposing upon the classes who received these great benefits the same burden which is imposed upon all other classes. Of course it requires no very great ingenuity to find some sort of objection, theoretical or practical, to every kind of tax; and I am sorry to have to say that those who are loudest and most unreasonable and impatient in their demands that Government should take upon itself the liability of relieving and preventing famine, and of constructing extravagant works of irrigation, are the first to put into the mouths of the people reasons why no one should contribute towards such a purpose. But the money has to be raised, and this being so, I must congratulate your Excellency's Government on the substantially fair and even manner in which this liability has been distributed.'

The so-called famine taxation, though it is convenient for some purposes to treat it as a whole, was actually imposed partly in 1877, and partly in 1878. The additional cess on the land in Bengal was originally imposed in 1877, as a part of the modified financial arrangement under which the provincial revenues were required to bear the charges incurred on account of the canals and railways constructed for its benefit, and for its protection against famine. The Bengal taxation differed in this respect from that imposed in Northern India. Its character was provincial and not imperial; and whereas in the other provinces the whole of the proceeds of the new rates on the land have gone into the imperial treasury, a large portion of them has, in Bengal, been left at the disposal of the Local Government, over and above the amount paid to the Government of India. The Bengal Public Works cess yielded in 1878–79, 355,590*l.* In 1878 the new rates were imposed on the land in the North-Western Provinces, Oudh, the Punjab, and the Central Provinces; they yield about 170,000*l.* Thus the total amount of new taxation on the land was about 525,000*l.*

The licence tax on traders was first imposed in 1877

in the North-Western Provinces, and in the following year the licence Acts, which, with modifications to be noticed, are still in force, were applied to the whole of India. They yielded at their maximum about 820,000*l.* net. The total amount of what has been called the famine insurance taxation was therefore about 1,345,000*l.* Subsequent exemptions of the poorer classes have reduced it to about 1,000,000*l.*

The attempt to make the commercial and trading classes, by means of the licence tax, contribute something towards the expenses of the State, was, on the whole, financially and otherwise, successful. The greater part of the tax, in by far the greater part of India, was assessed and collected without difficulty or opposition. But experience showed that, as originally introduced, it descended too low, and fell on large numbers of people on whom the imposition of direct taxation was not expedient or profitable.

The lower limit of liability to the tax, which varied in different provinces, had been in every case virtually determined by the Local Governments; in some instances, however, the Government of India interfered to make the limit higher than the Local Governments proposed, for some of them would have gone lower than annual incomes of Rs. 100, the minimum actually fixed. In the North-Western Provinces, Oudh, and Madras, traders whose annual earnings amounted to Rs. 200 were originally liable to the tax; in Bengal, Bombay, and the Punjab, the limit was Rs. 100. After nearly two years' experience, the Governments of Madras, of Bengal, and of the North-Western Provinces concurred in the opinion that about Rs. 250 might properly be adopted as the minimum. Sir Richard Temple, the Governor of Bombay, and Sir Robert Egerton, the Lieutenant-Governor of the Punjab, would have made little or no change in the existing limit of Rs. 100. They informed the Government of India that the tax was working well, that collections were made without trouble or complaint, and that the difficulties which had at first been felt had ceased.

Notwithstanding these opinions, given by such high authorities, the Government, towards the close of 1879, decided that it was desirable to raise throughout India the limit of liability to the tax. Statistics received from all parts of India showed that we were raising by direct taxation from more than a million of people no larger sum than about 340,000*l.* a year, and it was clear that this was neither financially nor politically wise.

The lower limit of liability to the tax was consequently fixed at an annual income of Rs. 500. This decision was not arrived at on the ground, often maintained by persons possessing little knowledge of the country, that the licence tax fell upon the poor. Speaking on this subject in the Legislative Council, in denial of the assertion that the tax would fall on the poorer classes, Sir Ashley Eden, the Lieutenant-Governor of Bengal, said—'It may be difficult for men who know nothing of the country to realise that practically a native with an income of Rs. 100 a year is in a better position than a trader or mechanic in Europe with an income of 100*l.* a year. I am sure that every one really acquainted with native habits and modes of life and requirements will agree with me that this is so.'

There now remain in all India not more than 250,000 traders liable to the tax, and it is expected to yield, in the present year, something over 500,000*l.*

When it was decided that the imposition of a

general income tax was impracticable, and that measures of class taxation must consequently be adopted, it was inevitable that whatever were the measures actually taken they would be open to objection on the ground of inequality and unfairness in their incidence. Such objections were raised by the mercantile classes in the Presidency towns, and by others, early in 1878, shortly after the licence tax was imposed, and the injustice of exempting the official and professional classes from taxation was strongly urged.

The Government of India, although it had thought it necessary, in the first instance, to restrict the operation of the new taxes, had no desire permanently to maintain any such exemptions; in the latter part of 1878 it made a definite proposal to extend to the professional and official classes taxation similar to that already imposed on the traders and agriculturists, which was approved by the Secretary of State. Various circumstances rendered the postponement of the measure necessary, and it was not until November 1879 that a Bill to carry it out was introduced into the Legislative Council. The extension of taxation to the official classes was supported by every local Government in India.

But from causes which need not be stated in detail, the proposal was dropped, a step which, though I myself accepted it as inevitable, I now regret; and I think the Marquis of Hartington was right when, in his despatch of August 5, 1880, he said that he could not 'approve of the withdrawal of the measure for the extension of the licence tax to the official and professional classes, which had been recommended by the Government of India and sanctioned by the Secretary of State as being likely to remove from the minds of the other classes a sense of being subjected to unequal treatment, and which, while thus desirable in itself, would have avoided a loss of 240,000*l.* a year.'

The existing licence Acts impose, or, with modifications such as those proposed in 1880, would impose, without minute inquisition, and in a manner little open to objection, a virtual income tax, at an average rate of about 1½ per cent., on the richer members of the professional, commercial, and trading classes. They are estimated to yield in the present year 515,000*l.*

With the extension of taxation, at 1½ per cent., to all the higher salaries, the richer officials would contribute at a rate similar to that already paid by the traders. The fund-holders and house-proprietors would remain untouched. Under existing circumstances, while India is every year borrowing money for the construction of productive public works, the exemption of the fund-holders from new taxation has much to recommend it. With regard to house-proprietors, according to the income tax returns for 1871–72 there were, in all India, only 3,100 persons deriving incomes exceeding Rs. 1,000 a year from houses alone, and a tax on them of 1½ per cent. would have yielded about 18,000*l.* In the absence of a general income tax, it would not be worth while to impose fresh taxation on this class.

The new rates on the land, now yielding 525,000*l.* a year, impose an approximately equal burden on the agricultural portion of the community in the Bengal Presidency, and, there is no reason why, with certain restrictions which the different tenure of land and other considerations would render proper, similar taxation should not be imposed in Madras and Bombay, especially on the permanently settled zemindars of Madras, if at some future time it should become desirable. But it would be very unwise on theoretical grounds of uniformity to impose any such fresh taxation when financially it is not wanted.

Although I have always regretted the loss of the income tax, and recognise that its reimposition at the present time is impracticable, rather from the strength of adverse opinion than from any fundamental objections of principle or policy, yet I am satisfied that it will be wise to continue, in regard to the question of direct taxation, to act on principles similar to those which during the last four years have been followed by the Government of India.

I do not propose to discuss at length the advantages of an income tax, or of other forms of direct taxation. In a note to this chapter a quotation is given from Mr. Bazett Colvin's valuable paper on Indian taxation, because it expresses the views which I hold. Although under existing circumstances I do not advise that practical effect be given to them, I must repeat Mr. Colvin's observation that they are in accordance with those of very many of the most distinguished men in modern Indian administration.

Foremost among these is that of my honoured master and friend, Lord Lawrence, who never, while he was in India, or after he left it, wavered in his opinion on this subject. No man knew India better than he, and never was there a man who would have more strongly and indignantly refused his consent to measures which he thought must entail injustice and oppression on the people. He believed that there are some classes of the community which have borne no proper part of the public burdens, although no classes are better able than they to bear their share; that it is by direct taxation alone that they can be reached; and that with reasonably good administration, which it is certainly within our power to secure, there is no necessity whatever for any gross abuses in the assessment and collection of taxes of this kind, particularly if a high minimum of taxable income be adopted. On the very last occasion on which I saw Lord Lawrence, he spoke to me to this effect.

Indirect taxation, in a country like India, is in itself no doubt preferable to direct, but many erroneous ideas are prevalent on the subject. Direct taxation on the trading classes has been imposed in India from time immemorial, and there is at this moment no important Native State in which it is not a recognised part of the fiscal system. There is probably no country in the world in which so large a proportion of a great revenue is raised by direct small payments as India. As a matter of fact, the greater part of the land revenue of more than 20,000,000*l*. is raised by what are virtually direct payments from an immense number of persons; and obviously it matters little to the millions of small proprietors and cultivators, who pay the greater portion of this revenue, what name we give to their payments. So, again, nearly the whole of the local taxation in a great part, perhaps in the greater part, of India, is received in the form of direct and not indirect payments.

If, however, any plan of direct taxation is to become successful, the fast-and-loose system which has hitherto been followed must be abandoned. As Mr. Rivers Thompson has observed, ever since the days of Mr. Wilson licence taxes have succeeded income taxes, certificate taxes have followed licence taxes, in various forms and shapes, and each in turn has been abandoned through an entire absence of any settled continuity of administration in our finances. No agency could be perfected under such constantly recurring changes.

It was forcibly pointed out, some years ago, by Mr. Alonzo Money, that in the assessment of direct taxation throughout the greater part of India a system resembling, in some respects, the periodical settlement of land revenue ought to be adopted. The character of the population is so stationary and unchanging that there is little variation from one year to another in the income and profits of the great majority of the persons called on to pay an income or licence tax, and, excepting in the large commercial centres, no necessity exists for annual assessments. Sir William Muir, when Lieutenant-Governor of the North-Western Provinces, laid much stress on these considerations. 'As in the assessment,' he said, 'of landed profits, so in the assessment of incomes, the more fixity and permanency arrived at, the greater will be the feeling of rest and of confidence. In proportion as such a state of comparative permanency can be approached, the suspicion and irritation, the fraud and oppression, and the other evils incident to the tax, would be diminished, the pressure on the people would be lightened, and the action of the Government would be better understood, and its motives more fully appreciated.'

The question may here fairly be asked, whether, granting that the imposition of this new taxation was right in 1877, its maintenance is necessary now, when the condition of the finances has become so far more satisfactory than it was, and when there is declared to be a large surplus of revenue over ordinary expenditure?

Before replying to this we should remember what are the classes on which this new taxation actually falls.

There are, first, the landlords of Bengal, the richest class in the richest province of the Empire, who now pay in taxation almost nothing, and in land revenue an amount altogether inadequate. They have succeeded in throwing upon the tenants a portion of all the cesses hitherto imposed on the land, and if this could be prevented I for my part should be glad. I can therefore conceive no more unwise or unjustifiable measure than the exemption of the Bengal zemindars from their share of this burden, the only fault of which, in relation to them, is that it is too light, while so much remains to be done for the relief of the poorer classes from taxation. Secondly, the new taxation falls, at the rate of 1 per cent. on their gross rental, on the landlords of Northern India. It has been shown how well they can afford to pay this demand, no portion of which is payable by the tenants. At the same time their case is altogether different from that of the landlords of Bengal. Although their assessments are very moderate, they nevertheless contribute largely towards the necessities of the State, and I should see without regret relief given to them by the remission of the rates imposed three years ago. The loss of revenue would be about 170,000*l.* Nor would there be any inconsistency in retaining the rates in Bengal and remitting them in Northern India, because, independently of the fact that Bengal is incomparably better able to pay, the rates were, as already explained, imposed at different times and for different purposes; and although it has been thought convenient to consider the Bengal public works cess as a part of the so-called famine taxation, it has been treated quite differently from the rates imposed in Northern India. Thirdly, the new taxation falls on the richer class of traders, touching no one whose annual profits are less than Rs. 500 a year, a limit equal perhaps to 400*l*. or 500*l*. a year in England. This class, if the licence tax were remitted, would pay literally no obligatory taxes at all, except indeed an annual 7*d*. a head for salt. The total number of persons paying the licence tax in all India is about 250,000. Considering that the population of British India exceeds 190,000,000, it is an abuse of language to talk of such a tax being unpopular. Of all the taxes that are levied in India, there will be none more just or more necessary than this, when, as I trust may soon happen, similar taxation has been extended to the official and professional classes in the way that has been proposed.

Indignation is always aroused in India by every attempt to relieve the poorer classes from taxation at the expense of the richer. 'Such a change,' it has been observed by an accomplished writer, 'is inevitably denounced with more vigour and outspokenness than are available for its defence. Those whom it relieves are for the most part persons who accept the decrees of Government, whether for better or worse, as providential dispensations which it is in vain to question, and as to which silent endurance is the wisest policy. On the other hand, it touches the pockets of a class of persons who have both the will and the power to make their troubles known, and are by no means inclined to let their interests suffer for want of courageous advocacy. Indian journalism of the more respectable and influential order is closely allied with the official world, and reflects with undeviating accuracy the feelings and the tastes of those from whom it draws its inspiration, and on whose patronage it depends. The English merchants, too, at the presidency towns have no difficulty in stirring the sympathies and guiding the convictions of writers whose interests are in many particulars identical with their own. The consequence is that every measure which imposes on the official or mercantile classes a larger share in the taxation of the country, is denounced by the Indian press with a vehement unanimity which an inexperienced observer would be tempted to value at more than its true worth. It implies really nothing more than the natural pang which every conscious contribution to the public treasury occasions: and its political importance is certain to be exaggerated, because we hear nothing of the silent millions whose opinion, were they capable of expressing it, could not fail to be in favour of a measure which transfers a portion of the burden of taxation to sturdier shoulders than their own.'[1]

Thus temptations are never wanting in India for Governments to earn for themselves an easy and apparent popularity by a refusal to impose taxes on the richer and more influential classes of the community; and while these, the only audible critics, approve, it will never be difficult to find acceptable reasons for a course essentially impolitic and unjust. Statesmen should never forget that the real foundations of our power in India do not rest on the interested approval of the noisy few. They rest on justice, on the contentment of the millions who may not always be silent and quiescent, and on their feeling that, in spite of the selfish clamour of those who profess to be their guardians and representatives, they may place implicit trust in the equal justice of our Government, and in its watchful care of the interests of the masses of the people. The exemption of

[1] Although the general truth of these remarks is undeniable, there is one notable exception. The justice and liberality of view shown by the public and by the press of Bombay in regard to all these questions of direct taxation have long been remarkable.

the richer classes from taxation is a political mistake which, as time goes on, and knowledge and intelligence increase, must become more and more mischievous.

When taxation is diminished, these, then, are not the taxes with which we ought to begin. As I have endeavoured to show in another chapter, further reductions in the salt duties are, on all grounds, desirable, both for the benefit of the people and of the finances. Further reforms in the customs tariff, involving a loss of present revenue, but certain to be most beneficial to the country, should also be made. The court fees, which are taxes on the administration of justice, ought to be reduced. The capitation tax in Burma ought to be abolished. These are among the taxes of which the reduction or remission are first required.

NOTE TO CHAPTER XII.

Extract from a Paper by Mr. Bazett Colvin on Indian Taxation.

An income tax is not an untried resource, or a doubtful experiment. In one shape or another it has been imposed, at intervals, during the last twenty years, and the arguments for and against it are familiar to most people in this country.

. . . .

I am aware how much there is to be urged against an income tax, and know its defects not from hearsay but from experience, having been personally engaged as a district officer, in assessing and collecting every direct tax upon incomes, except one, which was imposed between 1860 and 1872. I do not deny that there are serious defects in it; but it does not follow that those defects are beyond remedy; or, even if they were, that an income tax would be worse than any of the other forms of taxation which we have been examining. Our choice in the case supposed would lie among evils; and, this being so, the real question is, whether an income tax is not the least that we can choose.

The chief argument that is used against an income tax by its opponents is its unpopularity. It is, no doubt, greatly disliked both by Europeans and Natives. The European aversion from it is due, in some measure no doubt, to its incidence as a direct tax upon themselves; but the official dislike to it should (I think) be chiefly ascribed to the defects of its assessment, and to an Englishman's reluctance to be concerned in anything like arbitrary taxation. Natives object to it, less, perhaps, because its assessment is faulty, than because it is a direct tax, and because they hate all taxation of which they are conscious. Whatever the motives may be, I am not prepared to dispute the fact of its unpopularity. But I believe that much more importance has been conceded to this unpopularity than it deserves. The classes who cherish hostility to an income tax are, of course, the classes who feel it—in other words, the European community, and the educated and well-to-do portion, which is a very small portion, of the native population. These classes have every opportunity of making their dissatisfaction heard, and are, indeed, the only classes whose voice is audible. But they are, of all people, the least likely to carry their dissatisfaction to the point of disaffection towards the Government, and of any active desire to disturb order. The political importance, therefore, of the hostility displayed to the tax is really much less than it seems. The great mass of the people do not pay it, and are utterly indifferent about it. A tax on tobacco, or one on houses, or marriages, would stir the people with a far greater force, and to a much lower depth.

Putting aside the unpopularity of an income tax with the few whom it affects, there seem to be no other objections to it which are entitled to much weight. The inquisitorial mode in which it was at first assessed was abandoned after a short trial, and was no longer a characteristic of the tax when it ceased to exist. It is hardly disputed now that there was exaggeration in the charge made against it, that it afforded facilities for great corruption and oppression on the part of subordinate officials. Moreover, if an income tax became a permanent part of our financial system, there is no reason to suppose that these defects in its working, so far as they actually exist, could not be remedied as well in this as in other branches of the administration.

On the other hand, whatever may be said against an income tax, this, at least, in its favour, is true—that it would be no doubtful experiment, but a measure of which the result is known, and the success certain. Again, it is no less true that an income tax is a just form of taxation, and that it is the only way in which the mercantile wealth of the country can be made to contribute to the cost of the Government. It is notorious that this wealth, which is considerable and daily increasing, pays very little, in proportion to its means, for the protection and the great advantages which it enjoys under British rule. It is no small recommendation of a tax that it should redress the great injustice which this immunity of so many rich men causes to all other tax-payers. Admitting, also, that its assessment has been hitherto defective, this evil might certainly be remedied, if the number of persons liable to it were largely reduced, which, as I hope to show, is possible, and if the tax were made permanent. Nor must we forget that, however great the alleged evils of an income tax may be, they have not prevented a great many of the most distinguished names in modern Indian administration from expressing their approval of it.

CHAPTER XIII.

THE SALT AND SUGAR DUTIES.

SOURCES OF SALT SUPPLY IN VARIOUS PROVINCES—SYSTEM OF LEVYING DUTIES—ORIGIN OF DUTIES—ABOLITION OF OLD INTERNAL CUSTOMS DUTIES—SALT AND SUGAR EXCEPTED—RATES OF DUTY VARIED IN DIFFERENT PROVINCES—PREVENTIVE LINE ACROSS INDIA—RESOLUTION IN 1869 TO EQUALISE DUTIES AND ABOLISH CUSTOMS LINE—LORD MAYO'S MEASURES—FURTHER STEPS TAKEN IN 1878—DUTIES PARTIALLY EQUALISED—RAISED IN BOMBAY AND MADRAS—REDUCED IN NORTHERN INDIA AND BENGAL—FINAL REDUCTION TO 2 RS. 8 ANS. EXCEPT IN BENGAL—ARRANGEMENTS WITH NATIVE STATES IN RAJPUTANA—SINDH—ABOLITION OF CUSTOMS LINE IN 1879—GENERAL RESULTS ON PRICE—CONSUMPTION AND REVENUE—POSSIBLE FURTHER REDUCTION OF DUTY—SALT IN BURMA—ADMINISTRATION OF SALT DEPARTMENT—SUGAR DUTIES—THEIR ABOLITION IN 1878.

THE changes carried out during the administration of Lord Lytton in the system of assessing and collecting the salt duties in India have been extremely important, and, notwithstanding large reductions over the greater part of India in the rate at which the duties were levied, they now yield a revenue exceeding by nearly 1,000,000*l.* that which they yielded in 1877–78, four years ago.

Properly to appreciate the measures that have been taken, and the policy by which those measures have been guided, it is necessary to understand the condition of things which previously existed.

And first it must be explained that the circumstances under which the salt duties are raised vary greatly in different parts of India. Bengal and Assam, with 70,000,000 people, now get nearly the whole of their salt supply from England. Almost the only local source within easy reach, from which Bengal can obtain salt, is the sea, but owing to the damp climate, and the large body of fresh water brought down by the numerous rivers which intersect the delta of the Ganges, the natural facilities for making salt on the northern coasts of the Bay of Bengal are not great. On the equalisation of the duty on salt manufactured locally and on that imported by sea, the latter almost completely supplanted the former.

In Madras and Bombay, on the other hand, which contain about 47,000,000 people, the manufacture of salt from the sea is cheap and easy; and for these presidencies, as well as for the greater part of the Central Provinces and the Native States of Southern India, the sea is the great source of supply.

In Northern India the Punjab possesses inexhaustible supplies of rock-salt, which is consumed by about 16,000,000 people. Throughout the North-Western Provinces and Oudh, and in a portion of the Central Provinces and of the Punjab, although there are many places where more or less impure salts can be produced by washing the soil, the home sources for the supply of good salt are altogether insufficient; 47,000,000 of our subjects depend almost entirely for their salt on the Native States of Rajputana, or on places on the confines of those States, where lakes or springs impregnated with excellent salt occur.

The system under which the duty is levied also varies in different provinces. In Madras the duty is mostly collected under a monopoly by which all salt is manufactured on behalf of the Government, and sold at a price which gives a profit equivalent to the duty. In Bombay the duty is chiefly levied as an excise. In Lower Bengal it is levied chiefly in the form of a sea customs import duty. In the Punjab the duty is included in the selling price of the rock-salt, which is dug and removed from the mines and sold by the Government. For the rest of the upper provinces, until 1879 the duty was collected when the salt imported from Rajputana crossed the British frontier; it is now levied at the places of production, where it is prepared by evaporation from the brine by a Government establishment.

The origin of the Indian salt duties is well explained in the following quotation, taken, with some unimportant omissions and alterations, from a speech by Lord Lytton, made in the Legislative Council on February 9, 1878:—

'The taxation of salt is a part of the fiscal system which the British Government inherited from the Native rulers of India. The history of our present salt duties is a separate one for each province. Except in one respect, which I will mention immediately, these provincial duties have had no connection with each other; and hence that irregularity in their rates which the Government of India has always desired, and is now endeavouring, to rectify. The only historical connection between these local salt duties is to be found in the common origin of additions made to them in connection with the abolition of a mass of most vexatious transit duties with which the whole surface of this Empire was formerly covered. Under Native rule, tolls were taken on all roads and navigable rivers; and, in spite of their irregularity, these early transit duties were probably less harassing to trade than the forms which they subsequently assumed under the regulations of the East India Company; for those regulations added to the original tolls all the refinements and checks of an elaborate customs system. About half a century ago the Government, recognising the intolerable inconvenience of these multiplied checks upon internal trade, decided to abolish them and substitute for them higher rates of duty upon salt. This great reform is mainly due to the enlightened advice of Sir Charles Trevelyan, than a member of the Bengal Civil Service. The extinction of the condemned imposts involved a loss of revenue, in the Bombay Presidency, amounting to more than 345,000*l.*, whilst the enhanced duty on salt yielded only a revenue of less than 215,000*l.* In Madras the loss of revenue was still greater. The transit and inland customs duties had yielded a net revenue of about 310,000*l.*, while the increase in the salt duty yielded less than 95,000*l.*

'The history of the southern salt duties is thus not one which the Government of India has any reason to recall with self-reproach. A similar policy has been pursued in Bengal and the upper provinces of India. The Bengal transit duties were abolished by the Act of 1836, and the Bengal salt duty was fixed in the following year at Rs. 3–4 per maund. The Act of 1843 abolished all import and export duties on the frontiers of the North-Western Provinces, with the exception of the duties on salt, sugar, and cotton; and the cotton import duty was abandoned in 1855; the salt duty in the North-Western Provinces having been fixed in 1843 at Rs. 2 per maund, with an additional assessment of R. 1 on all salt passing eastward of Allahabad. The annexation of the Punjab was followed by an increase of the salt duty in that province; but that increase was part of a general measure which extinguished simultaneously all the export, import, transit, and town duties previously levied. It will thus be seen that the present system of comparatively high salt duties in British India is the result of an enlightened and beneficent fiscal policy, which has relieved British India from a multitude of mischievous and vexatious imposts on internal commerce; imposts described by a competent authority as being "so full of inequalities, and anomalies, and complications, that it would be vain to inquire from what objections or what abuses they were free."

Thus the salt duties levied in the different provinces of India had little real connection with each other, and the rates at which they were imposed varied greatly from time to time. From 1869 to 1877 the duty in Lower Bengal was Rs. 3-4 per maund (82 lbs.); in the upper provinces Rs. 3; and in Madras and Bombay Rs. 1-13.

So long as there were no railways, and the means of communication were imperfect, the inconvenience of these different rates of duty in different provinces was comparatively little felt. But to secure the levy of the duty on the salt imported from Rajputana, and, as communications were improved, to prevent the ingress of salt taxed at lower rates into the provinces where it was more highly taxed, preventive measures were necessary, and there grew up gradually a monstrous system to which it would be almost impossible to find a parallel in any tolerably civilised country.

A customs line was established, which stretched across the whole of India, which in 1869 extended from the Indus to the Máhánadi in Madras, a distance of 2,300 miles; and it was guarded by nearly 12,000 men and petty officers, at an annual cost of 162,000*l.* 'The line,' the commissioner of inland customs wrote in his report for 1869–70, 'is divided into 110 beats, each presided over by a patrol, and watched from 1,727 guard-posts. A very perfect system of patrolling exists, and, except in some wild portions of the Central Provinces (where tigers bar the way alike to smuggler and customs officer after dark), goes on with unabated vigilance night and day.'

Before the latest changes were made this inland customs line had been partially reduced, but still extended from a point north of Attock on the Indus to the frontier of Berar, a distance of more than 1,500 miles, and was guarded by some 8,000 men. If put down in Europe, it would have stretched from London to Constantinople. Along the greater part of its extent it consisted of a huge material barrier, which Mr. Grant Duff, speaking from personal observation, said could be compared to nothing else in the world except the great wall of China; it consisted principally of an immense impenetrable hedge of thorny trees and bushes, supplemented by stone walls and ditches, across which no human being or beast of burden or vehicle could pass without being subjected to detention and search. A similar line, 280 miles in length, was maintained in the north-eastern portion of the Bombay Presidency, from Dohud to the Runn of Cutch.

It may be easily imagined what great and inevitable obstruction to trade, what gross abuses and oppression, what annoyance and harassment to individuals, took place. The interference was not confined to the traffic passing into British territory; for, owing to the levy of an export duty on all sugar passing from British territory into Rajputana, which had been retained after all other similar inland duties were removed, and to which I shall again refer, the same obstructions were offered to the traffic passing in the other direction. In spite, however, of the evils inseparable from the existence of an inland customs line, it was impossible to dispense with it so long as we levied our salt tax at different rates in different provinces, and had no means of controlling the manufacture and taxation of salt produced in Native States and brought thence into our own territories.

The flagrant evils arising from this state of things were long recognised by the Government of India, but nevertheless, until ten or twelve years ago, it acted as if it had little interest in applying a remedy, or in facilitating the supply of salt to the people. Thus, for example, salt from the Sámbhar Lake, the most important source of supply to the North-Western Provinces, had to find its way two hundred miles through Native States, with no roads or bridges, on the backs of pack-cattle or camels, and subjected to imposts and exactions and hindrances of every kind, until it came to the greatest hindrance of all, our own customs line.

In 1869, Lord Mayo's Government, with the concurrence of the Governments of Madras and Bombay, raised the salt duty in those presidencies by five annas a maund, and this was done not merely to increase the revenue, but chiefly as a step towards the equalisation of the duties throughout India, and the abolition of the inland customs line. A still more valuable measure taken by Lord Mayo, in the same direction, was the acquisition by the British Government, under an amicable arrangement with the Native States of Jaipur and Jodhpur, of the lease of the Sámbhar Salt Lake, the most important of the salt sources of Rajputana. To Lord Mayo also belongs the honour of commencing, as the first instalment of the projects for railway extension then happily conceived, the lines from Agra and Delhi to the Sámbhar lake, thus providing railway transport between the salt sources of Rajputana and our own territories. With the means of communication which formerly existed, it was physically impossible to bring into Northern India a supply of salt sufficient for the wants of the people. During the administration of Lord Northbrook the same policy was followed, and, although the rates of duty remained unaltered, the extension of the railways in central India admitted of a further great step in advance, by the abolition in 1874, with practically no loss of revenue, of about 800 miles of the customs line in the Central Provinces and Behar.

When Lord Lytton became Viceroy, the whole question of the salt duties was reconsidered, and the result was the declaration by the Government of India not only of the policy which it intended to follow in connection with the equalisation of the duties and the abolition of the inland customs line, but of the principles by which the administration of the salt revenue ought in future to be regulated. What those principles are, what has been done towards carrying them into effect, and what still remains to be done, will now be stated.

There can be no doubt that salt is, in itself, a proper subject of taxation in India. The following extract from a despatch by the Duke of Argyll, dated January 21, 1869, expresses, very clearly and accurately, what appears to be the true doctrine :—

'On all grounds of general principles, salt is a perfectly legitimate subject of taxation. It is impossible, in any country, to reach the masses of the population by direct taxes. If they are to contribute at all to the expenditure of the State, it must be through taxes levied upon some articles of universal consumption. If such taxes are fairly adjusted, a large revenue can be thus raised, not only with less consciousness on the part of the people, but with less real hardship upon them than in any other way whatever. There is no other article in India answering this description upon which any tax is levied. It appears to be the only one which at present, in that country, can occupy the place which is held in our own financial system by the great articles of consumption from which a large part of the imperial revenue is derived. I am of opinion, therefore, that the salt tax in India must continue to be regarded as a legitimate and important branch of the public revenue. It is the duty, however, of the Government to see that such taxes are not so heavy as to bear unjustly upon the poor, by amounting to a very large percentage upon their necessary expenditure. The best test whether an indirect tax is open to this objection is to be found in its effect upon consumption.

'I observe that several of those officers whose opinions upon this question have been given in the papers before me, found that opinion upon what they have heard, or what they have not heard, in the way of complaint among the native population; but this is a very unsafe ground of judgment; it is one of the great advantages of indirect taxation that it is so mixed up with the other elements of price that it is paid without observation by the consumers. Even at home, where the people are so much more generally educated, and more accustomed to political reasoning, the heavy indirect taxes formerly levied upon the great articles of consumption were seldom complained of by the poor; they were not themselves conscious how severely they were affected by those taxes, and how much more of the articles they would consume if the duties were lower. But whilst this peculiarity of indirect taxation makes it a most convenient instrument of finance, it throws additional responsibility upon all Governments which resort to it to bring the most enlightened consideration to bear upon the adjustment of taxes which may really be very heavy and very unjust, without the fact being perceived or understood by those on whom they fall.'

In Sir John Strachey's financial statement made in March 1877 it was declared that the main object of the Government, and the basis of its whole policy in regard to this question, was 'to aim at giving to the people throughout India the means of obtaining, with the least possible inconvenience, and at the cheapest rate consistent with financial necessities, a supply of salt the quantity of which should be limited only by the capacity of the people for consumption. There can be no doubt that, in the interests of the revenue, the best system would be that under which we should levy throughout India a low rate of duty on unrestricted consumption.'

Although it cannot be truly asserted that there was any part of India in which the actual supply of salt was insufficient for the preservation of the health of the people, and although it is an exaggeration to say that the salt tax anywhere pressed with extreme severity on the poorer classes, yet it was not open to question that very large numbers of our subjects failed to obtain a full supply of salt, and that the system under which high duties were levied on a restricted consumption had not even the merit of being financially profitable. In the Madras and Bombay Presidencies, where the duties were lowest, and salt was cheap and abundant, the average consumption of the people per head was double that of the people in Northern India, where salt was dear, where the duty was high, and the supply limited; and financially, the results in the former case were far more satisfactory than in the latter. The salt duties yielded, relatively to the population, a larger revenue in Madras than in any other part of India.

The Government would have desired that the duties throughout the whole of India should be at once brought down to the rates in force in Madras and Bombay, but the immediate loss of revenue would have been at least 1,500,000*l.*, and some years must have elapsed before increased consumption restored the revenue to its former amount. It was clear that the equalisation of the duties throughout India was impracticable, unless while reducing the duties throughout the greater part of India some additions were made, for a time at least, to the low duties in Madras and Bombay.

Although the financial difficulties in the way of dealing with this subject in a thoroughly satisfactory way were greatly increased by the necessity, which arose in 1877–78, of imposing fresh taxation to meet the liabilities caused by famine, that necessity at the same time diminished the practical difficulty of enhancing the salt duties in Madras and Bombay, and prevented much opposition which would otherwise have been inevitable. Throughout the rest of India, rates were imposed on the land, as a part of the so-called famine taxation, but, although no pledges were given that the exemption would be maintained, no such rates were imposed in Madras and Bombay, in consideration of the increase made in those Presidencies to the salt duties. This fact has been systematically misinterpreted, and it is still often asserted that the salt duties were raised in Madras and Bombay as a part of the famine taxation, though the contrary was distinctly stated at the time. The measure was a step towards the equalisation and ultimate general reduction of duties throughout India.

It is not necessary to state in detail the measures taken, from time to time, during the last four years, for carrying out this policy, but the main facts will be described.

In the beginning of 1878 the duty on salt in the Madras and Bombay Presidencies was raised from Rs. 1-13 to Rs.2-8 per maund. In Northern India it was at the same time reduced from Rs. 3 to Rs. 2-12, and in Bengal from Rs. 3-4 to Rs. 3; a further reduction was made in July of the same year to Rs. 2-8 in Northern India, and Rs. 2–14 in Bengal. In 1878 agreements were completed with the Native States of Rajputana under which the British Government obtained leases of all the more important remaining salt sources, and on April 1, 1879, the whole customs line, with a small exception on the Indus, was abolished, and its abolition led to a direct saving of expenditure on the preventive establishments of about 100,000*l.* a year. The leases of the salt sources were framed on the precedent of the lease sanctioned by Lord Mayo, under which the Sámbhar Lake had been managed for nine years, without any friction with the Native States, and with most beneficial results on the price of salt. Ample compensation was paid to manufacturers and others interested in the salt-works. The chiefs were treated with liberality; they were fully compensated for all loss of revenue, and there is every reason to believe that they were and are well satisfied with the terms which they obtained. But, as an unavoidable consequence of the new system, and one without which the relief of our own subjects would have been impracticable, the people of the Native States in question became generally liable to the payment of the British salt duty; a portion, however, of the population still obtains salt free of that duty, and another portion pays only half the usual rate. Efforts were made, in carrying out these indispensable measures, to give to the people, as far as possible, compensation for the new salt tax so imposed on them. In four of the States, all transit duties on goods of every kind were abolished, and in all the States with which agreements were made it was stipulated that no transit duties on salt should continue to be imposed. Relief was also given by the removal, from April 1, 1878, of the duties formerly levied on all sugar exported across the customs line from our own territories, which fell mainly on the people of the Native States of Rajputana. These sugar duties will be more particularly referred to hereafter.

In Central India the new arrangements have worked very satisfactorily. Some difficulties have occurred with the Maharaja Holkar alone, certainly through no fault or want of liberality on the part of the British Government. The Maharaja Scindia, and all the other chiefs with whom agreements have been made, have declared themselves thoroughly satisfied. 'Salt,' wrote the Governor-General's Agent, Sir Henry Daly, on November 20, 1880, 'is cheaper in Indore than it was in 1875, and in all the eastern parts of Central India the benefit to the consumers has been great. The salt, except in Holkar's State, is untrammelled by petty dues; and to the poor is at a price before unknown. Scindia admits that he has been handsomely treated; and I have heard no chief with whom we have dealt say otherwise. I urged liberality in every case; and liberality was observed. . . . Everywhere throughout Central India the price shows that salt is a commodity within the reach of the poorest.'

In Rajputana the Agent to the Governor-General, Colonel Bradford, wrote, December 4, 1880, that 'the salt arrangements are working most satisfactorily.' The price of salt was necessarily increased in some of the States where salt is produced, but in this respect matters go on improving as trade adjusts itself to the new conditions. That the income of the chiefs is greater now than before the new arrangements were made, is said by Colonel Bradford to be indisputable.

In connection with this subject, it must be remembered that the British Government has now nearly completed, entirely at its own risk and at a cost of some 10,000,000*l.*, the railways running through the Native States of Rajputana and Central India. The benefit thus conferred on the people of these States has been enormous. No part of India was formerly more completely cut off from communication with the sea-board and with the great trading marts of the country. The transport of every article of trade has now been cheapened; and wherever the railways have displaced road traffic, the onerous transit duties on almost every article of consumption, from which the people of these States have long suffered, have ceased to be collected.

These measures, by which the British Government obtained the control of the salt manufacture in Rajputana, and without which the abolition of the inland customs line would have been impossible, were not expected to give any direct profit to our revenue. On the contrary, they were expected, in the first instance, to lead to an annual loss of about 48,000*l.*, which it was believed would in time be made up by increased consumption in British territory, following the reduction in the cost of salt. It is too soon to speak confidently, but it now appears probable that the additional revenue received from the salt consumed in the Native States, together with the amount saved by the abolition of the customs line, will considerably exceed the annual expenditure on account of compensation to the States, and the loss on account of sugar duties, which have also been relinquished.

If this anticipation should be fulfilled, and the new arrangements, independently of their effect on the people of our own territories, should prove financially profitable, it will be cause for satisfaction. It has been generally felt that the Native States throughout India ought to make much larger contributions towards the general expenses of the Empire than we now receive from them. For the maintenance throughout India of peace and tranquillity, they pay, for the most part, almost nothing, and these inestimable benefits are mainly provided for them at the cost of our own subjects. In many cases, however, a partial remedy has been supplied by the operation of our salt duties. Thus the States of the Nizam, all the Native States of the Punjab, and others in other parts of India, derive their supplies of salt wholly or in part, from sources where the British duty has been levied, and these States thus contribute indirectly towards the revenue of the British Government. Hitherto, with unimportant exceptions, no contributions of this or any kind have been made by the Native States of Rajputana, and if the new arrangements should give some direct financial gain to our treasury, they will in truth cause the partial removal of an injustice, not inflict one.

The great customs line ceased to exist in April 1879, and there was an end to those artificial obstructions to the free development of trade which had so long checked the supply of salt to the people. With it disappeared one of the greatest opprobria of British rule in India. Lord Lytton, speaking on this subject in the Legislative Council in February 1878, said that the maintenance of this line was 'a great commercial and political scandal,' and that he 'sincerely trusted that the history of his administration might be associated with its removal.' It is a cause of great satisfaction that this hope has been fulfilled.

The salt revenue in the province of Sindh was, before 1878, raised by a system of sale by contract. This system was extremely defective, led to much smuggling, and produced a revenue very small in proportion to the population. At the beginning of 1878, the system in Sindh was assimilated to that in Bombay, and the duty was raised to the same level, namely, Rs. 2-8 per maund.

The general result of all these measures was, that while the Government was compelled, for a time only as it believed, to increase the rate of duty on the salt consumed by 47,000,000 of our subjects, the rate was reduced throughout the greater part of India, to the relief of 148,000,000.

Complete figures to show the difference between the present prices of salt in various parts of India, and those which prevailed before the first steps in the new policy were taken, cannot be given, but the following facts are interesting.

At the chief salt mart in Northern India, Agra, in January 1868, good average Sámbhar salt was selling wholesale at Rs. 5-8 per maund. In 1869 the price was Rs. 6. In 1876 it had fallen to Rs. 4-6, and in 1880 to Rs. 3-3. Thus, a reduction of about 40 per cent. in the price of the most important salt in Northern India has been secured at the cost of a reduction of 16¼ per cent. in the duty. The increased duty in Southern India has necessarily increased the price of salt there, but to a smaller extent than might have been anticipated. In 1877, before the last increase of duty, the average price of salt in the Madras Presidency was Rs. 2-12 per maund, while in 1880 it was Rs. 3-5. This signifies, taking the average annual consumption at 12 lbs. per head, that each person has to spend in the whole year upon salt about 2*d.* more than he spent before. The increase of price in the Bombay Presidency has been nearly the same as in Madras. On the other hand the extension of railway communication has done much to lessen the price of salt over a great part of the country. In the speech already quoted, Lord Lytton observed—

'Nor should it be forgotten, I think, when we come to consider the practical incidence of the existing salt duties upon the poorer portion of the population, that the extension of railway communication has done much to cheapen the virtual price of salt to the people. For instance, the lines which now connect Bombay with Beypur and Madras, on the one side, and Jabbalpur and Nagpur on the other, and those which connect Negapatam with Tuticorin, carry salt from the sea-coast to the interior at the rate of one anna ($1\frac{1}{4}d.$) per maund for about every fifty miles. Thus the carriage of a maund of salt from Madras or Bombay to any intermediate railway station does not now exceed eight annas, which is considerably less than the old cost of carriage by road, and may be fairly reckoned in favour of the consumer, against the corresponding increase of duty.

'Similarly, in the Bengal Presidency, the present railroads have placed a great part of the country in immediate communication with the sea-coast and internal salt sources; so that, in spite of the continued imposition (in the past) of comparatively high duties, the development of railway communication has cheapened the price of salt over a great part of the country; and further reductions in the price of salt may consequently be expected from further progress in the development of railway communication.'

The effect of these measures on the consumption of salt and on the public revenue will next be shown.

In 1870–71 the total consumption of duty-paying salt in India was 23,031,000 maunds,[1] and the net salt revenue was 5,686,335*l.* In the three years preceding 1877–78, when the rates of duty were altered, the total average annual consumption was 24,218,000 maunds, and the average net revenue was 5,739,460*l.* Since the alteration in the duties, the total consumption and the total revenue have steadily increased. In 1879–80 the consumption had risen to 27,861,000 maunds, and the net revenue had risen to 6,895,713*l.*, an increase in three years of more than 1,000,000*l.* In 1880–81 there has been a decline in the consumption to 27,240,000 maunds, and of the net revenue to 6,572,000*l.* This is attributed partly to an artificial stimulus given to the sale of Sámbhar salt in the previous year, and partly to the ordinary fluctuation of trade.

[1] The maund equals $82\frac{2}{7}$ lbs.; a ton contains $27\frac{2}{9}$ maunds.

The reform commenced in the course of the year 1877–78, and was not completed until the end of the year 1878–79. It will therefore be best to compare the average consumption of the years 1875–76 and 1876–77 with that of the years 1879–80 and 1880–81. It will be found that the increase has been universal. In Bengal, where the duty was reduced from Rs. 3-4 to Rs. 2-14 per maund, the average consumption has risen from 8,014,000 to 8,877,000 maunds, but there has been a loss of duty amounting to 48,000*l.* In Northern India where the duty was reduced from Rs. 3 to Rs. 2-8, and the place of levy removed from the customs line to the sources of production, the consumption has increased from 4,517,000 maunds to 6,155,000 maunds, and the duty levied from 1,334,000*l.* to 1,519,000*l.* In Madras and Bombay, which should be taken together, since the west coast of Madras is chiefly but not wholly supplied with salt from Bombay, while Madras chiefly but not wholly supplies Mysore and the Nizam's territory, the duty was raised from Rs. 1-13 to Rs. 2-8 ; nevertheless, the consumption has increased from 10,678,000 maunds to 10,923,000 maunds, and the duty from 2,001,905*l.* to 2,727,800*l.* For the whole of India the average annual consumption rose from 24,424,000 maunds in 1875–77 to 27,550,000 maunds in 1879–81, the revenue increasing at the same time from 5,996,000*l.* to 6,834,000*l.*

The maintenance and even increase of the consumption in spite of the increase of the duties in Madras and Bombay is remarkable. The increase of annual taxation which the measure involved was estimated at about two-pence a head, distributed over the year by almost daily instalments, each of them infinitesimally small. The fact appears to be that, when, in consequence of the abundance of supply and lowness of price, the people of a country have become accustomed to consume a considerable quantity of salt per head, a small increase in the cost of salt will have a very slight effect in altering their habits and diminishing the quantity which they consume, and will interfere little with the growth of consumption following increased population, and extended cheap railway transport.

Such considerations as these indicate another and a very important conclusion. It appears highly probable that if the policy that has been described is followed for some years to come, the average consumption per head of the population will increase in the other parts of India to an amount as high as that which already prevails in Madras and Bombay ; and that with a uniform duty throughout India, at a rate lower than the lowest now in force, and coincidently with a general reduction in the price of salt to the people, the revenue will become several millions larger than it is at the present time. If these anticipations should be fulfilled, the Government will have in its hands a financial engine of immense power ; for it will be able, for the purpose of meeting any serious emergency, to obtain temporarily, by a small increase of duty, a large increase of revenue, and this almost without the people being conscious that any addition has been made to their burdens. But these results will only be attained if we steadily persevere in the course that has lately been followed ; we must finally abandon the erroneous notion that it is profitable to levy the salt tax at a high rate on a restricted consumption, and resolve to act at all times on the only sound principle, that the interests of the people and of the public revenue are identical ; for we shall receive the largest possible revenue when the salt duties are low, and when the people throughout India obtain 'an unlimited supply of salt at the cheapest possible cost.' No time could be more favourable than the present for taking another step in this direction, by a large and general reduction in the salt duties. The condition of the finances is so prosperous that a temporary loss of revenue could well be afforded, but this would rapidly diminish, and the salt revenue would before long be in a far more satisfactory condition than any which has hitherto existed.

Although the wisdom of these reforms is plainly shown by their results, it must not be supposed that the increased consumption of salt and the improvement in the revenue have been exclusively due to the reduction and equalisation of the duties, and to the removal of the hindrances to trade caused by the inland customs line. The extension of railways, the general improvement in the means of communication, the opening out of new markets, and the increasing prosperity of the country, have all powerfully contributed to the results which have been obtained; and without support of this kind the policy which has been adopted could not have succeeded. Until the last few years the means of supply and transport throughout the greater part of India were most imperfect, and the quantity of salt available for consumption was limited by material causes, and not by the requirements of the people. So long as this was true, many of the essential conditions of success for a policy which aims at raising the salt revenue without placing any avoidable restrictions on the consumption of the country, were absent.

The amount of duty is obviously only one among the numerous causes by which the price of salt is affected, and it is clear that it can by no means be assumed that reduction of duty will always be at once followed by reduction of price; but it is equally clear that, although in some particular place and province the price of salt may be as high after the reduction of duty as it was before, this affords no evidence that the reduction was unwise. Whatever may happen for a time, it is certain that if trade be free, and the means of communication sufficient, every reduction of duty must ultimately contribute to a reduction of price and to an increase of consumption.

During the last eight years the average rate of duty for the whole of India has only varied between a minimum of Rs. 2·43 per maund in 1875–76 and a maximum of Rs. 2·56 per maund in 1878–79, the mean for the entire period being Rs. 2·48. It was in view of this that in the measures of the last four years, which aimed at establishing throughout India a uniform duty, the Government adopted as nearly as possible the existing average rate; thereby alike avoiding any loss of revenue which could not then be spared, and any increase to the average burden on the people. The rate fixed was therefore Rs. 2-8 per maund, equivalent to five eighths of a penny per pound. This rate is now in force everywhere except in the Trans-Indus territory of the Punjab, in the greater part of Lower Bengal and in British Burma.

Most of the salt produced Trans-Indus is exported into Afghanistan, and is charged with extremely low rates of duty for reasons chiefly of a political character. This, however, involves the maintenance of a customs line for some 400 miles along the Indus. There seems to be no sufficient reason for not raising the duty to the rate prevailing in the Punjab, which would enable the Government to get rid of this last fragment of the customs line.

The duty in Bengal, which is now Rs. 2-14 per maund, should be immediately reduced by 6 annas. Increase of consumption would soon make good the temporary loss of revenue. It must not be forgotten that the difference between the rate of duty levied on Liverpool salt in Bengal and that imposed on salt produced in Northern India was formerly 4 annas and is now 6 annas a maund. The Salt Chamber of Commerce of Cheshire and Worcestershire represented early in 1880 that Liverpool salt had thus been placed at an unfair disadvantage, and that it had been driven out of markets formerly supplied by it.[1] The latter statement is perhaps a mistake, but it is impossible to deny the general justice of the complaint. Lord Lytton was very anxious at the commencement of 1880–81 to apply an immediate remedy, but, pending further inquiry, this was delayed. It is impossible to defend the maintenance of this differential duty, and there can be no doubt that the Liverpool and the Indian salt ought, in respect of the rate of duty, to be placed on precisely the same footing.

In British Burma an important reform remains to be carried out. Salt is now taxed at the nearly nominal rate of three annas per maund. It has long been recognised by the most experienced local authorities that it would be highly desirable to abolish the present objectionable capitation tax, and impose a duty on salt at the Indian rate. A salt duty could not, while the population of the province remains small, produce so much revenue as the capitation tax, but it would replace it to a considerable extent. Indeed, there would probably be no loss at all, if the people of Upper Burma, who now obtain their chief supplies of salt from our

[1] See Financial Statement for 1880–81, paragraph 94.

territory, were obliged to contribute to our revenue by paying duty on the salt which they consume. 'I do not see,' Sir C. Aitchison, the Chief Commissioner, wrote in 1878, 'any objection to the enhancement of the salt duty in Burma. The ordinary objection to a tax on necessaries, as lowering the condition of the labouring classes, hardly applies to the present circumstances of the country. The standard of comfort of the labouring class is higher than in other Indian provinces. The rate of wages is very considerably higher, while the staple food of the working classes is not correspondingly dear. From certain calculations I have made of the relation of wages to the price of various staple articles of food, I estimate that, roughly speaking, a labouring man in Burma is twice as well off as his fellows in the North-Western Provinces, the Central Provinces, or the Punjab; he gets far more from his labour, and does not pay very much more for his food.'

No such enhancement of the salt duties is at the present time possible, because the British Government is obliged, by its treaty engagements, to supply salt to Upper Burma at the rate of 1 per cent. *ad valorem*, or about one-half pie, or a small fraction of a farthing, per maund. Upper Burma is almost entirely dependent on us for its salt supply, and, while the treaties remain in force, we could not largely increase the duty in our own territories without the certainty that our attempts to raise a higher revenue would be, to a great extent, frustrated by smuggling from Upper Burma. It is to be hoped that a revision of the treaties may before long remove this obstacle to an important fiscal reform, and meanwhile the subject ought to be kept in view by the Government.

Before leaving the subject of Salt, it must be observed that one great improvement still remains to be carried out. The salt department throughout India ought undoubtedly to be administered by the Supreme Government, and not by the Local Governments as is now the case in the greater part of India. The evils of divided management are strongly felt. There are, of course, some most important functions which the Local Governments can alone exercise; they alone can judge how far it is wise and right to enforce the salt laws in their absolute rigour; they alone can take care that the operation of the tax does not become oppressive, and they alone can suggest efficient measures for mitigating its severity by the improvement of the communications, by the encouragement of local manufacture, or other means of a local kind. But, without depriving the Local Governments of their jurisdiction, or exempting them from their obligations in such matters, justice to the taxpayers throughout India requires that the salt tax should be in the main regulated and administered by the Central Government.

The Salt Department is already administered directly by the Government of India in the North-Western and Central Provinces, Oudh, and the Punjab, and in Central India and Rajputana, and with most satisfactory results. Conflicts between the Local Governments and the Salt Department or the Central Government are unknown. It would be most desirable to apply the same procedure to the rest of India, and thus to utilise for the general advantage the experience gathered in various parts of the country. Another reason for making the administration of the salt revenue imperial is the fact that the revenue brought to account in each province is not the duty levied upon the consumption of salt within the province. Bombay supplies salt to Madras,

Bengal, the Central Provinces, and the Native States of Central India. Madras salt goes to Mysore and Hyderabad, as well as to the Central Provinces. The Imperial Government can alone administer the salt revenue with a view to the interests of those provinces where the salt is consumed as well as of those where it is produced. Difficulties and disputes have not unfrequently arisen from the contention of these interests.

The fact that the inland customs line was used, until the year 1878, for the purpose of levying duties on Sugar as well as on Salt, has been already referred to; and the abolition of these duties, which were more than once characterised as 'the most discreditable relic of the dark ages of taxation that exists in India,' must be mentioned among the useful measures of Lord Lytton's administration. The following description of them, and of the considerations which led to their extinction, is taken from Sir John Strachey's Financial Statement for 1877–78:—

'I have alluded to the duties levied on sugar exported across the inland customs line. These are one rupee per maund on refined sugar, and six annas per maund on unrefined sugar, or saccharine produce. Except where the line runs along the left bank of the Indus, exports across it are taken to Native States; but, when it passes the Indus, the sugar is merely taken from one part of British territory to another. This sugar is all the produce of our own people in the North-Western Provinces, Oudh, and the Punjab; it is one of the most important agricultural staples of those provinces; and it is important not only to agriculturists and manufacturers and consumers, but directly to the Government, which looks greatly to sugar cultivation for its irrigation revenue.

'While we are taxing heavily our own sugar grown on the east of the customs line for the supply of the country beyond it, we admit into the same country the Mauritius sugar, which is imported largely to Bombay, taxed at a much lower rate. It is calculated that the inland customs duty is equivalent to 10 per cent. on the value; but the incidence of the duty varies considerably, particularly on refined sugar. In the cheaper kinds the duty is equivalent to more than 20 per cent. on its value. The sea import duty on Mauritius sugar is 5 per cent. *ad valorem.* I do not assert that there is, at present, any great competition between the sugar of the upper provinces of this presidency and foreign sugar; but as far as competition exists, the inland customs duty acts as a protective duty in favour of foreign and against our own sugar; to this extent the duty must fall on the producer within the customs line. The competition will be more apparent and severe when the connection of the Rajputana State Railway with the Bombay and Baroda line is completed.

'Little or no sugar is grown in Rajputana or Central India; and the increase of price caused by the inland customs line must tend to diminish consumption, and so, still further, to injure the producer. It is impossible to estimate the injury to the people and to the Government caused by placing artificial obstructions on the export of one of the great agricultural staples of the country; and such obstructions obviously affect not only the export but the import trade as well. The Government of India has repeatedly urged upon Native States the policy of abolishing their transit duties, but it is difficult to see with what consistency we can do this, so long as we retain sugar duties. They yield about 165,000*l.* a year.'

These duties were altogether abolished on April 1, 1878, with the approval of everyone who could appreciate their mischievous and discreditable character. Arguments were used in their defence, it is true, founded on the belief that their existence was probably unknown to the sugar growers in our provinces, and that they were virtually paid by the consumers in Rajputana. But the ignorance of the peasants of the North-West Provinces did not affect the interference of the duties with the growth of sugar, nor did the incidence of charge on the people of Rajputana diminish the real obstruction they caused to the salt trade which, it was so important to develop.

CHAPTER XIV.

OPIUM.

OPIUM REVENUE HOW RAISED—MANUFACTURE IN BENGAL—EXPORT DUTY AT BOMBAY—MISTAKEN IDEAS AS TO UNCERTAINTY OF REVENUE—CAUSES OF FLUCTUATIONS—GREAT VARIATIONS IN SALES BEFORE 1867—NECESSITY FOR REGULARITY IN SUPPLY AND SALE—FORMATION OF RESERVE—VARIATIONS DUE TO CROP AND SEASON—INCOME STEADY AND INCREASING—CHARGES OF YEAR NOT PROPORTIONAL TO QUANTITY SOLD—EXCESS REPRESENTS VALUE OF RESERVE—CORRECTED NET INCOME—UNCERTAINTY CAUSED BY UNDER-ESTIMATE ORDERED BY SECRETARY OF STATE—IN PRESENT YEAR ONE-AND-A-HALF MILLION—RISKS ATTENDING OPIUM REVENUE FROM ENGLISH OPINION THAT TRADE IS IMMORAL—TRUE POSITION OF CHINA IN RELATION TO OPIUM—SIR THOMAS WADE'S TESTIMONY—ACCOUNT FROM SHANGHAI—FACTS DO NOT JUSTIFY INTERFERENCE—PROBABLE EFFECT OF SUBSTITUTING EXCISE FOR MONOPOLY—RELATIVE FISCAL RESULTS FROM BENGAL AND MALWA SYSTEMS—EQUIVALENT DUTY CORRESPONDING TO PRICE—IMPORTANCE OF MAINTAINING A RESERVE—POSSIBLE FURTHER EXTENSION OF CULTIVATION—AN ADVANTAGE TO BENGAL AGRICULTURE—OBJECTIONS TO REDUCED SALES—IMPORTANCE OF AVOIDING CHANGES OF POLICY IN ADMINISTRATION.

NEXT to the land revenue the most productive head of revenue in India is opium, the net receipts from which are now little less than 8,500,000*l.* a year. The greater part of this sum is derived from the opium exported to Eastern Asia, and chiefly to China. Less than 200,000*l.* is obtained from opium issued to the excise department for consumption in India.

The revenue from opium is raised in two ways. In Bengal a strict monopoly is maintained by the Government; the poppy may not be grown and opium may not be prepared except for the Government. The cultivation of the poppy is voluntarily carried on in certain districts, under a system of advances, without interference in details, nor is any pressure exercised for its promotion. Its extent depends chiefly on the increase or decrease of the price offered by the Government for the produce, the rate being regulated so as to secure the quantity required for manufacture. The crude opium thus obtained is carefully prepared at the Government factories, sent to Calcutta, and sold there by auction without reserve to the highest bidders. The quantity sold annually is now 56,400 chests, or 4,700 at each of the monthly sales which take place regularly throughout the year. The Government is pledged not to alter this quantity without giving at least twelve months' previous notice. The difference between the cost price of the opium and the auction price constitutes the revenue from Bengal opium.

Another part of the opium revenue is raised by the levy of a fixed duty on all opium exported from Bombay. This opium, commonly known as Málwa opium, is produced in the Native States of Central India. The British Government has no concern with either the cultivation of the poppy or with the preparation or transport of the drug; it exercises no control over the quantity exported, otherwise than by the levy of the duty on every chest of opium before its export from Bombay is allowed. The present rate of duty is Rs. 700 per chest. The average quantity annually exported is now about 45,000 chests.

Thus, rather more than half the total quantity of the opium exported from India is derived from the Government monopoly in Bengal, and rather less than half from the produce of the Native States of Central India.

There is a general impression that this source of

revenue is peculiarly uncertain, that its fluctuations have been extremely great, and that its maintenance is in a high degree precarious. That such opinions were fifteen or twenty years ago to some extent justified by the facts cannot be denied, but there is no room to doubt that nearly all the serious oscillations which at that time took place in the opium revenue were directly caused by administrative mistakes, and by the absence of any settled policy on the part of the Government. At the present time the only serious doubts in regard to the stability of the opium revenue are those suggested by the hostility of influential classes in England, a hostility inspired by respectable motives, but based on ignorance or complete misconception of the facts, though not for that reason less formidable.

Between 1794 and 1838, when the commercial monopoly of the East India Company was abolished, the gross opium revenue rose pretty steadily from an insignificant sum to more than 2,000,000*l.* sterling. In 1839 the first Chinese war took place; this caused a temporary depression, which, however, was of short duration. By 1842 the revenue had recovered its position, and it went on steadily and constantly rising until 1855–56, when it amounted to 5,197,000*l.* During this period there were only two fluctuations of importance; the first in 1847–48, when the second Chinese war reduced the revenue, for a single year only, by nearly 1,000,000*l.*, and the other in 1850–51, when the rebellion in China led to a not very serious disturbance in the regularity of its progress. Until 1855–56 no important branch of revenue could, in any country, have increased more steadily. The supply of opium brought to sale in Bengal had been gradually increased, the number of chests rising from 18,362 in 1842 to 33,561 in 1852. During this period the fluctuations of price were small. In 1843 the price per chest was Rs. 1,345 ; in 1852 it was Rs. 1,110.

After 1852 a great change came over the management of the opium department. For reasons which are not apparent, the system which had worked so satisfactorily was abandoned ; frequent vacillations of policy took its place, and then began the great fluctuations in the opium revenue from which came that reputation of precariousness which has not yet been lost, although under a better system it has ceased to be deserved.

In the three years following 1852 the sales were increased very rapidly, the number of chests sold in 1855 having been 53,319, an increase of nearly 20,000 chests in three years. In 1856 the number was again diminished to 41,492, in 1857 it was 43,903, in 1858 it was 32,676, in 1859 it was 27,173, in 1860 it was 21,363. After this the number of chests sold was raised again as rapidly as it had before been reduced. In 1861 it was 21,423, in 1862 it was 29,393, in 1863 it was 39,240, in 1864 it was 49,646, and in 1865 it was 64,111. In 1866 it was once more suddenly reduced to 40,000, and in 1867 raised again to 47,999.

That the violent fluctuations in the quantities sold during this period of twelve years should have been accompanied by equally violent fluctuations in the price at which the opium was sold was no more than might have been expected, a rise taking place as the quantity was reduced, and a fall as it was increased. Thus the price, which had fallen to Rs. 737 a chest in 1855, on the great increase of the sales in the two preceding years, rose to Rs. 1,871 in 1861,[1] with the great reduc-

[1] For three months in this year the prices were Rs. 2,280, Rs. 2,470, and Rs. 2,507.

tion of quantity, and fell again to Rs. 956 in 1865 with the next great increase. This time was one of constant and violent speculation in the export trade, caused almost entirely by the absence of any settled policy on the part of the Government as to the quantity offered for sale year by year, and the fluctuations in the opium revenue were, as a necessary consequence, very great also.

The gross revenue from Bengal opium was during this period as follows :—

Year	Revenue	Year	Revenue
1855-56	£4,172,000	1862-63	£4,813,000
1856-57	3,825,000	1863-64	5,347,000
1857-58	5,216,000	1864-65	5,255,000
1858-59	4,671,000	1865-66	6,390,000
1859-60	4,314,000	1866-67	4,948,000[1]
1860-61	4,200,000	1867-68	6,565,000
1861-62	3,914,000		

Its amount directly depended on the price and on the quantity of the drug brought into the market. The price in great measure followed the quantity, which depended on the extent of the crop and produce, and this in turn varied with the season and the area under cultivation. The opium crop is very much influenced by irregularities of season, which are incessant, while the area under cultivation at this time constantly changed, being regulated on no uniform system.

The true principles upon which the opium revenue ought to be administered were first clearly laid down by Sir Cecil Beadon, Lieutenant-Governor of Bengal, in a minute dated April 18, 1867. 'Vacillation or uncertainty,' he wrote, 'in regard to the quantity of opium to be provided and brought forward for sale, not only acts injuriously upon the market and encourages

[1] From a change in the commencement of the financial year, 1866-67 embraced only eleven months.

gambling, but deprives the State of the full profit of its monopoly, and causes great fluctuation in the revenue. It also deranges the condition of agriculture over a wide extent of country, and discourages the ryots from engaging in a cultivation which, though more profitable than that of ordinary crops, they may at any time be required to abandon. It is not desirable that the area under poppy cultivation should be in excess of what on an average of years is found sufficient to produce the desired quantity of opium. . . . If in any year the produce of opium exceeds the quantity which it is thought desirable to bring forward for public sale, the excess should be held as a set-off against the temporary increase of expenditure involved in its purchase, and as a reserve against failure in future seasons; but if in any year the crop be a short one, and there is no such reserve, the quantity to be brought forward for sale must of necessity be limited to the actual supply, and, though there may be some saving in the expenditure of the year, the net revenue must either decline or be maintained only by such an increase on the selling price as will stimulate competition from abroad. Unfortunately the vicissitudes of season are so great, and the crop so precarious, that it is impossible to estimate beforehand, within a range of several thousand chests, what the actual produce of a given area will be; but though the yield under the most favourable circumstances cannot exceed a certain limit, it may, under very unfavourable circumstances, such as a prolonged drought or the prevalence of hail-storms during the brief gathering season, be reduced almost to nothing.'

Sir Cecil Beadon showed that the quantity of opium brought to market ought to vary very little from year to year, and that with the maintenance of a permanent reserve, from which the deficiencies of bad seasons would be supplied, the regulation of this quantity could always be secured. He showed that the quantity sold ought to be determined by the price obtained, and that the price to be aimed at was one that should neither provoke the competition of foreign countries in the Chinese market, nor stimulate the production of opium in China itself. His conclusion, based on all available facts, was that Rs. 1,200 per chest might be looked on as a safe average price, but that anything much above this was dangerous to the revenue. He considered that at the time he wrote, in 1867, not less than 48,000 chests should be brought to sale annually, and that when a sufficient reserve stock had been accumulated this quantity ought to be gradually and cautiously increased. Thus, he believed, the stability and steady progress of the opium revenue would be insured. The wise policy recommended by Sir Cecil Beadon was accepted by the Government of India in 1867, and it has been acted upon ever since. Owing, however, to bad seasons, it was a long time before the necessary reserve stock could be collected, and it was not until 1875–76 that full effect could be given to the new system. Its introduction was completed by the notification of March 8, 1879, when the Government abandoned the system of varying yearly quantities, and announced that a certain fixed amount would be brought to sale every month, and that this amount would not be altered without due notice.

This policy has been highly successful, and there can be no doubt that the great and constant increase of the opium revenue for some years past has been to a large degree due to the steadiness of the supply brought into the market, which the accumulation of a reserve stock has rendered possible, and to the consequent comparative steadiness of price and diminution of mischievous speculation in the trade. The Government, in this respect, now acts on the principles which are universally observed in the supply of agricultural produce by prudent traders. A wine merchant, for instance, would find it impossible to carry on his business if he acted on the plan formerly followed by the opium department in India, and neglected to keep in store a stock sufficient to guard him against the accidents of season.

The foregoing observations refer exclusively to the Bengal opium revenue. The Bombay portion of the revenue has been much more stable. The quantity exported has not varied greatly or suddenly from year to year, while a fairly gradual increase has taken place. Nor have Bombay prices been subject to violent change, though they have been perceptibly affected by great fluctuations in the Bengal market, and have thus acted on the export trade, and therefore on the revenue. The uncertainties of the gross revenue receipts directly due to the want cf method in the Bengal administration during past years, have in this manner been not a little increased.

Whatever may have been the case before the present system was established, it is a complete error to suppose that the opium revenue has at the present time any special character of uncertainty; on the contrary, during the last twelve years there has been no branch of the revenue which has been generally more steady, and during the last five years its growth has been rapid.

The gross and net opium revenue in each year since 1869–70 have been, according to the published accounts, as follows:—

	Gross	Net
1869-70	£7,953,098	£6,132,387
1870-71	8,045,459	6,031,034
1871-72	9,253,859	7,657,187
1872-73	8,684,691	6,870,415
1873-74	8,324,879	6,323,395
1874-75	8,556,629	6,214,782
1875-76	8,471,425	6,252,026
1876-77	9,122,460	6,280,781
1877-78	9,182,722	6,521,337
1878-79	9,399,401	7,669,032
1879-80	10,319,162	8,249,808
1880-81	10,498,000	8,466,000

These figures show that the net revenue presents rather larger fluctuations than the gross, but that the progress of the revenue receipts has been in reality continuous and steady notwithstanding these fluctuations

The fact is often not duly appreciated that the fluctuations which, from time to time, are seen in the account of the net opium revenue are caused to a very great extent, not by fluctuations in the Chinese demand or in the price obtained, but by the greater or smaller out-turn of the crop, and the consequent variations in the expense of gathering it; that is to say, that they are often not due to fluctuations in the income, but in the charges upon it.

The greater part of the expenditure is due to the cost of purchasing and manufacturing the opium in Bengal. But (as was explained in Chapter V.) the actual expenditure in each year does not depend on and has no direct relation to the quantity of opium sold in that year. Advances on account of the crop are first made in August or September, when preparations for the sowings commence, and these advances are continued, from time to time, until all the opium is delivered, weighed, and taken over by the Government Opium Agent, that is, until May or June. It is evident that the expenditure must vary with the extent of the crop, and since the year of cultivation is not conterminous with the financial year, the expenditure incurred in the financial year is on account of two crops; the chief part of the expenditure on the crop actually sold in any financial year will have been incurred in the previous financial year, and the actual expenditure in the financial year chiefly depends on the character of the season commencing six months after the estimate is framed. The quantity of a crop depends entirely on the season, and the seasons are very variable. For instance, in 1875–76 and 1876–77 the seasons were favourable, and the amount of opium produced in each of these two years was about 72,000 chests, while in 1877–78, there was a poor crop, from which only 47,700 chests were manufactured. These facts were reflected in the expenditure incurred, which was 2,841,647*l.* in 1876–77, 2,661,266*l.* in 1877–78, and only 1,698,730*l.* in 1878–79. The result of these variations is seen in the recorded net revenue of the three years, which was as follows:—

1876-77 . . .	£6,280,781
1877-78	6,521,337
1878-79	7,699,032

It might be supposed from these figures that there had been in the last year a great and sudden increase in the demand for opium, but in reality there was no increase or fluctuation at all. The high net revenue of 1878–79 was due to the shortness of the crop and the consequent diminished expenditure, while the net revenue of 1876–77 and 1877–78 was greatly reduced by the bumper crops of the years next preceding.

If we adjust the expenditure to the real cost of the opium sold during the three years, we find that the real net revenue remained steady, as follows:—

1876–77	£7,069,533
1877–78	7,208,820
1878–79	7,276,610

It was before stated (as was explained in Chapter V.) that during the last twelve years we have paid 1,105,299*l.* more than the actual cost of the opium sold, and that this sum is represented by the reserve stock of Bengal opium actually existing at the end of 1880–81. Unless these facts are properly appreciated, it is not possible to understand the real position of the opium revenue, nor can any comparison be made between the amounts yielded in different years. Setting off each year the actual cost of the opium sold against the amount received from the sale, the real net revenue for each of the last twelve years has been as follows:—

1869–70	£6,170,484	1875–76	6,496,450
1870–71	6,117,919	1876–77	7,069,533
1871–72	7,161,438	1877–78	7,208,820
1872–73	6,829,225	1878–79	7,276,610
1873–74	6,468,395	1879–80	7,981,682
1874–75	6,583,164	1880–81	8,409,763

Going further back, and taking the figures as they appear in the published accounts, the progress of the net revenue during the last twenty years has been as follows:—

	Total net revenue.	Annual average.
1861–62 to 1865–66	£27,251,241	£5,450,248
1866–67[1] „ 1870–71	31,668,832	6,333,767
1871–72 „ 1875–76	33,317,805	6,663,561
1876–77 „ 1880–81	37,188,958	7,437,792

There has thus been a constant increase in the net revenue from opium, and the annual net receipts are now nearly 2,000,000*l.* more than they were twenty years ago. In the last three years the increase has

[1] In this year there were only eleven months, which reduces the annual average for the five years by about 100,000*l.*

been very marked; no reason is apparent why it should not be maintained.

These facts conclusively show that the opinion frequently expressed as to the instability and precarious character of the opium revenue is, so far at least as the present time is concerned, completely incorrect, and that no branch of the revenue has shown a more steady development. They show also that there has been no reason for the practice constantly followed for many years past, and constantly urged upon the Government of India by successive Secretaries of State, of greatly under-estimating the opium revenue in making the financial arrangements of the year. This practice has been the consequence of the mistaken ideas that have prevailed in regard to the instability of this branch of revenue, and those ideas have been encouraged by the constant divergences between the estimates and the actual receipts from opium, which are the necessary consequence of deliberate under-estimates. There is no single year since 1870–71 in which the opium estimate has not proved greatly too low. The deficiency in the estimate has never been less than 270,000*l.*, and its average amount in the last twelve years has been 941,000*l.* In the Budget estimates for 1881–82, lately published, the net opium revenue is estimated, in accordance with the Secretary of State's orders, at 6,500,000*l.* This is less than the average revenue of ten years ago; it is 1,500,000*l.* less than will probably be realised, and at least 1,000,000*l.* below what would have been an estimate of moderation and caution. There is no justification for continuing this practice.

Even if it be admitted that there is real cause for doubting whether the opium revenue will be permanently maintained on its present scale of productiveness, it cannot for a moment be asserted that any danger exists of its immediate and sudden collapse, and deliberately to under-estimate it is as great a mistake as deliberately to under-estimate any other branch of the revenue. It is, of course, impossible to speak with equal confidence of the future, but the Indian opium revenue runs, in my own opinion, one serious risk only, and this arises, not from any action likely to be taken in China, but from the well-meaning but misinformed prejudices of those people in England who believe it to be morally wrong that the Government should derive a large part of its income from such a source.

It is proved to demonstration that although excess in opium, so far as the effect on the individual consumer is concerned, is as bad as excess in alcohol, for it cannot be worse, opium is to the immense majority of the Chinese, who use it in moderation, as harmless as any other of the stimulants which enter largely into the consumption of the world. Excess in opium-smoking is less common in China than excess in drinking in Great Britain, and, however ruinous it may be to the individual, it is much less injurious to his neighbours. It destroys his health, but it does not lead to violence and to crime, and it seems certain that the consumption of opium in China is infinitely and beyond all comparison less productive of evil than the consumption of alcoholic drinks in our own country. So long as the principle of repression by the State in these matters is not accepted for our own countrymen, Englishmen should surely hesitate before they proceed to apply it arbitrarily to others.

Opium, like all other stimulants, is mischievous when taken in excess, and harmless or beneficial when taken, as it ordinarily is, in moderation. Evidence can be produced to any extent on both sides of this question, but it is not proposed to quote it. One fact, however, must be noticed which has an important bearing on the subject, because it has received little attention in the discussions regarding the results to which the moderate consumption of opium leads.

There has practically been very little restriction, either under the Native Governments or under our own, on the cultivation of the poppy in the Punjab, and there has always been a very large consumption of opium in the province, especially among the Sikhs, who are prevented by religious prejudices from smoking tobacco. The opium is chiefly consumed in the form of a decoction of the poppy heads called *post*. Its use, although general among the Sikhs, has never been asserted by any competent authority to be injurious; the people who use it are physically the first race in India, and it would be difficult to find finer-looking men in any part of the world. 'It is the abuse,' wrote the Financial Commissioner of the Punjab, 'not the use of the products of nature that deserves the condemnation of the moralist. From the poppy is extracted a valuable sedative, largely used by the Sikh nation, than whom there is not a people of India of finer physical development, of more manly character, more excellent health, or more prolonged life.' The same may be said, with little exaggeration, of the Chinese.

The common notion that China mainly depends on India for her supply of opium, and that if Indian opium ceased to be imported the Chinese would cease to consume the drug, is a complete delusion. India, Lord Mayo observed, possesses conditions of soil and climate which give her the monopoly of opium of the highest *cachet*. She is in this respect situated as France is in respect of wines. The superiority of her produce enables it to defy competition in the Chinese market, but the Chinese would no more give up the consumption of opium if the Indian supply were to fail, than the people of France would cease to drink wine if the rare vintages of Burgundy and Bordeaux were no longer to be produced. Opium was largely consumed in China long before the trade in Indian opium became important, and the belief that it was the introduction of large quantities of opium from India which led to the general use of the drug in China is altogether without truth. The richer classes in all parts of China, and more particularly in the maritime provinces, consume Indian opium, but the bulk of the opium-smoking population has always been dependent on the supplies produced at home. If everything that is said regarding the demoralisation of the Chinese by opium were true, instead of being, as it is, without foundation, the fact would remain that the total abandonment of the Indian opium revenue would confer no benefit upon China, for the consumption of opium would remain, for all practical purposes, as great and general as before.

Nor is there any solid foundation for the common belief that the Chinese Government is anxious to prohibit and discourage the cultivation and consumption of opium. It is doubtful whether at any time any serious objection was felt to it by the Chinese authorities on moral grounds, although these were often urged, as a matter of expediency, in their controversies with the British Government. It is historically false, although frequently asserted, that we have made war with China with the object of forcing our opium upon her against her will, and in spite of her protests that the opium trade was demoralising her people. The first Chinese war was caused by the desire of the Chinese Government to prevent the exportation of silver, which was believed to be impoverishing the country. The second war had nothing to do with opium. But, whatever may have been the case in former times, it is certain that there is now no wish on the part of the Chinese Government to put a stop to the trade. It obtains a large revenue from duties on Indian opium, and as this goes directly into the central treasury at Pekin, it is one of the most certain and highly-prized sources of the State income. It is far more difficult for the Central Government to get the benefit of the taxes levied by the provincial authorities on the home cultivation of the poppy. The Chinese Government sees that the Government of India derives an immense revenue from the opium exported to China, and it is naturally and not unreasonably anxious to obtain for itself a larger share of profit. This, and not the prohibition of the trade, is what it is really aiming at, and it would be right and politic for our Government to consider in a liberal spirit any proposals brought forward with this object, the adoption of which would not seriously injure Indian interests.

A very significant statement of the views of the Chinese Government was made by the ministers in January 1881 to Sir Thomas Wade, and quoted by the Marquis of Hartington in his speech on April 29 in the House of Commons. 'I went,' Sir Thomas Wade reports, 'on the 16th to speak of various matters. Four ministers received me. Adverting to opium, I observed that the authorities in some places were taxing opium, native and foreign; in others they were trying to increase both sale and consumption of both. Without at all denying the right of the Chinese Government to do as it chose, I said I should wish to know which course the Government approved. They said the question was embarrassing. The Chinese Government would be glad to stop opium smoking altogether, but the habit was too confirmed to be stopped by official intervention. No idea of abolishing the trade at present was in the mind of the Government. Alluding to the desire of well-disposed people at home to see England withdraw from the trade, I asked if it would be of any use to diminish yearly the exports from India. They said, so long as the habit exists, opium will be procured either from India or elsewhere. Any serious attempt to check the evil must originate with the people themselves.'

The conditions under which opium is produced and consumed in China, and the results of the introduction of Indian opium, have lately been described by a writer who is evidently well acquainted with all the facts, and possesses the great advantage of knowledge acquired on the spot; and his accounts are so full and to the point that it will be useful to quote them here:—

'The British public is told that England taught China to smoke opium, and thereafter insisted upon supplying her with the drug at a handsome profit to the Government of India, at first whether the Chinese Government would or not, and latterly by virtue of a tariff rule legalising its importation attached to the Treaty of Tientsin, which was extorted from the terrified Chinese commissioners by force of arms; that Lord Elgin, in extorting the permission through his secretaries, was simply carrying out the brutal and bullying policy of the English Government of the day, whose servant he was, but that the policy itself was to him distasteful and to the Chinese plenipotentiaries odious; that the production and consumption of opium by its subjects have always been abhorred by the Chinese Government, and that they have shown this by their persistent and consistent efforts, at all times and in all provinces, to root up the poppy crops; that, deeply sensible of the evils which opium-smoking entails on the country, they have ever been vigilant to minimise the mischief by limiting the consumption to the amount of the Indian drug imported; that the whole policy and the only policy of the Chinese Government with regard to native opium has been and is one of hostility, prohibition, and punishment; that these efforts are rendered futile and this policy is paralysed by the increased importation of the Indian drug; and that, in sum, Christian England, turning a deaf ear alike to the prayers of the Chinese Government and the groans of the people, is directly responsible for the slow poisoning of heathen China.

'Now the instincts of an ordinary Englishman, whether with regard to his family, his country, or the world generally, are in the main those of the *bonus paterfamilias* of the Roman Law, and an accusation of this kind brought against his country, especially when reiterated with all the fervour of religion and the vehemence of burning truth, will certainly arrest his attention. Neither the fervour nor the vehemence has of late been wanting. The proceedings of the society whose gospel I have just given are rapidly reaching the stage of organised agitation, and as public opinion in England, given the initial impetus, forms and shapes itself with dangerous rapidity, this question of the Indian opium revenue may come prominently before Parliament and the country at any time. To help my countrymen to decide whether we are as a nation the immoral wretches the anti-opium society say we are, I have been at some pains to collate certain broad facts regarding the production and consumption of opium in China, a knowledge of which will tend to illumine the question by the light of common sense.

'The habit of opium-smoking is common all over China, but it is in the West, in the comparatively unknown half of China west of the 110th meridian, that it is most prevalent. In some parts of Western Hu Pei and Eastern Szechuen it is all but universal; there are few adults in any station of life who do not take an occasional whiff, and the very streets of the towns and villages reek with opium fumes. The practice is there indulged in in the most open manner, and no more stigma or disgrace attaches to it than to smoking tobacco. Mr. Watters, Her Majesty's Consul at Ichang, made careful inquiries last year into the origin of the practice, and he found that it had been indulged in for several hundred years, long before either the present reigning dynasty or foreign merchants and their opium were ever dreamt of. The custom, generations ago, passed into the family *sacra*, and at funerals in the West of China, among other gifts which are transmitted into the next world, by burning paper fac-similes of them in this, for the solace of the departed, is a complete set of opium-smoking requisites—pipe, lamp, needle, &c. By the people themselves the habit, so far from being regarded as a curse, is looked on as *sine quâ non* for a Chinaman who wishes to make the best of both worlds. The whole of the opium consumed in the West is locally produced, and Indian opium does not come higher up the Yangtsze than the districts contiguous to the port of Hankow, nor is it imported by any channel into Western Hu Pei, Szechuen, or the other provinces of the West. Above and beyond the enormous quantity there grown for local use there is a large trade in the drug, mostly contraband, from West to East. Indian opium is consumed in the provinces adjacent to the treaty ports, and, being an expensive article as compared with native opium, is mostly smoked by the well-to-do classes. The common people in these provinces smoke the native drug, which is either grown on the borders of Kiang Su and Ho Nan or is smuggled overland from the West. All Western China, therefore, and the lower classes in Eastern China smoke native-grown opium, and it is most important for English people who are asked at meetings to say whether they think Indian opium is forced by our Government on the Chinese or not to know to what extent and under what official conditions the production of native opium is carried on.

'Regarding the opium districts of Eastern China—that is, the borderland of Chih Li, Ho Nan, Shantung, and Kiang Su—I have no personal knowledge. But with the West, and especially the section of it I have mentioned as the centre both of consumption and production of the native drug, I have not only had some acquaintance myself, but I have lately been able to avail myself of the experience of the two Englishmen who have had the best opportunities and means of procuring information regarding the native opium of the West—Mr. Colborne Baber, who was for four years Consular Agent in Szechuen watching the trade there, and Mr. Watters, who was our Consul at Ichang, the port of Western Szechuen, until the other day. I can, therefore, speak with authority and confidence. The production of opium in Szechuen has been exceedingly underestimated hitherto. Mr. Davenport gives it as 50,000 chests for 1878, basing his estimate probably on Chinese official information. But all such statistical information on this point is misleading. I have been assured by officials both of Szechuen and Kweichow that for every *picul* (133 lbs.) of opium returned to the Government, 2½ to 3 *piculs* are produced and sold contraband. Mr. Baber, living and travelling among the Szechuen people, has been able to hear and see for himself, and he has obtained ample evidence that the production of Chinese opium in this one province is greater than the whole Indian crop, Malwa, Patna, and Benares put together. Of the amount produced in the hill country of Hu Pei, Mr. Watters has not been able to give me any figures, but he says that in Ichang alone there is an opium restaurant to every thirteen inhabitants, where nothing is consumed except the native drug, produced in one or other of the four western provinces, and that in the outlying parts of the two adjacent prefectures the officials admit of a production, on which they receive revenue, of 2,000 *piculs*. All over Western China the conditions of poppy culture, as far as the officials are concerned, are those of perfect freedom, and even open encouragement. All the grower has to think of is his profit. Opium is a more risky crop than cereals, but it pays seven times as well. If he chooses to run the risk of a failure in the crop, or of inability to buy rice with the money he gets for his opium, he is at liberty to grow opium if he likes. In ordinary circumstances a poppy crop subjects the grower to no interference on the part of his officials beyond paying the customary taxes: and in many districts where opium in manufacture or transit is the sole source of revenue its culture is encouraged.

'There is one risk, however, which the native grower of the poppy must take into account, although it is a small one, and that is the risk of destruction of his crop by an official in some part of whose jurisdiction there may be a famine. When cereals fail in China the places which have, cannot come to the relief of those which have not, and neither money nor opium can be exchanged for bread, owing to the defective means of inter-communication in the country. It is customary in such circumstances to order the rooting up of the poppy crop, and the orders are carried out in proportion to the sincerity and energy of the official. But as soon as the time of scarcity is past the poppy is allowed to bloom over the land again, and the reforming official, whose thorough-going patriotism has in the meantime been reported to and dilated on by the anti-opium society, reaps the usual reward in an enhanced revenue. Proclamations against the culture of the poppy, whether emanating from high or low officials, the grower may at all times disregard or 'contract' himself out of by valuable consideration in the shape of bribes. During the past twelve years I can only recollect one case where a crusade against the poppy was carried on by an honest and a determined reformer with a single eye to the good of his country, and being honest and determined he was thoroughly successful, as a local official in China must be in any legitimate scheme of local government he may choose to enforce with energy.

'Regarding the effect of opium on the Chinese nation, there is by no means a consensus of opinion that it is thoroughly bad. That it enslaves, enfeebles, and may kill all who take it in excess is incontestable. That it impoverishes all except the well-to-do is equally incontestable. But there are two things that may be said in favour of it. As it is a pleasure, or a vice, which it is quite possible to enjoy moderately, the vast majority of smokers take their opium as most Scotchmen do their whisky—in moderation; and a Chinaman stupefied is a much less terrible person than a Scotchman drunk.

'Be this as it may, so long as the Chinese do not interfere with the production of opium within their own borders in any manner which can be considered either genuine in purpose or effective in deed, the question of the supply by India to China of opium hardly comes within the domain of practical politics. So long as the Chinese not only allow the free cultivation of the poppy by their people, whether in the west or the east of China, but regard native-grown opium as a valuable and legitimate source of revenue, the cry that England is forcing opium on

China is unfair and untrue, and statements such as that made by a now responsible member of the present Government, that 'the opium traffic gravely imperils our friendly relations with the Chinese Empire,' are unmeaning. The present attitude of the central and provincial Governments of China regarding native opium, as judged by their acts and forbearances, not their words, and the present state of poppy cultivation in Western China, must be taken into account by anyone who wishes to decide for himself the question which the Society for the Suppression of the Opium Trade is placing before the country; and the society itself, in not fully informing itself of either one or the other, seems to be basing its case more on the sands of prejudice than on the rocks of truth.'

In a subsequent communication the same writer makes the following statements :—

'All over the west of China, in the provinces of Szechuen, Kweichow, and South-Western Hu Pei, opium cultivation is everywhere tolerated, and in most places encouraged by the provincial officials. The production there is not only sufficient for the entire consumption of a population among whom the habit of opium-smoking is universal and who have never even heard of Indian opium, but is leaving a yearly increasing surplus for the supply of the east. Although this is mostly carried from west to east in a contraband manner, the quantity sent is enormous and is driving out the Indian drug in the inland cities of this and the neighbouring provinces. Two travellers, missionaries belonging to the China Inland Mission, have recently arrived from Bhamo, on the upper Irrawady. They report the province of Yunnan to be rapidly recovering from its state of waste and desolation, and the universal form of the new cultivation to be a winter crop of opium. In February last the province was ablaze with poppies. The fact is that the supply of opium from India is a small part of the total consumption of this country; it is mainly obtained from her own fields, and the cultivation of and trade in the drug are participated in by the Government of the country, in the west at least, in the most open manner. Under the circumstances, the language which the Government at Pekin have recently

should be to give up the Bengal monopoly and throw open the trade. An export duty could not possibly be regulated with that undeviating maximum severity of pressure which a monopoly secures. If it is legitimate, then it is also desirable, that we should obtain from opium the highest possible revenue, and this end can only be attained by a monopoly. If, on the other hand, it be true that the interests of morality are involved, then those interests and the interests of the treasury coincide in demanding the maintenance of the monopoly. For to abandon the monopoly would be to sacrifice a great revenue with the probable result of a speedy development of the opium exports. In either case the substitution of a monopoly of Málwa opium for the present export duty, under conditions suitable to the joint interests of the British and Native Governments, would be preferable.

As a consequence of the discussion on the Opium question in the House of Commons last session, the Secretary of State has lately invited the attention of the Government of India to the general position of this branch of the revenue, more particularly with reference to the possibility of transforming the present monopoly in Bengal into a system of excise. The question is not a new one, and until now the suggestion referred to has received very little support in India. My own opinion is decidedly adverse to entertaining it, but beyond what has been said on the general subject it is not necessary now to go.

The question of the relative fiscal advantages to British India of the Bengal and Málwa systems is one of great importance, and the facts on which the answer to the question depends will be explained.

A chest contains, everywhere, the same gross weight of opium—namely a fraction over 140 lbs. avoirdupois weight. This is equal to a Chinese *picul* ($133\frac{1}{3}$ lbs.), plus 5 per cent. which is appropriated by the middlemen in trade perquisites. The different chests, however, contain different weights of what is technically called 'fine[1] opium,' as follows:—

	lbs. avoirdupois.
A chest of Behár, consistence 75, made at Patna contains .	105·107
A chest of Benares, consistenee 70, made at Gházipur contains	98·1

The 'consistence' is the percentage of 'fine opium,' excluding all water. The weight of fine opium in a chest of Málwa opium varies, because this opium is not prepared and packed under any responsible supervision or upon any uniform system; but the fixed rate of duty favours a high consistence, and it is usually assumed that Málwa opium contains from 90 to 95 per cent. of fine opium. At the lower of these two consistencies, a chest contains 126·128 lbs. In other words, a chest of Behár opium contains, at most, ·83, and a chest of Benares opium, at most, ·78, of the contents of a chest of Málwa opium.

Thus, in order that the three kinds of opium might contribute, equally, to the British Indian Treasury, it would be necessary that, for every Rs. 100 of duty levied on a chest of Málwa opium, a profit of, at most, Rs. 83-5-4 should be obtained on a chest of Behár opium, and a profit of, at most, Rs. 77-12-5 on a chest of Benares opium.

The actual cost of a chest of Behár opium, including a liberal allowance for interest on the capital employed,

[1] 'Fine opium' is opium dried to powder on a steam table at 200° Fahr., and then weighed whilst a little warm, *i.e.*, before moisture can be reabsorbed from the atmosphere.—*Opium Manual*, 1875 edit., paras. 68 and 73.

and for all indirect charges, is Rs. 436, and of a chest of Benares opium Rs. 373.[1]

The following table shows the least duty which it would be necessary to levy on a chest of Málwa opium to obtain from it a revenue as large as that derived from a chest of Bengal opium at various prices :—

Price of a chest of		Corresponding Duty on a chest of
Behár opium.	Benares opium.	Málwa opium.
Rs.	Rs.	Rs.
936	840	600
978	879	650
1,019	917	700
1,061	956	750
1,103	995	800
1,144	1,034	850
1,186	1,073	900
1,228	1,112	950
1,269	1,151	1,000
1,311	1,190	1,050
1,353	1,229	1,100
1,394	1,267	1,150
1,436	1,306	1,200
1,478	1,345	1,250
1,519	1,384	1,300

With these facts before us, we must remember in proceeding further to consider the fiscal advantages of the two systems, that, apart from the direct revenue which reaches the treasury, the cultivation of the poppy, both in Behár and in the North-Western Pro-

[1] *Cost of a chest of Behár opium.*

	Rs.
68 seers 2 chittacks opium @ 75% consistence = 73 seers @ 70% consistence,—@ Rs. 5 a seer . . .	365
Cost of manufacture and packing, interest on capital, percentage for pensions and leave allowance of officers, &c. .	71
	436

Cost of a chest of Benares opium.

68 seers 2 chittacks @ 70% consistence,—@ Rs. 4-8 a seer .	307
Miscellaneous items as before	66
	373

vinces, is, notwithstanding the monopoly, very profitable to the agricultural population directly engaged in it, and to the landholders who obtain a high rent for land upon which the poppy is grown. This is an established fact, denied by no one. The cultivation is extremely popular, and there is no doubt that it leads to no objectionable consumption of opium by the people who carry it on.

On the other hand, although we fix the export duty on Málwa opium at our discretion, we have never objected to the Native States in which the opium is produced obtaining revenue from this source. Opium has always been one of the chief branches of their income. It is impossible to say how much per chest is, on an average, thus levied; we do not know the true cost of the production of a chest of opium in Málwa; and the numerous Native States concerned impose their dues partly in the shape of increased revenue upon lands on which the poppy is cultivated, and partly as transit duties. If it should be found possible, at some future time, to substitute for the present system in Málwa a monopoly, the profits of which might be divided in suitable proportions between the British Government and the Native States, there would be great advantages in the change; but there are serious difficulties to overcome before it could be made.

Meanwhile, it is clear that, chest for chest, the Bengal opium monopoly yields us much more revenue than the Málwa export duty, so that we gain largely upon every chest of Bengal opium which is substituted for Málwa opium. This may be shown as follows:— About 45,000 chests of Málwa opium are now exported yearly, upon which we levy, at the present rate of duty (Rs. 700 a chest), 3,150,000*l.* At the rates obtained at the sale held in November, 1880, in Calcutta, the profits on the same quantity of Behár opium would have been 5,081,400*l.*, and of Benares opium 5,635,300*l.*[1] Even at the much lower average prices of the whole year 1879–80, the profits would have been, at Behár prices, 4,158,000*l.* and at Benares prices, 4,402,000*l.*[1] These calculations include the recent increase in the price paid for Behár crude opium, and all indirect charges.

Significant as these figures are, they do not tell the whole tale. There is every reason to believe that the taxation of Málwa opium by the Native States is not sufficient to make the whole burden upon it equal to that borne by Bengal opium under the monopoly. To whatever extent the aggregate British and native duties on Málwa opium fall short of the Bengal monopoly profits, the Málwa opium must compete on unfairly favourable terms with Bengal opium, and the tendency of this competition must be to reduce the Bengal monopoly profits.

Accordingly, the established policy, in the management of the opium revenue, is to regard our chief interest as concentrated in the Bengal monopoly, and to regulate our action in respect to Málwa opium with

[1] Thus calculated:—

45,000 chests @ 90 % consistence = 54,000 chests @ 75 % = 57,857 chests @ 70 % consistence.

	At the sale in Nov. 1880.		During the whole year 1879-80.	
	Behár.	Benares.	Behár.	Benares.
	Rs.	Rs.	Rs.	Rs.
Average price of a chest . .	1,377	1,347	1,206	1,134
Cost price	436	373	436	373
Profits	941	974	770	761

54,000 chests × 941 = Rs. 5,08,14,000 and × 770 = Rs. 4,15,80,000
57,857 chests × 974 = Rs. 5,63,53,000 and × 761 = Rs. 4,40,29,000

a primary regard to that interest. For this reason, on a comparison of the prices of Málwa and Bengal opium, the duty on Málwa opium was raised, in July, 1877, by Rs. 50 a chest, and, again, in September, 1879, by another Rs. 50 a chest. The export duty on a chest of Málwa opium is now Rs. 725 when paid at Ajmír[1] and Rs. 700 when paid elsewhere. At present Bengal prices, a chest of Málwa opium is taxed Rs. 429 less than an equal quantity of Behár opium, and Rs. 552 less than the same quantity of Benares opium.

The high level of Bengal prices which has lately prevailed has been regarded as to some extent accidental, and to it has been attributed the dulness of the Málwa trade. A further increase to the Málwa duty was therefore not proposed. But, if present Bengal prices should be maintained, and, especially, if the Málwa trade should revive without a simultaneous collapse of Bengal prices, there is no doubt that the duty on Málwa opium should be further increased.

It is difficult to lay down any principle upon which to fix the difference which should be allowed in favour of Málwa opium as a margin for Native State taxation, but probably it need not, under existing conditions, be more than Rs. 250 a chest; that is to say, the duty on Málwa opium should, as a rule, exceed the present rate of Rs. 700 in the proportion of Rs. 100 for every Rs. 83-5-4 by which the permanent average price of Behár opium exceeds Rs. 1,228 a chest. On the other hand, the existing duty of Rs. 700 need not be reduced unless the average price of Behár opium falls permanently below Rs. 1,186 a chest.

The policy of maintaining a reserve of Bengal opium,

[1] The exports from Ajmír are insignificant. The duty there is enhanced, because we do not wish to divert opium to Ajmír from the neighbouring Native States.

in order to prevent fluctuations in the supply sold month by month, has already been described, and is not now, it is hoped, likely to be seriously questioned; but there is still enough speculation in the opium trade to make it probable that, from time to time, pressure will be put upon the Government to induce it to revert to the plan of yearly notifications, with all its attendant inconveniences. A deaf ear should be turned to all such demands. The chief hope of getting rid of the speculative element in the trade lies in a steady perseverance in the system of fixed monthly sales, subject to as unfrequent variations as possible.

The Government of Bengal has sometimes been disposed to favour a dangerous reduction in the amount of the opium reserve. Such influences also should be resisted. Tne minimum reserve on December 31 should be 30,000 chests, besides the whole of the crop last gathered, and a still larger reserve might be desirable. The reserve on December 31, 1880, was only 25,183 chests, and it is not yet clear that it will be possible to maintain permanently the present fixed monthly sales of 4,700 chests; experience only can decide this.

The supply of Bengal opium should certainly be developed to whatever extent may be found possible. This matter has, from time to time, received much attention. Some years ago, the Opium Agent at Gházipur was deputed to inquire whether the poppy could be profitably cultivated in the Punjab and Sindh. His reports were not encouraging, and, according to present information, it seems likely, not only that the production of Bengal opium cannot be much increased, but that in order to maintain the present production, it may be necessary to increase the price paid to the cultivators for crude opium. The price was raised in 1880 in the Behár Agency, from Rs. 4–8 to Rs. 5 a seer of 70 per cent. consistence. There should be no hesitation about any needful increase of price, as occasion arises.

The views of those who object on economical grounds to the extension of the cultivation of opium need not be discussed at length. About 500,000 to 550,000 acres of land are now cultivated with poppy in Bengal, on much of which a second crop is grown. The poppy takes the place, for the most part, of garden crops, not of cereals. The appropriation of half or three-quarters of the productive capacities of half a million of acres, or, say, including Málwa, of a million of acres or more to this valuable commodity, is far from being a matter for regret upon economic principles; on the contrary, the discovery of fresh staples, other than food crops, which can be profitably grown in India, a country so essentially dependent on its agricultural produce, is a constant desideratum.

It has been contended by some authorities that a larger net revenue would be obtained by the sale of a limited supply of Indian opium at a higher price, than by the sale of a larger supply at a lower price. It is not worth while to examine this hypothesis. The Government of India wisely concluded, many years ago, as already noticed, that its opium revenue would be endangered if the price of Bengal opium should rise, for any length of time, above Rs. 1,200 a chest; but, with all its efforts to extend the cultivation and discourage speculation, it has not been able to prevent this limit being constantly passed. It can hardly be conceived that the Government of India will ever be so foolish as to restrict its opium exports otherwise than under necessity.

In conclusion, it must be urged that the opium revenue should be directly administered by the Government of India itself, and that, while the co-operation of the local governments should be encouraged and even insisted upon, these Governments should not interpose between the Government of India and the Opium Agents. The care and ability with which the Government of Bengal has discharged its duties in respect to the management of this department is fully acknowledged; but its hands are full of other work, and an increasing proportion of the Bengal opium is produced beyond the limits of Bengal. The interests at stake are so vast, and the risk of some misunderstanding, involving a disturbance of established policy, is so considerable, that it cannot be doubted that the management of the opium revenue should be in the immediate charge of the Government of India, every precaution being taken to preserve its traditional policy unbroken.

Illustrations could be given of the dangers to which the opium revenue is exposed. On one occasion, not very long ago, orders were actually issued for the reduction of the cultivation in Bengal, which, if they had not been cancelled, would in all probability have prevented the formation of the long contemplated reserve and the recent large increase of the revenue. It is very desirable that, while leaving all needful freedom to the Government of India as to details, Her Majesty's Government should peremptorily forbid any innovation in the management of this department without the previous sanction of the Secretary of State in Council. The conservative instincts of the India Office would in this case have a very valuable influence.

CHAPTER XV.

THE CUSTOMS DUTIES.

GENERAL RATES OF DUTY BEFORE 1875—REDUCTIONS MADE BY LORD NORTHBROOK—PUBLIC OPINION IN INDIA INDIFFERENT OR UNFAVOURABLE TO FREE TRADE—LORD SALISBURY'S ORDERS FOR REMOVAL OF IMPORT DUTIES ON COTTON GOODS—DECLARATION OF PRINCIPLES BY LORD LYTTON'S GOVERNMENT IN 1878—SPECIAL IMPORTANCE OF FREE TRADE TO INDIA—DIFFICULTY OF FRAMING AN UNOBJECTIONABLE CUSTOMS TARIFF—REMOVAL OF IMPORT AND EXPORT DUTIES IN 1878 AND 1880—DUTY ON RICE ALONE REMAINS AMONG EXPORTS—LORD SALISBURY'S ARGUMENTS FOR REMOVAL OF COTTON DUTIES—HIS ORDERS REPEATEDLY CONFIRMED BY HOUSE OF COMMONS—FIRST STEP TAKEN BY EXEMPTION OF GOODS WITH WHICH INDIAN MILLS COULD COMPETE—FURTHER EXEMPTIONS IN 1879—THEIR EFFECT—ENORMOUS INCREASE OF IMPORTS OF DUTY-FREE GOODS—INCREASED PROSPERITY OF INDIAN MILLS—NECESSITY FOR EARLY EXTENSION OF REMISSIONS TO ALL GREY GOODS—AFTER WHICH COMPLETE EXEMPTION SHOULD FOLLOW—REMAINING CUSTOMS DUTIES THEN OF SMALL IMPORTANCE—ALL INDIAN PORTS SHOULD BE THROWN OPEN.

GREAT changes were made during the Viceroyalty of Lord Lytton in the customs tariff, and in the practice which the Government of India had previously followed in regard to its commercial policy. The merits of those changes have been, and will be, very differently estimated, but no one doubts their importance. They must produce, for good or evil, great effects on the commercial and manufacturing interests of India, and on the financial position of the Government.

There has been much acrimonious discussion of these questions, and much has been said in the heat of controversy, which reasonable men will agree had better be forgotten. In order to avoid the repetition of such errors, it is desirable to enter as little as possible into fresh argument, but rather to give a dispassionate account of what has been done or proposed, and of the results actual or anticipated.

It is not necessary to follow, in any detail, the history of the commercial legislation of India during the last ten or twenty years. It has already been referred to in Chapter II. Until 1860 almost everything imported or exported was taxed. In 1860 the general rate of duty on imports was 10 per cent. *ad valorem*, and on exports 3 per cent. Various changes, of which some only of the more important need be noticed, were subsequently made from time to time. In 1864 the general rate of duty on imports was reduced from 10 to 7½ per cent. Between 1860 and 1867 many articles were exempted from export duty, and in the latter year a large number of minor articles were placed on the free list of imports. In 1871 the articles subject to export duty were reduced to eight in number,—cotton goods, grain, hides, indigo, lac, oils, seeds and spices.

In 1875 important changes in the tariff were made by the government of Lord Northbrook. The general rate of duty on imports was reduced from 7½ to 5 per cent., and the only articles which remained liable to export duty were rice, indigo and lac. This was the state of things when Lord Lytton became Viceroy.

In his speech in the Legislative Council, on the 5th August, 1875, Lord Northbrook gave an explanation of the general views which he held on the subject of customs duties in India. He in no way expressed approval of customs duties in themselves as a means of raising revenue in India. He accepted them as the lesser of two evils, and did not disguise his regret that in his opinion circumstances prevented him from carrying out thoroughly in India those principles of free trade, the universal truth of which he fully recognised. In this aspect of the subject there was little or no difference between the principles of Lord Northbrook and those of Lord Lytton, although there was a wide difference in the action taken by them. While Lord Northbrook admitted the objections to which customs duties were open, he considered that we could not afford to abandon the revenue which they yielded, and that as it was impossible to replace them by other taxes which would not be more objectionable, they must be retained.

These views found general acceptance in India both among the official and unofficial classes. As a general rule, subject to rare exceptions, few people in India think much about economic questions, and public opinion regarding them is almost always in favour of the policy of leaving things alone, which too often is also the most ignorant and unenlightened policy. This reproach has no special applicability to India, for, excepting perhaps England, there are few countries which do not equally deserve it. Hence the practical application to the Indian customs tariff of free trade principles might have been delayed for an indefinite period, however satisfactory had been the general condition of our finances, had not the interests of the English manufacturers of cotton goods forced the matter into prominence.

Whether it might not be right to impose fresh taxes for the purpose of getting rid of the cotton duties, or other parts of the Indian customs tariff, if they could be got rid of in no other way, is a question on which opinion differs, but it need not now be discussed. Lord

Salisbury, when he was Secretary of State for India, and Lord Lytton as Viceroy, repeatedly declared that no such course would be adopted by the Government. Nor was it suggested by those who thought it might have been legitimate, because they were satisfied that these and other necessary fiscal reforms could be carried out without fresh taxation. This anticipation has been justified by the event.

Lord Salisbury, however, was not satisfied with Lord Northbrook's conclusions. In a despatch dated May 31, 1876, he declared his conviction that the true interests of India, as well as the legitimate claims of English industry, required a reconsideration of the matter; that the complete removal of the duties on cotton goods was essential as soon as the condition of the finances would allow, and that they could not be relied upon as a permanent source of revenue.

Lord Lytton was prepared to act in complete accordance with these views, and if his Government had not fallen upon evil times of famine and of great financial disturbance caused by the depreciation of the value of silver, there would now be no cotton duties, and not many other customs duties, in India. It was not until the beginning of 1878 that any action became possible, when an important step was taken by the public definition and authoritative declaration of the principles, which the Government adopted and intended to carry out gradually as circumstances allowed. This declaration was made in Sir John Strachey's financial statement for 1878–79, as follows:—

'The Government deems it right to place on record the principles on which its action is at the present time guided, and by which it desires to be guided in the future.

'It is not necessary now to discuss the advantages to a

country of free trade and the disadvantages of protective duties. It is sufficient to say that these have been admitted for many years by the statesmen who, of whatever party, have guided the policy of the United Kingdom. In pursuance of the principles thus accepted, the tariff of the United Kingdom, which, less than thirty years ago, subjected to duty more than one thousand different articles, has been brought down by various stages to some half dozen, of which the only important ones are wine and spirits, tea and tobacco. At the same time all export duties have been abolished.

'The principles on which the customs legislation of the United Kingdom has been based are now admitted axioms by all who recognise the theoretic advantages of free trade. They must be regarded as a part of the national policy which Great Britain has finally adopted, and which the Secretary of State for India, with the deliberate approval of the House of Commons, has required the Government of India in this country to carry out.

'These principles are, as regards imports:—

'1. That no duty should exist which affords protection to native industry; and, as a corollary, that no duty should be applied to any article which can be produced at home, without an equivalent duty of excise on the home production; also, that no duty should be levied except for purely fiscal purposes.

'2. That, as far as possible, the raw materials of industry and articles contributing to production should be exempt from customs taxation.

'3. That duties should be applied only to articles which yield a revenue of sufficient importance to justify the interference with trade involved by the machinery of collection.

'As regards exports—that duties should be levied on those commodities only in which the exporting country has practically a monopoly of production.

'These principles are of general application; but, in the case of India, they possess a peculiar significance. India is a country of unbounded material resources, but her people are a poor people. Its characteristics are great power of production, but almost total absence of accumulated capital. On this account alone the prosperity of the country essentially depends on its being able to secure a large and favourable outlet for its surplus produce. But there is a special feature in the economic conditions of India which renders this a matter of yet more pressing, and even of vital importance—this is the fact that her connection with England, and the financial results of that connection, compel her to send to Europe every year about 20,000,000*l.* sterling worth of her products without receiving in return any direct commercial equivalent. It is this excess of exports over imports which, in the language of the economists, is described as tribute. It is really the return for the foreign capital, in its broadest sense, which is invested in India, including under capital not only money, but all advantages which have to be paid for—such as the intelligence, strength and energy on which good administration and commercial prosperity depend. From these causes the trade of India is in an abnormal position, preventing her receiving, in the shape of imported merchandise and treasure, the full commercial benefit which otherwise would spring from her vast material resources.

'The comparatively undeveloped condition of the trade of India may be illustrated by the following figures:—The value of the imports and exports, taken together, per head of the population is in the United Kingdom about 20*l.* In British India it is about 10*s.* The customs revenue on the few articles now retained in the import tariff of the United Kingdom is about 12*s.* per head; while that of India, on all the articles of its lengthy tariff, is about 3*d.*, showing that small as is the proportion of the foreign trade of India to that of England, the proportion of customs revenue derived from it is smaller still.

'Here then is a country which, both from its poverty, the primitive and monotonous condition of its industrial life, and the peculiar character of its political condition, seems to require from its Government, before all things, the most economical treatment of its resources, and, therefore, the greatest possible freedom in its foreign exchanges.

'Under these circumstances, what are the conditions of production and consumption in India? How far is it possible to construct a tariff of import and export duties which will comply with the accepted canons of taxation? And how far does the existing tariff conform to those canons?

'In answering these questions, it will be found that India, by the extent and favourable conditions of its territory, is capable of producing almost every article required for the use of man. If, therefore, the import customs tariff be maintained, it will involve the evils of protection, unless an excise duty to countervail the customs duty be imposed upon almost every item which the tariff now includes. Now, as excise duties are generally costly, vexatious, and inconvenient forms of taxation, and would be in most cases impracticable in India, this of itself is a reason against the permanent retention of the existing customs tariff, and one which interposes a very serious difficulty in the way of constructing one that shall be free from objection. Since almost every article that is now on the tariff, or that could be named, is either produced or is capable of being produced in India, it follows that import duties must in every case be actually or potentially protective, while, with the exception of liquors and salt, none of them are subject to an excise.

'Again, the people of India are too poor to consume many luxuries. The import trade merely consists of what may be considered either the materials of industry or the necessaries of life. It will accordingly be found that nearly all the heads of customs revenue which are of any importance are derived from one or other of these descriptions of commodities, and that the revenue derived from other articles is so insignificant as neither to justify the machinery of collection nor the interference with the trade.

'The total amount of import duties was, in 1876–77, 4,170,947*l.*, or, deducting erroneous collections, refunds and drawbacks on re-exportation, 4,098,296*l.*: of this latter sum there was realised—

From salt	£2,491,010
From liquors . . .	331,761
Total . .	£2,822,771

On these articles there is an internal excise duty countervailing the customs duty.

'Deducting the duty on these two articles, there remains

1,275,525*l*. Deducting again from this the revenue realised from cotton goods, or 811,340*l*., there remains 464,185*l*., which is thus distributed:—

Copper	£65,624	
Iron	17,096	
Other metals	30,020	
		£112,740
Silk, raw and manufactured		43,727
Woollen manufactures		38,068
Provisions		32,901
Apparel		25,658
Hardware and cutlery		21,049
Spices		18,724
Sugar		13,886
Glass		13,244
Railway materials		11,335
Articles, each group of which gave less than 10,000*l*.		132,853
Total		£464,185

'Many of the numerous articles in the last class yield each an insignificant revenue, and nearly the whole are, or can be, produced in India. The duties on them are thus indefensible in principle, and cannot consistently be maintained longer than financial exigencies require their retention.'

When making this declaration of principles the Government of India added that it would not hasten, by imposing fresh taxation, the fiscal reforms thus declared to be necessary, and that it confidently expected that the normal growth of the revenues would place at its disposal the necessary means.

In March, 1878, twenty-nine out of the sixty-two major heads under which the customs tariff was classified, comprising a larger number of sub-heads and a multitude of articles, were swept away. This remission of duties involved an estimated loss to the revenue of 51,400*l*. The inland duties on the export of sugar to Native States, to which reference has already been made, were at the same time abolished, with a loss of 150,000*l*.

In February, 1880, the export duties on indigo and

lac were removed. The average amount derived from the export duty on indigo was 42,000*l.* The export duty on lac yielded about 9,000*l.* With the exception of the duty on rice, no export duties now remain on the Indian tariff.

The effect of the duty on the manufacture of indigo may not actually have been great, but the progress of scientific discovery is now so rapid that any day this industry might have been seriously threatened by some chemically prepared substitute, and we should then have been exposed to the deserved reproach of having stimulated competition by the suicidal folly of our fiscal legislation. Even as these words are written, this possibility has been so far realised that the artificial preparation of indigo has become a fact, though its high price for the present may preclude its use. Export duties enjoy the credit of having deprived India of an almost exclusive trade in saltpetre; they were taken off when it was too late to repair the mischief, and the Government of India did not choose to run any longer a similar risk with indigo.

The only remaining export duty is that on rice, grown for the most part in British Burma, but partly in Bengal and Madras. It yielded in 1879–80 a revenue of 590,000*l.*, and in 1880–81, 718,000*l.* The economical objections to this duty are undeniable, and it is to be hoped that the time is not far distant when it will be abolished, and an amount equivalent to the duty levied in British Burma raised by a readjustment of the land revenue. Sir C. Aitchison, the chief commissioner of the province in 1878, said: 'The country is now in a state of transition, making gigantic strides every year. Existing taxes do not apparently check that progress to any appreciable extent. I would, therefore, let well alone; but hereafter, when the country is fairly populated, when the enormous area of cultivable waste is brought under the plough, and the province has become ripe, generally, for a regular revenue settlement, I am of opinion that the rice duty and the capitation tax ought to disappear and give place to an improved system of land assessment.' At the same time, there can be no doubt that the export duty on rice is, at the present moment, practically less objectionable than many of the import duties. Although it cannot be said that India and Burma have a complete monopoly of the supply of rice to Europe, they have something closely approaching to it, and so long as this is true the injurious effect of the duty on Indian interests is less serious. It is impossible, however, to say how long this may continue; the export duty on rice should certainly not be counted upon as a permanent source of revenue, but while more urgent fiscal reforms remain to be carried out, there is no immediate necessity for surrendering the large sum which it yields.

The measures taken with a view to the removal of the duties on cotton goods were of far more importance than those just described, both on account of the large interests directly at stake, and the indirect consequence almost necessarily involved, of the ultimate complete extinction of all Indian customs duties. The reasons which led to the adoption of those measures were stated by Lord Salisbury in a despatch to the Government of India, and are quoted at length in a note to this chapter. They were most forcibly and lucidly stated, and will, without any doubt, be conclusive to every one who accepts the principles of free trade. Lord Salisbury's orders were emphatically confirmed by a Resolution of the House of Commons, adopted without a division on July 11, 1877, in the following terms :—

> 'That, in the opinion of this House, the duties now levied upon cotton manufactures imported into India, being protective in their nature, are contrary to sound commercial policy, and ought to be repealed without delay so soon as the financial condition of India will permit.'

The position of the import trade of British cotton goods must here be explained. The Indian manufacture is at present confined to the coarser yarns, and to goods made of such yarns; it was clear, therefore, that the 5 per cent. import duty served to protect these yarns and goods against competition from without. It was asserted by many that the duty was so low that it could have no appreciable effect, but that it was protective in theory was denied by no one, and the Government of India considered that the first step towards the gradual removal of the cotton duties should be the remission of this undoubtedly protective portion of them.

The Indian manufacturer could compete with certain descriptions of grey or unbleached English cotton goods, which contained only the coarser yarns such as the Indian mills could produce. It was, therefore, decided to begin by exempting some of these classes of goods which were similar in character to goods actually manufactured in India, and which did not contain finer yarn than that known as 30s. This measure was carried out in March 1878, at the same time with the remission of the duties on minor articles above referred to. The step thus taken was avowedly of a temporary and tentative character; the estimated loss of revenue was only 25,600*l.*, and it affected only those qualities of goods on which the duties were directly and obviously protective. With any indirect protection which may have been given to the duty-free locally made fabrics, by displacing, to some extent, the finer dutiable imported goods, there was no attempt to deal.

The scope of the measure thus adopted was purposely very limited; it produced little effect, and the Government of India, in the beginning of 1879, appointed a Commission, under the presidency of Mr. T. C. Hope, to inquire further into the subject, in consultation with the mercantile community, from which various representations had been received. Their report showed that although the orders of the previous year had worked without much trouble or complaint, they were clearly open to this serious objection, that 'there was little essential difference between the cloths which had been exempted, and large classes of cloth, otherwise styled, which had not'; and the Commission stated its opinion that 'the only effective remedy obviously is to treat similarly, whether by exemption or taxation, all cloths of the same texture, irrespective of the lengths and widths in which they happen to be made up, or the names by which people may choose to call them.' The course thus proposed by the Commission had been more or less explicitly recommended by the Chambers of Commerce of Manchester, Bengal, and Bombay.

Some important facts were also established in illustration of the necessity of early action to relieve those imported goods which were exposed to local competition. It was shown that the falling-off in the imports of the coarser goods, on which much stress was laid by Lord Salisbury in the despatch mentioned above, was still going on, although there had been a large increase in the importation of goods of finer qualities. The effect of the import duty in leading to these results was estimated differently by different authorities, but the fact was indisputable that a branch of the trade which was once important had greatly fallen off, while on the other hand the Bombay mills had not only, in the four past years, increased their exports of yarn and piece goods to foreign countries by 26 per cent. and 51 per cent. respectively, but had more than doubled their exports to other parts of India. The total value of those exports, which was 432,000*l.* in 1875–76, had risen to 945,000*l.* in 1877–78.

The Report of the Commission was published with the Financial Statement for 1879–80, and its recommendations were adopted by the Government. It was decided to remit the duties on all grey goods, consisting of yarns not finer than 30s, a step which would remove the more urgent and immediate causes of complaint, and could be afforded at an annual loss of revenue estimated to range from 150,000*l.* to upwards of 200,000*l.*

Although, from the fact that India was at the time engaged in war and other adverse circumstances, the state of the finances was not such as to render this loss of revenue unimportant; yet the measure was held by Lord Lytton to be so necessary, both on economic and political grounds, that it could not rightly be delayed, and it was carried into effect on March 13, 1879. This important step was taken by Lord Lytton, in opposition to the opinion of a majority of his Council, but on the advice of Sir John Strachey, the Financial member. It was approved, on April 4, 1879, by the House of Commons in the following Resolution :—

'That the Indian import duty on cotton goods, being unjust alike to the Indian consumer and the English producer, ought to be abolished, and this House accepts the recent reduction in these duties as a step towards their total abolition, to which Her Majesty's Government are pledged.'

It was stated by one of the dissentient members of the Governor-General's Council, that there were not 'a dozen officials in India who do not regard the policy which has been adopted in this matter, as a policy which has been adopted, not in the interests of India, not even in the interests of England, but in the interests, or the supposed interests, of a political party, the leaders of which deem it necessary at any cost to retain the political support of the cotton manufacturers in Lancashire.'

Making allowance for some exaggeration of expression, this statement doubtless contained a good deal of truth as to the state of public opinion. The official and non-official classes of Englishmen in India have never been favourable to fiscal reforms based on the principles of free trade, and the natives of the country, even the richer and better educated, have not, with rare exceptions, arrived at the most elementary knowledge of such questions; nor were there wanting among all these classes those whose prejudices could attribute none but political or party motives to the advocates of the reduction of the cotton duties. The nature of this opposition satisfied Lord Lytton that he must carry out the measure himself, or acquiesce in nothing being done at all. He believed that the essential interests of India required it, and he was not to be deterred by the imputation of base motives. The case was one of those which had either to be settled by a bold and enlightened Viceroy, or be allowed to drift on to the serious discredit of the Government and injury of the country.

The measures thus taken were avowedly first steps towards that total abolition of the duties to which the Government of India is pledged, and which it has been ordered by Her Majesty's Government and by Parliament to carry out. They were intentionally given a form which at the outset placed them almost beyond the reach of opposition, except from avowed partisans of protection, though it did not affect their ultimate efficacy. If the object in view had been the mere reduction of the duties, and their maintenance for an indefinite period at a lower rate, it would have been a better mode of procedure to have made a general reduction of the duties on all classes of goods, instead of remitting the whole duty on the coarser kinds and retaining it on the finer. But as it had been decided that the cotton duties were producing mischievous effects on great Indian and English interests, that their maintenance for any length of time was impossible, and that their abolition could be effected without financial risk, it followed that the sooner they were removed the better. The knowledge that by the particular method chosen for dealing with them the difficulty of maintaining any part of them in any shape would be increased, was no objection, but rather a recommendation, to those who had made up their minds that everything was an advantage which helped to hasten the completion of a necessary reform.

The results have been greater and have come sooner than was foreseen, but they have entirely confirmed the accuracy of the conclusions at which the Government of India arrived. All present grounds for the complaint that we were levying protective duties in favour of the Indian mills, in their competition with English manufacturers, have been removed. Some classes of English goods are unduly favoured in comparison with other classes of English goods, but no protection remains for the special benefit of goods now produced in India.

It was anticipated by Mr. Hope's Commission and by the Government of India that the remission of duty on all goods made of 30s and under 'would probably soon effect a complete revolution in the piece goods trade.' In support of this opinion the Commission quoted the following passage from a report by Mr. Pritchard, the Commissioner of Customs in Bombay :—

'The remission will operate to create a new class of shirtings made of yarns 28 by 29 or 30, instead of the present standard quality of 32 by 36. This will pass free of duty, and, if it finds favour in the market, will take the place to a large extent either of the longcloths or of the shirtings now used, or of both.'

The Commission also quoted the following opinion of a mercantile firm :—

'There can be no doubt that a trade in cloth made of yarn just within the limit of exemption of duty would be fostered, and which might gradually become of considerable importance. Such cloth would probably be appreciated by consumers for its intrinsic value, as well as for its comparative cheapness, owing to there being no duty upon it; and, if this should be the case, it might do away with the importation of cloth made of yarns varying from 32s upwards.'

The immediate consequence of the exemption from duty of all goods containing no yarn of a higher number than 30s was the rapid development of the manufacture and import of a new class of goods made of 30s and lower counts. In consequence of their superior relative cheapness, these duty-free goods rapidly became popular, and, the experiment having thus proved successful, the tendency is now to make of the coarser yarns all cloth for which they can be used, and to substitute the coarser for the finer fabrics formerly made of yarns ranging from 30s to 40s. Within one year after the removal of the duties, this process had reached such a point that the duty-free shirtings and longcloths constituted more than 74 per cent. of those kinds of imported goods, and the dutiable qualities of some other classes of goods had almost disappeared from the market.

This rapid development of the trade in the class of goods exempted from duty has ever since gone on at an accelerated rate, and no one can now assert, as used formerly to be often asserted, that the 5 per cent. duty was so small as to have no appreciable effect upon the trade.

The changes that have taken place are illustrated by the following facts and figures. The year 1878–79, which immediately preceded the remission of duty on all the coarser sorts of grey cotton goods, was one of restricted and depressed trade, and the value of the imports of cotton manufactures, in particular, was smaller than it had been for many years. The following table shows the quantities and values of the various descriptions of cotton piece goods imported into India for the six years ending with 1880–81:—

	Grey		White		Coloured	
	Yards	Value	Yards	Value	Yards	Value
1875–76 . .	856,564,622	£10,639,712	174,290,998	£2,687,706	155,208,307	£2,837,250
1876–77 . .	840,605,329	10,125,258	193,453,866	2,887,534	152,240,661	2,709,820
1877–78 . .	992,537,579	11,562,852	215,624,360	2,936,108	150,548,913	2,454,103
1878–79 . .	775,120,394	8,648,844	192,098,379	2,559,904	160,377,489	2,588,335
1879–80 . .	908,630,133	10,391,903	226,483,857	3,052,057	198,457,802	3,129,947
1880–81 . .	1,170,467,629	13,544,719	285,358,911	3,690,800	318,051,544	5,147,639

It will be seen that there was a general recovery or increase under each head in 1879–80. The remission of duty came into force from the commencement of that year, but during the first three or four months the manufacturers and importers had not had time to arrange for supplying the market with goods of the kind exempted from duty. While for the first quarter of the year the proportion of duty-free goods to the whole quantity of shirtings and longcloths imported was only 16 per cent., it rose rapidly after August, and by the end of the year it had reached 82 per cent. Thus it was only during the last three quarters of the year that the remission of duty had any very great effect.

'The effect of the remission, however, was not so much to encourage a general increase in trade as to induce manufacturers and importers to substitute goods of the coarser and duty-free kinds for the medium and fair qualities which had formerly, when all classes were alike subject to duty, formed the bulk of the trade. In this respect, the results were much more decisive than was anticipated. It was of course expected that a certain proportion of the goods ranging from 30s to 40s would, in future, be made of yarns of 30s and under, so as to bring them within the limit of exemption. But what has actually occurred has been a complete revolution in the course of the trade in grey goods. . . . The removal of the duty on certain classes has enabled those classes to practically thrust out of the market the kinds still liable to duty, so far as these dutiable goods were consumed by the mass of the population.'[1]

During 1880–81 the same process continued. This is illustrated by the following table, showing the quantities of duty-free and dutiable grey piece goods imported into India in this and the two preceding years:—

Quantities in Yards.

	1878–79.	1879–80.	1880–81.
Duty free . .	21,796,881	374,360,464	815,792,705
Dutiable . .	753,323,513	534,269,669	354,674,924
Total . .	775,120,394	908,630,133	1,170,467,629

[1] *Review of the Maritime Trade of British India for* 1879–80, by Mr. J. E. O'Connor, published by the Government of India, Department of Finance and Commerce, 1880.

It will be seen at a glance that, while there has been a large increase in the total quantity of grey goods imported, the increase in the duty-free goods has been enormous, and that they alone now exceed in quantity the total imports of two years ago, and bid fair to supplant the finer sorts which are still liable to duty.

In the imports of the superior classes of piece goods known as white and coloured, on which the duties were not remitted, there was, as shown by the table given above, a large increase in 1879–80; and the increase in 1880–81 was still greater.

Simultaneously with the increase in the import trade, the cotton mills in India have been highly prosperous, and the evil consequences to this growing industry which we were often told would follow from the reduction of the import duties, have proved wholly imaginary. In 1880–81 the value of the exports of Indian cotton yarns and piece goods was 1,908,240*l.*, against 1,621,747*l.* in 1879–80, and 1,397,979*l.* in 1878–79. There has been a large increase in the number of looms and spindles working, and in the number of hands employed.

Notwithstanding the remission of duty on the coarser kinds of grey goods, the increase of imports, especially under the head of coloured goods, has been so great that the total revenue yielded by all cotton goods in 1880–81 was 732,265*l.*, being sensibly in excess of the amount received in 1879–80, viz., 681,768*l.*, and little below the receipts of 1878–79, 771,280*l.* The average amount received in the four years before any remission of duty was made was 890,362*l.*, so that the revenue from all cotton goods for 1880–81 is about 158,000*l.* less.

The average amount of duty collected on grey piece goods, for the four years ending with 1878–79, was 490,000*l.*, while the amount of duty collected on this class of goods in 1880–81 did not exceed 167,000*l.* The measures which have been described have therefore resulted in relief to the trade, and loss to the revenue of about 320,000*l.*; and it would apparently cost about 170,000*l.* more to complete the exemption from duty of all grey goods, without reference to the quality of the yarn of which they are made. But the loss would in fact be much less, for the supersession of the dutiable by the duty-free goods still goes on, and it is understood that the duty derived from grey goods in the current year will be less than 100,000*l.* This further exemption ought to be made as soon as possible. The necessity of distinguishing the grey goods still liable to duty from those which are duty-free, necessarily causes considerable trouble to manufacturers and importers, and many complaints have been made. Clearly, the present state of things is not satisfactory. As observed in a letter addressed to the Government by the Bengal Chamber of Commerce, the old conditions described by the Government in 1879, when it declared that 'it is not reasonable that certain goods should be admitted free while large quantities of goods of almost precisely the same character in everything but name remain liable to duty,' still exist, with this difference, that the hardship is now not caused by the competition between Lancashire and the local mills, but by competition amongst Lancashire manufacturers themselves. Nothing but financial necessity, which does not now exist, could justify the retention of the remaining duties on the finer qualities of grey goods. When these are given up, there will remain the duty on twist and yarn, on white and coloured piece goods, and on other sorts, which in the four years ending 1878–79 yielded, on an average, 360,000*l.*, and yielded, in 1879–80, 400,000*l.* It is to be hoped that this also may soon be abandoned, and it will then probably be found that the effect on these branches of the trade has been hardly less remarkable and satisfactory than that which has followed the remission of the duty on the coarser qualities of goods.

There has been a general consent of opinion among the most competent authorities, that one result of the remission of the duty on the coarser kinds of cotton goods has been that the poorer classes of Indian consumers obtain cheaper and better goods than they ever obtained before. The following quotation is taken from a letter written by one of the most important firms in Bombay:—

> 'The dutiable goods have gone so generally out of consumption latterly that the manufacturers for the Indian markets do not make them, and the prices quoted are only for old stocks of goods made before the full incidence of the remission was felt. . . . It is difficult to speak too strongly of the benefit that the consumer has derived from the change. The natives get cheaper, better made, and more durable cloths than they ever did before, and the remission of the duties has acted as a direct incentive to the manufacturer of *bonâ fide* cloth, as contrasted with the adulterated articles.'

The great development of almost all branches of Indian trade during the last two years has, no doubt, been due to general causes; but the foregoing facts show that removal of the import duties on the grey cotton goods has largely increased their sale, and that the Indian consumer has been greatly benefited by their free admission. At the same time that this result has been obtained, none of the remissions and reductions of duty made during the last twelve years have had any serious effect in diminishing the customs revenue as a whole. This will be seen from the following figures, which show the gross receipts from the sea customs duties, excluding salt, for each year:—

Import duties generally 7½ %:—

1869–70	£2,431,167
1870–71	2,401,696
1871–72	2,339,186
1872–73	2,447,629
1873–74	2,402,388
1874–75	2,476,502
1875–76	2,489,897

Import duties generally 5 %:—

1876–77	2,258,754
1877–78	2,441,547
1878–79	2,273,307
1879–80	2,229,947
1880–81	2,490,036

It appears clearly from this review that the policy followed by the Government of India during the Viceroyalty of Lord Lytton was one of absolute free trade, without reservation or qualification, and financial necessities alone prevented that policy from being carried out to the fullest extent. The proceedings of the last three or four years have, however, succeeded in rendering inevitable the almost total abolition of the customs duties, which of all Indian taxes are probably the worst. The cotton duties are virtually dead, and the other import duties cannot long survive them. How long a period may elapse before such a consummation is reached cannot be predicted, but the time is not very far distant when the ports of India will be thrown open freely to the commerce of the world.

The people of India consume at present hardly any foreign luxuries; and cotton goods, which are among the necessaries and not among the luxuries of life, are the only articles of foreign production which come largely into their consumption. There is no present possibility of deriving a large customs revenue from anything else. Putting aside the duties levied on salt and alcoholic liquors, which stand on special grounds, and on which internal excise duties corresponding with the customs duties are, and must continue to be, imposed, there will remain, when the cotton duties are removed, a very small amount of revenue derived from import duties. It is not likely to exceed about 500,000*l*., and apart from all other reasons in favour of a policy of absolute free trade, it will not then be worth while to keep up large establishments for the collection of so insignificant an amount. Further facts bearing on this subject will be given in the next chapter, and it will be shown that it is reasonable to anticipate that no permanent loss of revenue would be caused by such a general abolition of all customs duties in India, since any such loss would before long be made good by the expansion of trade and by the increase of the railway traffic receipts of the Government.

The reforms which have now been described will be remembered hereafter in the economical history of India, and they will be set down among the honourable titles of Lord Lytton's and Lord Salisbury's administration. They will be remembered not only because they were the first application to India of the principles of free trade, but also because they have been carried out in a manner which has made the adoption of any other policy virtually impossible in the future, and has rendered it almost a matter of certainty that, within a short period of time, the absolute freedom of Indian commerce will be accomplished. The authors of this book may be pardoned for recollecting the part they have taken in this work, and while on public grounds they must regret the almost universal opposition and disapproval in spite of which the policy they have so long maintained has been carried out, they cannot pretend that their personal satisfaction in the success which has been gained already, and in the greater future success which is inevitable, has been diminished by such considerations.

> Non tam portas intrare patentes
> Quam fregisse juvat.

NOTES TO CHAPTER XV.

I.

Extract from a Despatch from the Marquis of Salisbury, Secretary of State for India, to the Government of India, dated May 31, 1876.

I NEVER shared the belief which appears to have been entertained by the Government of India, that in this question there was any kind of real conflict between the interests of India and of England. On the contrary, while I was glad to feel assured that the measures which I recommended would have had for one of their effects the satisfaction of legitimate claims on the part of a most important British industry, I believed still more strongly that they were primarily required in the interests of the people of India.

I will not dwell again at length upon the political reasons which furnish, in my judgment, the weightiest arguments in favour of the course which I have urged upon Your Excellency's Government. I need hardly insist further upon the danger of keeping open between two great communities of Her Majesty's subjects an irritating controversy, which can be closed by one, and only one, solution. It is difficult to overstate the evil of permitting an industry so large as the cotton manufacture in India is certain to become, to grow up under the influence of a system which a wide experience has proved to be unsound, and which is opposed to the deliberate policy of England; nor can

I view without serious apprehension, unless it should be the result of natural causes, the gradual contraction of a trade which constitutes one of the strongest bonds of material union between England and India. But the urgency of these considerations is not denied by your Government; and I feel convinced that they will commend themselves to Your Excellency's mind with ever-increasing force.

The view of the Government of India appears rather to have been that the import duties on cottons, although protective in theory, are not so in practice, except to a very limited extent; that they are therefore not injurious to India, nor contrary to Imperial policy; that they yield a revenue which cannot be spared; that, regarded as purely fiscal duties, they constitute a more convenient tax than any which can be substituted for it; and that the relief which their remission might afford to a particular branch of British trade affords no sufficient ground for subjecting the people of India to a less popular form of taxation.

It is manifest that the strength of this chain of reasoning entirely depends on the assumption that the cotton duties are not protective. If this assumption is unfounded, the argument of the Government of India, derived from a supposed conflict of interest between India and England, falls to the ground, and the political objection to which I have referred revives in its full force. It is therefore to the examination of this question that I shall now address myself.

The opinion of the Government of India as to the operation of the cotton duties is stated to be derived from a report of a committee appointed to revise valuations and consider suggestions for the amendment of the tariff.

The method adopted by this committee in estimating the effect of these duties appears to have been to consider 'what proportion the particular goods which have to meet Indian competition bear to the whole cotton import duty;' and having satisfied themselves by an analysis of the importations of cotton goods, that only about four lakhs of rupees were levied on this particular class of goods in the year 1873–74, they arrived at the conclusion 'that to demand that, because one class of goods, represented by four lakhs of rupees duty in all India, has in one part of India to meet a local competition, the Government shall remit the remaining seventy-seven lakhs which competition cannot affect, was, in their opinion, quite unreasonable, and rendered it unnecessary even to inquire whether the finances could afford the remission.'

Upon this the Government of India, in their despatch of February 25 last, remark as follows:—

'We agreed with the committee that no sufficient reason had been shown for the removal of the import duties on cotton yarn and piece goods. The report of the committee showed that the cotton goods imported into India mainly consist of the higher qualities which cannot be manufactured from the cotton grown in India. Those who have the best opportunities of knowing the facts stated that the attempts made by Indian manufacturers to make the finer descriptions of cotton manufactures and yarn from Indian cotton had proved unremunerative, and had been abandoned. We believe that this has arisen, not as Your Lordship appears to think, from the imperfect development of the Indian manufactures, but from the inferior quality of the Indian raw cotton. It was shown by the committee that, in regard to the great bulk of the trade in cotton goods, the importers were subject to little or no competition from the Indian manufactures.'

These remarks are followed by a statement of the statistics of the cotton trade, which show that, in the four years from 1862–63 to 1865–66 the average value was 12,150,000*l.*; that value was in the next four years 17,966,000*l.*, and in the last four years 17,970,000*l.*, which, allowing for a reduction in valuations in 1869, would represent an advance of 250,000*l.* in the latter period against an advance of 5,816,000*l.* in the former period. It is true that, in the year 1874–75, the value of the imports increased to 19,387,000*l.*, which is, as your Government state, the highest return for any year since 1859; but in a review of the Indian Trade and Navigation Accounts for 1874–75 by the Department of Agriculture and Commerce, contained in your despatch of February 25 last, No. 7, Statistics, I find that the trade of this year is described as having been notoriously of an unsound and unprofitable kind, and the more recent accounts appear to show that it has not been sustained. I fail, therefore, to perceive any evidence of adequate or satisfactory progress in the general features of this branch of trade as exhibited in the foregoing figures.

With regard to the arguments of the Tariff Committee, I must observe that the facts which they adduce in support of their conclusion prove by themselves absolutely nothing.

The case of the importers of British cottons is that the trade in the coarse and low-priced goods has been so seriously injured by the operation of the duties, that it has in consequence become a comparatively small branch of their trade; and it is replied that, because the trade is comparatively small, it is unreasonable to ask that the duties shall be regulated with reference to it. From this point of view, the argument of the committee would have been still stronger if this branch of trade had been altogether destroyed by the duty; for it might then have been said that it was idle to discuss the question of a tax on a trade which had no existence. In other words, the more fatal the effect of the duty, the more complete would be the justification of its retention.

I should have been glad if your Government had supplied me with official means of inquiring how far the allegations of the importers have a foundation in fact, by supplying a statement of the importations of the particular goods in question, not only for one year, but for a series of years preceding 1873–74, as it is only by a comparison of its present with its past amount that any conclusion can be drawn.

Years	Cloth			Yarns		
	T cloths	Long-cloths	Domestics	Mules above 20s and under 30s	Mules 20s and under	Water 20s and under
	Pieces	Pieces	Pieces	Lbs.	Lbs.	Lbs.
1858	914,381	609,258	169,352	965,050	591,500	1,253.510
1859	910,481	304,705	179,409	925,085	445,640	1,443,205
1860	1,132,406	229,727	190,233	510,440	396,130	1,297,880
1868	1,023,335	113,348	119,980	412,245	80,510	507,480
1869	818,730	178,715	35,314	300,170	45,920	524,940
1870	1,080,743	94,746	46,792	342,115	96,990	857,480
1871	530,797	105,596	45,914	236,720	96,590	762,840
1872	527,831	83,229	9,639	458,270	15,060	198,315
1873	697,231	86,303	6,306	219,860	47,110	78,670
1874	588,872	148,376	10,950	137,190	27,350	337,390
Average per year—1858, 1859, 1860	985,756	381,230	179,664	800,191	477,756	1,331,531
Average per year—1872, 1873, 1874	604,645	105,969	8,965	271,773	29,840	204,792

But in the absence of official data, I have referred to a table furnished by the Bombay Chamber of Commerce in their letter to the Tariff Committee, of January 29, 1875, which is said to be compiled from Custom House returns, and the substantial accuracy of which I have no reason to doubt.

Comparing, then, the average per year of 1858, 1859, and 1860, the three years immediately preceding the American war, with the average per year of the last three years, viz., 1872, 1873, and 1874, we find the following decrease in each of these descriptions of cloth and yarns, viz.:—

T cloths	381,111	pieces
Longcloths	275,261	"
Domestics	170,699	"
Mule twist, above 20s and under 30s	528,418	lbs.
Mule twist, 20s and under	447,916	"
Water twist, 20s and under	1,126,739	"

These figures conclusively show that, so far as the import trade of Bombay is concerned, a serious decline has taken place in this branch of trade during the period in question; but their significance is increased by the considerations urged in the following extracts from the letter of the Chamber:—

'It should be remembered that this absolute decrease has occurred, after a lapse of fourteen years of profound peace and security, in the cloth and yarns principally consumed by the poorer classes, whose condition, it is well known, has immensely improved from a variety of circumstances, and during which period railway communication throughout the country was yearly extending. In 1860, 836 miles of railway only were opened in British India. In 1873 the number of miles of railway open had increased to 5,872. The progress of education, closer and more frequent contact with more advanced communities, and the wealth accumulated by the cotton cultivators throughout the Presidency during the American war and for several years subsequently, when the prices obtained showed enormous profits on the cost of production, combined to increase the demand for cloths and yarns of these descriptions to an extent far exceeding the demand which would have arisen at the ordinary rate of progress in ordinary years.

'The Chamber apprehend that, under the circumstances, a very great increase indeed in the present imports of low cloths and yarns over the imports of the years immediately preceding the American war would be necessary to show that the import duty has not been operating as a protective duty, unless experience proves, after the abolition of the import duty, that local mills are able to compete successfully on equal terms with the English manufacturers. As it is, it may be fairly assumed, however, that the duty is maintained at the expense of the consumers, principally the poorer classes, against whom it tells in this instance with particular hardship in a prime necessary such as clothing, and that it is injurious to the thousands of village handloom weavers throughout the country who are prevented from using the English yarns, which they might prefer, and are compelled to pay a higher price for what they do use, in consequence of its operation.'

I have taken from the same source, viz., customs returns, the following comparative table of the imports into Bombay of the finer cloths and yarns during the years 1872–74 and 1858–60, from which it appears that the progress of the trade in piece goods has been considerable :—

Statement of the Increase of Imports into Bombay of Fine Cloths and Yarn during the Years 1872–74, *as compared with the Years* 1858–60.

(From Custom-house Returns.)

Years	Shirtings	Yarns
	Printers, Jaconets, and Madapollams	Mule 40s and upwards Water 30s and upwards
	Pieces	Lbs.
1858	3,553,198	3,513,075 ?
1859	4,724,414	6,829,010
1860	5,540,166	4,028,499
Total	13,817,778	13,307,583
1872	6,280,269	4,330,202
1873	6,395,941	4,492,509
1874	6,697,472	4,690,642
Total	19,373,682	13,513,353
Average per year, 1858, 1859, 1860 .	4,605,926	4,456,861
„ 1872, 1873, 1874 .	6,457,894	4,504,451
Showing an increase of per year .	1,851,968 Pieces of cloth	47,590 Lbs. yarn

A similar result is shown by an examination of the returns of the importations of cotton piece goods into Calcutta, at which place they have not been hitherto exposed to the competition of native mills. From these it appears that the value of these imports has increased in fourteen years 77 per cent., while the corresponding advance in Bombay has been only 12 per cent.

It is difficult in the face of these indications to doubt that the protective action of the present tariff has had a marked effect in contracting within its present limits a trade which, if it had not been impeded by this obstacle, would have expanded to much larger dimensions.

But clearly as the protective operation of the duties is traceable in the past, I cannot but apprehend that their effect in the future will be even more decisive.

I have no belief in the existence of any cause of permanent disability on the part of the Indian mills to meet foreign competition to a far greater extent than has hitherto been in their power.

On the contrary, the information which I have received leads to the conclusion that the conditions of Indian production are such as to afford grounds for believing that the scope of the protective action of the present cotton tariff will at no distant time be so extended as to affect a very large proportion of the whole trade.

. . . . . .

It is estimated that about one-half of the cotton manufactures consumed in India is supplied by foreign importations, nearly the whole of which consist of British goods, representing an average annual value of 17,000,000*l.*

From the statements to which I have referred, it appears that two-thirds of this vast import trade, or at least a trade of a value of 10,000,000*l.*, is threatened by a competition which is rapidly becoming formidable, and which is artificially sheltered by a protective duty.

When the inevitable increase of consumption of mill-made cotton goods in India, consequent on the extension of the railway system and improved communication of all kinds, is taken into account, it becomes evident that, long before the point has been reached at which this large portion of the British export trade will have been superseded altogether by the products of the Indian mills, the area of the consumption of native products will have been so much enlarged that the people of India will be compelled to pay, for a first necessary of life, a price enhanced by all the incidents of protection; that a large industry, which it is of the first importance to place upon the soundest foundation, and the prosperity of which is a matter of national interest, will have grown up in India under influences which experience has shown to be in the highest degree injurious to its healthy and natural development; and that a revenue upon which the Government has been led to rely will year by year elude their grasp, until it altogether disappears.

Whether, then, the question be regarded as it affects the consumer, the producer, or the revenue, I am of opinion that the interests of India imperatively require the timely removal of a tax which is at once wrong in principle, injurious in its practical effect, and self-destructive in its operation.

II.

Extract from a Speech by Lieut.-General R. Strachey in the Legislative Council of the Governor-General of India, March 31, 1871.

THE first measure which the Government of India should seriously take up, after a permanently healthy condition of the finances has been established, is the complete reform of the tariff, and the removal from it of the blots which so greatly disfigure it.

The worst of these blots no doubt are to be found in the export tariff. And I should perhaps explain to the council why I have said that export duties are essentially bad, for no doubt those who first imposed them, and now retain them, thought and think better of them than I do. I regard it as an axiom in taxation that it shall, as far as possible, fall on the fund destined to supply consumption, and not on that which supplies production. An export duty necessarily falls on the producers.

To tax the export of rice is to do what is virtually equivalent to rendering the soil on which that rice was grown less productive. To tax the export of cotton goods manufactured in India is to do what in its result in no way differs from any material obstruction thrown in the way of such a manufacture. By the imposition of such taxes, the inducement to the production of the things taxed is reduced in India, and an additional stimulus is given to competition in other countries. It is of course true, that among export duties that is least noxious which is imposed on any article having a virtual monopoly in its markets. But as a fact all experience proves that nothing has such a monopoly. India can tell the tale of its saltpetre trade destroyed by export duties. Is India also to destroy its export rice trade? Will it stimulate to the utmost the production of other dyes to compete with its indigo? Will it drive its own sugar out of its own markets for the benefit of the Mauritius? Even in that commodity of which India apparently has the most important monopoly, opium, the competition of the local Chinese market is already beginning to be felt, and there are those who foretell the ultimate destruction of our export of this drug. Only to-day I have read of a commencement of opium production in the United States of America. But whatever is the immediate consequence of export duties in special cases, it is quite certain that the necessary tendency of the growth of knowledge, the spread of commerce, and the increase of competition, is to bring all producers more and more nearly to a level, and to reduce more and more the special advantages of any of them. Under such a competition, the law which has for other purposes been called a law of natural selection, will eventually destroy the industry which is weighted the heaviest, and export duties will thus constantly be tending to destroy the commerce of the country that imposes them.

The gross receipts from the export duties for the year 1870–71, reckoned from the actual accounts of the first eight months by adding one half, would be 528,000*l.* Of this, two articles, grain and seeds, paid 465,500*l.*, and all others 62,500*l.* Among these last have a place, by a refinement of barbarity, two of the very few manufactures of which India can boast. Cotton goods and leather pay 21,000*l.* together. Indigo, oils, lac, and spices, articles requiring either to be manufactured or specially dealt with, to fit them for the market, figure for 28,500*l.* I confess that I am at a loss to supply the arguments by which the retention of such duties can be justified in preference to refusing an infinite variety of petty administrative demands, among which I am quite content to class requirements for public buildings and such matters, which have been allowed to swallow up the money that, to my mind, would so vastly better have been applied to getting rid of these senseless and positively mischievous hindrances to the growth of the wealth of the country. . . .

I do not know that I should be disposed to agree with my honourable friends who have spoken of the grain duties as being those which most demand attention, though I fully assent to their condemnation of them absolutely. I regard that duty as the worst, which is most in the nature of a class duty, and which at the same time is least productive. Now all these little productive export duties are essentially class duties, and inflict special injury on a small body of persons employed in particular trades. Inasmuch as the rice duty falls on a large area it is less obnoxious and not more, and it partakes more of the character of a general tax on agriculture. I fear that the true reason we hear more of it than of other worse duties, is that it affects a greater number of influential persons who can complain, and not that it is really more obnoxious to censure.

And here I would say a word as to how bad a test of the character of a tax is mere absence of complaint. The sugar production of the North-West Provinces, to take an instance that has been lately referred to in this room, may be utterly strangled by export duties levied hundreds of miles away in the Punjab, Central Provinces, and Rajpootana, of which the grower of the cane probably never even heard. And so it may readily be with all industry. The poison is absorbed into the system imperceptibly, and the victim dies without a struggle it is true, but not the less surely.

The sugar duties of which I have just spoken are without doubt the most discreditable relic of the dark ages of taxation that yet subsists in India. A 10 per cent. *ad valorem* duty is deliberately retained on the export of British sugar into Rajpootana, and into our own territories on the wrong side of the customs line drawn across Northern India, by a Government which has for many years past preached to the very states on whose borders this tax is levied the impropriety of doing this very thing which is justified in our own case, because it yields 120,000*l*. or 130,000*l*. which it would be inconvenient to give up. I have rejoiced to hear the head of the Government (the Earl of Mayo) say that he thinks this is among the matters first to be put to rights, in any future revision of the public burdens, and I cannot see how there can be a difference of opinion on the subject. These sugar duties have been defended, by persons who should have known better, on the ground that no one complained of them. It shows a truly melancholy want of insight into, or consideration of, the action of such imposts, on the part of those who supervise this part of the administration, to find these duties in existence at the present day, and I trust that another year may not elapse before some step at least is taken towards extinguishing them.

And before I leave these export duties, let me ask why is it that the cotton goods manufactured on one side of the Hooghly are taxed, while the jute on the other goes free? Why does the cotton grown side by side with the indigo escape the duty which the other staple pays? The reply is obvious. The customers of the jute mills and the purchasers of the cotton live in England, and can make themselves heard, and have made themselves heard and feared. Here, for such reasons as I have mentioned, and in the absence of the natural defenders of the suffering interests from the councils of the Government, the true principles of taxation have too long been neglected for the sake of obtaining a revenue really insignificant in amount, and the necessity for which might quite easily have been avoided by proper firmness in refusing the expansion of expenditure.

But I fear that my bill of indictment against the customs duties does not end with the export tariff. As I before said, the true test of character of a customs duty is that it shall fall on consumers. Now there are several items of the import tariff, and one an important one, that does not comply with this condition. The first on the list is metals. It is true that iron is taxed lightly at 1 per cent., but all other metals are taxed at 7½ per cent., and almost in all cases such metals are in truth used in manufactures, and are not in any true sense articles of consumption. Naval stores come under the same description, also hides, and paints, and colours, and there may be others, which for the most part stand at 7½ per cent.

Railway materials, I need not say, come under the same condemnation, but this duty is yet more objectionable, for it is either paid by the Government in the form of guaranteed interest in case of materials used on an open line, or if for a new line it is charged to the capital account of the railway, and is converted into debt bearing interest at 5 per cent. for ever. Now that the Government is about to commence railway construction, the absurdity of this duty will perhaps become more obvious, and I hope that it will not make its appearance in another tariff. The aggregate of the five items which I have named is 225,000*l.*

Excluding these items, I find that the ten largest amounts, of which the lowest is 15,000*l.*, yield together 1,444,000*l.*, and that all the rest, thirty-nine in number, together give only 134,000*l.* The whole list comprises fifty-four items. I cannot consider that it is desirable to maintain such a tariff as this, several of the items of which do not produce 1,000*l.* Among the most miserable of the list are the last two additions to it, the mere mention of which will, I think, sufficiently indicate the spirit which has governed the commercial policy of the Government in late years—corals and lucifer matches.

Many of the items in the import tariff are, moreover, open to objection as being class taxes. Such are the duties which exclusively, or nearly exclusively, fall on the Europeans resident in India, and of these a long list might be enumerated. Although it would, no doubt, be indefensible to place Europeans in a better position than the natives of the country in these matters, yet to do the converse is still more indefensible; and I consider that many of these duties press most unjustly on the class to which I belong, and I think that I should be neglecting my duty in this council, and to that class, if I did not say it in perfectly plain terms. The European has at least as much claim to my sympathy in matters of taxation as the sugar grower of Northern India, or the indigo grower of Bengal, or the cotton spinner of Bombay. In all these cases, I affirm, are grievances in the matter of taxation far more onerous than those of which we have, within the last few weeks, heard so much, and having this distinctive character that they are as real as the others were imaginary. And I may add that, for my own part, I should be glad to hear the voice of the House of Commons require the Government of India, if it were necessary, which I hope and indeed believe it will not be, to do what is necessary for the removal of evils such as I have mentioned in the interest of Great Britain, for she has a great interest in them, and may justly defend it, as well as in the interest of India itself.

I am, of course, quite aware that it is not possible in a summary way to take off these duties, and I am anxious not to be supposed to suggest such a course. But what I say is, that the first occasion should be taken to reduce the list, and to carry out the other reforms of which I have spoken; and that such an occasion can only be found by a resolute determination on the part of the financial administration that there shall be no addition to the expenditure which shall prevent these necessary fiscal reforms. A distinct and positive policy must be adopted and acted up to, or nothing in this direction will be possible. I am too well aware of the incessant and insidious demands for money for mere administrative purposes, and I know the difficulty of resisting these demands, and I repeat, therefore, with special emphasis, what I believe to be the only rule of action that can lead to success.

Neither am I satisfied that even this amount of reform is all that we can fairly hope to see carried out. I go further still.

And in the first place, I reject entirely the doctrine that we do well to maintain a high rate of duty on the piece goods imports. Whether Manchester be selfish or not—and no doubt it has been loudly asserted—it is not for me to say; but this I know, that the men of Manchester gave England free trade, and understand the real requirements of commerce and progress vastly better than those statesmen who put export duties on such products as tea, and coffee, and grain, as well as on the few manufactures India ever had, and who maintain transit duties in the heart of our own provinces to this very day. I say, then, that those who ask for a reduction of the duty on piece goods may at all events possibly, and to my mind actually, have a very substantial ground on which to base their argument, quite apart from mere personal interest, though no doubt this is one of the motives of those who object to high duties, and a motive which is a perfectly proper one.

The truth is—and it lies on the surface—that exports are best paid for by imports, and that if a fair return in the shape of imports is not taken, the export trade is carried on at a disadvantage. Everything which enlarges the consumption of imports opens the way for a further production of exports. Now, obviously the best way of enlarging consumption is to reduce price, and even a very small fall of price may in a very important degree influence the total amount of trade. In the particular case of piece goods, moreover, every increase of consumption tends to add to the demand for the raw material, and thus in another way to stimulate Indian production.

And let me here further remark that it by no means follows that a duty is not mischievous because it only adds one, two, or three per cent. to the cost of goods. It is precisely these small amounts which in the end determine whether trade is possible or not; and in the present condition of commerce, with its vast extent and close competition, it is altogether erroneous to say that a duty is not important because the rate is low.

Nor does this finish my demands in behalf of the commerce of India. I do not affirm that it can at present be said to be within the limits of the practicable to make all the ports of India entirely free; but this is certain, that there is hardly any sacrifice of present administrative progress that I can conceive of that would not be a reasonable price to pay for the vast benefit of complete freedom of the export and import trade of India. The customs duties at the present time are not of a magnitude to render this idea in any way chimerical. . . .

I need not speculate on the probable results of such a policy, if carried out; but I may point to the wonderful effects of the adoption of a modified form of free trade by England, and say that it seems to me certain that the greatest benefit would be obtained by following a like course in India.

III.

Extract from Financial Statement by Sir John Strachey for 1880–81.

ALTHOUGH I do not intend to discuss the propriety of the course that has been followed in regard to the removal of the duty on cotton goods, I must ask Your Excellency's permission to say a few words on what is, in some respects, a personal matter. We are constantly told that these measures have been adopted in disregard of the interests of the people of India, and in obedience to the selfish demands of the Manchester manufacturers. If we had, indeed, manipulated, in the interests of England or of any political party in England, the taxes paid by the people of India, our conduct would have been not only shameful and odious, but absolutely criminal, and I, as Your Excellency's chief constitutional adviser in the financial measures of the last two years, must have borne my share of the responsibility. But for myself, who have taken part in these measures, I wish to say that I hardly remember the time when I did not argue, in the interests of India, for the removal of these and all other restrictions on her commerce. I advocated the abolition of these duties before, to the best of my belief, Manchester had herself discovered that she was injured by them, and before Lord Salisbury had proved in his despatches, in a manner which seems to me unanswerable, the serious injury which they were inflicting upon this country. As I said in my first financial statement three years ago, I would not have accepted my present office if I had not hoped that I should have an opportunity of co-operating with Your Excellency in carrying out what I may say without exaggeration have been the convictions of a lifetime. I have had that opportunity. The cotton duties are, in my opinion, virtually dead.

CHAPTER XVI.

FOREIGN TRADE.

…E OF INDIAN TRADE SINCE 1834—COMPARISON WITH ENGLAND—EXCESS OF EXPORTS EXPLAINED—ANALOGY WITH UNITED STATES—EVIDENCE OF PROSPERITY RATHER THAN REVERSE—TOTAL TRADE IN RELATION TO POPULATION—COMPARED WITH STATES OF EUROPE—INCREASE SINCE 1840—RECENT INCREASE GREATLY DUE TO EXTENSION OF RAILWAYS—RESULTS OF CHEAP TRANSPORT—COMBINED WITH REDUCTION OF CUSTOMS DUTIES—INTERESTS OF TRADE DEMAND FURTHER REMISSIONS—NECESSARY GROWTH OF RAILWAY REVENUE WITH INCREASED TRADE—LOSS OF CUSTOMS DUTIES PROBABLY AT ONCE COMPENSATED THUS—EXPANSION OF IMPORT AND EXPORT TRADE EXTENDS TO ALL CLASSES OF GOODS—PROOF OF GENERAL INCREASED PROSPERITY—MUTUAL INTEREST OF ENGLAND AND INDIA TO REMOVE OBSTRUCTIONS TO TRADE CAUSED BY CUSTOMS DUTIES.

THERE is no more striking evidence of the progress of the material wealth of India than that furnished by the record of its foreign trade, as shown in the table at the end of this chapter.

The general volume of the trade of India at the present time approximates nearly to that of Great Britain between 1830 and 1840, but with the important difference that the Indian exports exceed the imports by about the same amount as that by which the British imports exceeded the exports. The British exports appear to have been in excess of the imports until about 1825, when the imports began to prevail more and more, and the excess at length reached the enormous value of 150,000,000*l.* or 160,000,000*l.* sterling.

Supposing the values recorded in the trade returns

to be substantially correct, which there is no reason to doubt, the excess of the value of exports over imports indicates approximately the sum which India sends to England to pay for all charges connected with the administration, the interest on English capital invested in India, and the profits of private trade and savings from salaries remitted by Englishmen, less the new capital sent out from year to year for investment in the country. The period from 1854 to 1864 was the time when the capital for the guaranteed railways was being raised. About 80,000,000*l.* was borrowed or raised in England; 30,000,000*l.* chiefly to meet the heavy charges of suppressing the Mutiny, and 50,000,000*l.* subscribed as railway capital for investment or expenditure in India, and there was hardly any surplus of exports during this period. In 1869 the heavy outlay on the guaranteed railways was coming to a close, and the system of construction by the State was beginning; and since that time, the large sums which India has had to pay as interest, now amounting to more than 5,000,000*l.* yearly, have exceeded the capital supplied from England for investment. The great rise in the export trade dates from that time, and for the last ten years the excess of exports has averaged about 16,000,000*l.* sterling, of which perhaps half may be regarded as the return on capital invested in railways and commercial enterprise, and half as the charge on account of the administration of India, which has to be met in England.

It has frequently been alleged that this excess of the exports over the imports signifies a drain on the resources of India which, to use the words of one of those who thus argue, 'must stop all real improvement, and eventually bring the country to pauperism.' The most conclusive argument, perhaps, that can be brought against such a view is the practical one, that the nation which probably of all others at present gives the greatest signs of progress and of increase of wealth and general prosperity—the United States of America—exhibits a balance of trade similar to that of India, but with a still greater relative excess of exports. In round numbers the average values of the exports and imports of the United States for the five years ending with 1880 were 140,000,000*l.* and 106,000,000*l.* sterling respectively, showing an excess of exports of 34,000,000*l.* The foreign trade of India for the last five years is almost exactly half this amount, but with an excess of exports of only 15,000,000*l.*, the proportions of the excess to the total export values being about 22 per cent. for India, and 24 per cent. for America.

It seems, indeed, hardly necessary to discuss seriously such a doctrine as this, which would inevitably lead to the conclusion that Great Britain, by the enormous excess of its imports, is rapidly bringing to pauperism the countries from which those imports are received, and is stopping all real improvement in them. The obvious truth is that the accumulating wealth of England seeks useful employment all over the world, and that the legitimate returns on the capital thus invested flow back in the form of the excess imports, to which India and the United States of America, with many other countries similarly situated, contribute their shares.

So far as the excess of Indian exports is due to the investment of English capital in that country, it is difficult to conceive conditions under which the remittance of interest on such capital judiciously applied could be onerous to the country which pays it; for the investment must necessarily lead to the outlay of a much larger sum than the interest sent away, which only represents the profits, the other portion of the gross receipts which supplies the cost of production or working expenses, remaining in the country. Thus, in the case of the guaranteed railways, about 100,000,000*l.* of capital has now been raised and spent in India, and say 5,000,000*l.* a year has to be paid in England as interest on that capital; the railways pay this 5,000,000*l.* by earning a gross income of 10,000,000*l.*, of which 5,000,000*l.* is spent in wages or other working expenses, and affords increased profitable occupation to the people of the country. The persons who voluntarily pay the 10,000,000*l.* for the use of the railways are themselves largely benefited by them, and would have had to pay much more had they been obliged to use ruder means of conveyance. The remittance of 5,000,000*l.* of interest to England, therefore, indicates the investment of a sum of money in India which, so far from causing a drain on the country, confers in numerous ways great direct and indirect benefits on it. The same may be said of the smaller investments in tea and coffee, indigo, cotton mills, and other industries which are mainly supported by British capital, the interest remitted on which does not imply the impoverishment but the enrichment of the country. As to the other half of the excess exports, which goes to pay the cost of English administration necessarily incurred out of India, there can be no room for doubt that it is to the advantage of India to pay the sum really necessary to secure its peaceful government, without which no progress and no accumulation of wealth would be possible; and so long as this condition is not violated it is not material whether a part of the charge has to be met in England, or whether it is all paid in India.

The aggregate export and import trade of India now amounts in value to nearly 140,000,000*l.* sterling; twenty-five years ago it had not reached 50,000,000*l.* Though the progress of India has been great, the trade, in relation to the population, is, however, still far behind that of even the more backward European countries, as the following figures (showing approximately the facts between 1878 and 1879) will indicate :—

Country	Population	Imports	Exports	Total	Rate per head
		£	£	£	£ s.
Great Britain	34,000,000	363,000,000	249,000,000	612,000,000	18 0
France .	38,000,000	184,000,000	127,000,000	311,000,000	8 2
United States of America	47,000,000	107,000,000	141,000,000	248,000,000	5 6
Russia . .	85,000,000	65,000,000	68,000,000	133,000,000	1 11
Austria . .	37,000,000	58,000,000	70,000,000	128,000,000	3 7
Italy . .	27,000,000	51,000,000	44,000,000	95,000,000	3 10
Spain . .	17,000,000	16,000,000	17,000,000	33,000,000	1 19
India . .	252,000,000	49,000,000	67,000,000	116,000,000	10

The imports of merchandise have increased from 14,000,000*l.* in 1856 to 53,000,000*l.* in 1880–81, showing an increased purchasing power of close upon 30,000,000*l.* yearly. The exports, which in the first-named year were 23,000,000*l.*, rose in the last to 74,500,000*l.*, showing an increased power of production of 50,000,000*l.* sterling. The steadily increasing amount of the imports during the last forty years affords conclusive proof that the power of purchasing for internal consumption, so far from having been unduly pressed upon by adverse influences, such as over-taxation or any general deterioration of condition, has been constantly improving. The decennial increases of the imports of merchandise have been as follows: 1841 to 1851, 3,000,000*l.*; 1851 to 1861, 12,000,000*l.*; 1861 to 1871, 11,000,000*l.*; 1871 to 1881, 18,000,000*l.*

It is surely time that the misconceptions on these subjects, if indeed they do not rather deserve the name of misrepresentations, should be abandoned. It is inexcusable on the part of any one who professes to enlighten the people of England on the condition of India, to allege that when persons in authority have referred to the excess of exports over imports as being 'without any commercial return,' they have admitted that the transaction has been without any proper consideration, and therefore injurious to India. And the confusion of thought thus displayed is commonly combined with another fallacy. It is tacitly assumed that some condition of things would be possible under which, by reducing to a 'minimum the cost of good government,' this excess export of produce could be avoided and its value retained by the people of India. Now it is obvious that the only way in which this could happen would be for India to repay all the foreign capital spent on her improvement, and herself supply all that is required in the future, at the same time furnishing a national government which should give all necessary securities for the peaceful and progressive administration of the country. When this becomes possible the time may arrive when India, without relapsing into barbarism and losing its foreign trade entirely, will find that her exports no longer exceed her imports.

That the development of Indian trade, to which attention has been directed, has for the most part been due to the increasing wealth of the country, and to the greatly improved means of communication both by sea and land, and especially to the extension of railways, cannot be questioned. In 1856 the first few miles of Indian railways had just been opened, and the total receipts from the goods traffic were only 47,000*l.* In the last year for which we have complete accounts (1880) the goods receipts were nearly 7,700,000*l.*, the quantity of goods carried having been almost 11½ million tons.

It is interesting to inquire, and the inquiry has an important bearing on all questions relating to Indian trade, what relative effect customs duties and the cost of inland transport have on the probable sale of imported merchandise.

Taking cotton manufactured goods as an illustration, we shall find that the value of 1 lb. of cotton manufactures may be roughly taken on the average at about half a rupee; 1 maund, or say 82 lbs., will be worth Rs. 40, on which the duty at 5 per cent. will be Rs. 2, or annas 32 (4*s.*). Further, the transport of the same quantity by rail for 500 miles will be about annas 10 (1*s.* 3*d.*), or one third of the duty. Also the cost of cart transport being about four times that of transport by rail, the saving due to the introduction of railways is three times the actual cost by rail for 500 miles, or about annas 30 (3*s.* 9*d.*).

Hence it appears that the virtual effect of substituting 500 miles of railway transport for cart transport is equivalent to taking off a duty of 5 per cent.; and, considering the great distances to which cotton goods actually travel in India, it may be reasonably said that this fairly indicates the actual direct effect of the railways on the trade in these goods during the last twenty-five years.

But there is a further most important result of cheap transport; for the imports have to be balanced in value by the exports. The cotton manufactures are worth about 100*l.* per ton, while the average agricultural export produce can hardly be worth one-tenth of that sum: it follows, therefore, that for every ton of the cotton manufactures imported, there will be at least ten tons of produce exported. Taking the present value of cotton goods imported at 25,000,000*l.*, and their weight at 250,000 tons, the export produce equal in value might weigh about 2,500,000 tons, on which the railway receipts will be about 2,000,000*l.* The saving in the cost of transport of this produce by rail, over the old method by cart, would be about three times the actual cost by rail, or say 6,000,000*l.* Thus a most important stimulus is given by the railways to the import trade, by bringing a largely increased quantity of produce within the range of the export market, while the cost of the imported goods is at the same time reduced, and they are consequently brought within the means of an increased number of purchasers. The importance of these considerations, which of course apply to all descriptions of imports as well as to cotton goods, is so great that it is matter of surprise that they have hitherto received so small a measure of attention from the intelligent classes interested in the extension of British trade in India, and that the influence of these classes has not been more powerfully exerted for the purpose of stimulating the development of railways, on which the increased sale of foreign manufactures in the great continent of India so immediately depends.

These general causes have been in operation for the last twenty-five years, during which the railways of

India have been by degrees coming into existence, and their effect has been largely aided by the gradual reduction in recent years of the general scale of import and export duties. What that effect has been is shown by the figures already given; and it may confidently be concluded that the further development of the commerce of India will be found directly and intimately to depend on these two influences—the reduction of the cost of inland transport by the extension of railways, and the reduction or total abolition of the customs duties, whether on exports or imports. That a considerable increase of the export trade of India in the last few years may have been due to the fall in the value of silver in relation to gold, is more than probable, but the discussion of this subject will be more conveniently deferred to a later part of this work.

And we are thus brought back to consider the serious question discussed in the preceding chapter, how far it may be desirable in the interests of the trade of the country further to give up or reduce the customs duties, and how far the financial exigencies of the Government will admit of such relief being given. The sole justification of the maintenance of any tax is that it is required in the general interests of the community. It would be a short-sighted and mischievous policy to allow the cotton duties or any other duties to stand in the way of the development of a trade measured in millions of pounds, unless the requirements of financial equilibrium could not dispense with the few hundred thousand pounds they produce. The remission of the remaining cotton duties might lead to a loss of 700,000*l.*, and if the other customs duties were given up there would be a further loss of 1,000,000*l.*, or rather more. The inquiry, therefore, arises whether India could safely accept the risk of this, and how such sums could be made good.

The growth of the railway traffic following the increasing trade leads necessarily to the growth of the railway receipts, and to a corresponding addition to the revenues of the State. Experience shows that Rs. 10 or 12, or say 1*l.* of the conventional Indian currency, may be taken as the average sum earned from all sources per ton of goods carried on Indian railways. The number of tons moved has gradually increased from 1,800,000 in 1865, to 3,400,000 in 1872, to 8,800,000 in 1879, and to 10,450,000 in 1880, the last year for which full accounts have been published. The increase of every million tons to the traffic will add approximately 1,000,000*l.* to the gross receipts. About half of this sum will be net profit, and of this not less than two-thirds would directly or indirectly add to the resources of the Government, either as a reduction of the payments for guaranteed interest, or as direct profit on the guaranteed or State lines. Hence, for every million tons added to the goods traffic it would be reasonable to expect that 250,000*l.* would be added to the revenue in the shape of railway receipts. There has been in the last five years an actual increase of 5,000,000 tons, and if a similar increase should take place in the next five years, the revenue would be increased by 1,250,000*l.* from this source alone, of which but a small part would be absorbed by increase of interest charge.

The steady and continued increase of the foreign and internal trade of India gives evidence that such anticipations as these are reasonable and moderate. The tonnage of the shipping employed in the foreign import and export trade, which in 1856 was about 2,800,000, had become 5,800,000 in 1877–78, and it now exceeds 6,000,000. The interportal or coasting trade employs about double that amount of tonnage. The foreign trade has increased in the last twenty-five years from 49,000,000*l.* to 138,000,000*l.*, and the interportal trade is now valued at nearly 60,000,000*l.* sterling. It is not possible that such a growth of the foreign trade should go on—and there is every indication of its continuance—without a corresponding growth in the internal trade of the country, and every stimulus given to the foreign trade by the remission of the duties imposed upon it, must necessarily be immediately felt in an increase of the railway receipts and in the public revenues. From these considerations it is reasonable to anticipate that the repeal of the remaining duties on cotton goods would be immediately followed by an extension of the import trade, combined with a corresponding addition to the exports, and that this would soon lead to an increase of railway traffic sufficient to cover the first loss of revenue. Even, therefore, if the state of the finances were less satisfactory than it is, there need be no hesitation in immediately abolishing all the imposts with which this branch of trade is burdened. This same resource, the growing railway income, would also unquestionably, if it were prudently managed, afford within a short period of time the means of freeing the whole import trade of India from taxation. It is impossible to doubt that the removal of all customs duties would have a very great and immediate effect upon Indian trade, and through it on the railway receipts and on the public revenue. The hope has been expressed in other parts of this work, that nothing may be done to throw away or jeopardise that most important of the future resources of the Government in India, the profits from the railways. The revenue from this source is obtained with an amount of interference with trade which is almost imperceptible, and in return only for services rendered and urgently needed; and all efforts to stimulate its growth would involve the satisfactory maintenance and extension of a cheap and efficient system of railway transport, on which the realisation of such a revenue would directly depend, and which would be no less essential for successful and expanding commerce.

How far the anticipations of the further steady increase of Indian trade are justified by the facts will be seen from the following figures, which compare the imports of foreign merchandise and the exports of Indian produce in the last year, 1880–81, with the average of the five years 1874–75 to 1878–79, and the year 1856. In no single instance, excepting the exports of silk, is there anything but a satisfactory increase. The following tables include all articles the annual values of which exceed 500,000*l.* :—

Imports.

Articles	1856	Average of 5 years from 1874–75 to 1878–79	1880–81
Cotton twist and manufactures	£6,362,000	£18,895,000	£26,579,000
Metals	1,543,000	3,265,000	3,780,000
Liquors	755,000	1,336,000	1,387,000
Coal	112,000	835,000	1,240,000
Sugar	168,000	819,000	1,611,000
Woollen goods	134,000	780,000	1,299,000
Railway plant and rolling stock	347,000	757,000	1,118,000
Silk goods	139,000	747,000	1,350,000
„ raw	274,000	653,000	1,067,000
Provisions	266,000	765,000	920,000
Apparel	328,000	565,000	658,000
Salt	275,000	556,000	666,000
Hardware	—	442,000	552,000
Spices	123,000	401,000	543,000

Exports.

Articles	1856	Average of 5 years from 1874-75 to 1878-79	1880-81
Opium	£6,201,000	£12,175,000	£13,590,000
Cotton, raw	3,315,000	11,515,000	13,242,000
" manufactured	—	905,000	1,908,000
Rice	2,598,000	6,363,000	9,057,000
Wheat	174,000	1,344,000	3,278,000
Pulse	124,000	256,000	275,000
Total grains	£2,896,000	£7,963,000	£12,610,000
Oil seeds	1,273,000	5,210,000	6,345,000
Jute, raw	329,000	3,201,000	3,935,000
" manufactured	—	663,000	1,127,000
Hides	432,000	3,095,000	3,733,000
Indigo	2,424,000	2,973,000	3,572,000
Tea	63,000	2,579,000	3,054,000
Coffee	120,000	1,432,000	1,600,000
Wool	483,000	1,036,000	1,224,000
Silk	1,049,000	851,000	771,000

It is materially impossible that the great progress thus shown, both in production and consumption, can have taken place without a corresponding development of the wealth and industry of the people; and the well-known facts of the increase of the area of land under cultivation in all parts of the country, indicate the principal source from which that increased wealth has been derived, and to which that industry has been applied. That there are evils and difficulties from which some portions of the population suffer, is no doubt true for India as for every other country; but that the very remarkable growth of all branches of the public income, which has taken place simultaneously with an equally striking advance in the internal and external trade, evinced by the imports and exports and railway transactions, should be compatible with anything but an advancing condition of the people, is directly contrary to all experience and reason.

The very evils, difficulties, and sufferings which it has been the lot of the people to endure, have afforded a proof of the improved condition of the community; for they have shown how vastly the recuperative powers of the country have increased, the period of its greatest apparent prosperity having followed immediately on a period of the most exceptional calamity. In the face of these positive and continued proofs of general progress, it is irrational to give attention to vague assertions of deterioration, of which no definite evidence is forthcoming, and which are based on misconceived generalisations from local and partial evils, such as are to be found in every human society however advanced. And considering how little has yet been done to give India the advantages which are certainly to be secured by the adoption of improved methods of husbandry, by the institution of industries suited to the local conditions of the country, and by calling in the aid of modern science and the outlay of sufficient capital, the success already attained in the development of its resources is most encouraging for the future.

There are some who doubt whether England will continue to stand fast in that faith in the efficacy of free trade which many, among whom the authors of this work desire to rank themselves, hold to have been one of the most powerful causes of the extraordinary advance in wealth which our country has made in the last quarter of a century; but so long as she does, India offers a wide field for the application of that faith, and for the diffusion of the benefits which it will certainly confer on those who follow it. Though other countries be more or less closed to the industry of England by hostile tariffs, we possess in India a continent the capacity of which, whether to supply us with agricultural produce, or to receive our manufactures in exchange, has only just begun to be developed, and the extension of which depends on our own conduct in throwing down the artificial barriers which we still permit to stand in the way of the free growth of the trade of that country. The progress of this trade in the past year alone goes far to justify the belief that in this direction should be sought, and may be found in a comparatively short time, a most valuable set-off against any temporary check or diminution of the progress of British commerce caused by the oppressive tariffs of protectionist nations.

The idea of tolerating, still less of stimulating, a war of tariffs between England and India is monstrous. Whatever may be our position in respect to other countries or colonies, here at least such an insane policy should not be permitted. The future prosperity of India and England alike demand the most complete freedom of commercial intercourse between them. It is not easy to decide which country suffers most by the obstruction to the sale of its produce caused by customs duties. on the one side such as the Indian duties on the import of English manufactures, and on the other such as the English duties on Indian tea and coffee; the duty on tea being at no less a rate than 50 per cent. on the value, and placing on this article alone a burden of more than one million sterling. In neither case can a plea of necessity be accepted, and to talk of reciprocity or compensating tariffs would be absurd. Both countries require free markets, and it is equally true for both that no form of taxation is so prejudicial as that which restricts the free interchange of the products of their industry. Whether the subject be viewed from the side of the interests of India or of England, the same conclusion must be come to, and it is singular enough that amid all the discussion which has arisen as to the exclusion of English goods from foreign markets by hostile tariffs, the mutually destructive customs duties of England and India should not have attracted more attention, and should have been tolerated so long.

ABSTRACT STATEMENT OF FOREIGN TRADE FROM 1834 TO 1881.

Dates	Annual Imports			Annual Exports			Excess of Exports above Imports	Percentage of Excess on Total Exports
	Merchandise	Treasure	Total	Merchandise	Treasure	Total		
Averages for Periods of Five Years.								
	£	£	£	£	£	£	£	
1834-39	4,971,000	2,345,000	7,316,000	11,072,000	251,000	11,323,000	4,007,000	35
1839-44	7,691,000	2,762,000	10,453,000	13,790,000	463,000	14,243,000	3,800,000	27
1844-49	9,136,000	3,073,000	12,209,000	15,675,000	1,321,000	16,996,000	4,787,000	28
1849-54	11,059,000	4,793,000	15,851,000	19,023,000	994,000	20,017,000	4,116,000	21
1854-59	15,577,000	11,275,000	26,852,000	24,925,000	922,000	25,847,000	*1,005,000*	—
1859-64	23,971,000	17,092,000	41,063,000	42,147,000	1,023,000	43,169,000	2,106,000	5
1864-69	31,697,000	17,618,000	49,315,000	55,863,000	1,802,000	57,665,000	8,350,000	14
1869-74	32,256,000	8,265,000	40,521,000	56,235,000	1,590,000	57,826,000	7,306,000	29
1874-79	38,364,000	9,858,000	48,222,000	60,325,000	2,810,000	63,135,000	14,913,000	24
Actual Results for Single Years.								
1874-75	36,222,000	8,141,000	44.363,000	56,359,000	1,625,000	57,985,000	13,622,000	24
1875-76	38,892,000	5,301,000	44,192,000	58,091,000	2,200,000	60,292,000	16,100,000	27
1876-77	37,441,000	11,436,000	48,877,000	61,014,000	4,030,000	65,044,000	16,167,000	25
1877-78	41,464,000	17,355,000	58,820,000	65,222,000	2,211,000	67,433,000	8,613,000	13
1878-79	37,801,000	7,057,000	44,858,000	60,938,000	3,982,000	64,920,000	20,062,000	30
1879-80	41,166,000	11,655,000	52,827,000	67,212,000	2,035,000	69,247,000	16,426,000	24
1880-81	53,087,000	8,997,000	62,084,000	74,541,000	1,440,000	75,981,000	13,897,000	19

CHAPTER XVII

OCTROI DUTIES

OCTROI DUTIES FOR MUNICIPAL PURPOSES—ORDERS IN 1868 TO PREVENT ABUSES—RELAXED IN 1871—LEGISLATION PROPOSED IN 1879—ITS OBJECTS—ABUSES POINTED OUT BY BOMBAY CHAMBER OF COMMERCE—EXTREME CASE OF KARACHI—DECISION NOT TO LEGISLATE—NECESSITY FOR FUTURE VIGILANCE.

CLOSELY connected with the subject of customs duties and trade, which have been treated of in the last two chapters, there is an important matter which must not be left unnoticed.

For many years past the Government of India has recognised the necessity of placing better checks on the system by which, through a large part of India, octroi duties and tolls are levied for municipal purposes. It has been a constant complaint that these duties become taxes on goods in transit, and affect injuriously the general trade of the country.

The orders on this subject issued by the Government of Lord Lawrence in 1868 contained the first clear statement of the principles by which the levy of octroi duties should be regulated. Their propriety has never been successfully impugned; and they are quoted here:—'Such duties should be restricted to articles actually consumed in the towns, and not imposed upon articles of general commerce or suffered to interfere with the natural course of transit trade. The Government of India has reason to believe that these sound principles, the truth of which has been established by the prolonged experience of those countries of Europe in which octroi duties form commonly a source of municipal revenue, have been frequently lost sight of, and that to meet the burden of an annually increasing expenditure upon police, education, or sanitary improvements, a wide-spread system of taxation has been introduced, injurious to interests on which the burden in a great measure falls, and standing in the way of the proper development of the commerce of the country. It is to little purpose that the Imperial Government reduces or abolishes customs duties in the interests of trade, if municipalities are permitted to levy duties on articles of commerce passing through their limits. In all parts of India municipal taxation is largely on the increase; and there is a growing tendency to overlook, for the sake of small local improvements, the real injury that is being inflicted upon important general interests.'

These orders also laid down practical rules by which the levy of octroi duties and tolls was to be regulated. It was declared that duties on articles of consumption must fall entirely on the population of the town for the benefit of which they were levied, and that a jealous guard must be kept lest they should apply to any article belonging to the transit or general trade of the country. The articles on which duties might and might not be imposed were enumerated.

In the first class were articles of food or drink; animals for slaughter; articles used for fuel, for lighting, or for washing; articles used in the construction of buildings; tobacco, and some minor articles of consumption. The second class, on which the levy of duties was prohibited, comprised articles liable to customs duty and imported into India by sea—salt, opium, liquors, and drugs liable to excise duty. The articles subject to duty were so chosen that municipal taxation should not encroach on imperial taxation, and that, in the words already quoted, important general interests should not be overlooked for the sake of small local improvements.

It was also required that provision should be made for the refund of duty when goods were re-exported from towns, for bonded warehouses, and other purposes. Rules were laid down regarding the levy of tolls, the principle being affirmed that they were not to be levied as a source of general municipal revenue, but only for the purpose of defraying the cost of construction of particular works, or for their maintenance.

These orders of the Government of India were received with general opposition by almost all the local authorities wherever octroi duties were levied; and for this plain reason, that their execution involved, in many cases, a serious curtailment of existing municipal income. In consequence of the pressure brought to bear by the local authorities, some relaxation of the orders was unfortunately allowed, in 1871, and authority was given to add the following classes of goods to those on which duties might be levied:—Piece goods and other textile fabrics, and metals and articles of metal, provided that the duty should not exceed $1\frac{1}{2}$ per cent. *ad valorem.*

With these exceptions, the orders of 1868 were supposed to remain in force; and for the last ten years the Government of India has been trying, not always very zealously, to get them carried out. The Government of India is, in theory, supreme; but when its orders are regarded by local authorities and by Provincial Governments as opposed to their interests, and the subject to which they apply is one on which the Supreme Government itself shows signs of lukewarmness or divided counsels, it is not difficult to treat such orders with so much passive obstruction and indifference that they are very imperfectly executed. So it has been with the orders regarding octroi duties. Matters are undoubtedly better than they were, but they are still far from satisfactory.

In 1879 the Government of Lord Lytton came to the conclusion that the only way by which a complete remedy for existing evils could certainly be found was by legislation, placing on all local authorities obligations impossible to be disregarded, which would prevent these duties operating as transit duties, or interfering with the general interests of trade, and which would guard against collision with imperial taxation, or with the general principles of our commercial policy. A Bill was accordingly introduced into the Legislative Council by Sir John Strachey for these purposes. The Secretary of State, however, doubted the necessity of legislating on the subject, not because he in any way differed from the conclusions of the Government of India, or from any want of sympathy with the objects in view, on the importance of which he had often strongly insisted, but because it seemed to him that the Government of India would be able, by its executive authority, to accomplish everything that was required. It may be doubted, judging from former experience, whether this expectation will be fulfilled; but it is hoped that the Government of India will be more in earnest and more successful in the future than it has been in the past.

Whatever measures, legislative or executive, be adopted, the necessity for reform in regard to this matter is obvious and pressing. The following extract from Sir John Strachey's speech, on introducing his Bill in 1879, will show the condition of things that has to be dealt with:[1]—

'I will first refer to representations which have been made from time to time by the Bombay Chamber of Commerce, a body which has always taken a most enlightened view of this whole question, and which has repeatedly pressed on the Government (I wish their representations had had the success they deserved) the necessity for reform.

'In an address presented to your Excellency by the Bombay Chamber of Commerce in December, 1876, the Chamber made the following remarks:—

'"In the year 1875 the Chamber instituted an enquiry into the nature and extent of the transit and town duties levied by municipalities in the interior of this Presidency. The results of this enquiry induced the Chamber to urge upon His Excellency the Governor of Bombay in Council the expediency of abolishing, in all municipalities of the Presidency, all transit duties and all town duties having the character of transit duties, and of confining town duties, in accordance with the principles of municipal taxation defined by the Government of India in its Resolution dated 15th November, 1868, to a few articles of local consumption, such as ghee, firewood, fruit, vegetables, fowls, eggs, and animals for slaughter, which did not enter into the general trade of the country. The Chamber, in its representation to the Government of Bombay, showed that transit duties in their native form were levied in Karáchí, Broach, and Surat; that in nearly every municipality in the mufassil, the town duties levied were converted into transit duties by the stringent and illiberal nature of the rules under which refunds were granted; and that the duties levied by certain municipalities on certain articles were very high. In Karáchí, for instance, the town duty on wheat was $2\frac{1}{2}$ to 3 per cent., and on wool 1 to $1\frac{1}{2}$ per cent., of the value; in Surat, the town duty on yarn was about 3 to $3\frac{1}{2}$ per cent., and on copper 5 per cent., in either case about the same as the imperial customs duty; while in Ahmadábád the town duty on yarn was no

[1] Speech in Legislative Council, November 14, 1879.

less than 6½ per cent., or nearly twice the imperial customs duty.

'"The town duty levied on yarn imported into Ahmadábád is particularly objectionable. It is, we believe, quite understood to be a protective duty in favour of the two mills in that town against other yarn, whether of English or of Indian manufacture: and constituted as the mufassil municipalities of this Presidency are, it illustrates the necessity of the strictest vigilance on the part of the Government with respect to the rate and incidence of every tax imposed by these municipalities. The town duty levied on yarn brought into Surat is open to similar objections, and we have mentioned a few instances in which the town duties in other places are much too high. We earnestly hope that Your Lordship will order an immediate revision of all the taxes imposed by the municipalities of this Presidency to be made, abolishing all transit duties, and all town duties having the character of transit duties, or which have a protective effect, and reducing those which are high, or press heavily on any article."

'Again, on the 14th March, 1878, the Bombay Chamber of Commerce addressed the Government. It said:—

'"It is, we believe, universally accepted that the great principles of an octroi duty are that it should be small, and that it should never be allowed to operate as a transit duty. Yet in numerous instances, whether the articles have already borne customs duty or not, the taxes levied, under the name of octroi, by district municipalities, are excessive, while the refusal to grant refunds when the articles are re-exported, or the limitations or restrictions imposed on the granting of refunds, have the effect of converting the town duties paid into transit duties."

'The Chamber then gave a list of cases in illustration of that statement, and they added:—

'"Numerous other instances could be furnished, but the Chamber has reason to believe that in almost every city and town municipality throughout the Presidency, excessive duties are levied, and on articles on which no municipality should have any right to levy a duty. It has, however, been specially brought to the Chamber's notice that at Bársi very heavy taxes have been levied on machinery erected there, and that at Viramgaum a duty of 4 per cent. was levied on hoop-iron sent there for the purpose of binding bales of cotton, and no refund was allowed. At Wadwán no duties appear to be charged on articles entering the town, but iron or similar articles cannot come out of it without being taxed at the rate of about 10 per cent.: a duty of Rs. 600 would be levied on the removal of an old cotton press. Other impositions, and of a similar character, are, it has come to the knowledge of the Chamber, levied in many parts of the Presidency."

'I have quoted these passages only as illustrations of what is liable to occur at the present time, and of things that, at any rate, were actually occurring only a short time ago. I do not say that in these particular instances the state of things thus described now prevails. The Government of Bombay, since Sir Richard Temple has been in Bombay, has been paying great attention to this subject, both in that Presidency and in Sindh, and I believe that things are much better than they were. But although, as I say, I only give these as illustrations, it is impossible to doubt that a more or less similar state of things exists in many places where octroi duties are levied. One of the most preposterous illustrations of this system was to be found not long ago at Karáchí. Karáchí, as we all know, has been—and we hope it will be a great deal more in the future—one of the chief ports for the export to Europe of Indian produce. One of the great staples of the country, which has its outlet towards the sea at Karáchí, is wheat, and with the object of removing all obstacles to the growth of this most important trade, the duty on the export of wheat was everywhere abolished by the Government of India. Two years ago, it was found by the Government of India that one of the very largest sources of municipal revenue at Karáchí was an octroi duty (levied at the railway station, and on goods which never came within municipal limits, but were shipped directly from the station) at the rate of from $2\frac{1}{2}$ to 3 per cent. on all the wheat brought down from the Punjáb and Sindh for export to Europe. I think no terms can be too strong in reprobation of such a state of things. It has now happily ceased; a better system has been introduced in spite of the strong protests of the municipality of Karáchí, which naturally liked very much having its local wants supplied at the expense of other people. This is, of course, an extreme case, and I do not mean to say that such cases are common; but, nevertheless, it is an illustration of what has been going on.

'Now, if such things be allowed, it is really useless for the Government of India to attempt to establish proper principles of commercial legislation, and it may save itself the trouble of trying to reform its customs tariff; for when we have taken off duties and carried out the principles of free trade, at a serious loss perhaps to the imperial revenue, traders and manufacturers may find that, after all, they are no better off than before, and that heavier burdens than those from which they have been relieved have been imposed or are maintained by local municipalities for local purposes.

'We are often told that the great merit of taxation of this kind is that it is popular; that the people have long been familiar with it; and that it is inexpedient to force municipalities to substitute unpopular taxation for imposts that are not practically felt by the people. Now, up to a certain point, this is perfectly true. The Government of India has no desire to embark in any general crusade against octroi duties. It has not objected to octroi duties when they are properly managed. Going back to the principles laid down in 1868 by the Government of India, from which, in regard to this matter, there has since been no departure, it was said:—

'"If these principles be strictly acted upon, and the duties be moderate in amount, the Governor-General in Council is of opinion that there is in many parts of India nothing objectionable in this system of taxation for local purposes. In wealthy communities like those of Europe, it may be admitted that the balance of argument is in favour of raising municipal revenues by direct taxation only, and leaving the local trade entirely free. But in so poor a country as India, it will, in the judgment of the Governor-General in Council, be more commonly the best course to combine direct with indirect taxation; for by this means alone can a sufficiently broad base be secured for raising a sufficient income without undue pressure on individuals. So long as octroi duties on grain and other articles of consumption are kept at a moderate rate, they do not injuriously affect small retail transactions with which the poorer classes are mainly concerned. That such duties are commonly far more popular in India than any direct taxation is a strong argument in their favour, and the prejudice against them, founded on the common practice of England, should not be allowed to prevent their introduction under suitable limitations where there is reason to think that the general feeling would be to prefer them to other forms of taxation."

'The Government of India still holds this view. It makes no objection to octroi duties so long as they are properly regulated, but it refuses to allow them to become taxes on the general trade of the country. With reference to the question of their popularity, I may add that it often happens that the greater the popularity of those taxes the more objectionable they are, for often in practice this popularity—as in the case I have just given of Karáchí—only means that the people of the town have managed to provide for their own local wants without placing any burden on themselves; that they have transferred their own proper burdens to the shoulders of other people, and thus the popularity of the tax leads sometimes to its being grossly abused.'

The foregoing remarks apply more especially to octroi duties strictly speaking, but it is understood that the system of levying tolls on vehicles and goods entering a town, in return for no services rendered, as a source of municipal revenue, has been carried in some parts of Southern India to an extent of which the Government of India was not aware when the Bill just mentioned was introduced, and to an extent which must certainly lead to the serious obstruction of trade.

When it was decided that these evils were not to be remedied by legislation, further executive orders were issued in the sense of the proposed Bill. The subject, however, is one which, to secure any effectual reform, demands not only the future vigilance of the Government of India, but also of those commercial interests which are being injured to a far greater extent than they now suspect. It may seem, at first sight, a not very serious hardship that English piece goods, for example, which have paid nothing to the imperial customs, should pay a tax of $1\frac{1}{2}$ per cent. on their value on entering a municipality. Every one, however, who knows anything of the operations of trade will be aware how mischievous a tax of even this small amount may be; and when octroi duties become transit duties, they may be levied in half a dozen places before the goods reach their destination, so that the taxes actually paid from first to last may greatly exceed the maximum amount which is nominally chargeable.

CHAPTER XVIII.

WEIGHTS AND MEASURES.

REFORM OF WEIGHTS AND MEASURES NEEDED IN INTEREST OF TRADE—QUESTION HAS LONG ENGAGED ATTENTION — ENQUIRY IN 1867 — ITS RESULTS—CONDITION OF WEIGHTS AND MEASURES IN VARIOUS PROVINCES—TOTAL ABSENCE OF UNIFORMITY OR DEFINITE STANDARDS—REMEDIES PROPOSED—ADOPTION OF ENGLISH POUND AS UNIT OF WEIGHT REJECTED—REASONS FOR PREFERRING KILOGRAMME—NEARLY EQUAL TO ORDINARY INDIAN SEER—CONVENIENCE FOR FOREIGN TRADE—CONCLUSION ACCEPTED BY SECRETARY OF STATE—ACT PASSED IN 1870 TO ESTABLISH METRICAL STANDARDS—MODIFIED IN 1871 SO AS TO EXTEND ONLY TO WEIGHTS AND MEASURES OF CAPACITY—ACT NOT BROUGHT INTO OPERATION BUT STILL IN FORCE—SERIOUS OBJECTIONS TO PRESENT ABSENCE OF PROPER STANDARDS.

AMONG the reforms required in the interests of Indian trade there is none more urgent than that of the weights and measures; a reform which has been talked about for years, and the real necessity of which every one admits, but which cannot get itself accomplished. The powers of prejudice, and of those obstructions which meet every change however beneficial, have in this case proved too strong to be overcome up to the present time. Although future Governments may find the subject as difficult to deal with as their predecessors have done, and although there seems little probability of immediate action, it may be useful to give some account of the conclusions which have been accepted in principle, though to no practical effect, by the Government of India.

For more than forty years this question of weights

and measures has, from time to time, engaged the attention of the Government. The need of reform was a matter on which there had, for many years past, been no difference of opinion. It was admitted on all hands that it would be difficult to exaggerate the inconvenience caused by the confusion and diversity of the existing weights and measures, or, what was still worse, the fraudulent practices from which the poorer classes are constantly suffering, owing to the want of all proper standards by which the weights and measures of retail dealers can be tested and regulated. But it was not until 1867, when Lord Lawrence was Viceroy, that it was seriously taken up with a determination to settle it.

In that year a committee was formed to consider the subject, on the evidence from all parts of the country that had been collected for the purpose. The general condition of the weights and measures of India, as it then was and as it still is, was thus described by General Strachey, who had been nominated President of the Committee of Enquiry:—

'The diversity among the weights and measures used in various parts of India is as great as is well possible. Throughout India the old standard of weight seems almost universally to have been the current coin of the locality, and the multiplicity of coinages has been, and is still, accompanied by an equal or even greater multiplicity of weights. Not only do the weights vary from province to province, but from town to town, and even within the same town or rural district. Different weights are used in various trades in the sale of different commodities, and in wholesale and retail transactions.

'In Northern India the usual unit of weight is the tola, which is the weight of the current rupee. The seer is a given number of tolas, varying from 70 to 100. The man (by the English commonly called maund) is usually 40 seers. The rupee of the British Government weighs 180 grains; the seer of the British Government being 80 tolas is equal to $2\frac{2}{35}$ lbs.

avoirdupois, and the Government maund is $82\frac{2}{7}$lbs. avoirdupois, or 100lbs. troy. Local seers and maunds vary on either side of 2lbs. avoirdupois and 80lbs. avoirdupois.

'In Southern India the original unit of weight commonly used was the pagoda, a coin no longer current. The common seer was 80 pagodas, and was equivalent to 24 current rupees. The maund of Southern India usually contains 40 such seers, and is commonly divided into eight viss, or five seer weights, and 40 pollums. The candi, of 20 maunds, is another weight in ordinary use. At Madras, the Government some years back endeavoured to establish a local system of weights, on the basis of the rupee weighing 180 grains. The seer was not acknowledged in this system, but would be 0·617lb. The viss was 3·086lbs. and the maund 24·686lbs. This system, however, never came into use. In practice the commercial maund in the town of Madras is taken at 25lbs. avoirdupois, and the viss and candi are modified accordingly; but beyond the municipal limits other weights are used.

'The weight in common use in Burma is called viss also; it is 3·65 lbs. and is subdivided into 100 ticals, each of 252 grains.

'In Guzerat a seer of 40 local rupees weight, a maund of 40 such seers, and a candi of 20 maunds are the common weights. These maunds vary from 37 to 44lbs., and the seers are about 1lb.

'At Bombay the old seer was about 10 or 12 ounces avoirdupois, being reckoned equal to 30 pice (copper coins). The maund being 40 such seers is nearly 28lbs., at which it is now commonly reckoned. This maund is the usual one also on the Malabar coast, south of Bombay; but the seer is the Madras one of 24 rupees weight, so that the maund consists of 46 to 48 seers instead of 40. At Bombay and in the Deccan the subdivision of the seer is into 72 parts, called tank. The Deccan seer is commonly 80 local rupees, or about 2lbs. The maund varies greatly. In the Deccan the weights seem to merge into the Madras system on one side, and into the systems of Málwa and Northern India on the other. The candi, at Bombay and the neighbouring commercial centres, varies for almost each separate article of merchandise.

'Measures of capacity are hardly known in Northern India. In Bengal and Southern India they are more frequently used, and, as a rule, are intended to be equivalent to certain determinate weights of grain. In Burma grain is universally sold by measure. There is, however, such great variety among measures bearing the same name that it would be useless to refer to them in detail. No liquid measures are believed to exist anywhere.

'The usual lineal measures are the cubit, or hăth, and the yard, or gaz, the latter being divided in North India into 16 girahs or 24 tassus. The háth varies from 14 to 20 inches, the gaz from 28 to 40 inches. Thirty-three inches is the length assumed for the gaz in fixing the official land measures in the North-Western Provinces. The coss is now sometimes taken to be 4,000 gaz, about $2\frac{1}{4}$ miles, and sometimes half that distance; but 5,000 gaz, equal to about 4,500 yards, or $2\frac{1}{2}$ miles, would seem to have been the old coss of North-Western India.

'Measures of area are commonly based on the háth or gaz, but vary so exceedingly from one district to another that no general account can be given of them. Frequently the denomination of the land measures is the same as that of the grain measures, it being understood that the quantity of grain in a given measure will sow the area of land having the same name. It is common in Southern India to find the land measure of the same name differ considerably, according as the crops are irrigated or unirrigated. For all Government purposes the English acre has now almost universally been adopted, and the revenue records are, I believe, almost everywhere drawn out on this basis, though the local measurement is at the same time still recognised.

'The immediate conclusion forced upon us, on a review of such a condition of things, is, that to establish uniformity it would be necessary to set aside what may practically be said to be the whole of the existing weights and measures of all sorts.'[1]

The Committee of Enquiry were not able to agree on the course to be recommended to the Government,

[1] *Proposals relating to the Introduction of new Standards of Weight and Measure in British India*; by Colonel Strachey. October, 1867.

and alternative plans were proposed for remedying the existing evils by establishing a uniform system of weights and measures. The first of these proposals was based on the assumption that it was desirable to assimilate the Indian system to that of England, and the plan which received most favour among those who held this view was to take the English pound as the new unit of weight. The second proposal advocated the adoption of a new unit which should approximate, as closely as possible, to the existing Indian seer, the most generally known of all Indian weights. The average weight of the seer had been ascertained by enquiries all over India to be about $2\frac{1}{4}$lbs. avoirdupois. This being almost exactly the equivalent of the kilogramme of the metric system now in force throughout the whole of civilised Europe, with the exception of England, it was proposed that a seer of this value, or 2·205lbs., should be the basis of the new Indian system.

Although in deciding between two proposals of this description reasons of a theoretical or scientific character could not be disregarded, yet Lord Lawrence wisely insisted that it was essential that our conclusion should be based exclusively on a consideration of the convenience of the people of India, and that we are bound to select a system which shall be in all respects thoroughly and permanently convenient to them.[1]

The decision of the Government was communicated to the Secretary of State in these terms:—

'We are of opinion that the adoption of the English system of weights is not advisable. Neither the English pound, nor any multiple of it, can be a convenient unit of weight for India. It has been almost universally admitted that the new unit should

[1] Despatch from the Government of India to the Secretary of State, dated November 6, 1868.

approximate to the existing Indian seer, the average weight of which is about 2¼lbs. To reduce the seer to 2lbs. would be extremely unpopular and objectionable. On the other hand, the kilogramme of the metric system, which weighs 2·205lbs., at once provides a seer, which would certainly be as acceptable to the people as any that could be chosen. Further, we consider that on account of its simplicity and its symmetrical form, the metric system of weight, in its integrity, will be more convenient for India than any other. While it will be perfectly suitable for the internal wants of India, it will be in harmony with the system which has been already adopted in the greater part of the civilised world, and which may ultimately be adopted by England herself. In any case it will be more convenient for commercial transactions between England and India than any other system not really commensurable with that of England.'

The following is a summary of the reasons which led Lord Lawrence's Government to these conclusions.

The only system of weights recognised by the Government, but never generally introduced for trade purposes, was created by Regulation VII. of 1833, a law which in fact served only as a basis for the currency. It adopted as the standard unit, the tola, equal in weight to the rupee, or 180 grains; the seer was declared to consist of eighty tolas, and the maund of forty seers. Thus the seer was commensurable only with the troy pound, and was equal to $2\frac{2}{35}$lbs. avoirdupois, and the maund was equal to $82\frac{2}{7}$lbs. avoirdupois, or 100lbs. troy.

Although these weights, being the only ones recognised or defined by any Indian law, were to some extent introduced in Government transactions, and adopted in towns containing a large English community, no serious attempt was ever made to bring the system into use in the country at large, and it has never been generally known or used. The seer of 80 tolas was inconveniently less than the weights of that name in use in the country at large, and there can be no doubt that this insufficient weight of the Government seer is one of the main reasons which have made it disliked by the people, and which have prevented it from being more commonly adopted.[1] The system, which from an Indian point of view had little to recommend it, was, as General Strachey wrote in 1867, in its relation to English commerce inconvenient in the extreme. It is founded on troy weights, which are only used for the sale of drugs in retail, and of gold and silver, and it has no exact equivalent in avoirdupois weight, which is exclusively used in commercial transactions. For these reasons the universal adoption of this system did not seem desirable.

No reasonable person would propose to adopt in India the English system in its integrity. Every one, even in England itself, has always admitted that the English system of weights and measures is, in itself, most complicated and inconvenient, and that the only reasons that can be given for maintaining it are that the unit (the pound) has been clearly defined, that the system has existed for centuries, and that the people of England have become accustomed to it. Any proposition to impose such a system on India would deserve no discussion.

A proposal which met with much favour, however,

[1] In the debate on this subject in the Legislative Council on September 5, 1871, the Lieutenant-Governor of Bengal, Sir George Campbell, said, with regard to the impropriety of calculating the seer at 2lbs. avoirdupois, that 'he remembered in Lucknow serious discontent being caused by the introduction of a seer which weighed only 2lbs. The local seer weighed a fraction over that amount. The dealers took advantage of the fact of a new seer being introduced, and charged the same price for the new seer as they had for the old, and so got the advantage of the difference between the two seers. Every purchaser accordingly found himself mulcted to a corresponding amount, and serious dissatisfaction resulted.'

was the adoption of the English pound as the new unit of weight, without the rest of the English system. Two pounds avoirdupois would then make a seer.

The objections to this plan were considered by Lord Lawrence's Government to be decisive. For, in the first place, the pound, although nominally the unit of English weight, is not conveniently commensurable with the ordinary weights used in wholesale dealings, with which alone external commerce is concerned. We cannot assimilate the Indian weights to the ton and the hundredweight, the commercial weights of England, by any scheme which takes the English pound as its unit. To establish in India a system in harmony with the system of weights in use in commercial transactions between the two countries, we must take the ton and not the pound for our starting point. Further, the adoption of the pound as the unit of weight would be inconvenient to the people of India in their internal transactions, the seer of 2lbs. being much smaller than the seer in common use. It cannot be said that the general belief of purchasers, that loss is entailed upon them by a diminution in the standard of weight, is merely fanciful. That belief is really an expression of the fact that prices often depend not only upon competition but on custom.

By adopting for the new unit a seer equal to the kilogramme, or 2·205lbs., a weight was obtained which differed little from the thousandth part of a ton, and the fiftieth part of the hundredweight, while it approximated well with the average Indian seer.

These views were otherwise supported in a minute [1]

[1] This quotation is taken from a minute dated August 4, 1868, with which Sir Henry Maine expressed his concurrence 'on all points;' and the conclusions stated in it, so far as they referred to weights, were entirely accepted by Lord Lawrence.

written by Sir John Strachey, from which the following extracts are taken :—

'There can be little doubt that, in the interests of the people of India, the best unit of weight to adopt would be a seer weighing about $2\frac{1}{4}$lbs. avoirdupois. Such a seer would be almost identical with the kilogramme of the metric system, which weighs 2·205lbs. All the advantages therefore which may be claimed for a seer weighing 2·24lbs., or the thousandth part of an English ton, as the unit of retail trade in India, belong equally to the kilogramme. The difference between the two is little more than half an ounce, or $1\frac{1}{2}$ per cent., a quantity that, with ordinary scales and weights, and in the ordinary transactions of life, is hardly appreciable. So far as the unit of weight is concerned, it may be confidently affirmed that, for the purposes of retail trade, no value more generally convenient to the people of India, or more popular, could be given to the seer than the value of the kilogramme.

'It remains to consider the interests of the wholesale and external trade of India.

'If we were to look only to the present, we should come to the conclusion that the most convenient plan would be to take the English ton as the basis of our system, in the manner already suggested. But we must not look only to the present. In the interest of the people of this country it would, as Colonel Strachey has urged very forcibly, be altogether unjustifiable to make any organic change in the weights of India, unless we are satisfied that it will be virtually final, and that there is no probability that further organic changes will be required hereafter.

'It therefore becomes necessary to take into consideration the probabilities of England abandoning its existing weights, and ultimately adopting the metric system.

'Every country in civilised Europe has to a greater or less extent gone through the same process which we seem to be now going through in England. The first feeling which has everywhere prevailed has been one of absolute and universal hostility to the introduction of any new system of weights and measures having its origin in a foreign country, however inconvenient the existing system may be. The next step has been that men of science have come generally to the conclusion that the metric system ought to be adopted. Then, after, for the most part, a long interval, the leading men of the commercial classes have said the same. Opinions in favour of the change have gone on gradually but constantly spreading, until at last the change has been, with more or less completeness, actually made. England will apparently be, before long, the only country in the civilised world which will not have assimilated its weights and measures to those of the metric system. It is shown by these papers that this system has been adopted in its integrity by France, Belgium, Holland, Italy, the Papal States, Spain, Portugal, Greece, Brazil, and the South American Republics; and that Austria, the Southern States of Germany, Switzerland, Sweden, Norway, and Denmark have adopted it in part. Even during the last few months, progress in the same direction has been going on. We have lately learned that Prussia and the whole of the States of the North German Confederation have, by a law passed by their parliament, adopted the metric system without modification, and that it will be brought into compulsory use from the commencement of the year 1872, and optionally from 1870. Considering the dislike which at the present time prevails throughout Germany towards everything that is French, there can be no more remarkable instance than this of the irresistible progress of the conviction that the metric system is the only system suitable to the wants of a civilised nation. . . . When we see what is going on in all parts of the civilised world towards bringing about conformity of weights and measures and coinage; when we see how much progress has actually been made; and when we consider the unanimity of men of science upon this subject in all countries (for, in spite of a few great English names that may be quoted in support of other opinions, this unanimity really prevails), it seems impossible to believe that England, whose system of weights and measures is probably as inconvenient as any existing in the world, will remain permanently content to leave matters as they are. . . . The metrical system has the great practical advantage of being based on proper scientific principles, of being the only such system actually in use, and of being in operation, at least partially, over the most advanced part of Continental Europe. These advantages are such as to satisfy me that it will never have any real competitor when the day for change has come. The true importance of international uniformity in these things is at last beginning to be properly estimated, and the movement which has commenced in its favour cannot cease until it has been successful. . . . If the ultimate adoption by England of the metric system is inevitable, it would be altogether wrong to force India to adopt the existing English system. Even if my anticipations be thought too strong, and the probabilities of the introduction into England of the metrical system be really far more remote than I suppose, it can hardly be said that they are so remote that it would be reasonable to leave them out of consideration. It would be better to do nothing at all, and to let the weights and measures of India remain in their present state of confusion, than to run the risk of having, at some future time, to go through the process of altering them again.

'If we take the kilogramme for our unit of weight, we may be satisfied that we are laying the foundation of a system which will be perfectly convenient for the internal wants of India; which will be in harmony with that of the greater part of the civilised world; which will probably be eventually adopted by England herself; and which in any case will be more convenient for the transactions between England and India than any other system can be which is not really commensurable with that of England. A very large and increasing part of English commerce is with nations using the metric weights, and this system is therefore necessarily familiar to all English merchants. To extend it to the Indian trade would be attended with less annoyance than to introduce any altogether new system. . . .

'The question may perhaps be raised whether it would not be better to defer any action until all doubt has been removed as to the course that England will pursue. Now the adoption in India of the existing English system being out of the question, the practical issue thus raised is the following:—

'First, whether India should at once take as the basis of her weights the metric system, which she might do with complete internal convenience; with a reasonable expectation that England herself will before long adopt it also; and with the knowledge that its introduction into India will in no way cause inconvenience in commercial transactions with England greater than that which exists already; or—

'Secondly, whether all reform should be delayed for an indefinite period, with a view to India shaping its course in conformity with that which England may ultimately adopt. The urgency for the removal of the evils of the present state of things in India—evils universally acknowledged to be real and serious—has to be balanced against the possible inconvenience that may be caused by a future difference in the system of weights in India and in England. This difference would certainly never be greater than that which has always existed, and which now exists, and in all probability it might before long entirely cease.

'The conclusion is easy that delay should not be permitted for such a reason. It is certain that the longer we delay in laying the foundation of a uniform system, the greater will be the difficulties with which we shall have to deal. The evils which result from the present state of things must necessarily be felt more and more with the improvement of the means of communication, and with the progress of the country in wealth, education, and civilisation. It is easier to make the commencement of a change now than it will be hereafter, when fresh interests have grown up, and when the power and inclination to create opposition to the introduction of any new system will have become far stronger than they now are.'

For these reasons Lord Lawrence's Government reported its conclusion to the Secretary of State that 'the new unit of weight should be a seer equal to the kilogramme, or 2·205lbs. avoirdupois.'[1] The conclusion was approved by the Duke of Argyll, who was then Secretary of State, and in 1870 an Act was passed to give it the force of law. Lord Mayo was then Viceroy, and the Legislative Council had the advantage of the presence of commercial members of much eminence. The measure received the warm approval of Lord Mayo, and it was passed by the Council without a dissentient voice.

[1] Despatch to Secretary of State, dated November 6, 1868.

It had been agreed by the Government of Lord Lawrence and by the Secretary of State that it was expedient, in the first instance, to deal with weights only, and not with measures of length, the latter being a subject of less urgency. It was, however, thought desirable by Lord Mayo's Government, partly for technical reasons, to take the opportunity of also defining in the new law the standard of length, on which, under the metrical system, the unit of weight depends. The metre was declared to be the official unit of length, because it was apparent that the unit of weight being that of the metric system, the unit of length must almost of necessity follow the same system. The Secretary of State, however, thought that the original conclusion was the better; that no reference to measures of length should be made in the Act; and he thought also that certain sections containing compulsory powers in regard to weights went further than was desirable. A new Bill was, therefore, introduced by Sir James Stephen, containing the modifications which the Secretary of State desired, and it became law as 'the Indian Weights and Measures of Capacity Act, 1871.'

The Regulation of 1833 having been repealed as obsolete, the Act of 1871 is the only law on the subject actually in force in British India. Its principal provisions are as follows. It declares that 'it is expedient to provide for the ultimate adoption of a uniform system of weights and measures of capacity throughout British India;' that the primary standard of weight shall be a seer, equal to the French kilogramme; that the unit of weight shall be the seer, and the unit of measures of capacity a measure containing one seer of water; that other weights and measures of capacity may be authorised by the Governor-General in Council, subject to the condition that they must be integral multiples or sub-divisions of the prescribed units; that proper standards and sets of weights and measures of capacity are to be provided for use in the various districts. The Act then declares, with various provisions which need not be quoted, regarding the appointment of warders, the verification of local standards, and other matters, that whenever the Governor-General in Council considers that proper weights and measures of capacity have been made available, he may order that, after a fixed date, all or any of such weights and measures shall be used in dealings and contracts by any Government office, or municipality, or railway company.

This last provision defines the only power given to the Government for carrying the new law into effect. It was from the first decided by Lord Lawrence, and the decision was never altered, that the new system ought not, in regard to private trade and dealings, to be forced upon any class of the public, until that class was prepared to receive it with approval. Whatever new system might be adopted, this would be equally expedient. It is visionary to suppose that even if the Government were inclined to do anything so foolish, it could force upon the people of India, within any definite period, the adoption of any new system of weights and measures. The views of Lord Lawrence's Government in regard to the steps to be actually taken were explained as follows in the minute already quoted:—

'All who have studied the subject have agreed that the proper way of beginning the introduction of any new system would be to adopt it in all Government and municipal departments, and on the railways. When we consider the manner in which India is being covered with a network of railways and canals, which will carry an enormous proportion of the trade of the country; and when we remember the magnitude of the operation of the Government in the Public Works, the Commissariat, the Post Office, the Customs, and in other departments, it is reasonable to anticipate that, in a not very distant future, the country would have become so far accustomed to the new units, that the measures necessary for their general introduction could no longer be properly called compulsory. I believe that it may be confidently said that not many years would elapse before this would be true at least of the wholesale traders in all of the richest parts of India, and that they would gradually, for their own convenience, adopt the new system almost without pressure on the part of Government. When the wholesale traders had become accustomed to the change, its gradual introduction into the operations of retail trade would be attended with comparatively little difficulty.'

In pursuance of this plan of proceeding, Lord Mayo opened communications on behalf of the Government with the principal railway companies. The East Indian and some other companies had gone so far as to alter their weighing machines to make them suitable to the new system, and Lord Mayo confidently expected to see the first steps towards this reform, in which he had taken a great interest, successfully carried out. After his death a stop was put to further proceedings, and although from time to time attempts have been made to renew them, they have always, through various causes, come to nothing, and matters remain in the same unsatisfactory condition in which they were found by Lord Lawrence fifteen years ago. We must be satisfied, for the present, with the knowledge that it is something even to have failed in the accomplishment of a wise undertaking, when the failure may help to prepare the way for success hereafter.

It need only be said further that the existing absence of all recognised legal standards of weights and measures in India is not merely extremely inconvenient and objectionable for trade purposes, and conducive to fraudulent transactions among an ignorant population, but also is most mischievous in relation to the collection of trustworthy statistics of any kind. It is to be hoped that a more intelligent view of this really important subject may before long prevail, and lead to the adoption in practice of the system which, having been authorised by the law, only requires the action of the Government in the manner that has been indicated to bring it into early general use. It may confidently be asserted that the acceptance of a sound and uniform system of commercial weights and measures would be hardly less important and valuable to India than was the adoption of a uniform system of currency. The public inconvenience and injury caused by the neglect of this matter have gone on far too long, and must continue to increase as the country becomes richer and trade more active.

CHAPTER XIX.

POSSIBLE SOURCES OF NEW TAXATION.

PRODUCTIVE TAXES IN INDIA FEW—NEW SOURCES OF REVENUE MAY BE FOUND—RATES ON LAND—IN BENGAL—THE PERMANENT SETTLEMENT—ITS SERIOUS EVILS—RATES ON LAND IN OTHER PROVINCES—INCOME TAX—REGISTRATION—EXTENSION OF PRESENT SYSTEM DESIRABLE—SUCCESSION TAX—DIFFICULTIES IN WAY OF ITS ADOPTION—TOBACCO TAX—OBJECTIONS TO IT—SUGAR DUTY—MORE PRACTICABLE—HOUSE TAX—NOT RECOMMENDED—ON MARRIAGES—RAILWAY TRAFFIC—OTHERS—CONCLUSIONS—NOTE ON DARBHANGA ESTATE.

THERE seems, as already explained, no present cause for anticipating that it will become necessary to impose upon the country any new or onerous taxation. On the contrary, there is every reason for believing that we shall continue to see a steady improvement in the finances, and a diminution of the public burdens; provided always that we continue to improve the administration of the existing sources of revenue; that we spare no efforts in developing the immense natural resources of the country; and refuse to listen, both to those who tell us that India cannot afford to provide herself with railways and canals, and the other machinery without which it is impossible she should be really prosperous, and to those who, under the name of promoting independent enterprise, desire to divert to foreign capitalists the profits of such undertakings, which should become one of the most important sources of the national wealth. It may nevertheless be useful, independently of any questions of present or future financial necessity, to place on record some account of the schemes by which it has, at various times, been suggested that the revenues might be improved by fresh taxation, for it is an obvious defect of the Indian financial system that the productive sources of taxation are so few. This defect is one of the inevitable consequences of the monotonous and primitive conditions of Indian social life and industry, and of the comparative poverty of the people, but it is, at the same time, an element of financial weakness which it is wise to bear in mind and, from time to time, to remedy, so far as this is possible without falling into the far worse evil of worrying and alarming the people with new and unnecessary imposts.

But although new forms of taxation may be difficult to devise, it would be a great error to suppose that the limits of possible taxation have been nearly reached in India. The country is, beyond a doubt, one of the most lightly taxed in the world, and there is not only no foundation for the assertion that taxation has of late years been increasing, but, on the contrary, it has positively been reduced. It may be added, that whether we look to the incidence of the land revenue, or to the total burdens imposed on the people, there is certainly no considerable native state in India where the taxation is so light as it is in our own territories; and this relative advantage must in most places be much increased by the greatly improved means of communication, and the greater freedom and expansion of trade in the British provinces.

It would undoubtedly be possible, therefore, to increase largely the income of the State without serious injury to the industry of the country, and without political danger, in the event of any great financial emergency; such, for instance, as might conceivably though most improbably, arise if we were suddenly to lose the greater part of our opium revenue, or if the difficulties caused by the fall in the value of silver in relation to gold should attain very alarming dimensions.

Rates on Land.—Among possible sources of additional revenue the first to be considered is the Land; and if circumstances should arise in which the application of heroic remedies became not only justifiable but necessary, there can be little doubt, if regard be had to the true interests and reasonable wishes of India herself, that one source from which those remedies would, in part at least, be drawn is the land of Bengal.

Nearly ninety years ago Lord Cornwallis carried out the permanent settlement of Bengal.

It is not overstating the facts to say that, in consequence of this settlement, which has been well described as 'one of the most unfortunate but best-intentioned plans that ever ruined a country,'[1] at least 3,000,000*l.* of revenue is lost every year with no compensating advantage.

According to the official returns the total rental of Bengal at the present time is more than 13,000,000*l.*, and it is certain that the actual rental exceeds rather than falls short of this sum. If land revenue were paid at the rate prevailing in those provinces of Northern India where the assessment is universally admitted to be light, the amount yielded by it in Bengal would be at least 6,500,000*l.*, while a settlement made on the system followed in the most prosperous parts of the Bombay presidency would yield a very much larger amount. The actual land revenue of Bengal being

[1] Niebuhr, quoted by Mr. O'Kinealy.

only 3,700,000*l.*, it is a moderate computation, and one really much below the mark, to say that we are now losing 3,000,000*l.* a year from this cause.

The time will inevitably come when the intelligent portion of the community in the rest of India will appreciate the fact that, in consequence of an arrangement ignorantly made nearly a century ago, the richest class in the richest province of the Empire bears far less than its just share of the public burdens; that the other provinces, all of them comparatively poor in natural resources, are therefore paying several millions a year of taxation from which they would otherwise be exempt, and that, what they lose from this arrangement, the people of Bengal do not gain. When this is understood and admitted, except by the zemindars, in Bengal itself, the application of the needful remedies will be an easier matter than it seems now.

It must not be supposed, from what has thus been said, that it is desired in any way to deny or undervalue the moral obligation which rests upon us, of respecting the pledges given by Lord Cornwallis, at the permanent settlement, to the zemindars of Bengal. As Sir James Stephen has said in one of his admirable speeches :—

'Those to whom we succeed, and whose policy laid the foundations of the power which we possess, deliberately gave to a large and influential class of the population, over which we exercise that power, a pledge on the faith of which relations have grown up which modify the whole framework of society. No one is more strongly impressed than I with the importance of scrupulously maintaining the pledges given at the period of the permanent settlement.'[1]

[1] Speech in the Legislative Council, April 6, 1871. This opportunity may be taken of expressing the hope that Sir James Stephen will some day

But what we are bound to respect are the rights which were really bestowed upon the zemindars, and which they have lawfully enjoyed; and if the conditions of the permanent settlement be altered to the detriment of the zemindars, just compensation must undoubtedly be given to them for the loss of such rights, not for the loss of that gain which has been wrongfully usurped, and to which their claims have never been admitted by the Government or the law.

The preposterous claim of the zemindars, based on non-existent and imaginary stipulations in the permanent settlement, to be exempted for ever from all liability to every form of taxation, whether for general or local purposes, on their property in land, though still vehemently asserted by members of this class, have passed finally away from discussion by reasonable men. The last ten years have seen the imposition, with the full approval of every Lieutenant-Governor, every Viceroy, and every Secretary of State, of cesses upon the land in Bengal for local and provincial purposes, yielding nearly 700,000*l.* a year. If the example be wisely followed hereafter, the application of heroic remedies, so far at least as merely financial considerations are concerned, may be avoided, however necessary they may be for other and possibly more important reasons.

And to such reasons, though they lie beyond the strict limits of the present discussion, a short reference must be made. The Report of the Commission recently appointed to consider the question of the amendment of the rent law in Bengal, which included some of the

give us the means of easy reference to his speeches and minutes, which are now scattered about in inaccessible places. They will be a storehouse of practical wisdom to all interested in India.

ablest and most experienced men in the service of the Government of Bengal, and whose conclusions have been generally accepted by that Government, furnishes a melancholy commentary on the condition of things which has grown up under the permanent settlement in this great province, containing nearly 70,000,000 of people, the vast majority of whom are dependent on the land for their support. It would be out of place to give here any opinion on the particular remedial measures proposed. But there can be no doubt that if the views of the Commission were adopted, and the legislation which it advises were carried out, something like a revolution would be brought about in the relations between the zemindars of Bengal and the cultivators of the soil, and in the social condition of the province. It will not be without a long and arduous struggle that these questions will receive even a partial solution. Meanwhile the bounty of nature happily counteracts the folly and injustice of man, and Bengal cannot cease to be the richest and in some respects the most prosperous province of India, although a large proportion of her people are condemned to poverty which, if justice had been done, they would not now be suffering, and although a large proportion of her wealth has been uselessly thrown away.

The spirit of the views adopted to a great extent by the Commission may be gathered from the following passage, quoted from a paper appended to the Report by Mr. O'Kinealy, a distinguished officer of the province, and one of its members. The accuracy of his statements will doubtless be called in question by those who admire the permanent settlement and the existing system of landed tenure in Bengal, but they cannot be passed over in silence.

'The Government revenue of the permanent settlement was about 2,858,000*l.*, and eight-tenths of the gross rental. One-third of the land was waste, it is said. On these conditions, if the whole of Bengal had been under cultivation, the gross rental would be 4,764,000*l.* According to the report of the Board of Revenue, it was in 1877 equal to 13,037,000*l.* In other words, the rates of rent which were intended to be fixed by the permanent settlement have been trebled, and the ryots are now being compelled to pay an excessive exaction of 8,273,000*l.* yearly. If this annuity be valued at twenty years' purchase, it appears that we have deprived the cultivators of this enormous sum of 165,000,000*l.*, and given it to the zemindars, who still cry for more. What large portions of this enormous income are squandered by "mismanagement, extravagance, and want of self-restraint" may be gathered by a reference to the Report on Wards' Estates for 1877–78 and other years. During the last few years the Government has spent crores on famine. Every Administration Report since 1873 dwells on the bad feeling existing, and the riots and murders which have occurred through disputes between landlords and tenants. An Act to prevent agrarian disturbances had to be passed, and a committee appointed to enquire why the ryots in Behar had abandoned their holdings and fled to Nepal.'

The not uncommon supposition that nearly the whole of the land of Bengal is in the hands of a comparatively small number of very rich zemindars is, of course, erroneous. A great number of middlemen has grown up. But, notwithstanding the existence of a multitude of subordinate interests in the land, the fact remains that in the midst of the people whose condition has been described in the foregoing extract, and whose patient industry has created and maintains the great wealth of this magnificent province, we have the spectacle of men whose annual income, given to them originally by the British Government in return for nothing, is sometimes reckoned, not metaphorically but literally, in hundreds of thousands of pounds, who discharge none of the duties of landlords towards those whose rights have been confiscated for their profit, and contribute almost nothing towards the requirements of the State. A note to this chapter contains a Resolution lately published by the Government of Bengal, regarding the vast estate of the Maharaja of Darbhanga, in Behar, which affords an excellent example of the consequences which have followed from the permanent settlement.[1]

The destruction or non-recognition of the rights of the masses of the agricultural population has been by far the most serious and lamentable of the evils which have followed in the train of the permanent settlement of Bengal. If it had given prosperity and comfort to the millions who cultivate the soil, there might have been sufficient compensation for the sacrifice of the revenue directly derived from the land, but this sacrifice, while it has failed to benefit the people of Bengal, causes permanent injustice to the whole of India, and unduly increases the burdens of the entire people.

It is not only in Bengal that it would be possible, in case of serious emergency, to obtain, without injury to the agricultural interests of the country, a larger contribution from the proprietors of the land. It would be cause for regret should it become necessary to place further taxation on the landholders of Northern India, and it is very unlikely that such necessity will arise during the currency of the existing settlements; but it cannot be doubted that ample means to bear

[1] As an amusing but unfortunately true illustration, the following story may be quoted:—'The bailiff of a wealthy landholder in Bengal lately wrote to his law agent in Calcutta as follows: "His honour my master purposes to raise the rents on his estate 5 per cent., in consequence of the recent providential fall of rain; and 2 per cent. more to meet the cess which the Government has imposed on him in order to diffuse the blessings of education amongst his tenants."'

additional burdens, if these should become unavoidable, have been left to them by the liberality of the Government. In treating of the new famine taxation, and elsewhere, enough has been already said on this part of the subject.

Income and Licence Taxes.—The income tax as it existed in 1870–71, yielded, at the rate of $3\frac{1}{8}$ per cent. on incomes exceeding Rs. 500, a little more than 2,000,000*l.*, and with the better administration which could be secured, it would certainly, at that rate, now yield very much more. A large sum could, however, without difficulty or the slightest political danger, be raised, in case of necessity, by the simple plan of increasing the existing licence tax and cesses. By doubling their present rate, which would still not bring them up to the rate at which the income tax was on more than one occasion levied, and extending their incidence to the official and professional classes in the manner that has been proposed, we should obtain at least 2,500,000*l.* a year, or 1,500,000*l.* more than the revenue now derived from these sources. This is obviously the easiest and best way of obtaining, in case of emergency, an immediate increase of revenue, and it shows very strongly the importance of holding this resource in careful reserve. If the existing system of direct taxation be wisely administered and improved, it will become, not only one of the least objectionable among present sources of revenue, but would, if necessary, be capable of great expansion hereafter.

Registration.—There is one plan by which a not unimportant increase of revenue might almost immediately be obtained, and which is so little open to objection that it might, in my opinion, be at once adopted. It was suggested in 1879 by Mr. F. R.

Cockerell, and consists in the development into a source of revenue of the present system under which fees are levied on the registration of documents.[1]

Under the existing law affecting registration in India, all written instruments are divided into two classes,—those which must be registered, and those of which the registration is optional.

It may be said generally that the first class comprises documents affecting immovable property, and that the second includes all other documents. Fees are levied on all instruments brought for registration. When registration was in its infancy, it was necessary to its success that it should be as cheap as possible, and the system has hitherto been worked on the assumption that it is not to be a source of revenue. It has now, however, been for some sixteen years in common use; it has become thoroughly familiar to the people; the practice of registration has become almost everywhere greatly developed, and there is no reason to fear that a moderate enhancement of the fees now charged would check its progress. There has been a general agreement of cpinion, on the part of the Local Governments and officers who were consulted, that these fees are a most proper source of revenue, and a committee of experienced officers, appointed to consider Mr. Cockerell's proposals, reported in favour of them. These proposals were, first, to abolish the limit of Rs. 100, below which value the registration of documents affecting immovable property is not now compulsory, and thus to enforce the registration of all documents affecting such property; and, secondly, to raise the fees for all registration, from two-fifths to one per

[1] The following account of these plans is taken from Mr. Bazett Colvin's note on taxation in India, and very often in his own words.

cent. on the value of the property affected by the registration.

As a financial measure, the first proposal has little importance, but on administrative grounds it is highly desirable that it should be adopted. It has been proved by experience in India to be necessary to provide for the authentication of all written instruments; every Local Government in India has supported the proposal, and it can hardly be doubted that, apart from financial considerations, it will before long be carried out.

The second proposal, that the fees on all registrations should be raised, is financially more important, and there has been a general consent of opinion among the authorities consulted that this measure might be adopted without objection.

Mr. Bazett Colvin, who was President of the Committee of Enquiry into the subject, has stated, in the note to which reference has been made, his reasons for believing that we might obtain in this way a gross annual revenue of about 700,000*l.*, and, taking the probable expenditure at about 200,000*l.*, there would be a clear gain to the treasury of say 500,000*l.* a year. It is possible that this estimate would prove too high at first, but, on the other hand, it is probable that it would ultimately be exceeded. This is one of the best suggestions yet made for adding to the revenue; there is complete evidence to show that it could be collected without dissatisfaction, and that no important objection of principle to it exists. In France, the revenue derived from the registration of assurances amounts to upwards of 18,000,000*l.* a year, and although any comparison between the two countries would be absurd, there is in some respects, and especially in the minute sub-division of property in land, an analogy between the social circumstances of France and of British India, from which instructive lessons may sometimes be drawn.

Succession Tax.—A form of new taxation frequently talked about in India has been a succession tax; but the belief in its expediency and suitability for India has been given up by every one who has studied it. Little can be said regarding it which has not already been said by Sir J. P. Grant, Sir Henry Maine, Mr. Colvin, and others.[1] No machinery exists for collecting such a tax in India. In England, a legacy and probate duty is levied without difficulty, because all property must pass at its owner's death into the hands of executors and administrators, who have no interest in defrauding the State, and can be used as quasi-public functionaries for the collection of the tax. Almost all personal property in England takes the form of investments, which constitute a debt payable to the deceased person's estate. The law has only to declare, as it does, that no debt due to an estate can be discharged except by payment to the deceased's personal representative, and the debtor's private interest is at once enlisted on behalf of the public revenue. He will not expose himself to loss by paying his debt into the hands of any one but an executor or administrator.

In India these conditions are almost reversed. Personal property seldom takes the form of investments. Capital is laid out not in scrip, stock, insurances, &c.,

[1] See in particular (1) Sir J. P. Grant, in letter from Government of Bengal to Government of India, dated May 29, 1860; (2) Memorandum on succession duties, by Mr. J. Strachey, dated October 19, 1865; (3) Minute by Hon. H. S. Maine, dated August 12, 1867; (4) Note on the possibility of further taxation in India, by Hon. B. W. Colvin, 1880. Nearly all that is here said regarding a succession tax is taken from these papers, often in the words of their authors.

but in cash, bullion, and precious stones; nor is there any possession of these by temporary representatives through whom a duty can be collected. They pass, in domestic secrecy, on their owner's death, into the hands of his heirs, and are not even seen by anybody but the persons interested. Sir Henry Maine's conclusion was that 'no approach to fairness could be made in the assessment of such a tax, unless the procedure were made to the last degree inquisitorial.' This impossibility of justly assessing personalty is alone an insuperable objection to a succession duty. Unless personal property can be reached, it would be paid almost exclusively by landed proprietors.

Another important argument against a succession tax has been forcibly stated by Sir Henry Maine. It has been said that a tax on inheritances is levied at a time when its payment is little felt. This would not be true in India. Joint ownership by families, clans, and communities, still prevails largely. When a member of such a community dies, his co-proprietors gain so far as his requirements for personal expenditure go, but lose by the produce of his labour. In a poor community his earnings usually exceed his expenses, and thus a man's heirs are commonly made poorer instead of richer by his death. The argument that a succession duty is a well-timed tax, which is often untrue in England, would be almost always so in India.

No form of direct taxation would be more unpopular or more difficult to assess. One suggestion, however, was made by Sir Henry Maine which still deserves consideration. He said that, although a succession tax was unsuitable for India generally, it might be practicable in Lower Bengal, where there is a nearer approach than elsewhere in India to the English law of probate and administration, and a greater tendency to substitute the individual for the family as the unit of ownership.

It must be added that the changes in the law of probate and administration, now under the consideration of the Legislature, may, in process of time, cause important change in the present condition of things; better data than now exist for the assessment of personalty may become available, and a succession tax may become, in many parts of India, a more suitable tax than it would be at present.

Tobacco Tax.—Another tax which has been frequently recommended for India is a tax on tobacco. Everything seems at first sight to recommend tobacco as a subject of taxation. It is not a necessary of life. It is consumed by a very large proportion of the population, and the effect of a moderate duty would scarcely be distinguishable among the fluctuations to which the price of tobacco is constantly liable. Frequent attention has been given to this subject, and during Lord Lytton's administration it was carefully reconsidered. The same conclusion, however, has always been come to, that the idea of raising a large revenue from this source must be abandoned.

We may put aside, as impracticable, except under the pressure of some financial catastrophe so great that it would justify almost any experiment, the idea of establishing a Government monopoly of the sale of tobacco throughout India. Such a monopoly might doubtless, if it were possible, yield a large revenue, perhaps 3,000,000*l.* or 4,000,000*l.* a year; but no approach has hitherto been made to the suggestion of a scheme by which this could be done.

The only other plan that has been seriously proposed, and the only one which has seemed to offer any real chances of success, is to place a special tax on the cultivation of the plant. This is by no means impossible, but the objections and difficulties would be great. The amount and value of the tobacco produced on different soils varies so much, that a uniform rate on cultivation, sufficiently high to be profitable, could hardly be imposed without pressing very heavily on the poorer soils, while differential rates of duty would afford great facilities for corruption and fraud. The yield of tobacco in Bengal is said to range from 160lbs. to 3,200lbs. per acre, and the cost of cultivation from Rs. 4½ to Rs. 50 per acre, while prices vary from Rs. 2 to Rs. 22 per maund (82lbs). It is another serious objection, that, although ultimately paid by the consumer, the tax would have to be advanced in the first instance by the producer. It would thus be levied in the most inconvenient and objectionable way possible; and considering the comparative poverty of the majority of the Indian agricultural population, their ignorance, and their general dependence on the money-lender, not only would this payment in advance of a tax which they had to recover from the consumer, be extremely distasteful, but there can be little doubt that a portion of the impost, or an addition to it, would ultimately rest upon them, and that they would be unable to pass on the whole of the burden. All these objections would be increased, in many parts of India, by the great difficulty of preventing the introduction into the markets of tobacco from Native States, or by other methods of smuggling; and to whatever extent tobacco that had not paid duty might enter into general consumption, the tax would to a corresponding extent fall upon the producer, and would be irrecoverable from the consumer. The same would probably happen whenever accident of season or other cause might lead to the total or partial loss of the crop upon which the duty had been paid in advance; for it would be hardly possible, in practice, in most parts of India, to make refunds of the duty on such grounds.

Another fact must not be forgotten. Tobacco is almost universally consumed, and is looked upon as almost a necessary of life. Whatever means were adopted, the tax would only be largely productive if it fell ultimately on the classes which form the great mass of the community. It would be paid by the same classes which now pay the salt tax; and if it should become necessary to increase the burdens which they already bear, this object would be more easily and economically gained, and with far less vexation to the people, by increasing the existing tax upon salt than by imposing a new tax upon tobacco. That any increase in the rate of the salt tax would be one of the greatest possible mistakes, unless in most exceptional circumstances, and, on the other hand, that its present reduction would be financially a most desirable measure, has been shown in another chapter.

Sugar Duty.—Another tax which has been suggested is an excise duty upon sugar. 'If,' writes Mr. Colvin, 'it should be desired to raise a considerable sum of money by indirect taxation, an excise laid upon sugar, accompanied by a corresponding import duty, would no doubt supply it. There is, indeed, no other indirect tax which, if levied at an equal rate, would bring in such large returns. It would fall upon an article which is perhaps more of a luxury than anything else that is generally consumed in this country. Moreover, it would be a tax upon more than one luxury; for in most, if not all parts of India, the tobacco that is smoked by the people is mixed with an equal weight of sugar. Smokers, therefore, would pay a tax, which would be equivalent to a tobacco tax, upon the sugar which they consume in this form, in addition to the tax levied from them for the sugar that they eat.' Mr. Colvin thinks that we may assume, although the data are very imperfect, that the total value of the sugar consumed in British India in a year is about 20,000,000*l.*, and an *ad valorem* duty of 5 per cent. would yield about 1,000,000*l.* of revenue. The average incidence of such a tax would be less than three farthings per head of the population. It has been suggested that it might either be levied by a licence fee on the boiling pans, or by a licence fee on sugar mills, or by an acreage rate on cane cultivation and date groves.

This would be on the whole a better tax than one on tobacco, but it would be very unwise to adopt it without extreme necessity. It is unnecessary now to discuss its merits and demerits; it is obviously open to nearly all the objections which have been urged to a tax upon tobacco.

House Tax.—In theory, a house tax has much to recommend it; but it has been shown by experience that among all Indian taxes there is perhaps no one so universally unpopular as this. The following remarks are taken from Mr. Colvin's paper:—

'A house tax in India is peculiarly open to the great objection which lies against direct taxation in all countries, viz. that it cannot be fairly assessed. As the tax is at present levied, it is assessed in one of two ways: either by a rate upon the assumed rental or value of the house, or by one calculated upon the supposed means of the house-owner. Now, in India, there is no certain rental on which to base a calculation. A house is built for occupation by its owner and his descendants; hardly ever for the purpose of being let. Renting, except in large towns, is unknown, and there is no recognised letting value of buildings in other places. In the absence of any actual rents, the assessors are driven to conjecture them. It is not to be expected that assessors, being at liberty to guess, should always care to guess fairly, and much injustice is done, no doubt wilfully. Even when they endeavour to be fair, the tax is not made palatable because its assessment may be equitable. A native of this country can never recognise any justice in an assessment so calculated. He can understand, though he does not like, a tax that is calculated on income, or one that is calculated upon actual expenditure; but a tax reckoned upon his imaginary rental seems to him to be neither one nor the other, but simply exaction. . . . It might be supposed that the house itself would furnish no bad indication of its owner's means. But in India, where men do not at once change their houses with their fortunes, this is not the case. It is notorious, on the contrary, that such a test would be very delusive. A prosperous trader in this country will often be content to occupy a mere cluster of sheds, whilst an honourable, but ruined, family will continue to live in a substantial house, built, by wealthier ancestors, long after it has become much too large for their diminished means. . . . Another important objection to a house tax is that, with all its unpopularity, it would not produce much. It would, I have no doubt, be found that the agriculturists must be exempted from it. They already contribute their fair share to the public revenue; and though it might not be unjust, perhaps, to impose a house tax on them, this tax could not, I am persuaded, be levied from them without danger. . . . If the tax did not extend to the agricultural community, three-fifths of the whole number of taxpayers would be exempted. The proceeds of the tax would not be diminished in quite the same proportion, as the rate of incidence would be less in the country than in the towns; but as much as one-third or one-half of the income would probably be lost.'

Marriages.—It is unnecessary to discuss at length the propriety of a tax upon marriages, though some authorities have advocated it, on the ground that it would produce a large revenue and that it might check, to some extent, the excessive expenditure often incurred on marriage ceremonies in India. Mr. Colvin has clearly shown that such a tax could not yield much revenue, except at the cost of extreme unpopularity; for to be profitable it must reach the masses of the people. It has been calculated that it would affect four millions of families every year, and that it would affect the entire population of the country, or thirty-six millions of families, in the course of every nine years, while three-fourths of it would be paid by the poorest classes in the country. These figures are alone sufficient to condemn the proposed tax.

Railway Traffic.—The only other tax which has been suggested, which it is necessary to mention as a possible source of imperial revenue, is a tax on railway fares and freights, similar to that levied in France and some other countries in Europe. In the existing circumstances of India, and considering that a large and increasing proportion of the railways belong to the State, this would be a questionable tax; but there is no doubt that it could be made to yield a considerable sum, say 500,000*l.* a year, and that it would be collected without any difficulty, and almost without expense. In the event of the complete abolition of all customs duties, such a tax as this might in the future afford a useful and equitable means of bringing the growing trade of the country under contribution, in a form that would be as little open to objection as any such tax could be.

Miscellaneous.—Other taxes have been suggested which might sometimes be levied without objection for local or provincial purposes, and which might thus be useful, but which, as general sources of imperial revenue, would financially be hardly worth imposing or would not be otherwise suitable. Mr. Colvin has noticed all the more important of them. Among them, he mentions one tax which, under proper regulations, would be open to no objection whatever,—a tax on the privilege of carrying arms. Taxes on conveyances and beasts of burden, taxes on retainers and servants, taxes on betel-leaf or pan, and some others, might also, in some provinces, be imposed without hardship or serious unpopularity; they would sometimes give useful aid to provincial resources.

General Conclusions.—The general conclusions which seem to be established are these: first, that the existing revenue is so prosperous, and its main sources so certainly increasing in productiveness, that there is no reason to suppose that recourse to new and untried methods of taxation will become necessary; secondly, that there would be little difficulty, in case of necessity, in almost immediately increasing the revenue, yielded by existing and other taxes of a little objectionable nature, to the extent of at least 2,000,000*l.* a year; and thirdly, that if a much larger sum than any which could be provided by such means, or by the growth of existing revenues, should be required in consequence of some great financial catastrophe, the income of the State could certainly be increased by several millions a year without injury to the country; but that before any measures were taken in such a view the whole question of taxation in Bengal should be reconsidered, with the object of placing on that province that fair share of the public burdens which it now fails to bear.

NOTE TO CHAPTER XIX.

Extract from a Resolution of the Lieutenant-Governor of Bengal, dated June 24, 1880.

THE Durbhunga estates were taken over by the Court of Wards on the death of the proprietor, Maharajah Maheswar Sing, on October 20, 1860, and were released on September 25, 1879, when the present Maharajah, Luchmeshwar Sing, attained his legal majority.

The estates comprise an area of about 2,410 square miles, with a population of 750,000 souls, and are scattered over the districts of Durbhunga, Mozufferpore, Bhagulpore, Purneah, and Monghyr. The bulk of the population is rural and agricultural; the Hindus being to the Mahomedans in the ratio of ten to one; and, of the Hindus, one in every nineteen being a high-caste Brahmin.

When the Court of Wards took charge in 1860, the condition of the property seemed almost hopelessly bad. The late Maharajah had left a daughter, Rajeshuree Daee, and two minors sons, Luchmeshwar Sing and Rameshwar Sing, aged respectively two years and under one year. The gross annual rental of the estates was nominally Rs. 16,39,357 (163,000*l.*) and the Government revenue only Rs. 4,07,484 (40,000*l.*). But the management had for years been left entirely in the hands of underlings. All the villages were leased to farmers, most of them relatives of the Raj servants, who had got their leases on favourable terms. Others were outsiders. men of straw, who had nominally undertaken to pay rents far above the value of the lands, and who made what they could by rack-renting the ryots and levying illegal cesses, without attempting to satisfy the Raj demand. Security for payment was never taken from the farmers. Pottahs and kabuliats [1] were seldom interchanged. The correct rental of the villages was nowhere recorded. Putwaris' [2] papers were seldom forthcoming. The outstanding arrears of rent, at first unknown, proved to amount to Rs. 56,44,972 (564,000*l.*). There were other debts due to the

[1] Leases and their counterparts.

[2] Village accountants.

estate, aggregating Rs. 3,37,775 (33,000*l.*). The debts due by the Maharajah to creditors amounted to a crore of rupees, of which the Court of Wards was compelled to admit Rs. 71,88,427 (718,000*l.*). The estates were destitute of roads and bridges. The palace was neglected and in ruins; its courtyards quagmires; its environs a hopeless waste of jungle, pools, and filth. Notoriously all the epidemics of the town took their rise in the Rajbaree. There were no refuges for the sick; no resting-places for travellers; not a school on the whole estate. No reproductive works of any kind had anywhere been attempted.

On the surrender of the estate to the Maharajah last year, all this had been changed. The rent-roll had been re-adjusted; and although reductions of rental had been made amounting to Rs. 5,92,323 (59,000*l.*), the gross rental (including that of a few small properties purchased) was Rs. 21,61,885 (216,000*l.*). The outstanding arrears of rent due to the estate were Rs. 18,51,397 (185,000*l.*) (less than a year's demand), of which Rs. 14,51,664 (145,000*l.*) were good, and in process of realisation. All debts had been paid off long ago. There was a cash balance in hand of Rs. 2,75,733 (27,000*l.*), besides Government securities of the value of Rs. 38,54,500 (385,000*l.*). Over 150 miles of road had been constructed and bridged (in many places with screw-pile viaducts); upwards of 20,000 trees had been planted along their sides. Feeder and village roads had been made and improved. In Khurrukpore extensive irrigation works, securing that property against famine, had been made and opened. A large bazaar had been built at Durbhunga, including a handsome public serai.

. . . . . .

In lieu of the ruinous system of farming leases, the whole estate had been brought under direct management. Collections were made without friction or difficulty. The outlying zerat[1] lands had been equitably settled with indigo-planters, while those in the vicinity of villages had been reserved for the ryots, thus putting an end to the constant disputes between the factories and the cultivators. Hundreds of small embankments, water-channels, tanks, and wells had been constructed from advances made without interest to the tenants. Complete surveys had

[1] Cultivated lands.

been made of the greater part of the property, and a considerable area had been re-settled to the advantage both of the estate and of the cultivators. Twenty vernacular schools had been established by the Raj, educating 1,000 children, aid being at the same time given to other educational institutions not belonging to the estate. Three admirable hospitals were kept up for the use of the tenantry, while assistance was also afforded to six charitable dispensaries in various places near. Above all, both the Maharajah and his brother had received a thorough English education, were proficient in manly exercises and free from the vices which are too often the ruin of native magnates. The Maharajah had been trained to manage his own affairs and to take a lively interest in the welfare of his people, while his brother had been deemed fit for appointment to the Civil Service of the province, in which he is now an assistant magistrate. They had both travelled over the greater part of Upper India, and made the personal acquaintance of the Viceroy, Lieutenant-Governor, and other high officers of State, as well as of many native potentates, to all of whom they commended themselves by their unassuming intelligence and gentlemanlike demeanour.

During the incumbency of the Court of Wards, the aggregate demand of rent due to the estate amounted to Rs. 4,26,79,578 (4,267,000*l.*). Of this, Rs. 3,54,66,458 (3,546,000*l.*) or 83 per cent. was collected, and Rs. 55,39,610 (553,000*l.*) remitted. The total receipts from all sources during the management were Rs. 4,84,50,669 (4,845,000*l.*), and the total disbursements Rs. 4,80,86,228 (4,808,000*l.*), of which Rs. 32,90,934 (329,000*l.*), or only 6·7 per cent. of the receipts, represents the cost of management. Rs. 80,41,113 (804,000*l.*) were expended in payment of Government revenue, and Rs. 31,98,000 (319,000*l.*), or 6·5 per cent. of the receipts, in the allowances of the family, including social and religious ceremonies.

. . . . . .

The Lieutenant-Governor observes, however, with regret that while the Court of Wards has done so much for the proprietor of the estate, it is frankly admitted by the manager that the condition of the Raj tenants is not generally prosperous.

Many of them are said to be living merely from hand to mouth, having suffered much from successive bad seasons. It is urged that they would have been much worse off had it not been for the good roads made, enabling them to take advantage of the high prices of produce; the liberal remissions of rent in famine years; and free advances of money given without interest. They have also, it is stated, been relieved of multifarious illegal cesses, and from the unjust exactions of ticcadars or petty leaseholders, are more alive to their legal rights, and less in debt than they were in former years. Granting all this, there can, Sir Ashley Eden fears, be little doubt that the cultivators on the Durbhunga estates are suffering from the same causes which in long course of years have reduced the peasantry of Behar generally to a lower level than that of the ryots in Central and Eastern Bengal. There has been in years gone by, under the Court of Wards, the same kind of rack-renting, the same ignoring of ryot right, the same unwillingness to recognise occupancy tenures, the same resort to illegal distraint, that have been found and condemned in every district of Behar. The traditions of the Court of Wards have from the time of its institution been essentially proprietary. The chief aim of its management in every estate has been to make the most of the property for the benefit of the owner; and although it has, in its relations to the tenantry, been incontestably a better and a wiser landlord than the ordinary run of native zemindars, it is only within the last few years that anything has been done by it to improve directly the position of the cultivators. The most important measure of this kind in the Durbhunga estate, which has been actually carried through to completion, has been the survey and settlement of Allapore. This was, it may be said, forced upon the Court by the report of the Special Commission which enquired into the condition of the pergunnahs of Allapore and Nareedigur, after the drought of 1875. It then appeared that 'a large number of the tenantry had fled from their houses to avoid the burden of debt due to enhanced rent which lay upon them too heavily.' The re-settlement of the pergunnah under the supervision of Mr. Finucane, C.S., led to a re-adjustment of rents which, while affording considerable relief to over-assessed ryots, actually led, by the discovery of lands concealed by the putwaris and head ryots, to an increase of the Raj receipts. Mr. Finucane has now nearly completed a cadastral survey of the whole of the Tirhoot and Bhagulpore estates, and the Maharajah has been allowed to retain his services to bring the work finally to a close. But in these proceedings no attempt is being made to revise the rates of rent. The Maharajah is left to make his own arrangements for this at his own time. The Lieutenant-Governor trusts that, in any action which the Maharajah may take in this direction, he will remember that it will be his wisest policy to endeavour to secure upon his estates a substantial well-to-do tenantry, able to meet the ordinary vicissitudes of season, self-respecting and jealous of their own rights, while recognising and satisfying the just and moderate demands of their landlord. In the long run it is far more profitable to the landlord to leave in the hands of the cultivators such a share in the profits of the soil as will enable them to face even the worst season without actual suffering, than to take from them all that they have, with the certainty that enormous sums will have to be expended by him in years of famine in maintaining the ryots on his estate. It may be taken as certain that the Legislature must ere long interfere for the protection of the Behar peasant against arbitrary ejectment and undue exaction of rent; and those landlords will suffer least from the intervention of the State who have themselves entered into equitable arrangements with their tenants, and admitted of their own free will those substantial rights which, under the old law and custom of India, every resident cultivator undoubtedly had, and which the frequent recurrence of famine among the poverty-stricken population of Behar seems to make it a matter of imperial necessity once more to revive. The Lieutenant-Governor, from what he knows of the Maharajah, believes that he will prove himself an active landlord. But he also believes him to be an upright and benevolent landlord, strongly impressed with a desire to improve the condition of the poorer classes residing on his estate. It is hardly necessary to impress upon him that the best practical way in which he can do justice to his education and responsibilities, and show his appreciation of the care which has been bestowed by Government on him and on his estate, will be by showing himself the friend and protector of his ryots and by setting an example to the neighbouring landholders, and using his influence with them to bring about a reform of the undoubted evils of the land system of Behar.

CHAPTER XX.

CURRENCY AND EXCHANGE.

METALLIC CURRENCY OF INDIA—GOLD COIN NOT CURRENT—PAPER CURRENCY—IMPORTS OF BULLION AND COINAGE—COMPETITION BETWEEN SECRETARY OF STATE'S BILLS AND SILVER AS A MEANS OF REMITTANCE—EXCHANGE VALUE OF RUPEE DEPENDS ON MARKET PRICE OF SILVER—RELATION BETWEEN EXCESS OF EXPORTS AND SECRETARY OF STATE'S BILLS—COMBINATION OF STERLING AND RUPEE EXPENDITURE IN PUBLIC ACCOUNTS—ADOPTION OF CONVENTIONAL RATE OF EXCHANGE—OBJECTIONS TO THIS—REASONS FOR RETAINING IT—AMOUNT OF LOSS BY EXCHANGE—HOW FAR REAL—ADJUSTMENT OF ACCOUNTS BETWEEN INDIA AND ENGLAND—ARRANGEMENT WITH BRITISH GOVERNMENT—GUARANTEED RAILWAY TRANSACTIONS—EVILS CAUSED BY FALL IN RELATIVE VALUE OF SILVER TO GOLD—EFFECTS ON FOREIGN TRADE OF INDIA—DIFFERENCE OF STANDARDS OF VALUE IN INDIA AND ENGLAND THE REAL CAUSE OF ALL THE DIFFICULTIES—NECESSITY FOR OBTAINING UNIFORMITY—COMPLETE REMEDY ONLY ATTAINABLE BY INTERNATIONAL AGREEMENT—FAILING BIMETALLISM THE ADOPTION OF GOLD STANDARD BY INDIA ESSENTIAL.

THE metallic currency of India was established on its existing basis in 1835. It consists primarily of the rupee weighing 180 grains, $\frac{11}{12}$ths fine, and therefore containing 165 grains of pure Silver; with silver coins of the same standard, representing the half rupee or 8 annas, the quarter or 4 annas, and the eighth or 2 annas. The rupee and half rupee are legal tender for any amount, the other coins only for fractional parts of the rupee. Silver is coined without limit, on payment of a seignorage of 2 per cent., and, when necessary, the cost of refining.

The Copper coins in use are the half anna, quarter anna, and one pie or the $\frac{1}{12}$th part of the anna. Copper is given and received by the public treasuries in exchange for silver, in amounts of not less than Rs. 2.

The currency law authorises Gold coins to be struck at the Mints, but they are not legal tender, and are not used as money. The coinage of gold has gradually diminished during the last twenty or thirty years, and has now virtually ceased. The authorised gold coins are the Mohur or 15-rupee piece, weighing 180 grains, $\frac{11}{12}$ths fine, and therefore equal in weight to the rupee; and corresponding coins to represent Rs. 10 and Rs. 5

The opinion has been expressed that gold money is not used in India because the people prefer silver, by reason of the small amount of their transactions. There is, however, no real evidence of this, the fact being that, for three quarters of a century at least, gold coin has either not been a legal tender, or has been improperly valued, so that either it could not come into circulation, or could not remain in circulation, in competition with the silver rupee, which has always been the standard coin. Towards the end of the last century gold coins circulated freely, with silver, in most parts of Bengal, and about half the revenue was paid in gold. Forty years ago gold coins were still to be found in use in some of the districts of Madras. Gold, however, everywhere gradually went out of circulation, and for a great many years has, for all practical purposes, ceased to be employed as money.

At various times gold coins have been received in payment of Government demands, at varying rates, but under the law of 1835 they ceased to be a legal tender. After the great gold discoveries, on some tendency appearing towards an accumulation of gold in the public treasuries, its acceptance was stopped; but, with the subsequent recovery of the value of gold in relation to silver, attempts were made to bring gold into use as money, by the Government offering to accept the sovereign at a specified rate, though not making it a legal tender. The great fall in the relative value of silver had, however, already begun, and these attempts all failed from the undervaluing of the gold; and coins of this metal, though commonly procurable in small quantities from the bankers, are used only for hoarding or for export in foreign trade.

The paper currency of India is established on a purely metallic basis. Notes are issued, by the Government alone, at one or more offices in each province, in exchange for current coin or bullion, a limited portion of the amount thus received, Rs. 60,000,000, being invested in Government securities, and the rest retained in coin by the currency department. The notes are convertible into coin on demand at the office of issue, and at the chief town of the presidency if issued elsewhere. The circulation of notes is at present about fourteen or fifteen millions.

During the last twelve years the gross imports of bullion by sea have amounted in all to 30,463,988*l.* of gold, and 80,804,579*l.* of silver; or on the average 2,538,666*l.* of the former, and 6,733,715*l.* of the latter yearly. The net imports, after deducting the exports by sea, were 23,981,589*l.* of gold, and 61,811,392*l.* of silver; or at the average rate of 1,998,382*l.* of gold, and 5,150,949*l.* of silver yearly. The total value of the silver coinage in the same period was 68,752,475*l.*, or at the rate of 5,729,373*l.* yearly. The net import of gold since 1835 amounted in value to 107,991,012*l.* The total amount of silver money coined since 1835 is somewhat more than 250,000,000*l.* sterling, and including the old coinages the quantity in existence no doubt exceeds that value; but of course a large part of this is hoarded.

The occasional excess of the coinage over the net imports of silver, is doubtless in part due to hoarded silver coin or bullion being brought to the Mint, and partly to the recoining of worn or defaced coin, but it is probably mainly caused by the export of newly coined silver. During the last three years the average yearly export of silver to Mauritius, Ceylon, and Aden, at which places the rupee is the current coin, amounted together to 812,277*l.*, which more than accounts for the excess in question during those years.

The import of silver into India, like that of any other commodity, of course depends on the demand, which in the nature of the case chiefly depends on the requirements of the country for silver coin, either to be hoarded or brought into active circulation. From the obligatory nature of the Government remittances, the sale in London of a large amount of bills on India, drawn by the Secretary of State, is necessary, for in the present state of things this is the only means of making remittances on any considerable scale; this comes to much the same thing as offering rupees for sale, and a competition is therefore established between the Secretary of State's bills and the silver bullion offered for sale in the European market, the coining of which in India is unrestricted. In these circumstances the exchange value of the rupee bills of the Indian Government is immediately, and almost solely, determined by the price at which the holders of silver bullion are prepared to sell it. After the adoption of a gold standard by Germany, the coining of silver in Europe virtually came to a standstill, and at present the United States and India may be said to be the only two countries that coin this metal, the former to a limited amount, by the State, the latter without limit for all comers. The United States being the great producer of silver, India affords almost the only market for the metal on a large scale. Hence the export of silver from India as a means of remittance becomes impossible, and, as above said, the government is driven to making its remittances by the forced sale of its bills, the value of which is controlled by the market price of silver, which again is depressed by the present limited demand for coinage, and the competition with the Secretary of State's bills, the amount of which has been much increased during the last few years. The great fall in the exchange which has occurred, and the fluctuations which still take place, have no important relation to variations of trade demand; and if the condition of the Indian currency admitted of specie remittances the effect of those variations on the exchange would be insignificant, and could never exceed in amount the cost of a bullion remittance from India and of re-coinage in Europe.

There is a close connection between the amount of the Secretary of State's bills and the excess of the Indian exports over the imports. The value of the excess exports indicates in fact the total amount which India has to remit to foreign countries in discharge of her various obligations to them; those obligations consisting chiefly of the payments to be made in England on account of the Government, for the public services, interest on debt, railway capital, and so forth; and of the savings and profits of foreigners employed or trading in India. After setting off the value of the imports of all descriptions against that of the exports, the difference must be paid to the Indian producer or his agents in coin. The foreign exporter purchases bills on India, or some other form of transferable security, with the proceeds of the sale of the exports, from persons desiring to exchange rupees in India for sterling in London, or for francs in Paris, and so forth. The bills or securities thus serve a double purpose—for the remittances from India, and for the payments for the excess exports. As the remittances are chiefly to England, it is by bills sold in London that they are for the most part made; and, the Government being the principal remitter, the bills are mainly those drawn by the Secretary of State. The difference between the actual sum realised by the sale of these bills, and their nominal value, assuming the rupee to be equal to two shillings, is what is spoken of as the loss by exchange on the Secretary of State's remittances.

During the twelve years from 1857–58 to 1868–69, inclusive, the aggregate excess of exports was 45,470,000*l.*, the bills of the Secretary of State paid in India having been 45,420,000*l.* In the following six years, the excess of exports having been 96,334,000*l.*, the bills paid amounted to 66,865,000*l.*; and in the last six years ending in 1880–81, the excess exports were 92,826,000*l.* and the bills 91,265,000*l.* For the whole series of twenty-four years the average value of the excess exports was 9,776,000*l.*, and the average of the Secretary of State's bills has been 1,295,000*l.* yearly less.

The serious effect which the fall in the exchange value of the rupee has had on the finances of India has more than once been dwelt upon in the earlier chapters of this book. The manner in which it affects the public transactions, and how it is dealt with in the public accounts, will now be considered in more detail.

The transactions of the Home treasury being necessarily conducted and recorded in sterling, while those of the Indian treasuries are necessarily in rupee currency, a system has to be settled for the combination of the accounts. Even before the amalgamation of the Home and Indian accounts, a head 'Loss by exchange,' or its equivalent, had a place in the accounts between the two countries to make allowance for the exchange value of the rupee in taking credit for remittances from India by the sale of bills, or adjusting payments of various descriptions.

Until the Mutiny in 1857 the bills on India never amounted to so much as 4,000,000*l.* in any year; the deposits of guaranteed railway capital between 1850 and 1870 contributed on an average about 4,000,000*l.* yearly to the Home treasury, and the transactions with the companies were regulated by an arbitrary rate of exchange fixed under the contracts; after the Mutiny recourse was had to borrowing on a large scale in London, and the bills up to 1870 only once exceeded 7,000,000*l.* Up to this time also the exchange value of the rupee had hardly fallen below 1*s* $10\frac{3}{4}$*d.* The loss by exchange, therefore, had not become of very material importance, and the divergence of the amount of the Home charges reckoned in sterling, from their true amount converted into rupees at the actual rate of exchange, attracted no particular attention. It was in these circumstances that the system of combining the Home and Indian accounts, on the conventional basis of treating ten rupees as equal to 1*l.*, and correcting the discrepancy by the adjusting entry 'Loss by exchange,' was adopted almost without discussion, and the practice of stating Indian revenues and expenditure in conventional pounds sterling at this rate of exchange tacitly grew up.

The rapid and serious fall in the gold value of silver after 1870, followed by the corresponding fall in the exchange value of the rupee in relation to sterling currency, led to a great change in the magnitude and importance of the 'Loss by exchange'; and the question was raised by the Government of India in 1877, in which year this charge appears as more than 2,000,000*l.*, whether it would not be desirable to show the whole of the accounts in rupee currency, that being the true standard of value for India, and to convert the Home transactions into rupees at the actual exchange of the day.

It is obvious that under the present practice of combining amounts in rupees with others in sterling, at the conventional exchange of ten rupees to the pound, no charge which is not incurred either wholly in England or wholly in India will be correctly stated, and the amounts so combined cannot represent any precise facts. For instance, a bridge for which iron-work was procured from England at a cost of 10,000*l.*, while the Indian expenditure was 120,000 rupees, would appear in the accounts as having cost 22,000*l.* If the actual exchange when the iron was bought was 1*s.* 8*d.* per rupee, its true cost would have been 120,000 rupees, and the whole cost of the bridge 240,000 rupees. The Public Works' accounts, however, would only show a charge of 22,000*l.*, the remaining 2,000*l.* (20,000 rupees) being included under the general adjusting head, 'Loss by exchange,' and there left undistinguished.

Another practical illustration of the confusion likely to arise from this system may be found in the statements made as to the cost of the Afghan war, and the share of it to be borne by England. Excluding the frontier railways, which were not taken into account for this purpose, the net cost of the war appears in the Indian accounts as 18,748,300*l.*, while the English contribution of one-third is 5,000,000*l.* This discrepancy is accounted for by the circumstance that the former sum is stated in conventional currency, which at the actual rate of exchange for the time, 1*s.* 8*d.* per rupee, is reduced to 15,623,588*l.* in true sterling, in which currency the contribution paid by England is of course stated. Thus the cost of the war might at one time be said to be 18,000,000*l.* and at another 15,000,000*l.*, both sets of figures in fact representing the same amount.

But notwithstanding these defects and the acknowledged want of precision in the present system, it has been ruled by the Secretary of State that the proposed change was not desirable and should not be made. It was argued, that the conversion of the Home accounts into rupee currency would be very troublesome, if a varying rate of exchange were taken, and if an average rate were used, true precision would still not be attained. Further, it was considered that the results on the proposed plan would also in their turn be misleading, as they would give to fluctuations in the rupee equivalents of sterling payments, which are solely dependent on variations in the rate of exchange, a false appearance of reality, and would otherwise render comparisons with former years difficult or impossible.

The sterling payments made in England, it was urged, are not determined in relation to a scale of values fixed in rupees, and it was hence argued that for purposes of general financial control, which are those mainly sought to be facilitated by the combined statements of revenue and expenditure, the ready and clear exhibition of the actual transactions is more important than any account modified and complicated by the introduction of entries arising from loss or gain by exchange, which are contingent on circumstances in no way dependent on the administrative control of the actual expenditure.

Moreover, there is an inherent essential difference of character between charges such as these and all other items of expenditure in return for which some service has been performed, or advantage obtained. The loss by exchange is a contingency of the Indian currency being based on a silver standard; the causes which influence it are altogether independent of the nature of the services in connection with which it arises; and to combine it with the cost of those services might lead to serious and objectionable misconceptions. For such reasons the conventional system of treating the pound sterling as equivalent to ten rupees has been retained, and the necessary adjustment in the accounts is made in one sum, by a single entry under the head 'Loss by exchange,' instead of being distributed over the separate heads of service affected. The charge is thus treated as incidental to the administration generally, and not as falling on any particular branch or portion of the public outlay.

The combination of the accounts by the conversion of the Indian rupee transactions into sterling values at the current rates of exchange has not been seriously advocated by any one; and, without disputing that there may be sufficient justification for maintaining the present bastard system, it is hardly open to question that the currency of India should be made the basis on which the accounts of that country are stated, and that the more completely this is accomplished the better.

It has already been noticed, and the fact is indeed obvious, that the 'Loss by exchange' arises immediately in connection with the Home receipts and disbursements, which for the purposes of the present explanations may be grouped as those relating to the Indian Government and its officers, the British Government, and the railway companies.

The main element of the 'Loss by exchange' is, as before said, the difference between the actual sterling value realised by the sale of the Secretary of State's rupee bills, and their conventional value at the rate of 2*s.* It has been said, and truly, that it is an error to regard the whole of this difference as an absolute loss. In fact, there is no absolute standard by which to estimate gain or loss in transactions such as these. The Indian Government correctly describes the entry in the accounts under 'Loss by exchange' as an adjusting entry. All that can be said as to loss being involved, or otherwise, is comparative. Compared with the rate of exchange that prevailed twenty years ago, 2*s.* 2*d.*, there is a present loss at 1*s.* 7·8*d.* of more than 6*d.* in the rupee; but in that year (1881) hardly any bills were sold. From 1863–1866 the rate was 4*d.* better than now, and it was not till 1872–73 that it fell to only 3*d.* better, in that year bills having been sold to the value of 15,000,000*l.* It is probable, therefore, that if the gold value of silver had returned to 5*s.* per ounce, as it was in 1872–73, the loss on the Secretary of State's bills in 1880–81 (15,400,000*l.*) would not have exceeded $1\frac{1}{4}$*d.* per rupee, and the advantage to the Indian treasury would have been nearly 2,500,000*l.* As the bills in the future are more likely to exceed than to fall short of 16,000,000*l.*, the amount which India may fairly be said to be losing at present by the fall in the value of silver is rather more than 2,500,000*l.* yearly.

The transactions between the British Government and India, in respect to payments made for the former in India, are adjusted at a rate fixed before the beginning of each year, by arrangement with the Treasury, based on the value of silver, and the selling price of the Secretary of State's bills at the time. On these adjustments, which generally involve a sterling payment in England, the advantage appears on the side of India, as a gain by exchange. This same rate is commonly applied for settling accounts of officers' pay and the like. The amount at stake in these transactions is not important.

The guaranteed railway transactions are much larger. The old contracts provided that the rate of exchange for adjusting the accounts between India and England should be 1*s.* 10*d.* per rupee during their entire continuance. The effect of this agreement was certainly not foreseen.

Its operation in respect to the capital accounts began by causing an apparent loss by exchange of 2*d.* per rupee, which was charged in the Indian accounts on the whole amount remitted to India by the Secretary of State for the companies; this having been about 50,000,000*l.*, the total loss by exchange would be its $\frac{1}{11}$th part, or about 4,500,000*l.* But this loss can only be regarded as having been real to whatever extent the actual exchange was better than 1*s.* 10*d.* It was therefore an effective charge till 1874–75, from which time, the exchange having been worse than 1*s.* 10*d.*, the remittances for the railways to India have been really profitable, though still appearing as a nominal loss.

For some years past, however, most of the companies have been paying back to the Government in India sums on capital account, obtained chiefly by the sale of stores paid for from capital, or by their transfer to the revenue account; these payments are credited at the rate of 1*s.* 10*d.* per rupee, and the Government nominally gains 2*d.* in the rupee, which appears accordingly as 'Gain by exchange.' But this gain is not real unless the actual exchange is above 1*s.* 10*d.*; and, in fact, these transactions at present really involve a loss, leading as they do to the companies receiving sterling credits in London at the rate of 1*s.* 10*d.* on account of rupee receipts in India, which the Secretary of State can only remit at 1*s.* 8*d.* or less.

The revenue accounts lead to different results. The companies obtain credit for their 'net traffic' receipts at the rate of 1*s.* 10*d.*, so that on the accounts the Government gains 2*d.* in the rupee on their whole amount. Up to the end of 1879 the net traffic receipts thus dealt with had aggregated rather more than 50,000,000*l.*, so that the gain by exchange in this direction had at that time nearly balanced the loss on the capital remittances. The gain on the revenue receipts until 1879–80 was deducted from their actual amount, and was shown as 'Gain by exchange,' as stated in Chapter VII. This procedure has been recognised to be inaccurate. In the accounts with the companies the net rupee receipts are rightly shown at the exchange of 1*s.* 10*d.*; but in the public accounts the actual sums received in rupee currency should be shown without deduction; and since 1879–80 this system has been adopted. Thus the railway income now appears relatively larger than before, and the gain by exchange to the same extent less, or the loss so much more.

There has been another recent change of practice which has led to a more correct way of treating the home expenditure of the railway companies on revenue account. Heretofore the funds to meet this outlay were supplied by the Secretary of State from the capital deposits, and the transfer in account was made at the contract rate; whereby, after the actual exchange fell below the contract rate, the Government has borne a loss which was not required by the contracts. The adjustments are now made at the actual rate of exchange, by which a sum of about 123,000*l.* was saved in 1879–80.

It is a necessary consequence of the manner in which the loss by exchange is treated in the public accounts—it being, as already explained, dealt with altogether apart from the effective expenditure under the various heads of service—that the accounts give no indication of the real extent to which the railway transactions influence the charge under 'Loss by exchange.' The complicated adjustments that have been explained have reference only to the remittance operations, which under the contracts are undertaken by the Secretary of State for the companies, and do not influence the financial results of the working of the railways, so far as these appear in the public accounts. It was, however, before noticed, and it may here be repeated, that the railway obligations probably cause at least one-third of the whole loss by exchange, and that this share of the burden is now little less than 1,000,000*l.* yearly.

The general result of the exchange adjustments for 1879–80 is shown below, and will indicate the main features of the charge under this head:—

Loss by exchange on Secretary of State's bills, being the difference between 2*s.* per rupee and the actual rate of sale . . .		£3,088,190
Loss on gold remittances . . .		120,221
Total loss on remittances .		3,208,411
Loss on miscellaneous transactions .	£38,572	
Gain on " " .	110,345	
Net gain . . .	71,773	
Gain on railway capital . .	87,215	
Gain on railway revenue . .	123,020	
Total gain . . .		282,008
Net loss		£2,926,403

It should be understood that what is here described as *gain* is, in fact, no more than the refund of the *loss* arising on payments made by the Secretary of State on account of other parties.

Whatever may be the real economical effect on India of the burden thus caused, on which point more will be said hereafter, it is an obvious fact that it has led to the necessity for maintaining the taxation of the people of India at an amount at least 2,500,000*l.* more than would have sufficed if the exchange value of the rupee had remained as it was nine or ten years ago. It may confidently be affirmed that if it had not been for the fall in the value of silver, no additional taxation would have been thought necessary in 1877, no difficulties would have arisen in removing the cotton duties when the necessity for that step was first admitted, and that apart from this fall not only those duties, but the whole of the customs duties, could have been removed, and the financial position of the country would still have been better than it now actually is. This statement will show how great a practical misfortune the recent alteration in the value of gold and silver has been to India. The evil has come in a form which placed it wholly out of the power of the Indian Government either to foresee or to avert, and leaves the future open to the gravest doubt and anxiety. Measures of improvement which the otherwise thoroughly satisfactory condition of the finances would reasonably suggest, must be regarded as more or less hazardous, and progress will inevitably be much retarded, not only in respect to the action of the Government, but in all directions, so long as the existing state of uncertainty as to the future of the Indian currency continues.

There is some difficulty in tracing the effects of the change in the value of silver in relation to gold on Indian interests other than those which appear on the surface; namely the increased taxation, the uncertainty as to the result of all permanent investments in India in the future, and the serious injury to those who have invested in former years, or who are dependent on Indian sources of income payable out of the country. It is of course apparent that these evils arise from the sudden actual or possible fall in the exchange value of the rupee, not from any particular rate of exchange being in itself desirable or better than any other. What is required for the future is fixity in relation to the gold currency of England, though obviously the injury inflicted in relation to the past can never be fully remedied, nor even partially, unless there is a substantial return to the old relations of value.

There is hardly room to doubt that the foreign trade of India has been stimulated by the increase in the value of gold, which has almost certainly accompanied the depreciation of silver where that metal has ceased to be coined. There is at present no evidence that the purchasing power of the rupee in India has been injuriously affected, and it is reasonable to suppose that under the actual conditions of Indian trade its volume has been increased by the increase of the silver value of the gold employed in the foreign trade. Approximately this increase of value will be represented by the loss by exchange on the remittances required to settle the trade accounts of India, and may therefore be reckoned at 2,500,000*l.* or 3,000,000*l.* sterling. Contrary to what is commonly taught by economists as to the consequences of such a condition of trade, there is no evidence from the returns of any special improvement of the exports as compared to the imports, and it is therefore probable that the import and export trades are to so great an extent interdependent that the advantage is distributed between them.

If this view be correct, the trade of India at the present time may be regarded as being carried on with the stimulus of a bounty of some 3,000,000*l.* yearly, or about 2½ per cent. on its total value, supplied by general taxation, and rendered necessary by the currency of India being based on a silver instead of a gold standard.

The same conclusions might be otherwise stated as follows. By reason of the relative higher value of gold, India is now required to export a larger quantity of merchandise than formerly to discharge her foreign obligations. This increased quantity of exports corresponds in value to the 'Loss by exchange' on the Indian remittances, and, so far as this loss has to be met by the Government, it of course falls on the taxpayer. The export trade is therefore increased by this amount at the cost of the general revenues. Should any change of circumstances arise by which the exchange value of the rupee were raised to its old amount, the revenues would gain by the amount of the present loss by exchange to the disadvantage of the traders; and it would seem that the most appropriate way of dealing with the improved financial position, which would then admit of a large reduction of taxation, would be as far as possible to apply it to the removal of general burdens on trade, such for instance as the customs duties. The interests of trade would thus be best compensated for any injury caused by a sudden change of the conditions under which it had lately been conducted.

Speaking generally, the financial difficulties, or, as they may almost be called, dangers, which have now been discussed, are wholly due to the want of uniformity in the standards of value in England and India. The vast transactions between the two countries are disorganised by the difference of standard, causing very great and constant administrative difficulty and anxiety to the Government, and almost more serious injury to private interests, with extreme and undeserved hardship to the large and meritorious class of European officials. The position, in truth, is hardly less irrational than it would be to maintain a silver standard of value in Scotland or Ireland, with a gold standard in England. That there is a difficulty to be overcome in supplying the remedy is not to be disputed, but this is no sort of justification for refusing to supply it. The responsibility for the present state of things rests with the British Government, India, which is the real sufferer, not being allowed to help herself. It is beyond belief that any independent government would tolerate the continuance of such a state of affairs, and that India has so long been compelled to bear it is wholly the result of her dependence on England.

It would be beyond the scope of this work to enter at length on a discussion of the best means of obtaining the uniformity of standard between the currency of

India and that of England which is certainly necessary. The authors, however, find no difficulty in adopting the conclusion that the best, and only complete remedy, would be in the acceptance by India of bimetallism, as it is now commonly understood ; and that, if England were so disposed, the means of accomplishing this might be found without sacrificing the single gold standard which she has adopted for herself. The evils that have arisen in connection with the fall in the value of silver are essentially due to the want of proper harmony between the standards of value of different nations, and those evils have specially affected India on account of the peculiar divergence of her monometallic silver standard currency from the currencies of all other civilised countries, these having more or less completely adopted a gold standard. The remedy for these evils should therefore be sought in an international agreement that shall establish the requisite harmony, which is equally important to all nations.

If, from whatever cause, such a solution of the difficulty is not attainable, then it would only remain for India to protect herself, which she should do by making such a change in her currency law as would give her a gold standard of value in place of the present silver standard. How this should be arranged in detail could only be usefully considered with reference to the exact circumstances at the moment, after the decision had been arrived at that it was necessary actually to apply remedial measures. But attention may be drawn to the fact before noticed, that during the last twelve years the imports of gold into India have been as much as 30,000,000*l.* sterling, or nearly three-tenths of the whole bullion imports ; and as during the last forty-six years the total net imports of gold have been very nearly 108,000,000*l.*, the conclusion is suggested that if gold were required for currency purposes in India it might probably be obtained within the country itself, in sufficient quantity for present use, and that, by the introduction of a gold coinage on a sound basis, the available volume of gold money in the world might be considerably increased instead of being diminished.

CHAPTER XXI.

FUTURE REQUIREMENTS OF PUBLIC WORKS AND FINANCE.

FURTHER EXTENSION OF RAILWAYS ESSENTIAL—PRESENT POLICY OF GOVERNMENT TO FAVOUR PRIVATE ENTERPRISE — OBJECTIONS TO STATE ACTION CONSIDERED—MR. MILL'S OPINION—ITS APPLICATION TO INDIA—IMPORTANCE OF ESTABLISHING LOCAL AND NATIONAL OWNERSHIP OF RAILWAYS—REGULATION OF MONOPOLIES—AGENCY OF COMPANIES HOW FAR EXPEDIENT—OBJECTIONS TO SYSTEM OF GUARANTEE—STATE WORKING NOT DESIRABLE—LOCAL MANAGEMENT IMPORTANT—OBJECTIONS TO BORROWING FOR PUBLIC WORKS—THEIR INCONCLUSIVE NATURE—REASONS FOR NOT THROWING ENTIRE COST ON REVENUES—CONSIDERATIONS WHICH SHOULD DETERMINE DISCHARGE OF DEBT—NECESSITY FOR ECONOMICAL CONSTRUCTION—NEEDLESS COMPLICATION OF EXISTING RULES FOR UNDERTAKING PUBLIC WORKS—ECONOMY NOT SECURED BY RESTRICTIONS ONLY—PROVINCIAL RESPONSIBILITY DESIRABLE—IMPORTANCE TO REVENUE OF INCOME FROM RAILWAYS—CHECK OF PUBLIC OPINION ON PROVINCIAL FINANCIAL ADMINISTRATION SUGGESTED—NECESSITY FOR MORE EQUITABLE ADJUSTMENT OF TAXATION—RISK OF REACTION AGAINST RECENT MEASURES —IMPORTANCE OF REMISSION OF IMPOSTS ON COMMERCE—CONCLUSION.

THE principal object with which the preceding chapters have been written is to supply an account of the actual financial position of India, and of the results of the public works policy followed during the last twelve years; but discussions of the principles on which the action of the Government has been based have often necessarily formed a part of the narrative, and it appears desirable, in some cases, to extend the examination into those principles, with more special reference to the course to be followed in the future.

The recent remarkable progress of India, which

has been placed beyond every reasonable doubt, may without hesitation be traced up to the natural productive powers of the country, for the development of which greatly increased facilities have been given by the extension of railways and the cheap transport they afford; and it is indisputable that there is still a wide scope for further progress, through the continued development of the internal means of communication, and the general amelioration of the administration.

Although much has already been done, and with very great advantage to the country, there remains nevertheless more which is urgently needed for the protection of the people against famine and the results of drought, altogether apart from any question of merely adding to the wealth of the community.

Competent Indian opinion has long ceased to be divided on this point, and whatever differences exist relate to the manner of accomplishing the object, not to the object to be accomplished. The views of the Famine Commission,[1] which have virtually been accepted by all authorities in India, including the Supreme Government, are thus expressed:—

'Until the whole country is more completely supplied with railways or canals by which food can be transported rapidly, cheaply, and in large quantities to every part where severe want may exist, the possibility of some unusual demand for Government interference in particular localities, or for special classes of people, cannot be shut out, nor the danger of the occurrence of a great calamity altogether removed. It is, therefore, to the improvement of the internal communications and the removal of all obstructions to the free course of trade, accompanied by the extension of irrigation in

[1] See Report, Part I. par. 165.

suitable localities and an improved agriculture, that we look for obtaining security in the future against disastrous failures of the food supply in tracts visited he drought.'

The Famine Commissioners have estimated the length of railway which might suffice to meet the requirements of the country in the above sense at 20,000 miles, of which about 10,000 miles already exist or are in progress, and 10,000 miles are needed; and they consider it probable that less than one half of the length above named, or 5,000 miles, in addition to the existing lines, would go far to remove all future risk of serious difficulty. Nor will any smaller scale of construction commend itself to any one who carefully considers the facts of the case. In respect to irrigation works also, there are still large areas liable to utter devastation by drought, which could certainly be protected with great direct profit to the agricultural community, and ultimate full return to the State; and no single year has passed since the great calamities of 1876–77 without giving additional evidence of the absolute necessity of doing all that is possible to extend irrigation.

This is no time to cry 'Rest and be thankful.' Year after year runs silently by, and the fatal term will only too soon be reached when another terrible catastrophe will suddenly arise, though exactly where and when we know not. It is in the intervals of prosperity which are granted to us that we must prepare for the inevitable future; and if the lessons of the past still continue to be neglected, the responsibility for the consequences will rest upon those who, having the power to avert them, have failed to do so. For any hesitation or delay in carrying out the works which alone can give the country the protection it requires, there is no valid argument to be found either in the probability of their causing financial difficulty, or in their insufficiency for meeting the end in view. So far from this being the case, judicious expenditure on these works will certainly supply the only assured means of preventing frightful mortality and ruin, and of avoiding the future waste of millions on ineffectual famine relief with no corresponding permanent benefit to the country; and such works, while thus affording protection in time of difficulty, will constantly increase the resources of the people and render them more and more capable of resisting pressure when it arises. Past experience, both in what we have done and what we have left undone, points to these conclusions.

The practical point for consideration, therefore, is simply, how the means should be obtained for carrying out these essential works. Should we continue in the course adopted with complete success till lately, or should the former policy be given up and a new departure taken? The Government, it would appear, has within the last year come to the conclusion that, so far as railway construction is concerned, a change should be made, that the restrictions which have gradually been imposed on the prosecution of these works with borrowed money should be increased, and that what is termed private enterprise should henceforth be principally looked to for what is required. This decision is one of the gravest importance to India, and the question to which it is designed to give a practical answer calls for the most serious consideration.

To clear the ground certain preliminary matters call for attention. First, it is evident that India must long continue to look to this country for most of the capital by means of which her progress is to be secured, and, this being the case, we must be prepared to find that the profits earned on that capital will be remitted to England. As such investments of capital increase in amount, these remittances must go on increasing also; their growth will, it is true, indicate growing wealth in India, and not, as has often been asserted, a drain of wealth from India; but it must not be overlooked that it would certainly be far better for India if these works of improvement could be carried out with Indian capital, so that they should be wholly national, their management being conducted in India, and the whole of their profits retained in India, including the return on the capital as well as the profits derived by the community from their use. In considering this subject we are bound to place ourselves in the point of view of a national Indian government, and not of the English capitalist. Though we should not hesitate, if no alternative were left to us, to accept the works subject to the disadvantage of the whole or greater part of the direct profits being drawn away to England, and the chief management placed there, yet if it be possible to secure for India the entire income from the investment of the capital expended on its railways, and the complete control over them, we are certainly bound to do it.

Now experience has established beyond dispute that it is within our power both to construct and work railways economically through State agency; and without attempting to discuss such a question as the relative excellence or economy of management by the State and by a company, it may without hesitation be said that in the case of lines yielding a profit (to which alone this argument is applicable), the amount which would be carried out of the country by a company of foreign capitalists, including as it would both interest on capital and profits, must be greater than the charge incurred under Government management, which would consist of interest only, since the profits, even if smaller, would all remain in India.

In the financial interests of India, therefore, it will *primâ facie* be better for the State to become the owner of the railways, undertaking their construction with money borrowed at the low rate of interest which it credit permits, and receiving the excess of the profi over that interest, instead of allowing those profits to enrich foreign capitalists. To whatever extent the profits are retained by the State for the necessary charges of the public administration, there must be a corresponding diminution in the burdens placed upon the people.

This, of course, applies only to works that are profitable. But it may be confidently said that private capitalists will not undertake any railway in India unless the conditions are such as to render it certain that the profits will exceed the interest which would have been paid on the borrowed capital, if the line had been undertaken by the State, or would even suffice to pay off the capital debt within a moderate time. Further it must be remembered that to complete the railways which are admitted to be necessary for the safety of the country, many lines must be undertaken the profits of which will be small and the growth of the traffic slow, or which may be finally unremunerative when considered simply as investments. If, therefore, we give up the whole of the profitable lines to private enterprise, the burden of constructing the unprofitable ones will fall on the State without that set-off which could otherwise be secured; and the difficulties of the situation would be aggravated, as has often been pointed out, by the discredit thus thrown on the State by its management of lines necessarily unproductive, compared with the management by the companies of lines as necessarily productive.

The foregoing argument goes far to show that the intervention of companies of foreign capitalists must in every case lead to an increase of charge on the country; and as it is a self-evident proposition that the duty of the Government requires it to do all in its power to provide India with railways at the least possible cost, the adoption of the more costly in preference to the cheaper system would demand some preponderating obligation to justify it.

The policy which has been followed for the last ten years has been opposed on various grounds. First, it is argued that it is beyond the proper function of the Government to undertake such works as railways, which should be left wholly to private enterprise; and further, that the evils of borrowing the requisite sums are so great, that it will be preferable either to leave the country, for a time at least, without railways, or to accept the necessary additional cost of employing companies.

The first of these objections, it is true, has not been put forward openly or unconditionally in the official discussions on the policy of public works construction in India, but it is incontestable that it has largely influenced the latest conclusions. All arguments on this subject adduced by Indian officials would doubtless be discredited, and fail to convince persons who, being ignorant of India, its wants, and capacities, insist on conducting its affairs on the model of England, and applying economical and political maxims suited to one of the most artificial, advanced, and wealthy communities in the world, to a totally different condition of society. The matured opinions of one who was certainly among the ablest advocates of rational freedom and the foremost opponents of the undue extension of Government action, will, however, have a force of authority which must command attention and respect.

'In the particular circumstances of a given age or nation,' says Mr. John Mill,[1] 'there is scarcely anything, really important to the general interest, which it may not be desirable, or even necessary, that the Government should take upon itself, not because private individuals cannot effectually perform it, but because they will not. At some towns and places there will be no roads, docks, harbours, canals, works of irrigation, hospitals, schools, colleges, printing presses, unless the Government establishes them; the public being either too poor to command the necessary resources, or too little advanced in intelligence to appreciate the ends, or not sufficiently practised in conjoint action to be capable of the means. This is true, more or less, of all countries inured to despotism, and particularly to those in which there is a very wide distance in civilisation between the people and the Government: as in those which have been conquered and are retained in subjection by a more energetic and more cultivated people. In many parts of the world, the people can do nothing for themselves which requires large means and combined action; all such things are left undone, unless done by the State. In these cases, the mode in which the Government can most surely demonstrate the sincerity with which it intends the greatest good of its subjects, is by doing the things which are made incumbent on it by the helplessness of the public, in such a manner as shall tend not to in-

[1] *Political Economy*, vol. ii. 4th ed. p. 575.

crease and perpetuate, but to correct, that helplessness.'

It is obvious that these opinions were specially directed to the actual condition of India, with the administration of which Mr. Mill had been connected for a great part of his life; their wisdom is beyond dispute, and it would be impossible to say anything more to the point.

The full acceptance of Mr. Mill's principles, when applied to the case of India, leads immediately to the conclusion that progress should be sought by the application of the superior knowledge and resources of the State, but in such a manner as gradually to accustom the people to manage their own affairs, and to entrust them with such management as soon and as far as it is practicable. This holds true in dealing with economical as well as with political matters. To speak of the operations of foreign capitalists in India as though they were identical with the spontaneous working of what is commonly described as private enterprise in our own country, is a manifest confusion of thought, and every argument based on such an assumption necessarily involves a serious fallacy. The intervention of great companies of foreign capitalists, having their seat of business out of the country, differs little, indeed, in its ultimate effects, from the establishment of a strong foreign despotism.

Mr. Mill very truly implies that the proper course to follow in matters such as these must depend on circumstances of time and place and other varying conditions peculiar to each case; and it is not intended in what is said above to lay down any absolute or invariable rule of action. Circumstances formerly led, almost unavoidably, to the general employment for railway construction of companies of British capitalists, constituted and managed in England; and it may still be found desirable to make use of companies, though under modified conditions. But it is the duty of the State when accepting this form of agency to provide the means of eventually replacing it by a truly local and national system, without undue cost to the public; and to secure at the same time for India the greatest practicable share of the profits, the whole of which are ultimately derived from the industry of the people of India and the natural resources of their country. The true interests of India demand that foreign enterprise should be regarded as a temporary and not as a permanent resource; and so far as it is necessary or expedient to accept such aid, this condition should never be lost sight of. Even in the case of a company which asks for no pecuniary assistance whatever from the State, or which exclusively employs national capital, the mere fact of authorising it to undertake such a work as a railway, places it under obligations to the community which the Government is bound to enforce. On this point also the authority of Mr. Mill[1] may be adduced.

'In many analogous cases,' he says, 'which it is best to resign to voluntary agency, the community needs some other security for the fit performance of the service than the interest of the managers; and it is the part of the Government, either to subject the business to reasonable conditions for the general advantage, or to retain such power over it that the profits of the monopoly may at least be obtained for the public. This applies to the case of a road, a canal, or a railway. These are always, in a great degree, practical monopolies; and

[1] *Political Economy*, vol. ii. p. 557.

a Government which concedes such monopoly unreservedly to a private company, does much the same thing as if it allowed an individual or an association to levy any tax they chose, for their own benefit, on all the malt produced in the country, or on all the cotton imported into it. To make the concession for a limited time is generally justifiable, on the principle which justifies patents for inventions; but the State should either reserve to itself a reversionary property in such public works, or should retain, and freely exercise, the right of fixing a maximum of fares and charges, and, from time to time, varying that maximum. It is perhaps necessary to remark that the State may be the proprietor of canals or railways without itself working them; and that they will almost always be better worked by means of a company, renting the railway or canal for a limited period from the State.'

The new arrangements made for working the East Indian Railway, which are elsewhere explained, are in substantial accordance with these last suggestions. Some extension of the general principle they imply appears to afford the best solution of the much-vexed question of how to secure for India the necessary development of railways, with a minimum of Government interference in detail; the legitimate interests of the State, and of the capitalists whose funds are required, being at the same time guarded.

Up to the present day no attempt has been made to carry out a railway in India without Government aid, and it remains very doubtful whether English capitalists will venture to invest in these undertakings otherwise. The failure of the irrigation companies, which were unaided or very slightly aided, and the extremely inconvenient and costly financial burdens they have occasioned, should induce caution in handing over to a private company a monopoly which the interests of the public may probably force the Government to take over on very disadvantageous terms, in the event of want of success in the enterprise itself, or of inability of the promoters to carry it out to completion. There can, however, be no reason why any substantial scheme for constructing a railway on a true basis of private enterprise should not be favourably received, subject to such conditions as have been referred to, among which should invariably be found an arrangement for the ultimate transfer of the ownership to the State, on equitable terms.

But the really practical question for consideration, after all, is how to deal with those cases in which unassisted private enterprise is not forthcoming, yet in which the Government considers that an undertaking is necessary either for the protection of the country from famine, or to supply requirements of other sorts, its cost being too great to be met from current income. The earliest conception was to offer a guarantee of interest on the capital required; but this system was deliberately given up ten years ago, and until the present time its resumption has been rejected with substantial unanimity. It now, however, has reappeared as one of the suggested forms of action, though with some pretence of disguise under the much abused name of private enterprise.

Of the objections to the old form of guarantee it is not necessary to say much. Its possible results are well shown by the position of such an undertaking as the Madras Railway. The original share of 100*l.* has involved the Government in a steady net yearly charge of about 2*l.* 10*s.*; wholly by reason of the Government guarantee the present value of the share has risen to 126*l.*, and this sum the Government may eventually have to pay to the shareholder for a property not worth half the amount. Under a system of guarantee of interest on capital all the inducements to economy and good management are reduced to a minimum. But perhaps the worst feature of this system is that it offers a constant stimulus to the companies to be lavish in their expenditure and to expand their capital. In the nature of the case the stock is at a premium, and there must therefore be a certain profit in adding to it. The Government is always at a disadvantage in any discussion involving its financial interests, and there is no real power of enforcing control where the management is not inclined to acquiesce in it. A system of guarantee being once established, it is impossible to withdraw from, or limit it; capital can be procured on no other terms, and as a continued expansion of the capital is unavoidable with the progress of traffic, the liability under the guarantee goes on constantly increasing.

Comparing any possible system of guarantee, even for a limited term of years, or on a limited capital, with State construction from borrowed funds, it may confidently be said that the former will be more onerous than the latter. The refund of the guaranteed interest would be contingent on the shareholders receiving a part of the surplus profits, which in the other case would be all taken by the Government. Again, if the line be made by the State it becomes State property at its actual cost; in the other case, if a power of purchase be reserved (which should be considered obligatory), a considerable premium would be required; and on the transfer of the property, whatever precautions were taken, it would almost certainly happen that it would be found in a less satisfactory condition than if it had throughout belonged to the State. In the one case the whole character of the works and the general scale of the outlay during construction is under the complete control of the Government; in the other, the company and its engineers decide all questions of this sort, and are likely to view the subject in a very different light. Neither could it be hoped that any limitation of the guarantee would effectually protect the Government against dangers of increased expenditure in excess of a sum first named as a maximum; for, if the works were not completed within that maximum, the Government could not practically compel the company to supply the requisite funds without help; nor in the event of any other failure to perform the contract could any real remedy be found besides that of taking possession of the undertaking, which in such circumstances would infallibly involve a considerable sacrifice. The history of the Madras Irrigation Company conveys a serious caution in this direction; and that more difficulties of the same sort have not been apparent in dealing with the railway companies, may reasonably be attributed to the almost complete absence of restrictive clauses from their contracts.

It is then to be earnestly hoped that no return to the old and very objectionable system of giving a guarantee of interest on capital will be permitted, and that all proposals to re-introduce it under the disguise of aided 'private enterprise' may be wholly rejected. If private enterprise is to take a part in the provision of railways for India, let it be what it calls itself, and not something else under that designation. Any departure from this strict rule will infallibly lead to the eventual total disregard of it; and all expectation of the healthy operation of private enterprise truly deserving the name, not only in railway construction but in all directions, will be still further indefinitely postponed, as it certainly has hitherto been retarded, by the continued grant of guarantees of interest to the large amounts of capital required in one form or other for the old guaranteed railway companies.

The exclusion of factitious private enterprise does not, however, necessarily involve the more direct forms of State construction or working, and least of all the continuance of these operations under the immediate direction of a central department of the Government of India. Though the transition from the old system of guaranteed companies led to this as a temporary expedient, there are many serious objections to the railways of India being worked as parts of a great State department. The objections to State construction are less; but even this might often, with advantage, be relegated to other agencies. The case of the East Indian Railway shows that the agency of companies, under a lease for a term of years, may be employed advantageously for working lines owned by the State; and there is no apparent reason why a company might not also be employed for the construction of railways with capital to be provided by the State, as well as for their subsequent working.

Local effort, as elsewhere mentioned, has already been usefully exerted, and would without doubt have done much more had it not been unfortunately arrested at the outset. To it all reasonable assistance should be given. Economy and convenience are generally secured by placing a considerable length of railway under one management; but this condition will often be counterbalanced by others, and too great weight should not be attached to it. Wherever it is possible, local co-operation should be sought in some shape, and trustworthy persons, having a knowledge of local wants and resources, might profitably be associated with the management, or with the Government control which in every case would be exercised in some form or to some extent. Another plan would be to conduct the management of State railways under the supervision of suitable public boards or trusts, such as have been constituted and work very successfully in the case of the ports of Calcutta and Bombay.

As to the other class of objections, those based on financial considerations, it must first be said that it is beside our present purpose to discuss the greater or less urgency of the demand for the extension of railways at the present time. The argument is based on the assumption of urgency (the proofs of which are to be found elsewhere), and what concerns us here is to ascertain the relative advantages and disadvantages of different ways of meeting the demand.

It is extremely difficult to understand how the assertion can be supported, that the policy of borrowing to construct public works, necessarily or probably involves results which must be ruinous, or, at the least, mischievous. To make the assertion is of course easy, and if its frequent and loud reiteration could prove it to be true, nothing more need be said on the subject. But there has been no attempt made to support it by fact. On the other hand, the evidence which has been repeatedly brought forward for some years past, and which is again presented in this volume, of the results of experience up to the present time, conclusively establishes the certain and great financial advantage which has actually been derived from the prosecution of public works with money directly borrowed or applied under a guarantee of interest by the State.

And it is a point of great importance in considering this with reference to the future, to bear in mind that the obligations imposed on the Government under the original contracts with the guaranteed companies, were extremely onerous, so that it is certain that in whatever form the Government might undertake the construction of railways, its liabilities would be far less heavy, even after taking account of the circumstance that the old main lines occupy the richest districts, and would enjoy a larger traffic.

That the policy of borrowing for the prosecution of public works has not created a burden on the revenues, is no mere statement advanced on the personal authority of individuals which might be discredited. It is established on facts authenticated by the independent testimony of the published accounts, which cannot be set aside by any mere denial of their accuracy, unsupported by specific evidence to the contrary. It has been shown in the present volume, from the facts thus recorded, that, so far from this policy having caused any such burden, its financial success has been complete; that not only has there been no increase in the public burdens through its operation, but that those burdens have been largely diminished; that the expenditure on railways and canals has been in the highest degree profitable to the country; and that, while some 140,000,000*l.* of borrowed money has been invested in these works, the net charge on account of the public debt has been reduced in the last twelve years by nearly 3,500,000*l.* a year. The total net charge for interest on debt and productive public works outlay of every description does not exceed 3,100,000*l.* out of a net revenue amounting to 43,750,000*l.* The gross charge for debt is 6,100,000*l.* against a gross revenue of 68,000,000*l.*—or, say, 9 per cent. Even including the whole interest on the guaranteed capital, the total possible liability of the State on the supposition that the public works produced nothing, would not be more than 15 per cent. of the gross revenue. The charge for debt in our own country is 29,000,000*l.* upon a gross revenue of 85,000,000*l.*, or 34 per cent. It is also a fact completely established, that the credit of the Government has not been injuriously affected by the borrowing for public works during the last ten years. The rate of interest is now lower than it ever has been before, both in England and India, and no difficulty has been experienced in obtaining the sums needed. So far, then, as past experience affords a guide, it may safely be said that a judicious continuance of the policy adopted in the time of Lord Mayo, is not in the least likely to lead to inconvenient financial results hereafter.

As to the suggestion that rather than borrow we should do better to rely wholly on resources obtained from the current revenue, two things must be remarked. First, to carry out necessary works of permanent improvement from income alone, is in the nature of things impossible in India, as it is everywhere else. Accumulated capital must be applied to the task in some shape, either at the risk of the State, or of private persons. Secondly, the actual condition of India is certainly not one in which any justification can be found for adding to the burdens of present taxation for the purpose of giving advantages to a future generation. Nor can we, with this object in view, justly postpone or give up reductions of present taxation which otherwise would be practicable, and which are of immense importance in the interests of progress in all directions. It has already been pointed out that the benefits secured by the extension of railways will certainly be much greater some years hence than they can be while the works are under construction, or in an immature condition, or so long as the country is uninstructed in their use. To require their cost to be defrayed from the revenues of the year, to any considerable extent, would be most unjust to the present taxpayers, who will only partially realise their benefits. It is strictly in accordance with public equity, good sense, and sound finance to call in the credit of the State for the purpose of distributing over a series of years the burden of providing these great works of permanent improvement. There is no established fact which supplies a ground for the assertion that there is a present tendency to add to the actual burden of the public debt. Those who affirm this commit the absurdity of disregarding the income obtained from public works in estimating the charge which has been incurred for their construction. It is no doubt necessary to do in the future what was done in the past, namely, to be careful that the net charge for public works executed from borrowed money is not permitted to go beyond what the revenues can bear. To allege that the adoption of this principle is opposed to public policy because the charges cannot be so regulated, and because no proper control can be exercised over them, is in flagrant opposition to the experience of the last ten or twelve years, which shows that the exact reverse is true, and that such a control has been exercised, with the result of a great improvement in the financial position.

The regulation of the expenditure of borrowed money on public works by a consideration of the net interest charge incurred after setting off the income of the works, in relation to the available revenues, and treating any such excess charge as a part of the current expenditure of the year, has a complete economical justification. The position of the Government in carrying out works of permanent improvement is by no means that of the ordinary capitalist, nor can its action be properly determined by the same considerations. The capitalist looks only to the direct money return obtained from his investments. The Government, no doubt, cannot disregard the money return from its undertakings, but its essential object is the improvement of the public estate. Altogether, apart from, and besides the direct returns obtained from works and railways, the improvements in the country which they cause have a very real and a very large value, though this is not susceptible of being defined by a money standard, and can find no place in any financial statement. So long, then, as proper care is taken that the investments of borrowed money do not permanently increase the public burdens, the payment of interest on capital, while such works are not directly profitable, becomes a legitimate charge against the general revenues, in consideration of the indirect benefits which they secure.

In the present condition of India the considerations which support the conclusion that it is important to reduce the public debt, are almost exclusively political. Viewed financially, and in the interests of India itself, the charge for debt is not serious. But it is certainly inexpedient in the interests of England to encourage the unlimited expansion of the debt of India, which must be so largely held in England. It is, no doubt, very difficult to fix attention on possible dangers of that indefinite future when India may cease to be a British dependency, and on the risks of a failure of the income, derived from large investments of English capital in works or securities, dependent on India for its realisation. But these dangers and risks, though distant, should not be left out of sight.

Hence it will be a step in the right direction to acquire for India the full property in its great public works, and as far as practicable to apply their surplus income to the discharge of the capital outlay they have involved. But the obligations on the Government to place the country in a secure position for meeting the terrible disasters in the shape of famine, to which it is still subject, are paramount. Until this end has been attained, every other object should be regarded as secondary.

The need is urgent of securing a sound fiscal system for the future, of adjusting more equitably the burdens on the people, and of freeing the springs of wealth by removing existing obstacles to the expansion of trade. To attain all these objects a strong financial position is necessary. It is only with an assured surplus, derived from a revenue fairly contributed by all classes of the community, that the remission of objectionable taxes, and a prudent discharge of the public debt, can be secured without interfering with the provision of material improvements essential for present safety and future progress.

The necessity for restricting the expenditure to the smallest sum that will provide efficient works is obvious. The magnitude of the task to be accomplished in relation to the available means at our command, should enforce the strict limitation of the projects accepted for execution, to what is essential to meet the requirements of sound construction and provide for a moderate traffic; everything beyond this, whether of luxury, or in anticipation of future wants, should be postponed or discarded.

Complications have by degrees been introduced into the rules under which borrowed money is applied to public works, which are merely mischievous and misleading, and the sooner the original simple plan is reverted to the better it will be. This plan was to treat alike, in dealing with their income and charges, all works of the same actual character, irrespective of the sources which supplied the funds required for their construction, and to determine the extent to which funds should be obtained by borrowing, on a consideration of the urgency of the demand, and of the capacity of the revenues to meet the charges for interest in excess of the anticipated income of the whole of the works. Considerations which properly arise in respect of the manner of obtaining the funds for construction, have no legitimate bearing on the subsequent financial treatment of the works when constructed. Purely technical distinctions have now been created between works called 'productive,' 'protective,' and others, which, having identically the same actual characters, are called neither the one nor the other. Those works are held to be 'productive,' and are exclusively carried out with borrowed funds, which are estimated to yield, in a time arbitrarily fixed, an arbitrary rate of profit, on an outlay also estimated on arbitrary rules. Other works, absolutely identical in every respect, excepting that they cannot be brought within these precise limits, but will presumably afford protection against famine, have been called 'protective' and may be constructed out of revenue only. Nor is this all; for works, still identical in essentials, though not requiring borrowed money for their execution, nor calculated to give special protection against famine, fall into another category. Different rules are laid down for the sanction and treatment in the accounts of these various classes which are undistinguishable in any other way. The 'productive' work may quite possibly give a smaller net return than the 'protective'; and it has even happened that different portions of the same railway have fallen within different classes.

Such a system makes it extremely difficult, even for those most familiar with it, and conversant with the actual position of the various works, to acquire a proper insight into their operation; while to others, the result is hopeless confusion. It may perhaps appear incredible, but it is true, that under the existing rules, strictly applied, the East Indian Railway would have been proscribed, and the construction of the Ganges canal would have been impossible; nor is it wonderful that these artificial barriers are disregarded, however demoralising the practice, whenever the supreme controlling authority desires to find a plausible excuse for doing so.

It can hardly be too often or too plainly repeated that no real safeguard against the waste of the public resources is to be found in the multiplication of restrictions, which may wholly arrest the expenditure, but are powerless to control its economical application; nor in establishing checks exercised upon estimates only, by distant authorities—the Government of India and the Secretary of State—who can have but an imperfect knowledge of local wants and capacities. No provision is thus made for guarding against the actual consequences of error, nor for obtaining any self-acting system of check which shall throw back the burdens of ill-considered expenditure on those who recommended it.

The true method of obtaining the requisite securities in this, as in all other public expenditure, is to substitute for a merely restrictive financial policy directed by a centralised authority, one based on the recognition of the efficacy of local responsibility. The expansion of provincial financial authority would secure such a result. A healthy constitutional sense of responsibility would be established which should ensure the efficient performance of all local administrative services, and the punctual discharge of all local liabilities, without the interference in details of a central authority. It would be easy to define the limits beyond which the provincial revenue might not be charged by reason of interest on borrowed capital, and, that limit being reached, outlay should be stopped until by an increase of income or reduction of expenditure an available margin had been restored. Arrangements could be made for the discharge year by year of a fixed proportion of the debt incurred for carrying out local improvements, so that the burden of their first cost might be distributed over a term of years, while the indefinite accumulation of liabilities would be prevented. The whole of the charges and income of the works being localised, the provincial revenues would reap the advantage of economy and good management, while the consequences of insufficient estimates or other deficiencies would be immediately brought home to those responsible for them.

Reasons have elsewhere been given for regarding the State income derived from railways, as one of the certain and growing sources of revenue which it is of the greatest importance to retain and develop, and the hope may again be expressed that it will not be endangered by rash departure from a policy which has already given such substantial proofs of its wisdom. Doubtless the railways should not be worked with a view to obtaining from them any excessive income, or more than may fairly be asked in return for the services rendered. In fact increasing receipts, and relatively reduced expenses, will follow only on a moderate tariff, of which the evidence is as complete in India as elsewhere.

Little further remains to be said on these matters. Although the public interests imperatively demand that the great works, to which special reference has now been made, should be retained by the State as public property for the benefit of the people of India, it is impossible to doubt the inestimable importance of encouraging the application, by private enterprise, of English capital to purposes of Indian improvement. There is ample and almost boundless scope for such investments in undertakings, the successful prosecution of which is incompatible with Government interference in any shape, and in respect to which complete freedom of action is as essential in the public interest, as is State control in the case of railways and canals.

Full explanations have already been given regarding the development of provincial financial responsibility; and among the subjects discussed in this volume, there is assuredly none of greater practical moment. On one of its aspects, however, something remains to be said. It is one of the present inevitable conditions of Indian administration that it should be almost entirely free from the immediate control of what is commonly described as public opinion. To some small extent, indeed, this may be said to operate in the local legislative councils, on the branch of business which is there conducted. But in respect to the public expenditure, it still has to be called into action. There is no portion of the work of administration in which the expression of public opinion, even if it were not always intelligent, would be more useful, and measures by which it could be encouraged and called forth would not only be beneficial to the local government, but valuable as steps in political education. The larger authority which is now vested in the local governments in financial matters, would gain in efficiency if exercised with increased publicity, and local discussion by a body not wholly composed of officials would, no doubt, prove in India, as elsewhere, to be an important aid to the economical administration of the finances.

Nothing could be more foolish than to attempt to create assemblies having plenary power over the public income and expenditure. India is not a country for such experiments. What is really to be desired is not to weaken the action of authority, but to take a step towards the formation of a public opinion which shall assist the responsible Government for the advancement of provincial and local objects. Checks, which under different social and political conditions are useful and necessary, would be wholly out of place, and the object in view could probably be safely obtained by creating local consultative bodies, before which would be placed every year the provincial budget estimates of receipts and expenditure. The local government would be expected to set these forth in detail, and to explain any portion of the estimates the policy of which was challenged. Such a body should contain the chief executive officers of the local government, together with non-official persons of local knowledge, weight, and intelligence. Political discussion should under no circumstances be permitted, the business being restricted to the consideration of the estimates, so far as they lie within the limits of the authority of the local government. The existing constitutional law of India entrusts all questions of taxation to the final decision of the Government of India, and no infringement of this rule should be permitted. Further, to prevent misconceptions as to the scope of the functions to be performed, it would be inexpedient to entrust them to the existing local legislatures, or to combine with those legislatures such bodies as those which it has now been proposed to create.

The relation of the Government of India to the general financial administration of the whole country is so entirely different from that which subsists between the local governments and their financial administration, that no true analogy can be established between them; the chief arguments which go to support such proposals as have been made in respect to the provincial governments are therefore inapplicable in the case of the Government of India. No corresponding body could possibly be created in connection with the Supreme Government.

Among the other subjects already treated at some length, there are some of exceptional importance, in relation to which the policy adopted in the immediate future is likely to have dominant influence on the fiscal history of India.

Some advance has been made towards the more equitable adjustment of the public burdens, by giving greater relief to the poorer classes, and placing a fairer share on the rich. This is an object of incontestable importance, and for its more complete attainment the present improved condition of the finances offers fresh facilities. It would be a great misfortune if the surplus revenue, which has now been secured, were applied otherwise or dissipated. To abandon the measures which have been taken for the partial redress of these inequalities, such as the licence tax on the most wealthy class of traders, and the cesses on the land in Bengal, would be to sacrifice ground gained with difficulty in a most just cause.

But it is not to be concealed that there are powerful influences in operation, seeking such a movement, and that strenuous efforts will be required to resist it, and to secure, instead, the further remission of those burdens which still weigh in undue proportion on the great mass of the population. Among such burdens should be specially named the Salt duties. It has been shown in this work how successful have been the measures already taken for their reduction, and how essential it is, in the interests of the people and the finances, that those measures should receive a further and large development.

Not less grave are the considerations which demand the early remission of all imposts on trade. To ensure the application of the capital which India requires for her proper development, involving as this does the continued growth of the foreign remittances, already so large, wider markets will be necessary for her increased and more valuable produce, and these can only be profitably found in combination with a corresponding expansion of her import trade. The conditions under which her further progress is possible, demand the most complete removal of all obstacles to the freedom and growth of her commerce, both fiscal and material. How she responds to the removal of such obstacles is illustrated in a remarkable manner by the sudden creation of the wheat trade, following immediately on the remission of the export duty, and the opening up by railways of the irrigated wheat-producing districts.

Improvement in the material condition of the people of India, without which no other forms of progress can be assured, is to be obtained only through an accumulation of wealth accompanying a steady development of the foreign trade. The means of accomplishing this are obvious and quite within our reach; if we fail to provide them, we fail to fulfil a most imperative duty of the governors to the governed. These means lie, as this volume seeks to establish, in an intelligent extension of the great public works which the country requires, whereby will be ensured its future well-being, and the continued prosperity of its finances.

APPENDIX

CONTAINING TABULAR STATEMENTS OF THE PRINCIPAL ELEMENTS OF THE PUBLIC REVENUE, EXPENDITURE, AND DEBT, FROM 1869-70 TO 1880-1881.

STATEMENT No. 1.—*General Comparison of Total*

Head of Account	1869–70	1870–71	1871–72	1872–73	1873–74
	£	£	£	£	£
1. Gross revenue	56,243,003	56,559,337	56,451,028	56,617,394	57,766,171
2. Gross expenditure . . .	56,124,334	55,076,347	53,326,851	54,851,722	59,573,839
3. Gross surplus or deficit . .	118,669	1,482,990	3,124,177	1,765,672	*1,807,668*
4. Net expenditure on Afghan war, including frontier railways . . .					
5. Surplus or deficit, excluding line 4	118,669	1,482,990	3,124,177	1,765,672	*1,807,668*
6. Expenditure on famine relief	83,230	448	5,531	763	3,876,923
7. Surplus or deficit, excluding also line 6 . . .	201,899	1,483,438	3,129,708	1,766,435	2,069,255
8. Assets of military funds credited	244,953	472,329	331,308	252,505	366,471
9. Loss of exchange saved by short remittances .	75,323	190,273	78,189	*32,497*	• 87,581
10. Excess or deficient expenditure charged on Bengal opium	*38,097*	*86,885*	495,749	41,190	*145,000*
11. Total lines 8 and 9, less line 10	282,179	575,717	905,246	261,198	309,052
12. Surplus or deficit, excluding also line 11 . . .	*80,280*	907,721	2,224,462	1,505,237	1,760,203

STATEMENT No. 2.—*Net Revenue*

Head of Account	1869–70	1870–71	1871–72	1872–73
	£	£	£	£
(*a*). Land revenue, excluding capitation tax .	20,811,905	20,335,678	20,267,532	21,054,495
(*b*). Tributes and contributions from native states	765,126	719,421	744,036	741,465
(*c*). Forests	158,854	77,350	151,066	176,350
(*d*). Opium	6,132,387	6,031,034	7,657,187	6,870,415
(*e*). Miscellaneous	141,606	*389,044*	134,868	*73,122*
Total revenue other than taxes . .	28,009,878	26,774,439	28,954,689	28,769,603
(*f*). Excise on spirits and drugs . . .	1,991,039	2,079,853	2,231,238	2,189,003
(*g*). Capitation tax	201,395	202,727	203,647	212,442
(*h*). Assessed taxes	1,026,400	1,988,023	797,208	581,733
(*i*). Provincial rates	1,235,496	1,303,602	1,579,007	1,819,213
(*j*). Customs	2,167,797	2,353,555	2,341,449	2,402,335
(*k*). Salt	5,462,501	5,686,335	5,456,065	5,643,356
(*l*). Stamps and registration	2,280,670	2,391,883	2,387,314	2,543,064
Total taxes	14,365,298	16,005,978	14,995,928	15,391,146
Total net revenue	42,375,176	42,780,417	43,950,617	44,160,749
Total net expenditure (Statement 3) .	42,418,230	41,769,308	41,152,217	42,646,819
Net surplus or deficit	*43,054*	1,011,109	2,798,400	1,513,930
Add assets of military funds and deduct war and famine expenditure	161,723	471,881	325,777	351,742
Surplus or deficit as in Statement 1, line 3	118,669	1,482,990	3,124,177	1,765,672

N.B. Figures in Italics signify

Revenue and Expenditure from 1869–70 *to* 1880–81.

1874-75	1875-76	1876-77	1877-78	1878-79	1879-80	Estimate 1880-81	Total
£	£	£	£	£	£	£	£
59,121,089	60,158,035	59,227,533	62,073,948	65,201,569	68,484,666	70,783,617	728,687,388
58,801,892	58,489,090	61,410,311	65,617,035	63,167,323	69,667,615	77,003,382	733,109,741
319,197	1,668,945	*2,182,778*	*3,543,087*	2,034,246	*1,182,949*	*6,219,767*	*4,422,353*
				676,219	6,100,474	11,295,660	18,072,353
319,197	1,668,945	*2,182,778*	*3,543,087*	2,710,465	4,917,525	5,075,893	13,650,000
2,242,961	601,966	2,145,431	5,366,875	313,420	103,990	47,281	14,788,819
2,562,158	2,270,911	*37,347*	1,823,788	3,023,885	5,021,515	5,123,174	28,438,81[illegible]
362,178	413,627	283,270	281,688	349,940	213,943	27,000	3,599,212
284,037	82,559	299,831	724,083	*512,746*	81,662	415,132	1,773,427
368,382	*244,424*	*788,752*	*687,483*	422,422	268,126	58,237	*1,073,299*
277,833	251,762	*205,651*	318,288	259,616	563,731	500,369	4,299,340
2,284,325	2,019,149	168,304	1,505,500	2,764,269	4,457,784	4,622,805	24,139,479

from 1869–70 *to* 1880–81.

1873-74	1874-75	1875-76	1876-77	1877-78	1878-79	1879-80	Estimate 1880-81
£	£	£	£	£	£	£	£
20,772,672	21,036,606	21,212,412	19,577,827	19,741,198	22,187,183	22,125,807	21,414,000
768,544	724,972	726,188	694,934	675,120	703,660	702,451	751,000
231,458	152,073	274,551	156,373	236,036	149,451	208,933	223,000
6,323,395	6,214,782	6,252,026	6,280,781	6,521,337	7,699,032	8,249,808	8,466,000
95,000	627,660	242,678	90,794	84,570	25,872	*55,313*	31,000
28,191,069	28,756,093	28,707,855	26,800,709	27,258,261	30,70[illegible],198	31,231,686	30,885,000
2,189,011	2,252,669	2,403,809	2,426,506	2,356,424	2,525,575	2,714,064	2,967,000
221,829	228,364	222,440	235,707	241,065	252,237	261,117	266,000
29,517	17,382	14,336	14,063	96,898	837,312	696,651	497,000
1,740,840	1,785,167	1,788,112	1,839,567	2,205,357	2,544,507	2,826,562	2,731,000
2,374,090	2,422,114	2,470,391	2,220,028	2,348,729	2,060,905	2,026,513	2,269,000
5,651,482	5,732,371	5,699,483	5,786,526	5,874,071	6,503,031	6,895,713	6,573,000
2,635,792	2,649,704	2,740,363	2,756,761	2,935,702	3,065,378	3,149,358	3,243,000
14,842,561	15,087,771	15,338,934	15,279,158	16,058,246	17,788,945	18,569,978	18,546,000
43,033,630	43,843,864	44,046,789	42,079,867	43,316,507	48,494,143	49,801,664	49,431,000
41,330,846	41,643,884	42,189,505	42,400,484	41,774,407	45,820,198	44,994,092	44,335,000
1,702,784	2,199,980	1,857,284	*320,617*	1,542,100	2,673,945	4,807,572	5,096,000
3,510,452	*1,880,783*	*188,339*	*1,862,161*	*5,085,187*	*639,699*	*5,990,521*	*11,316,000*
1,807,668	319,197	1,668,945	*2,182,778*	*3,543,087*	2,034,246	*1,182,949*	*6,220,000*

deficit or excess expenditure.

STATEMENT NO. 3.—*Net Expen*

Head of Account	1869-70	1870-71	1871-72	1872-73
	£	£	£	£
1. Land revenue	2,790,375	2,733,589	2,759,595	2,806,371
2. Administration	1,434,728	1,367,390	1,475,832	1,478,308
3. Minor departments	190,575	247,962	301,967	377,217
4. Mint	*56,150*	32,859	*11,830*	31,949
5. Post office	33,409	17,324	*82,615*	188,877
6. Telegraphs	296,267	255,669	222,234	233,747
7. Law and justice	2,145,233	2,292,974	2,290,289	2,259,757
8. Police	2,223,837	2,103,048	2,172,329	2,176,640
9. Marine	989,793	426,966	379,839	356,832
10. Education	756,445	702,619	678,303	731,296
11. Ecclesiastical	161,126	153,553	158,190	156,881
12. Medical	445,360	522,287	498,774	549,982
13. Political	415,367	361,120	316,105	392,300
14. Stationery and printing	361,787	390,519	188,854	203,313
Total effective civil services	12,188,152	11,607,879	11,347,866	11,943,470
15. Furlough allowances	157,918	175,068	173,029	156,059
16. Superannuations	993,581	1,119,040	1,099,654	1,238,169
Total non-effective civil services	1,151,499	1,294,108	1,272,683	1,394,228
17. Allowances under assignments and treaties	1,863,615	1,756,973	1,724,510	1,749,890
18. Interest	5,245,187	5,496,101	5,598,011	5,340,483
19. Public works, including guaranteed interests	6,635,796	5,798,753	5,807,576	6,642,227
Total interest and public works	11,880,983	11,294,854	11,405,587	11,982,710
20. Exchange	102,786	341,536	172,612	463,674
21. Army	15,247,134	15,112,946	14,731,083	14,596,928
22. Provincial and local surplus or deficit	*15,939*	361,012	494,876	515,919
Total net expenditure	42,418,230	41,769,808	41,152,217	42,646,819

N.B. Figures in Italics signify

Statements Nos. 1, 2, *and* 3.—The gross revenues and expenditure in Statement No. 1, and the net revenues and expenditure in Statements No. 2 and No. 3, have been taken from the latest returns prepared by the Government of India, abstracts of which have recently been published as a Parliamentary paper dated June 2, 1881. For the ten years 1869-70 *diture from* 1869–70 *to* 1880–81.

1873–74	1874–75	1875–76	1876–77	1877–78	1878–79	1879–80	Estimate 1880–81
£	£	£	£	£	£	£	£
2,852,923	2,845,772	2,935,336	2,876,261	2,929,024	2,940,554	2,914,976	2,956,000
1,518,486	1,555,905	1,644,273	1,489,967	1,489,940	1,487,852	1,492,280	1,543,000
347,154	347,935	357,358	317,205	318,410	270,416	258,978	323,000
11,103	*26,414*	*2,863*	*128,253*	*311,776*	*68,344*	*121,020*	6,000
194,772	156,904	138,449	122,314	113,598	121,664	141,182	153,000
161,199	145,630	184,120	131,900	122,465	99,227	*54,409*	*35,000*
2,380,352	2,472,183	2,514,715	2,573,846	2,600,757	2,701,737	2,661,583	2,595,000
2,192,581	2,208,016	2,220,002	2,289,595	2,224,218	2,212,520	2,270,098	2,282,000
299,164	299,089	399,478	466,934	310,892	298,269	272,653	325,000
763,521	845,177	876,103	855,315	848,469	837,236	828,219	839,000
163,733	166,174	162,160	163,844	158,039	155,200	156,012	159,000
571,699	599,158	624,337	621,137	642,031	626,986	613,891	628,000
366,756	404,604	430,444	505,319	469,072	448,793	430,571	521,000
194,698	203,737	197,377	404,390	406,482	424,399	362,490	428,000
12,018,141	12,223,870	12,681,289	12,689,774	12,321,621	12,556,509	12,227,504	12,723,000
258,464	216,704	229,199	235,990	237,362	231,561	215,092	224,000
1,188,134	1,439,535	1,601,382	1,471,735	1,564,659	1,679,786	1,885,499	1,864,000
1,446,598	1,656,239	1,830,581	1,707,725	1,802,921	1,911,347	2,100,591	2,088,000
1,856,700	1,738,368	1,713,724	1,672,543	1,646,093	1,826,484	1,814,635	1,908,000
5,324,594	4,854,032	4,986,589	5,260,954	5,563,576	5,738,523	5,844,767	5,655,000
6,319,472	6,415,852	6,087,670	4,659,982	3,213,584	4,745,783	3,600,137	3,852,000
11,644,066	11,269,884	11,074,259	9,920,936	8,777,160	10,484,306	9,444,904	9,507,000
591,362	502,543	1,034,293	1,676,482	1,092,139	2,884,659	2,926,403	2,553,000
14,218,378	14,386,333	14,262,848	14,866,639	15,769,780	15,441,488	15,866,756	15,466,000
444,399	*133,353*	*407,489*	*133,615*	365,593	715,405	613,299	90,000
41,330,846	41,643,884	42,189,505	42,400,484	41,774,407	45,820,198	44,994,092	44,335,000

receipts in excess of expenditure.

to 1878–79, the finance and revenue accounts presented to Parliament have been revised, so as to include the provincial and local revenue and expenditure, which are now incorporated in the annual accounts on a uniform system. Any one desirous of making a correct detailed comparison of the finances for the past twelve years can only do so by reference to these revised accounts, which have been specially prepared by the Government of India for the purpose. The figures for 1880–81 are, in all cases, those adopted for the revised estimates, which are in most cases based on actual results for ten months.

The net revenue under each head in Statement No. 2 has been obtained by deducting from the gross revenue the refunds and charges under the same head, and the net expenditure under each head in Statement No. 3 has been obtained by adding refunds to the gross expenditure and deducting the receipts appertaining to that head.

The finance and revenue accounts for the year 1880–81 have not yet been closed. The figures for that year in these Statements are approximate; they have been taken from the Parliamentary return with certain modifications obtained approximately from such sources as were available, to provide for refunds, of which details are not given in that return.

In the case of land revenue, which appears both as revenue and expenditure, the gross capitation tax (which is shown net separately under revenue) has been deducted from the land revenue, under which head it appears in the public accounts, and the commission paid on the collection of that tax has been deducted from the expenditure under the same head. In the year 1869–70 the amount of this commission is not recorded in the public accounts, and has been assumed with reference to the amount recorded in the following year to have been 20,000*l.* The entries under this head also are made to include the land revenue due to irrigation, and therefore differ from the figures in the Parliamentary return above referred to, which show this part of the land revenue, though in an incomplete manner, as public works income after the year 1876–77.

The net receipts under 'Stamps and registration' have been thrown together in Statement No. 2. Before 1879–80 the registration receipts and charges were included in the accounts under the head 'Law and justice,' and are so shown in the Parliamentary return. In these Statements, however, they have been removed from the head 'Law and justice,' and the net receipts have been added to the net stamp revenue.

The head 'Miscellaneous,' which appears in the Parliamentary returns on the net expenditure side of the account, is shown in Statement No. 2 as net revenue, because the receipts usually exceed the expenditure.

In Statement No. 3, under the head 'Superannuation,' the assets of the Military funds, which were credited in the accounts, have been excluded, for reasons which have been explained in Chapters IV. and V. The annual details of these credits are given in Statement No. 1. From the head 'Army' has been deducted the net expenditure on the Afghan war, and the expenditure on frontier railways has been treated as a part of the war charges, the whole of which are excluded from Statement No. 3. The expenditure on famine has also been omitted from this Statement. The reasons for these omissions are explained in Chapter V. Details of the omitted expenditure will be found in Statement No. 1.

The entry under 'Interest' in Statement No. 3 includes the interest on the Productive public works debt, which is therefore here excluded from the head 'Public works.' In this respect the entries differ from the Parliamentary return, which shows the interest in question under 'Public works,' and also includes, though imperfectly, the land revenue due to irrigation, as before explained. With these modifications the entry in Statement No. 3, under 'Public works,' includes the whole net charges as shown in the Parliamentary return, excepting those on account of frontier railways, which are treated as an incident of the Afghan war, and therefore omitted from this Statement. The separate Statement No. 7 brings together all the elements of revenue and expenditure connected with Productive public works.

STATEMENT NO. 4.—*Gross Disbursements and*

Head of Account	1869–70	1870–71	1871–72	1872–73
GROSS DISBURSEMENTS.	£	£	£	£
Interest on debt	2,209,000	2,350,000	2,437,000	2,467,000
Civil :—				
India office	212,000	215,000	218,000	220,000
Civil furloughs	161,000	177,000	174,000	157,000
Superannuations	1,007,000	1,052,000	1,095,000	1,131,000
Departments in India	456,000	577,000	338,000	517,000
Total	1,836,000	2,021,000	1,825,000	2,025,000
Remittances :—				
Service funds	186,000	144,000	135,000	132,000
Postage	44,000	43,000	89,000	53,000
Family remittances	675,000	553,000	504,000	422,000
Miscellaneous	13,000	173,000	112,000	190,000
Total	918,000	913,000	840,000	797,000
Total civil administration	2,754,000	2,934,000	2,665,000	2,822,000
Army :—				
Effective	1,437,000	1,463,000	1,332,000	1,433,000
Non-effective	1,190,000	1,141,000	1,373,000	1,280,000
Total	2,627,000	2,604,000	2,705,000	2,713,000
Stores :—				
Civil and military	1,414,000	1,425,000	1,249,000	1,146,000
Public Works :—				
Capital	1,045,000	11,000		
Railway stores	124,000	38,000	111,000	297,000
Total	1,169,000	49,000	111,000	297,000
Guaranteed Railways :—				
Capital	2,897,000	5,344,000	2,499,000	1,467,000
Interest, &c.	4,138,000	4,353,000	4,546,000	4,619,000
Total	7,035,000	9,697,000	7,045,000	6,086,000
Advances	47,000	1,000	8,000	5,000
Debt discharged	501,000		5,000	
Grand total	17,756,000	19,060,000	16,225,000	15,536,000
GROSS RECEIPTS.				
Revenues	194,000	178,000	222,000	221,000
Advances repaid	1,615,000	245,000	106,000	615,000
Bills sold, &c.	6,980,000	9,015,000	10,310,000	13,939,000
Guaranteed railway capital	4,794,000	7,612,000	3,689,000	938,000
Debt incurred	4,039,000	2,424,000	1,413,000	
Total	17,622,000	19,474,000	15,740,000	15,713,000
Opening balance	3,026,000	2,892,000	3,306,000	2,821,000

N.B. The sum of 9,565,000*l.* was added to the Debt in 1879–80 in part purchase of the Eas 2,000,000*l.* under Advances repaid, in 1880–81, is part of the English contribution towards th

Receipts of the Home Treasury from 1869 *to* 1881.

1873-74	1874-75	1875-76	1876-77	1877-78	1878-79	1879-80	Estimate 1880-81
£	£	£	£	£	£	£	£
2,434,000	2,191,000	2,161,000	2,318,000	2,493,000	2,594,000	2,706,000	2,685,000
211,000	211,000	233,000	223,000	213,000	218,000	214,000	241,000
310,000	263,000	276,000	282,000	303,000	294,000	270,000	280,000
1,135,000	1,148,000	1,191,000	1,259,000	1,293,000	1,354,000	1,362,000	1,411,000
352,000	353,000	296,000	350,000	430,000	364,000	371,000	360,000
2,008,000	1,975,000	1,996,000	2,114,000	2,239,000	2,230,000	2,217,000	2,292,000
136,000	137,000	149,000	158,000	160,000	166,000	169,000	170,000
123,000	121,000	94,000	92,000	103,000	107,000	89,000	90,000
443,000	325,000	473,000	612,000	555,000	586,000	422,000	560,000
373,000	217,000	360,000	494,000	186,000	219,000	278,000	208,000
1,075,000	800,000	1,076,000	1,356,000	1,004,000	1,078,000	958,000	1,028,000
3,083,000	2,775,000	3,072,000	3,470,000	3,243,000	3,308,000	3,175,000	3,3-0,000
1,248,000	1,056,000	1,028,000	1,131,000	1,146,000	1,274,000	1,298,000	1,290,000
1,257,000	1,437,000	1,458,000	1,685,000	1,980,000	1,936,000	2,115,000	2,126,000
2,505,000	2,493,000	2,486,000	2,816,000	3,126,000	3,210,000	3,413,000	3.416,000
1,157,000	1,596,000	1,545,000	1,544,000	1,514,000	1,090,000	1,191,000	1,035,000
	84,000	4,000				9,566,000	
1,002,000	1,040,000	736,000	608,000	1,138,000	683,000	775,000	1,266,000
1,002,000	1,124,000	740,000	608,000	1,138,000	683,000	10,341,000	1,266,000
1,270,000	1,571,000	2,897,000	2,443,000	2,590,000	1,799,000	1,279,000	1,537,000
4,632,000	4,660,000	4,657,000	4,687,000	4,685,000	4,739,000	4,787,000	4,298,000
5,902,000	6,231,000	7,554.000	7,130,000	7,275,000	6,538,000	6,066,000	5,835,000
5,000	1,000	12,000	4,000	3,000	7,000	7,000	6,000
4,994,000	1,000		500,000		3,375,000	2,610,000	4,453,000
21,082,000	16,412,000	17,570,000	18,390,000	18,792,000	20,805,000	29,509,000	22,016,000
238,000	343,000	291,000	238,000	292,000	241,000	324,000	533,000
232,000	218,000	125,000	260,000	172,000	529,000	320,000	2,509,000
13,286,000	10,842,000	12,390,000	12,696,000	10,134,000	15,465,000	15,759,000	15,388,000
1,328,000	790,000	1,688,000	890,000	2,277,000	874,000	822,000	232,000
5,012,000	5,001,000	1,200,000	6,100,000	4,280,000	3,737,000	13,436,000	4,956,000
20,096,000	17,194,000	15,694,000	20,184,000	17,155,000	20,846,000	30,661,000	23,618,000
2,998,000	2,014,000	2,796,000	920,000	2,714,000	1,077,000	1,118,000	2,270,000

Indian Railway, and appears in that year also as a charge under Public works. The sum of cost of the Afghan war.

STATEMENT NO. 5.—*Abstract of Net Disbursements and*

Head of Account.	1869-70	1870-71	1871-72	1872-73
NET DISBURSEMENTS.	£	£	£	£
Interest on debt	2,209,000	2,350,000	2,437,000	2,467,000
Civil administration	2,754,000	2,934,000	2,665,000	2,822,000
Army	2,627,000	2,604,000	2,705,000	2,713 000
Stores, civil and military	1,414,000	1,425,000	1,249,000	1,146,000
Total administration	9,004,000	9,313,000	9,056,000	9,148,000
Guaranteed railways	2,241,000	2,085,000	3,356,000	5,148,000
Productive public works	1,169,000	49,000	111,000	297,000
Total	12,414,000	11,447,000	12,523,000	14,593,000
NET RECEIPTS.				
Revenues	194,000	178,000	222,000	221,000
Advances repaid	1,568,000	244,000	98,000	610,000
Bills sold	6,980,000	9,015,000	10,310,000	13,939,000
Debt incurred	3,538,000	2,424,000	1,408,000	
Total	12,280,000	11,861,000	12,038,000	14,770,000
GUARANTEED RAILWAY CAPITAL.				
Total received	86,522,000	91,427,000	93,722,000	93,837,000
Total issued	83,911,000	87,687,000	90,183,000	90,661,000
Balance	2,611,000	3,740,000	3,539,000	3,176,000

N.B. The amount of debt incurred in 1879-80 for the East Indian Railway

Receipts of the Home Treasury from 1869 *to* 1881.

1873-74	1874-75	1875-76	1876-77	1877-78	1878-79	1879-80	Estimate 1880-81
£	£	£	£	£	£	£	£
2,434,000	2,191,000	2,161,000	2,318,000	2,493,000	2,594,000	2,706,000	2,685,000
3,083,000	2,775,000	3,072,000	3,470,000	3,243,000	3,308,000	3,175,000	3,320,000
2,505,000	2,493,000	2,486,000	2,816,000	3,126,000	3,210,000	3,413,000	3,416,000
1,157,000	1,596,000	1,545,000	1,544,000	1,514,000	1,090,000	1,191,000	1,035,000
9,179,000	9,055,000	9,264,000	10,148,000	10,376,000	10,202,000	10,485,000	10,456,000
4,574,000	5,441,000	5,866,000	6,240,000	4,998,000	5,664,000	5,244,000	5,603,000
1,002,000	1,040,000	736,000	608,000	1,138,000	683,000	775,000	1,266,000
14,755,000	15,620,000	15,870,000	16,996,000	16,512,000	16,349,000	16,504,000	17,325,000
238,000	343,000	291,000	238,000	292,000	241,000	324,000	533,000
227,000	217,000	113,000	256,000	169,000	522,000	313,000	2,503,000
13,286,000	10,842,000	12,390,000	12,696,000	10,134,000	15,465,000	15,759,000	15,388,000
18,000	5,000,000	1,200,000	5,600,000	4,280,000	362,000	1,260,000	503,000
13,769,000	16,402,000	13,994,000	18,790,000	14,875,000	16,590,000	17,656,000	18,927,000
94,726,000	95,119,000	95,072,000	94,883,000	96,313,000	97,174,000	97,959,000	97,988,000
91,354,000	92,442,000	93,393,000	94,108,000	95,431,000	96,445,000	96,794,000	97,728,000
3,372,000	2,677,000	1,624,000	680,000	882,000	729,000	1,165,000	892,000

is excluded both from the net receipts and disbursements.

STATEMENT No. 6.—*Distribution of the Charges for Army and Stores,*

Head of Account	1869–70	1870–71	1871–72	1872–73
ARMY.				
Effective :—	£	£	£	£
Pay of British troops	756,000	578,000	614,000	674,000
Furlough allowances	403,000	469,000	438,000	423,000
Transport service	278,000	315,000	280,000	336,000
Stores	878,000	930,000	937,000	812,000
Total	2,315,000	2,392,000	2,269,000	2,245,000
Non-effective :—				
Indian army pensions	966,000	887,000	889,000	907,000
British army pensions	224,000	253,000	490,000	380,000
Total	1,190,000	1,140,000	1,379,000	1,287,000
Grand total	3,505,000	3,532,000	3,648,000	3,532,000
STORES.				
Army :—				
Clothing	232,000	185,000	203,000	238,000
Ordnance	287,000	373,000	424,000	289,000
Medical	41,000	59,000	56,000	38,000
Commissariat	318,000	313,000	254,000	247,000
Total	878,000	930,000	937,000	812,000
Public Works :—				
Ordinary	237,000	134,000	50,000	60,000
Productive works	124,000	38,000	111,000	297,000
Total	361,000	172,000	161,000	357,000
Civil :—				
Telegraph	5,000	75,000	42,000	92,000
Marine	110,000	77,000	89,000	66,000
Stationery	114,000	158,000	89,000	80,000
Stamps	13,000	23,000	15,000	9,000
Mint	13,000	7,000	6,000	4,000
Miscellaneous	44,000	21,000	21,000	23,000
Total	299,000	361,000	262,000	274,000
Grand total	1,538,000	1,463,000	1,360,000	1,443,000

N.B. The charges for stores under Army were increased in 1879–80 and 1880–81, by 170,000*l.* the details not being available. The sums under Productive works in 1879–80 and 1880–81,

Statements 4, 5, *and* 6.—These Statements have been compiled from the accounts of the Home treasury, and illus-

under the chief sub-heads, from 1869 to 1881.

1873-74	1874-75	1875-76	1876-77	1877-78	1878-79	1879-80	Estimate 1880-81
£	£	£	£	£	£	£	£
591,000	525,000	474,000	582,000	682,000	744,000	762,000	760,000
263,000	221,000	202,000	210,000	203,000	184,000	162,000	160,000
394,000	310,000	352,000	339,000	261,000	346,000	374,000	370,000
853,000	1,125,000	1,097,000	1,129,000	1,155,000	773,000	875,000	760,000
2,101,000	2,181,000	2,125,000	2,260,000	2,301,000	2,047,000	2,173,000	2,050,000
958,000	1,118,000	1,108,000	1,217,000	1,231,000	1,286,000	1,428,000	1,450,000
305,000	321,000	350,000	468,000	749,000	650,000	687,000	676,000
1,263,000	1,439,000	1,458,000	1,685,000	1,980,000	1,936,000	2,115,000	2,126,000
3,364,000	3,620,000	3,583,000	3,945,000	4,281,000	3,983,000	4,288,000	4,176,000
275,000	292,000	235,000	254,000	357,000	242,000	315,000	270,000
206,000	417,000	481,000	505,000	555,000	315,000	215,000	200,000
80,000	120,000	63,000	79,000	52,000	60,000	61,000	60,000
292,000	296,000	318,000	291,000	191,000	156,000	294,000	230,000
853,000	1,125,000	1,097,000	1,129,000	1,155,000	773,000	875,000	760,000
34,000	23,000	21,000	8,000	10,000	3,000	44,000	10,000
1,002,000	1,040,000	736,000	608,000	1,138,000	683,000	785,000	1,266,000
1,036,000	1,063,000	757,000	616,000	1,148,000	686,000	829,000	1,276,000
41,000	47,000	47,000	61,000	37,000	35,000	46,000	61,000
46,000	55,000	80,000	67,000	35,000	22,000	50,000	53,000
119,000	179,000	209,000	185,000	182,000	181,000	95,000	65,000
23,000	59,000	35,000	25,000	28,000	42,000	37,000	33,000
6,000	15,000	25,000	40,000	26,000	9,000	8,000	3,000
35,000	93,000	31,000	29,000	41,000	25,000	26,000	50,000
270,000	448,000	427,000	407,000	349,000	314,000	262,000	265,000
2,159,000	2,636,000	2,281,000	2,152,000	2,652,000	1,773,000	1,966,000	2,301,000

and 70,000*l.* respectively on account of charges for the Afghan war, entered under Commissariat, include respectively sums of 244,000*l.* and 695,000*l.*, for frontier railways, treated as war charges.

trate the discussions contained in Chapter VI. on the Home charges.

STATEMENT No. 7.—*Receipts and Charges on account of Productive Public Works including*

Head of Account	1868–69	1869–70	1870–71	1871–72	1872–73
GUARANTEED RAILWAYS.	£	£	£	£	£
Capital outlay	79,168,000	83,911,000	87,687,000	90,183,000	90,661,000
Gross guaranteed interest . . .	3,878,000	4,126,000	4,342,000	4,542,000	4,608,000
Charges for land, &c.		81,000	83,000	66,000	161,000
Net receipts less surplus . . .	1,966,000	2,618,000	2,557,000	2,877,000	2,554,000
Net charge or receipt . . .	1,912,000	1,589,000	1,868,000	1,731,000	2,215,000
STATE RAILWAYS.					
Capital outlay	553,000	744,000	1,193,000	1,838,000	3,252,000
Gross receipts	13,000	8,000	8,000	4,000	17,000
Working expenses	30,000	9,000	9,000	8,000	11,000
Net income	−17,000	−1,000	−1,000	−4,000	6,000
Interest on capital	10,000	30,000	40,000	61,000	115,000
Net charge	27,000	31,000	41,000	65,000	109,000
IRRIGATION WORKS.					
Capital outlay	688,000	2,695,000	3,414,00	4,398,000	5,169,000
Gross direct receipts	319,000	528,000	479,000	449,000	420,000
Share of land revenue	120,000	129,000	136,000	140,000	135,000
Working expenses	222,000	213,000	234,000	258,000	272,000
Net income	217,000	444,000	381,000	331,000	283,000
Interest on capital	69,000	114,090	171,000	206,000	228,000
Net receipts or charge . .	148,000	330,000	210,000	125,000	55,000
TOTAL PRODUCTIVE WORKS.					
Capital outlay	80,409,000	87,350,000	92,294,000	96,419,000	99,082,000
Net income	2,166,000	2,980,000	2,854,000	3,138,000	2,682,000
Interest	3,957,000	4,270,000	4,553,000	4,809,000	4,951,000
Net charge or receipts . . .	1,791,000	1,290,000	1,699,000	1,671,000	2,269,000
Net interest on ordinary debt . .	4,785,000	4,539,000	4,819,000	4,898,000	4,491,000
Total productive public works and debt .	6,576,000	5,829,000	6,518,000	6,569,000	6,760,000
Ordinary public works	6,471,000	5,311,000	4,125,000	4,213,000	4,532,000
Grand total	13,047,000	11,140,000	10,643,000	10,782,000	11,292,000

N.B. **Figures with (+) before them signify receipts in excess of charge.**

Guaranteed Railways, of Ordinary Public Works, and Interest on Debt, from 1868 *to* 1881.

1873-74	1874-75	1875-76	1876-77	1877-78	1878-79	1879-80	Estimate 1880-81
£	£	£	£	£	£	£	£
91,354,000	92,442,000	93,393,000	94,108,000	95,431,000	96,445,000	96,794,000	97,728,000
4,618,000	4,644,000	4,638,000	4,659,000	4,655,000	4,705,000	4,708,000	4,599,000
152,000	55,000	83,000	52,000	67,000	58,000		
3,241,000	3,455,000	3,729,000	4,433,000	5,397,000	4,023,000	4,924,000	4,936,000
1,529.000	1,244,000	992,000	278,000	+ 675,000	740,000	+ 110,000	+ 337,000
5,606,000	8,620,000	11,785,000	14,651,000	18,636,000	21,964,000	24,644,000	26,689,000
40,000	131,000	290,000	372,000	549,000	966,000	1,549,000	2,175,000
46,000	86,000	193,000	283,000	421,000	734,000	1,215,000	1,573,000
−6,000	45,000	97,000	89,000	128,000	232,000	334,000	602,000
168,000	284,000	410,000	530,000	664,000	918,000	1,058,000	1,210,000
174,000	239,000	313,000	441,000	536,000	686,000	724,000	608,000
6,367,000	7,603,000	8,708,000	9,652,000	10,458,000	11,252,000	11,851,000	17,806,000
460,000	460,000	487,000	564,000	534,000	650,000	724,000	656,000
159,000	111,000	141,000	130,000	149,000	118,000	602,000	701,000
268,000	245,000	285,000	291,000	298,000	310,000	415,000	430,000
351,000	326,000	343,000	303,000	385,000	458,000	911,000	927,000
290,000	330,000	374,000	416,000	454,000	540,000	574,000	851,000
61,000	−4,000	−31,000	−113,000	−69,000	−82,000	337,000	76,000
103,327,000	108,665,000	113,886,000	118,411,000	124,525,000	128,661,000	133,289,000	142,223,000
3,434,000	3,771,000	4,086,000	4,773,000	5,843,000	4,655,000	6,106,000	6,465,000
5,076,000	5,258,000	5,422,000	5,605,000	5,773,000	6,163,000	6,383,000	6,660,000
1,642,000	1,487,000	1,336,000	832,000	+ 70,000	1,508,000	277,000	195,000
4,376,000	3,910,000	3,867,000	3,971,000	4,140,000	3,952,000	3,846,000	2,898,000
6,018,000	5,397,000	5,203,000	4,803,000	4,070,000	5,460,000	4,123,000	3,093,000
4,926,000	5,382,000	5,344,000	4,594,000	4,202,000	4,528,000	4,337,000	5,312,000
10,944,000	10,779,000	10,547,000	9,397,000	8,272,000	9,988,000	8,460,000	8,405,000

Figures with (−) before them signify charge in excess of receipts.

STATEMENT No. 8.—*Showing Corre-*

Head of Account	1869–70	1870–71	1871–72	1872–73
	£	£	£	£
Net interest (Statement No. 3) . . .	5,245,000	5,496,000	5,598,000	5,340,000
Deduct service funds	612,000	516,000	483,000	556,000
Net interest on debt (Statement No. 10) .	4,633,000	4,980,000	5,115,000	4,784,000
Public works (Statement No. 3) . . .	6,636,000	5,799,000	5,808,000	6,642,000
Total	11,269,000	10,779,000	10,923,000	11,426,000
Deduct land revenue due to irrigation . .	129,000	136,000	140,000	135,000
Total public works and interest (Statement No. 7)	11,140,000	10,643,000	10,783,000	11,291,000

STATEMENT No. 9.—*Correction of Public*

Head of Account	1869–70	1870–71	1871–72	1872–73
	£	£	£	£
Loss by exchange (Statement No. 3) . .	102,786	341,536	172,612	463,674
Corrected amount, excluding gain on railway receipts	347,599	582,644	433,095	694,846
Difference	244,813	241,108	260,483	231,172
Net charge guaranteed railways (Statement No. 7)	1,589,000	1,868,000	1,731,000	2,215,000
Corrected charge for guaranteed railways .	1,344,000	1,627,000	1,471,000	1,984,000
Corrected charge for all productive works .	1,045,000	1,458,000	1,411,000	2,038,000

N.B. Figures with (+) before them

[Corre]spondence of Statements 3, 7, *and* 10.

1873-74	1874-75	1875-76	1876-77	1877-78	1878-79	1879-80	Estimate 1880-81
£	£	£	£	£	£	£	£
5,325,000	4,854,000	4,987,000	5,261,000	5,564,000	5,739,000	5,845,000	5,655,000
541,000	380,000	386,000	394,000	356,000	379,000	383,000	401,000
4,784,000	4,474,000	4,601,000	4,867,000	5,208,000	5,360,000	5,462,000	5,254,000
6,319,000	6,416,000	6,088,000	4,660,000	3,214,000	4,746,000	3,600,000	3,852,000
11,103,000	10,890,000	10,689,000	9,527,000	8,422,000	10,106,000	9,062,000	9,106,000
159,000	111,000	141,000	130,000	149,000	118,000	602,000	701,000
10,944,000	10,779,000	10,548,000	9,397,000	8,273,000	9,988,000	8,460,000	8,405,000

Works Account for Railway Loss by Exchange.

1873-74	1874-75	1875-76	1876-77	1877-78	1878-79	1879-80	Estimate 1880-81
£	£	£	£	£	£	£	£
591,362	502,543	1,034,293	1,676,482	1,092,139	2,884,659	2,926,403	2,553,000
882,718	785,820	1,355,861	2,059,311	1,554,922	3,225,831	2,926,403	2,553,000
291,356	283,277	321,568	382,829	462,783	341,172		
1,529,000	1,244,000	992,000	278,000	+ 675,000	740,000	+ 110,000	+ 337,000
1,238,000	961,000	670,000	+ 105,000	+ 1,138,000	399,000	+ 110,000	+ 337,000
1,351,000	1,204,000	1,014,000	449,000	+ 533,000	1,167,000	277,000	195,000

signify receipts in excess of charge.

STATEMENT No. 10.—*Capital and*

Head of Account	1868–69	1869–70	1870–71	1871–72	1872–73
CAPITAL.	£	£	£	£	£
Sterling debt	31,698,000	35,197,000	37,607,000	38,992,000	38,992,000
Rupee debt	65,681,000	65,965,000	68,627,000	68,560,000	68,116,000
Total	97,379,000	101,162,000	106,234,000	107,552,000	107,108,000
India stock in excess of guarantee fund	4,579,000	4,579,000	4,579,000	4,579,000	4,579,000
Grand total	101,958,000	105,741,000	110,813,000	112,131,000	111,687,000
DISTRIBUTION OF DEBT.					
Ordinary debt	100,033,000	101,598,000	102,684,000	101,957,000	99,045,000
Productive public works . .	1,241,000	3,439,000	4,607,000	6,235,000	8,420,000
Productive public works transfer for outlay from revenue .					
East Indian railway . . .					
Loans at interest	684,000	704,000	3,522,000	3,939,000	4,222,000
GROSS INTEREST—*excluding funds.*					
On sterling debt	1,528,000	1,579,000	1,720,000	1,807,000	1,837,000
Rate per cent.	(4·8)	(4·5)	(4·6)	(4·6)	(4·7)
On rupee debt	2,898,000	2,789,000	2,974,000	3,046,000	2,835,000
Rate per cent.	(4·4)	(4·1)	(4·3)	(4·4)	(4·2)
On India stock	630,000	630,000	630,000	630,000	630,000
Total.	5,056,000	4,998,000	5,324,000	5,483,000	5,302,000
NET INTEREST.					
On ordinary debt	4,785,000	4,539,000	4,819,000	4,898,000	4,491,000
On productive public works . .	29,000	94,000	161,000	217,000	293,000
On East Indian railway . . .					
Total	4,814,000	4,633,000	4,980,000	5,115,000	4,784,000
PRODUCTIVE WORKS.					
Net charge or receipts from guaranteed companies . . .	– 1,961,000	– 1,638,000	– 1,918,000	– 1,789,000	– 2,272,000
Net receipts state works . .	+ 199,000	+ 442,000	+ 380,000	+ 335,000	+ 296,000
Total charge or receipts . .	– 1,762,000	– 1,196,000	– 1,538,000	– 1,454,000	– 1,976,000
Total charge, productive works and debt, as in Statement No. 7	6,576,000	5,829,000	6,518,000	6,569,000	6,760,000

N.B. Figures with (+) before them signify receipts in excess of charge

Interest of Public Debt from 1868 *to* 1881.

1873–74	1874–75	1875–76	1876–77	1877–78	1878–79	1879–80	Estimate 1880–81
	£	£	£	£	£	£	£
41,096,000	48,576,000	49,776,000	55,376,000	59,656,000	60,008,000	68,835,000	71,335,000
68,217,000	71,667,000	74,602,000	73,762,000	76,836,000	79,069,000	84,598,000	85,814,000
109,313,000							
4,579,000							
113,892,000	120,243,000	124,378,000	129,138,000	136,492,000	139,077,000	153,433,000	157,149,000
97,240,000	98,730,000	98,206,000	98,684,000	100,164,000	97,319,000	98,767,000	93,839,000
11,973,000	16,223,000	20,494,000	24,303,000	29,094,000	33,476,000	36,840,000	39,656,000
							5,306,000
						9,730,000	10,208,000
4,679,000	5,290,000	5,678,000	6,151,000	7,234,000	8,282,000	8,096,000	8,140,000
1,804,000	1,993,000	2,161,000	2,317,000	2,492,000	2,593,000	2,740,000	2,685,000
(4·4)	(4·1)	(4·3)	(4·2)	(4·2)	(4·3)	(3·8)	(3·5)
2,815,000	2,842,000	3,017,000	3,092,000	3,248,000	3,390,000	3,467,000	3,411,000
(4·1)	(4·0)	(4·0)	(4·2)	(4·2)	(4·2)	(4·2)	(4·0)
630,000	198,000						
5,249,000	5,033,000	5,178,000	5,409,000	5,740,000	5,983,000	6,207,000	6,096,000
4,376,000	3,910,000	3,867,000	3,971,000	4,140,000	3,952,000	3,846,000	2,898,000
408,000	564,000	734,000	896,000	1,068,000	1,408,000	1,582,000	2,011,000
						34,000	344,000
4,784,000	4,474,000	4,601,000	4,867,000	5,208,000	5,360,000	5,462,000	5,253,000
−1,590,000	−1,300,000	−1,058,000	−331,000	+617,000	−782,000	+113,000	+626,000
+356,000	+377,000	+456,000	+395,000	+521,000	+682,000	+1,226,000	+1,534,000
−1,234,000	−923,000	−602,000	+64,000	+1,138,000	−100,000	+1,339,000	+2,160,000
6,018,000	5,397,000	5,203,000	4,803,000	4,070,000	5,460,000	4,123,000	3,093,000

Figures with (−) before them signify charge in excess of receipts.

STATEMENT 11.—*Abstract of Charges on account of Debt, adjusted for comparison, from 1868 to 1881.*

Head of Account	Averages of four years			First and last years	
	1869–73	1873–77	1877–81	1868–69	1880–81
CAPITAL.	£	£	£	£	£
Sterling debt	37,697,000	48,706,000	64,958,000	31,698,000	71,335,000
Rupee debt	67,817,000	72,062,000	81,579,000	65,681,000	85,814,000
India stock in excess of guarantee fund	4,579,000	1,145,000		4,579,000	—
Total	110,093,000	121,913,000	146,537,000	101,958,000	157,149,000
DISTRIBUTION.					
Ordinary debt	101,321,000	98,215,000	98,848,000	100,033,000	99,145,000
Productive public works . .	5,675,000	18,248,000	34,766,000	1,241,000	39,656,000
East Indian railway . . .			4,985,000		10,208,000
Loans at interest	3,097,000	5,450,000	7,938,000	684,000	8,140,000
GROSS INTEREST—*excluding funds.*					
On sterling debt	1,736,000	2,069,000	2,627,000	1,528,000	2,685,000
On rupee debt	2,911,000	2,941,000	3,379,000	2,898,000	3,411,000
On India stock	630,000	207,000		630,000	
Total	5,277,000	5,217,000	6,006,000	5,056,000	6,096,000
NET INTEREST—*adjusted.*					
On ordinary debt	3,999,000	3,681,000	3,530,000	4,097,000	2,898,000
On productive public works . .	429,000	888,000	1,696,000	267,000	2,011,000
On East Indian railway . .			94,000		344,000
Total	4,428,000	4,569,000	5,320,000	4,364,000	5,253,000
Net charge or receipts from productive public works . .	−1,541,000	−674,000	+1,134,000	−1,762,000	+2,160,000
Total charge for debt and productive public works . .	5,969,000	5,243,000	4,186,000	6,126,000	3,093,000

N.B. Figures with (+) before them signify receipts in excess of charge. Figures with (−) before them signify charge in excess of receipts.

Statements Nos. 7 to 11.—The sums shown as productive public works outlay in these Statements include the expenditure on state railways and irrigation works only, that on other works not properly coming into consideration in connection with the discussions contained in Chapters VII. and VIII. where full explanations are given on all points of importance.

The amount excluded consists of a sum of 1,133,362*l.*

advanced for improvements in the town of Bombay, and of a sum of about 350,000*l.* for the Madras Harbour, the last of which it has already been decided to deal with as a loan to the Harbour Trust.

The capital outlay on the Madras Irrigation Company's works has also been excluded from the account. It amounts to about 1,400,000*l.* of which 1,000,000*l.* is under a guarantee of interest at 5 per cent.

Statement No. 8 shows the causes of the differences between the entries in Statements Nos. 3, 7, and 10, and the Parliamentary return before referred to.

Statement No. 9 shows the correction that would have to be made in the accounts of years previous to 1879–80, in order to show the entries under 'Loss by exchange' on the system now adopted. This is explained in a note to Chapter VII., and more fully in Chapter XX.

The entries in Statement No. 10 are all explained in Chapter VIII.

Statement No. 11 is designed to show the adjustments of the charges for interest on debt, which are described in Chapter VIII. as being necessary for a proper comparison between different years.

The net interest on ordinary debt has been reduced by 450,000*l.* yearly, until 1873–74 inclusive, this having been the sum covered by the India stock guarantee fund.

The net interest on productive works debt has been increased and that on ordinary debt has been reduced by 238,000*l.* yearly (this being the interest on the sum transferred in 1880–81 from ordinary to productive works debt, on account of capital outlay on irrigation works supplied from revenue), in all years except the last, in which the charge for this interest appears in the published accounts under productive public works.